The Art & Science
of Technology
Transfer

The Art & Science
of Technology
Transfer

PHYLLIS L. SPESER

WILEY

John Wiley & Sons, Inc.

For general information on our other products and services, or technical support,
please contact our Customer Care Department within the United States at
800–762–2974, outside the United States at 317–572–3993 or fax 317–572–4002.

Wiley also publishes its books in a variety of electronic formats. Some content that
appears in print may not be available in electronic books.

For more information about Wiley products, visit our Web site at
http://www.wiley.com.

Library of Congress Cataloging-in-Publication Data:

ISBN-13 978–0–471–70727–1

ISBN-10 0–471–70727–9

This book is dedicated to my father, David, who taught me that marketing and sales is just a matter of walking in the other guy's shoes.

Contents

Acknowledgments

When you come to the end of an exercise like this book there is a moment of sadness and loss. After such a long time, you miss the regularity of writing. But the moment is immediately replaced by relief that the book is done and gratitude for the people who made it possible to finish.

Like every author, I find there are too many to thank by name, so I too will focus on those few who made the difference between quitting and continuing. Tops on my list is my Mom. Not only is she the woman who said "You can do this," she has spent countless hours editing the text. Next is my Dad, who has always been there to teach and support. Susan McDermott of John Wiley & Sons also deserves thanks for being kind when I was late and encouraging when I promised to finish.

I also want to express my gratitude to the citizens of Providence, RI, where I moved in January 2005. I have spent countless hours in restaurants outlining chapters or typing away at my notebook computer. To my amazement, people actually took an interest in what I was doing. They asked me to explain it, offered suggestions, and were supportive. Talk about being blessed! And special thanks to Mayor David N. Cicilline and his economic development team for encouraging us to move here. If you have a high tech company and are not sure where to locate, call me about Providence. I'm a happy camper.

I also want to thank Roland Tibbitts, who developed the first federal Small Business Innovation Research program at the National Science Foundation, and Bob Wrenn, who initiated—and for many years ran—the SBIR program at the Department of Defense. Roland and Bob, you have been an inspiration and friends.

We at Foresight have been fortunate to have awards from U.S. Department of Agriculture, the Department of Education, and the National Science Foundation SBIR programs to study how to do technology transfer better. I also want to thank the Office of Naval Research for supporting beta testing of our methods through their Long Term Scientific Research Broad Agency Announcement and Vinny Schaper, now retired, who was the Navy SBIR program manager who encouraged me to apply. Of course,

I need to add the findings and conclusions and recommendations in this book are mine alone and do not reflect the views of the government.

I also want to thank our customers at Foresight, with a special thanks to the following SBIR program managers: Jim Gallop of EPA, Charles Cleland of USDA, and Larry James of DoE who have encouraged us to experiment with our commercialization support program in order to better help their awardees attain commercial success. If you are a small company and do not know about SBIR, you need to find out. No matter what agency you work with, you will be fortunate to meet some of the finest people in the science, engineering, and technology community. All we can hope is that every federal civil servant is as dedicated to the wise use of the taxpayer's dollar.

A special thanks goes out to my son Arendt, and two of his buddies from Haverford, Joe Bender and Chris Penfield, who worked many vacations at Foresight when we hit overload. I also want to thank my daughter, Ariel. They spent countless hours around the dinner table discussing my research. What I have learned from "my three sons" and my daughter cannot be adequately acknowledged. How many people get to toss ideas around with amazing bright young folks who also love you?

Finally, I want to thank the people of my company, Foresight Science & Technology. Hillary Clinton was famous for saying "It takes a village to raise a child." I can tell you it takes a team to move technology. I have been honored to work with the best, the brightest, and the most fun-loving people in the world.

Phyllis Leah Speser
Providence, RI
October 28, 2005

Phyllis Leah Speser is the co-founder and team leader of Foresight Science & Technology (Providence RI), where she is the senior executive for the company and focuses on strategic planning and new product development. Dr. Speser holds a Ph.D. and a J.D., cum laude, from the State University of New York at Buffalo. She has supported commercialization of technologies in all fields, is the developer of the Technology Niche Assessment™ and Virtual Deal Simulation™ methods used by Foresight, She has served as Principal Investigator on numerous federal R&D awards focused on application of artificial intelligence to technology transfer and commercialization. She also has authored many other publications on technology transfer/commercialization and is a frequent speaker at professional society and trade association meetings.

Dr. Speser was the lead lobbyist for the Small Business Innovation Development Act, developer of the Small Business Technology Transfer Research program concept with Roland Tibbetts, and a lobbyist for the Technology Transfer Act of 1989. During her ten years as a lobbyist she was instrumental in enacting legislation protecting archaeological and environmental resources as well as serving as the point person for the science community on the federal budget as Executive Director of the National Coalition for Science and Technoloy.

Dr. Speser served two terms on the Board of the Technology Transfer Society, is a recipient of the society's Certificate of Appreciation (1991), was Chairman of its Task Force on National Technology Transfer Policy (1989–1991) and a co-author of the Best Paper at its 1987 annual meeting. She was a gubernatorial appointment to the Board of the Washington Technology Center from 1994 to 1997 and is a member of the Bar Association of the District of Columbia, the Licensing Executives Society, and the American Association for Artificial Intelligence and has been listed for years in numerous Who's Who publications. She has been active in public service, including helping to start and serving as the founding chairperson of the Glen Echo Park Foundation (now the Glen Echo Park Partnership for Arts and Culture Inc.) and the Olympic Peninsula Foundation (renamed the Northwest Natural Resource Group in recognition of its expansion to serve the entire Pacific Northwest).

The accomplishment she is most proud of is raising two wonderful children.

Preface

I was educated as a political philosopher and philosopher of law. My graduate work, in the SUNY Buffalo Department of Political Science and Law School, focused on problems of judgment and how we can make reasonable political judgments. I wrote a dissertation on the topic. So why am I writing this book? The short answer is that technology transfer is a problem in applied judgment. Deals are based on two parties agreeing on what is a reasonable exchange. Understanding how they come to this conclusion is an interdisciplinary problem that builds upon insights from the social scientific, economics/business, and legal literature interpreted in light of a healthy dose of practical experience.

The real reason, however, has to do with the contingencies of life. In the mid-90s I was living in Port Townsend, WA. I was *"equity tripping,"* a quaint term used on the Olympic Peninsula for living off the funds gained when a business is sold. In my case, I had done an asset sale of a government relations business in Washington, DC. I had started that business after graduate school, when the opportunity to make a difference seemed more attractive than studying about how others might make a difference.

As a lobbyist I had specialized in science and technology legislation. Among other legislation, I played key roles in the establishment of the Small Business Innovation Research (SBIR) Program government-wide, the Small Business Technology Transfer Research (STTR) Program, and the 1984 amendments to the Stevenson-Wydler Act. So I had a pretty good view of technology transfer from the policy side. I also had done some consulting along the way—things like helping to design university/industry centers and raising seed money for them. That activity gave me some insights into technology transfer from the hands-on side. Those insights were enhanced by work getting government R&D and procurement contracts for university and corporate customers, and licensing technology out of small high tech companies and into Fortune 500 corporations or other small companies.

I had sold my business because I needed a bone marrow transplant for leukemia. I was fortunate enough to have a sister, Louise, who was able to

xvii

be my donor. I was transplanted at Fred Hutchinson Cancer Research Center in Seattle. The Hutch is a bone marrow transplant factory and the people there are great. I was lucky in that my two doctors, Fred Applebaum and Mary Flowers, were research scientists. I got to spend many hours talking with them about the dilemmas of balancing the need for R&D funding with the best possible patient service. Part of that discussion addressed the role of technology transfer.

After leaving the Hutch I settled on the Peninsula and had, for the first time in years, the leisure to engage in reflection. Having worked on technology transfer legislation, done a bit of it as a consultant, and experienced its benefits as a bone marrow recipient, it is not surprising I began reflecting on how to do technology transfer better.

Then I got lucky. I was reflecting on the fact that I could market an optical technology as easily as a biomedical one. Why was that? There must be something generic in the technology transfer process that allows practitioners like me to cut across technologies and industries. At first it seemed that I must be following a set of rules, a kind of 1, 2, 3 linear process. Reflecting on just what those steps might be led me to write a proposal to the U.S. Department of Agriculture SBIR program on an expert system for technology transfer. I won a Phase I and Phase II award and built the expert system.

Then I got really lucky. No one wanted to buy the expert system. The software was unwieldy to use, required massive amounts of data, and the algorithms had limited utility since they had to be supplemented for each sector and technology. Clearly the 1, 2, 3 approach had limited utility. After struggling with this problem for about two years, an epiphany occurred.

The epiphany was this: Optimizing requires a single solution, hence the massive data problems and limited utility of the algorithms. But if we give up optimizing for *satisficing,* for a "good enough" solution, we can accept constrained data and analysis so long as our outcome provides an acceptable solution, however defined. That permitted a more generalizable methodology. My goal now became to find a satisfactory, rather than an optimal solution. Because the analysis could terminate with an acceptable solution rather than an optimal one, there could be, and likely was, more than one solution—just like in technology transfer.

Once I knew what I was looking for, I quickly discovered I was on a well trodden path. The trailblazer was Herbert Simon, who called his approach *bounded rationality*[1] Bounded rationality is a judgment process

---

[1] Herbert Simon, "Alternative Visions of Rationality," in Hal Arkes and Kenneth Hammond, eds., *Judgment and Decision Making,* (Cambridge University Press: 1992), pp. 104–106.

in which incomplete data and analysis can be utilized so long as the decision criteria and process can be described and shown to lead us to attain our objectives and goals. Because the set is bounded, it can be expanded or contracted over time, as new knowledge and experience justifies.

This book presents my reflections on my experience and on the social scientific and business literature I have read. I have used these reflections to create the model presented in this book and to draw from it the lessons on how to be more efficient and effective when doing technology transfer. Aristotle said somewhere that philosophy is not studied with benefit by the young as they have nothing yet to reflect upon. Fortunately, I have been doing technology transfer for about 30 years so I do have something to think about. Having said that, I am reminded that Samuel Coleridge once said the willing suspension of disbelief constitutes poetic justice. As this book is, of course, not poetry, *caveat emptor.*

Phyllis Speser
Providence, RI
October 2005

Introduction

This is a book about marketing technology. It explains how to get technology out of laboratories and into practical applications. It focuses on how to find and do deals since deals are, after all, what technology transfer is all about.

Research indicates that novices grasp concepts best when they have tools that help them gain insight into how experts cognitively grasp and pattern a situation. One such tool is emulating the expert, which, of course, is what occurs in apprenticeships. The novice replicates the expert's behavior in order to gain insight into the underlying cognitive pattern. It is the reason why so much mathematics is taught with the aid of doing the problems at the end of each chapter.

Let's try a mind experiment. Suppose you wanted to sell a technology (see Exhibit I.1). That means you probably want to be market driven. Why? A study of more than 300 Dutch firms from multiple industries found that to commercialize technology you must be market oriented. Market orientation is the key to product advantage which, although mediated by good launch tactics, is the most important variable leading to new-product performance and, through it, organizational performance.[1]

We will use an easy-to-grasp example: this book. After all, what is this book if not a commercialization of intellectual assets the author has built up over the years as a researcher and practitioner in the field? I will present the conceptual structure that is the core intellectual asset (IA). By embodying my model in this book, it becomes an expression. By being embodied in a physical medium, literally touchable, it becomes an object. Like other objects, we can meaningfully discuss who can touch it and under what conditions and in what contexts. The creative expression embodied in a physical medium becomes property due to the magic of a legally enforceable prohibition on replicating that expression. We call this

---

[1] F. Lanerak, E. Hultink, H. Robben, "The Impact of Market Orientation, Product Advantage, and Launch Proficiency on New Product Performance and Organizational Performance," *Journal of the Product Development Management Association* 21, no. 2 (March 2004): 89.

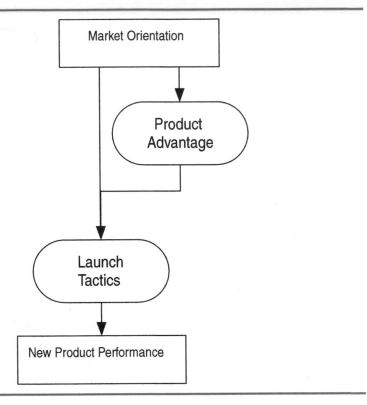

EXHIBIT I.1   Selling a Technology

legally enforceable right *copyright,* which is a kind of intellectual property (IP).

Now the research tells us to succeed at commercialization we need a market orientation. So who needs to know about technology transfer? Who will put their hands on this book and read it? Who is the audience? More generically, who is the end user? Answering the question, "Who needs it?" is the key to developing a market orientation. We want to know who will gain utility from reading this book. For those people, this book will be an asset, that is, an object with a value. Since the object will have value, at least in theory, I should be able to make some money by capturing some portion of that value. How much value I can capture is a matter of how much of the value the end user has to retain to make it worthwhile to acquire the book. But, I am getting ahead of myself.

One way to answer, "Who needs it?" is ask who does activities in which this book would be useful. In other words, market orientation occurs when a technology push-perspective (I have this knowledge about how to commercialize technology) is converted to a market pull-perspective (these folks want to know how to commercialize technology). If I can make this transition, a deal is possible. I can sell books.

As we will discuss, identifying relevant folks is a matter of mapping the performance, ease of use, and price of a technology against needs of potential end users. From this perspective, technology transfer is providing "*just-in-time knowledge*™" to those who need it. If I find the people who need the intellectual assets, then I will find the customers.

Technology transfer is the transfer of a technology from one person to another across organizational lines. Almost always, *technology* transfer involves early stage technologies that are just emerging from R&D or offer a substitute for technology recently introduced into a market niche. In technology *transfer,* the intellectual asset package that constitutes the technology is literally handed from one party to another. This transaction is called a deal. The deal commonly involves money, but as with any contract, it really does not matter what is being traded in exchange for the intellectual asset package.

Now, if technology transfer involves doing deals, then one market niche for this book should be people who do deals involving technologies. We can segment these professionals into at least four groups by where they work: university and non-profit technology transfer offices, government lab technology transfer offices, corporate licensing offices, and consulting groups, like my own company Foresight Science & Technology. On the other side of the deal equation we again have at least five segments based on the arena in which people work: corporate in-licensing offices, government R&D and procurement activities, venture capitalists and other investors, consulting firms that find and integrate technologies for customers (another activity of Foresight), and firms that buy or license in technology in order to further develop it and then sell it.

We can examine each of these customer segments in more detail to discover why they might be interested in this book. Since they are probably buying the book to learn something, it makes sense to understand their current knowledge and know-how in technology transfer. That way we can offer them something new. What we need to understand is their requirements for knowledge and know-how so we can design our book to map to their needs.

One reason for segmenting the market, as part of gaining a market orientation is that each segment will have more or less different requirements. For example, a major motivation for university technology transfer is to get faculty discoveries into practical use in order to stimulate social and economic benefit on the one hand, and on the other hand, to create honorific and monetary rewards for faculty and the university. Money is far more important for corporate out-licensing. General social and economic benefits are usually not success criteria for corporate offices. So it is likely that universities will be far more interested in learning how to do small deals that break even than corporate folks, as they have to create faculty satisfaction as well as make money. In other words, the requirements of end users reflect the activities they conduct and their motivation for those activities and thus shape what they will look for in a technology.

Comparing the training offerings of different associations highlights this difference. The Association of University Technology Managers (AUTM), which represents university technology transfer professionals, has courses like Basic Licensing, Start-Up Businesses, and Technology Operations and Organization Licensing Skills.[2] The major emphasis of training for university offices is how to move the technology out, sometimes in the context of bringing in research funding from industry. The Licensing Executives Society (LES), which represents corporate professionals, has courses like Licensing Fundaments, Intermediate, and Advanced but adds courses in intellectual asset management and business development.[3] For corporations, moving it out is important, but also important is bringing technology in and managing for profit. The Federal Laboratory Consortium, which represents labs run by the U.S. government, has courses analogous to those of universities, i.e. tech-out, with a subsidiary emphasis on forming research partnerships that bring in external funds and resources.[4]

In addition to activities and motivations, other factors influence end-user responses when they are confronted with new technology. As we shall see, especially important are the competencies and experiences of the practitioners of the activity. Obviously, experienced practitioners will seek more advanced material than novices. Lawyers will seek different material than marketing folks. Understanding who our end-users are, and what they do, helps us determine if our technology, in this case, this book, will likely be perceived as useful.

One place training is useful is where new people are entering a field. What was striking when I did the original market research leading to this book is that in every customer segment there was a demand for more training and education about how to do technology transfer. Why? Labor shortages! According to the U.S. Department of Labor's *Occupational*

---

[2] Association of University Technology Managers, "AUTM Events," n.d., http://www.autm.net/index_ie.html (accessed September 12, 2004).

[3] Licensing Executives Society, "LES Education programs," n.d., http://www.usa-canada.les.org/education/ (accessed September 12, 2004).

[4] Federal Laboratory Consortium for Technology Transfer, "T2 Education and Training," February 18, 2004, http://www.federallabs.org/servlet/FLCItemDisplayServlet?wItemID=2003–08–11–14–31–46–062-Item&wRgn=National&wUser=eportney (accessed September 12, 2004).

Handbook, marketing is a growth industry and in this rising tide, early-stage technology marketing is just one of the boats rising.[5]

Labor shortages suggest a new market niche: higher education. A quick Web search reveals the National Collegiate Inventors and Innovators Alliance, an association for entrepreneurship programs at universities and colleges. The members list is extensive—a good preliminary indicator of market opportunity.[6] As with the professional niche, we can segment the customers. For example, students in entrepreneurship programs likely will have somewhat different needs from students in engineering management, MBA programs, and technology transfer programs.

We end up with a market that has two niches plus a bunch of customer segments within each niche. Thus, we may have a dilemma as a technology that is designed to meet the needs in one segment or niche may not meet needs as well in another segment or niche. One way to focus on the best opportunities is to look at competition. It makes little sense to try to meet a need if the market is already locked up by competitors, or soon will be. A search of Amazon and Barnes and Noble revealed there appear to be few textbooks. There are lots of how-to books and some specialized studies, but it is hard to find a generic textbook.

Hey, hit me over the head with a market opportunity! So, this book is designed to exploit a gap in the market that is inadequately served: textbooks. But it is written in such a way as to be useful for technology transfer professionals who want to step back and think about what they do in order to work more efficiently and effectively.

Think about it. What you want is to sell your IP into a market where you can grab significant market share quickly, and thus attain takeoff. Then you want to leverage that initial market niche to penetrate follow-on niches. University courses are great for books like this one. Each time a professor specs the book for a class, you sell multiple copies. Because of the cost of redoing a course each year, you are likely to get multiple years

---

[5] See U.S. Department of Labor, "Advertising, Marketing, Promotions, Public Relations, and Sales Managers," *Organizational Handbook* (February 27, 2004), http://bls.gov/oco/ocos020.htm (accessed September 8, 2004); U.S. Department of Labor, "Market and Survey Researchers," *Organizational Handbook* (May 18, 2004), http://bls.gov/oco/ocos013.htm (accessed September 8, 2004); U.S. Department of Labor, "Demonstrators, Product Promoters, and Models," *Organizational Handbook* (February 27, 2004), http://bls.gov/oco/ocos020.htm (accessed September 8, 2004); and U.S. Department of Labor, "Management, Scientific, and Technical Consulting Services," *Organizational Handbook* (February 27, 2004), http://bls.gov/oco/cg/cgs037.htm (accessed September 8, 2004).
[6] For the NCIIA membership list see http://apps.nciia.net/WebObjects/NciiaResources.woa/wa/Members/ByLetter?l=A (accessed September 12, 2004).

of purchasing once the professor docs adopt your textbook. Heck, you can teach and have your own students buy it if sales are slow.

Educational use has another benefit. The first sales are always hardest to get. Once you penetrate one market, you can use it as a springboard to others. So, if I can get this book adopted as a text, it will have the credibility it needs to make it more likely that other professionals will buy it. But that means when you design the technology, in this case this book, it is necessary to do it in such a manner as to meet needs in both market niches—schools and professional continuing education.

Obviously, adapting the knowledge I have to meet the needs of my targeted readers will be critical for selling this book. Common sense says meet the most widely held need where there is not too much competing technology. So now we have the focus of this book: how to find customers and do deals; the tech-out side of the equation. This is an activity done across the board, whereas tech-in is primarily of interest in the corporate sector and, to a lesser extent, in government agencies with defense, space, or other mission foci.

Of course, writing a book that will sell sounds great, but before you opened the cover to read these words, somehow you had to be made aware of the book and convinced it was worthwhile buying. Then, you needed a place to buy it. Meeting these challenges is called marketing and sales. Launch tactics address this topic.

Before ending this introduction, I should say a few quick words about my publisher. As an author, a technology developer, I had a dual challenge. On the one hand, I had to write a book you would buy. On the other hand, since I am not a publisher, I needed to find a publisher, who would acquire my IP and then manufacture and resell it to you. (We call this party a commercialization partner or a target.) This structure is pretty common in technology transfer. On the one hand is the end user; on the other hand is the partner (a licensee, strategic alliance partner, investor, etc.). Usually both are needed to succeed.

If you know how to sell to the end-user, you can almost always sell to the partner. The reason is simple. If a potential partner is in business, if you can make money for them, they have an incentive to do the deal.[7] All you need to do is find someone selling to your end users (or wanting to sell to them), who has the ability to do what is necessary to sell to the end users, and who has a gap in their offerings that you fill. In my case, Wiley was the obvious target. They have a well respected series on intellectual property. Their books are bought for both university courses

---

[7] If the target is a government agency or nonprofit, the incentive is almost always a superior way of meeting a mission.

and professional continuing education. They do not have a marketing-technology book.

Technology, end users (buyers), competitive product, good launch tactics, appropriate partner. All we need to get this book into the market are two deals: the first one with the partner, the second one with you. And if you are reading this, well, thanks. That counts toward the royalty payments.

Throughout this book I have used Web sources for information as much as possible. My intent was to demonstrate that, with publicly accessible sources, you can do an amazing amount of research. The down side of using the Web is that sometimes information disappears as the page is taken down or moved. (That is the reason we always list the date we access a site in footnotes.) It is important to compensate for the Web's fluidity by capturing the data when you find it.

It is vital to recognize that Web information can be inaccurate and unreliable. Always consider the source creating it and maintaining it. Cross-check information by seeking multiple sources for the same information. Whenever possible confirm the information from the Web with interview data or other more reliable secondary sources (such as a referred journal accessed through a fee-for-service Web site). Use the Web to make your hypotheses and other sources to sustain or falsify your hypotheses.

Finally, please note that the copyright for all the graphics in the book is owned by Foresight Science & Technology and all are used here with permission.

So much for the introduction. Let us begin.

The Art & Science
of Technology
Transfer

The Game of Technology Transfer

CHAPTER 1

The Pieces

INTRODUCTION

In this part we introduce you to the cognitive framework for understanding and doing technology transfer. We use a game metaphor, as that is the easiest way to understand the model. As with other games, there are pieces and there is a board. In this chapter we introduce some of the key pieces. In the next chapter we explain the board. In Chapter 3, we discuss strategy.

Technology is simply an aid for conducting an activity which is repeated time and time again. It may be a tool, a technique, a material, etc. Because humans engage in activities that are repeated over and over again, it makes sense to build tools and other useful aids so we can do this activity more effectively and efficiently.

Consider a game in which the object is to move a technology out of the hands of one player into the hands of another in such a way as each player is better off after the technology has moved than before. In plain English: You win when you do a good deal. You lose if you do a bad one or do not get one at all. Since you have two ways to lose and only one to win, all other things being equal, simply relying on luck should lead to a loss.

Now, what makes technology-based aids different from those developed on the basis of experience or Eureka bursts of inspiration is that we can explain why we built the tool the way we did. Technology occurs where thought precedes action and is applied to the improvement of that action. In modern times, this thought is usually a scientific or engineering finding that explains why if you do X, you will get Y with some degree of confidence.

It is these aids we are trying to move from one player to another. Our game board is a geophysical-temporal space on which are laid out a series of channels. Players move messages, goods (including technology), and themselves through these channels. The channels run between nodes or arenas where the players live and work. If a channel does not exist, the players are allowed to construct one.

Players, messages, and goods can only be moved where relationships exist. Relationships exist where the players develop predictable patterns of behavior that is patterns that have some probability of occurring. These patterns involve interactions between two or more players.

Rules govern how you can bring players, messages, and goods into relationships by defining what constitutes coherence between attributes of those entities. By defining what constitutes coherence, that is, a permissible relationship, the rules also de facto define what is impermissible. The rules can change over time. By changing a coherence between attributes into an incoherence, players can block the movement of their opponents' players, messages, and goods.

Relationships can be described via equations. These equations use terms like "*constrains*" (–>), "*equals*" (=), or "*approximately equals*" ($\approx$) to describe how an attribute of one entity coheres with the attributes of another entity. For example, an equation can express the equivalence in value between a technology that is being offered to other parties and what other parties are seeking to exchange for technologies.

When players interested in a deal agree the values are equal (or close enough to equal), technologies can be moved from one party to another. This part of the book explains the game. The rest of the book is about how to win this game.

THE PROBLEM WITH MODELS ABOUT HUMAN BEHAVIOR

Like Monopoly™, this game purports to reflect certain aspects of reality. However, social science requires abstracting essential features out of the flux of everyday life. Just what is essential depends on what is being studied. Here we are studying human behavior.

Social scientists will tell you building models about human behavior is fraught with problems because the object of study is active, dynamic, and intelligent. There is a famous debate concerning the anthropologist Margaret Mead, who studied the differences between adolescent sexual behavior in South Pacific and Western cultures. The debate centers on whether Mead was subject to a hoax pulled by the Samoans she interviewed.[1]

According to Derek Freeman, two of the people Mead relied upon, Fa'apua'a and Fofoa, were kidding when they said they spent their nights

---

[1] See Bender, Humphries, and Michal, "The Margaret Mead and Derek Freeman Debate," n.d., http://members.fortunecity.com/dikigoros/meaddebate.htm (accessed September 11, 2004).

with boys. Freeman said Fa'apua'a told him that she never thought Mead would have believed them because it is a Samoan custom to joke and exaggerate about sexual behavior. For our purposes it does not really matter what was the truth. We just need to be aware that asking people about what they are doing or thinking does not necessarily lead us to the truth.

Unfortunately watching people may not be any better. Observation does allow us to develop statistical probabilities for behavior. But without an understanding of what motivates people, we have no way of knowing with any certainty if the behavior will continue. For example, in a study of workers at the Western Electric Company's Hawthorne plant in Chicago, various factors were changed to see if they had an impact on productivity. The factors were things like pay, light levels, and rest breaks. Curiously, every change brought productivity increases. Then, over time, in each instance the productivity increase dissipated. Finally the researchers came to the conclusion that it was not the factors being manipulated that led to the increase in productivity. Rather, it was the workers' awareness that they were being studied. As the studies wound down, so did the productivity gains.[2]

A third path is called *participant observation.* In this method, the scientist uses a carefully structured research protocol to analyze a situation in which the researcher is also a participant. The idea is that by participating, you share in the intersubjectivity of human experience and thereby are able to combine both the "*ask them*" and the "*watch them*" approaches. The problem is the tendency to "go native" and lose objectivity. Even if this problem can be avoided, by becoming a participant, the researcher can never be sure his or her presence has not skewed behavior and views from what they would be in the researcher's absence. It is the social scientific equivalent of the Heisenberg uncertainty principle.[3]

What this brief digression demonstrates is that any scientific method for collecting data on which to build a model has problems. So, I hope the reader will be sympathetic when I acknowledge this model is based on none of these approaches. Instead my approach is philosophic in the Platonic sense. This model is based on contemplation: reflection on my experiences, reflection on what I have read, and thinking about how to systematize the data.

---

[2] See Stephen W. Draper, "The Hawthorne Effect and Other Expectancy Effects: A Note," June 1, 2004, http://www.psy.gla.ac.uk/~steve/hawth.html (accessed September 12, 2004).
[3] See Sociology.org, "Participant Observation: Overview," n.d., http://www.sociology.org.uk/mpop.htm (accessed September 12, 2004).

CONSTRUCTS

Following Max Weber, I have created constructs or ideal types, which are then explored to create the model.[4] Constructs are objects (entities, model elements) that carry attributes and can be placed into relationships.[5] The attributes define (when instantiated) entities. The relationships use these attributes to link one contract or entity to other constructs. The constructs have no intrinsic merit. They merely are more or less useful, depending on how well they help us understand the phenomenon being modeled.

Science is premised on the assumption that with the right knowledge, we can form predictions of the form "if X then Y" with a reasonable level of confidence. If we can do that, then we can combine this knowledge of X and Y with other knowledge and know-how and end up with technologies of the form "do X and Z will result" with some level of confidence.

Assuming we want Z, then the ability to use X to get Z is useful. For example, I supported initial commercialization of a barnacle protein-based technology for Tufts University, based on a breakthrough by David Kaplan. The university's invention disclosure states:

> *The proteins involved in barnacle adhesion are useful in devising high-strength protein-based adhesives capable of curing under water, coating for prosthetic implants to serve as an interface between the prosthetic and the bone or other tissue, and methods of preventing biofouling of underwater surfaces. DNA and amino acid sequences of the adhesion proteins are provided and isolated nucleic acid sequences as well as microorganisms comprising such vectors and capable of expressing a barnacle adhesion protein are also provided.[6]*

As the above summary highlights, if we know specific proteins are involved in barnacle adhesion, (our "if X then Y") then we can use that

---

[4] For an overview of Weber's ideal type, see Coser, "Ideal Types," 1997, http://www2 .pfeiffer.edu/~lridener/DSS/Weber/Weberw3.html (accessed September 25, 2004). Note that for our purposes, we need not worry if our constructs are rooted in the current historical period and in modern socioeconomic systems since that is where technology transfer occurs.

[5] The entity, attribute, relationship approach has its root in Peter Chen's Entity-Relationship approach for unifying network and relational data base views. For an overview see University of Texas, "The Entity-Relationship Model," February 29, 2004, http://www.utexas.edu/its/windows/database/datamodeling/dm/erintro.html (accessed September 25, 2004). The E-R basis is important because ultimately we want a way to model technology transfer that is programmable. As we shall see, the E-R approach is one leg. It allows us to collect and store relevant data. The other leg is how we analyze, and thus make useful, the data. The methodology for that is coherence, which is discussed in the following paragraphs.

[6] Tufts.biz, "Novel Kinase and Mechanisms of Curing of Barnacle Adhesives," September 11, 2002, http://www.tufts.biz/cgi-bin/tech_search.cgi?full_report=1&case=37 (accessed September 11, 2004).

knowledge to invent a set of technologies (our if "X then Z" where X is our knowledge of the protein, and Z is some desired end, such as making glue, making a coating, or making antifouling paint). To make glues, we combine our knowledge of the amino acid sequence (X) with tools for synthesizing sequences. To make antifouling additives we combine our knowledge of those same sequences with knowledge of how to cut them or inhibit their formation and with tools for making those enzymes and chemicals. Assuming we want either under-water curing glues or antifouling coatings, knowing the amino acid sequences is useful. In other words, we can design "*how-to's*" if we have a reliable and replicable understanding of "*what-is.*"

Carrying this instrumental orientation back to our model, if we want to build a technology for technology transfer, one beauty of constructs is that they can be sustained or falsified empirically. You can go out and test to see if the attributes and relationships actually exist in the phenomenon being modeled, to see if they accurately reflect "what-is." A sustained construct is called valid—that is, to the extent we have tested, it is a fair abstraction of "what-is." If we create valid constructs, we should be able to improve the "how-to" involved in technology transfer.

PORTRAYING CONSTRUCTS

Before continuing, I need to take care of a housekeeping chore. I am going to use graphics to portray constructs. The graphic in Exhibit 1.1 is the legend for understanding the portrayals.

Note that to be included in a construct, an attribute must be capable of being measured. At least a yes/no, 0/1 scale must be conceivable. For us, technology transfer is a quantitative interdisciplinary social scientific field.

Also note that defining a relationship is never enough. There must be a special-temporal path, which, following the marketing and communication literatures, we call a *channel* through which the relationship can be formed and endure. While the ideas behind inventions and creations are critical, we always have to remember technology is embodied ideas. It is as physical as the people who sign the deal.

DEALS

We start with the basic assumption of transactions in market economies: Deals take place where the goods bought are (at least roughly) equal to what is given to obtain them insofar as the parties to the deal are concerned.

In technology transfer, the goods being sold are intellectual property—

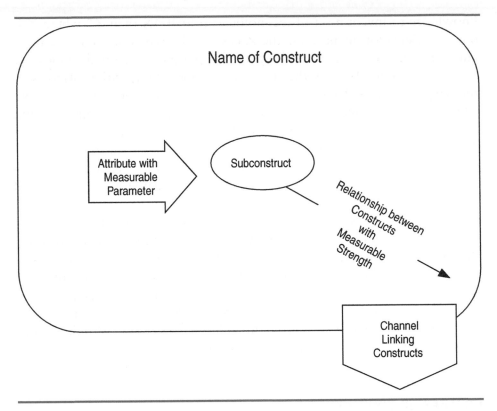

EXHIBIT 1.1   Components of a Construct

that is, ideas that have been reduced to an embodied format (paper, products, etc.) and that can be legally protected (patented, trademarked, copy-
righted, covered by trade secret, etc.), so the coercive power of the state
can be used to punish any party breaking the deal.

In market transactions, what we are saying is so much of X equals so
much of Y. Where two things can be put into this market equation, we say
they have equal value.

One way to visualize value is to think of breakfast cereal. How many
bowls of cereal would you want to sell your hat? How many bowls to sell
your car? How many to sell that great idea you had last night? Technology
transfer can be modeled as trading ideas for bowls of cereal. Using money
makes the calculation easier but changes nothing in the basics of
exchange. Return on investment is like a potlatch. When the deal is signed,
it's time to celebrate.

Now, how many bowls of cereal you want for your idea probably
depends on all sorts of things. Three factors often involved are: desirability, attachment, and available substitutes. Each of these is a relationship
between a player's needs and attributes of a technology.

Desirability measures how well your technology meets a player's criteria for acquiring it. What makes a laptop computer desirable may be its portability. But we can operationalize what portability means into a set of metrics. Operationalization leaves us with metrics for price, performance, and/or ease of use of a technology. These metrics reflect the preferences of the buyer.

Sometimes we need to add an additional set of criteria: aesthetic. Taste is an example. If you like sweet and nutty flavors, you will look forward to eating to your honey nut cereal more than your oatmeal. Such criteria are most commonly found where consumer goods are involved.

> Where taste enters into buying decisions, variation between goods often increases their value. Where taste is not a factor in decisions, variation almost always reduces the value of a good as it indicates a defect. The only question is what the acceptable range for variance is. Let's compare two process technologies. We did a project on introducing new manufacturing methods for near net shape forming making vanes inside jet engines. Here the issue was tolerance. Because the technology could eliminate a processing step while maintaining tolerances, it was a winner. In aviation, where variation can mean a plane falls out of the sky, increasing variation was a "no no" for new technology. Now compare that aviation technology to the introduction of new curing techniques for leather. In the Indian leather industry, tanning used to be accomplished with the aid of vegetable tanners. Today chromium salts are used. The adoption of salts required consumer education, which consisted primarily of adding a label that says "range marks and variation are signs of quality." (I guess consumers could not be trusted to understand each cow is a bit different from every other cow.) Variation in hand-made leather finishes is a "yes yes." Ideally, and perhaps ironically, what is wanted is controlled variation. That suggests sewing, design technology, information technology, etc. are likely to be more attractive to leather manufacturers than inspection or material handling, which have a higher likelihood of damaging the finish. It turns out that is the case.[7]

---

[7] See Sanbord and Becksted, "Technology Adoption in Canadian Manufacturing," August 1999, http://www.advancedmanufacturing.com/pdfs/technology.pdf (accessed September 25, 2004). The information on Indian leather tanning technology is from "Leather Technology," *Times Internet* (2002), http://learning.indiatimes.com/career/car_options/engg/leather.htm (accessed September 25, 2004); and an example of the plebeians' notice for leather buyers is at "A How-To Guide To Purchasing Leather Clothing at Leather Lollipop," n.d., http://leatherlollipop.com/leather_howto_buying_guide.cfm (accessed September 25, 2004).

For our purposes here it suffices to note that, all other things being equal, the more your technology is perceived as desirable, you are more likely to be able to charge a premium price. Alternatively, for any given level of desirability, the cheaper your technology, the more likely you are to sell it. Economists discuss this factor when talking about the elasticity of the demand curve, that is, how much shift in demand occurs per shift in price.[8]

An example helps. Bob Jaffee, as a young post-doc research scientist, discovered that by observing the growth rates and swimming behavior of single cellular organisms he could create a near real-time assay for non-specific toxic agents in water and air. (The organisms function like canaries in a mine. They die or get damaged before people do.)

Bob developed a field deployable unit. For years no one cared. After all, who needs quick analysis when you can collect samples and send them out to an analytical chemistry lab. But Bob believed in the significance of his work, even after his National Institutes of Health funding ended. He drove a taxicab in New York City to subsidize his research, conducted in a small lab in his apartment.

Shortly before 9/11 we met. I thought the work was pretty cool, and on investigating it further concluded it was good science. I found some folks at the Department of Defense who feared there was a coming terror-ist storm. They were funding research and development on a new genera-tion of tools to monitor and protect water supplies for troops in the field and people at home.

What Bob needed was someone who could build a machine he had conceived that did automated analysis of single celled organism swimming behavior. We contacted Woods Hole Oceanographic Institute because they had built equipment to study swimming behavior of plankton in the ocean. They agreed Bob had a good idea and together Jaffee and Woods Hole submitted a proposal to DoD that won a big slug of money. Shortly thereafter 9/11 occurred and no one questioned why we would want a near-real time way of determining the presence of nonspecific toxins in water or air. What had been undesirable was now very desirable.

> Never value a technology on why it is desirable to you. If the other party is clever they will point out they do not care. They only care about why the technology might be attractive to them and your focus

---

[8] For a quick tutorial on how quantity demanded changes in response to a change in price, see Neil Skaggs, "Price Elasticity of Demand," n.d., http://www.econ.ilstu.edu/ntskaggs/ECO%20105/readings/price_elasticity_of_demand.htm (accessed September 25, 2004).

on yourself indicates you have no real idea about that. "*Green*" technologies are commonly prone to this problem. For example, we assessed a nonvolatile organic compounds glue for bonding metal to rubber—something done frequently in the auto industry. But the non-VOC aspect had little interest until our customer produced test results demonstrating that the glue actually made superior bonds. Sounds silly but the key challenge for auto manufacturers is getting better bonding of rubber to metal, not removing the VOCs. The reason is that infrastructure is already in place to suck up and dispose of VOC fumes. The disposal cost is minimal and the infrastructure is sunk cost. Without the superior performance no-VOC just won't sell till that investment has been amortized.

Attachment measures how easily you will part with the good or how badly you want it. We assume the more emotionally difficult it is to part with the good or the more imperative its acquisition, the higher its attachment. Attachment thus links the relative importance of a player's needs with the performance, ease-of-use, or aesthetic features of a technology. Attachment weights the metrics of desirability

If you have a car and someone asks to buy it, you might think, well, if the price is above what it would cost you to replace it, why not sell? On the other hand, suppose the car is a 1971 silver blue Shelby Mustang that you have lovingly restored after finding it three years ago in a farmer's shed outside Oshkosh, Wisconsin? That car is *your* car, not just vehicle ID # so and so.

Now think about living in Manhattan where no-one needs a car and suddenly there is this 1998 Ford Escort you inherited from Aunt Jeannette, and it's parked outside on the street where every Tuesday that dang parking enforcement officer gives it a ticket because you do not have a garage and work late Monday night and somehow never wake up in time to move it to the other side of the street before the street cleaning machine comes down the road. The point is that replacement value only matters if you want to, and are willing to, replace the good. Or as Art Butler, a retired economic professor at the State University of New York at Buffalo likes to say: "My house is always for sale. It's just a matter of the price."

Never value technology on its development costs. If the other party is clever, they will tear you apart by exploring how you stupidly wasted money developing the technology, thereby artificially inflating your price.

Attachment is one factor for figuring out whether it is better for a company to license or buy from you as opposed to developing a competing product. One of our projects was for Areodyne, a well-respected developer of advanced scientific instrumentation for atmospheric research. The company was one of the first in its niche to market with a quantum cascade laser based spectrometer. The market is small for this kind of specialized atmospheric chemistry instrumentation and part of the key competition is in-house development by research teams. What matters to these buyers is getting a unit quicker and cheaper than they can develop it themselves, that is, they have negligible attachment. The appropriate method for pricing the unit was to determine the buyer's in-house development costs and beat it. That method placed the price below the value of substitutes for the buyer. The pricing is feasible because the development costs are being amortized over tens of units rather than a single unit.

We can even go further. Suppose our developer wants to form original equipment manufacturer (OEM) arrangements to sell their unit through vendors who would otherwise be competitors. For the developer, (e.g. Aerodyne in our example) OEM agreements enable increasing the number units sold, thereby increasing the base for amortizing costs, thereby effectively cutting the cost per unit. So long as an increased economy of scale can be attained, each additional unit produced should cut per unit cost, which will increase the profit on units the developer sells. Selling more increases gross revenues; earning more per unit increases net revenues. Profits rise. This is definitely a good thing for a company. Heck, even universities and government labs like money.

We can conclude it should be in everyone's best interest to enter such an OEM agreement so long as each competitor can beat the anticipated per unit profit margin it would have earned, had it run an independent development program, or partnered in a development program with someone else. No strategy a competitor might adopt would leave them better off. But, this conclusion only holds if we can assume attachment away. If the competitor feels demonstrating technical prowess or leadership is critical for long term success, it will be attached to its own technology, changing the calculus.

Attachment is a two way street. Maybe 30 years ago I was in London and walked into the Tate Museum and saw the Turners. I was knocked off my feet. The play of light in which the world dissolved; the use of water and sky as fluids that metaphorically danced with the fluidity of light. This year I was back in London again. The first place I went was to the Tate to see them again. And this time, being an older and wealthier person, I looked for an affordable Turner for sale in the galleries. In art there is an aesthetic attachment not found in most technology transactions. But the dynamic is the same. The more someone wants it, the more you can usually charge. If you don't believe this, Google Jerome Lemelson. You may have to drag them to the table kicking and screaming, but if they are really attached to what you are selling, they will buy it rather than not have it.

The final factor is the availability of substitutes. Substitutes create a benchmark for a technology's fair market value, or to be more precise, a market price range likely to be perceived as reasonable or fair by buyers. (Attachment can be used to suggest where in that range you should price your goods.)

The substitutes need not be direct replacements for what you have. All other things being equal, the value of a new sensor for detecting mercury emissions from coal power plants is likely equivalent to the value of a sensor used to detect equivalent parts per whatever of mercury being emitted from an industrial incinerator. Wander through the cereal aisle in the supermarket. The price of any vendor's cereal is constrained by the other cereals being sold, with the range smallest when comparing cereals with similar ingredients and taste.

Never value a technology above its substitutes unless you have brand loyalty. If the other party is clever they will make you feel stupid by pointing out they can buy an equivalent good for less. Now you have to come back cheaper or there is absolutely no reason to buy from you because you just got caught gouging.

Brand loyalty changes the equation because it enables you to price above substitutes for the same product. It is why people buy Honey Nut Cheerios rather than the store brand even when they taste the same, have the same nutritional value, and so forth. But, even brand loyalty can only take you so far. As Abe Lincoln said, "You can fool some of the people some of the time but you can't fool all of the people all of the time."

Substitutes create a framework for sticker shock. Because we want to avoid "You Want How Much!" when we go to enter the market, we can use the pricing of substitutes that adequately meet end-user needs to eliminate potential market entry niches.

Under contract to the U.S. EPA, we did a market analysis for a hand-held explosives detector designed for military use in Iraq. The EPA was funding the company that developed the unit to adapt it to sense biological toxins as well. The company thought they could commercialize the device, which cost around $26,000 for landfill use. Two problems: First, substitutable technology only cost a few thousand dollars. Second, landfills do not get the kind of budgets that an army at war can obtain. Our research indicated the focus of commercialization should be an industrial biotech, where buyers were used to paying prices in the $20 thousands. (Although sensing toxins was not needed, users did want a better way to detect closely related chemical compounds, making market entry contingent on one of those proverbial "simple matters of engineering.")

Substitutes also set a baseline for general acceptability. People normally make decisions on only a few criteria. You are buying a car. You want good fuel economy, comfort, and a price below $15,000. You do not specify what you want for tires or the lock on the trunk. These are important, in that a car without tires would not be very useful. But basically all you care about is that the tires be good enough, that is, within the general range of acceptability.

Now, the whole reason for this discussion is to point out we have to understand what people want to write an equation that works for a deal. Value is always the middle term in a market equation. This value presumes that the attachment to the good by the seller and buyer do not make a deal impossible, that it can be sold for a price within the range of substitutes (or if there are no substitutes for a price seen as reasonable), and that it is desirable enough that someone wants to buy it. Given such assumptions, the seller and buyer can agree on a price and you have a deal.

From this perspective technology transfer can occur where an attainable equation can be created, that is, you can define a transaction that both parties to the deal will find fair. That is the art and science of technology transfer: making sure the equation happens at the right time, in the right place, for you and your customer. All deal makers do is create attainable equations. These equations look something like this:

Royalties (x) = Some Percent of the Value of Technology for
Generating Savings or Profits (v) = Rights (y) Transferred via License

Capital (x) = Some Percent of the Value of Technology for
Building a Company (v) = Equity (y) Transferred

Cash (x) = Some Percent of the Value of Technology (v) for
Providing Services in this Context = Know-How (y) Transferred
in Consulting Contract

Now, implicit in these equations is the fact that the value received with a technology *is not* simply equal to what a buyer will pay:

$$\text{Value } (v) \neq \text{Cash } (x) = \text{Price } (\$)$$

The value of a technology has to be more than they will pay for it, or there is no reason to enter the deal. At best the buyer ends up running in place financially.

> Be aware. Not everything will sell. Sometimes a technology is early, sometimes it is too late, and sometimes it is just irrelevant because no one wants it even though it's brilliant science. But if you have a portfolio to move, you will almost always have some winners.

TECHNOLOGIES

Now that we know what a deal is, we can focus on what is being traded. To say we are trading embodied ideas is not precise enough. There are all sorts of ideas and all sorts of ways to embody them (see Exhibit 1.2). What makes a technology suitable for use in a deal?

Plato, in *The Republic*, says ideas are the essential core of reality. In the myth of the cave, he has Socrates describe a group of people chained in place. Behind them is a fire. Another group of people carry cutouts in front of the fire, but behind the backs of the chained people. That creates shadows on the cave wall. The chained people watch these shadows. They see birds, chairs, trees, and shadows made by whatever silhouettes are carried in front of the fire. They think what they see is the actual object, but it is just a representation. This representation is a metaphor for the idea of the object being carried.

In Plato's myth, the people are unchained and realize all they have seen are shadows. They think the silhouettes (these embodied ideas) are the real objects until they wander outside the cave into the sunshine and see the "real world." Plato's point is that even the objects in the real world are just embodiments of the eternal ideas of bird, chair, tree, etc. He wants you, the reader, to realize that there is more to life than what you can see and touch. He believes there is something outside any embodiment—the pure idea. Because it is outside any embodiment it is eternal. He believes what really matters is knowing those eternal ideas.

Whatever the merits of the Platonic argument, our concern in this book is more instrumental. For us, what matters is not the idea per se,

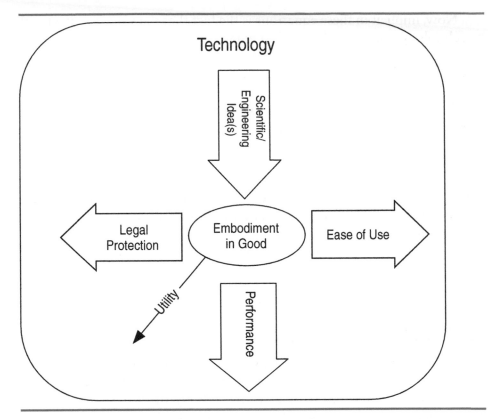

EXHIBIT 1.2   Attributes of a Technology

but its embodiment. It is the process of embodiment itself that concerns us—how an idea is made into something we can see, touch, feel, hear, or taste. The ideas that interest us are ideas that can become things we can sense. Technology transfer occurs down and dirty in the mud of human existence.

In this life, we wake up in the morning and are hungry. We want that bowl of cereal, and we want it without working too hard to get it. Suddenly we understand why technology transfer is important. It is important because we want to get our hands on tools that make it easier to get that cereal. We want combines to harvest wheat in Nebraska. We want ships to carry the sugar from Hawaii and ways to produce it out of sugar cane. We want trucks to deliver milk to stores in New York from farms in Wisconsin and refrigerators to keep the milk cold. We want bowls and spoons to eat with.

When we think about a way to satisfy a need, like eating, we can usually refine it into an ordered set of tasks. A task is one or more activities focused on accomplishing a specific goal.

When tasks are linked together in a particular order to conduct goal-directed behavior, we call that set of tasks a task sequence. Practices are made up of one or more task sequences. Dribbling a basketball is a task. The fast breakaway into a lay up is a task sequence. Playing basketball is a practice.

Technology is a physical embodiment of an ideal that is helpful for accomplishing a task. Technology can be tools, techniques, or materials. The kinds of tasks where it applies are almost always repeated tasks. After all, why buy or learn to use a technology for one time only. However, if the task is repeated, it makes sense to adopt a more reliable, most effective, and/or more efficient way for doing that repeated activity. Technology helps us manipulate the physical world to accomplish a predetermined end that is instrumental for fulfilling the reason for doing a repeated task.

Technology gets applied in task sequences in order to move the physical world in a manner that makes our life better. Our friend Plato would tell us there is an eternal definition of what makes life better. He calls this idea "*Good Life*." Given the idea of the good, its embodiment in life is the Good Life.

Markets are not so contemplative. In a market, it is just about goods. Goods are anything that anyone believes facilitates living a good life, however they define that. The ability of the good to contribute to that good life is measured as utility. But since what is the good life is entirely subjective, that definition does not help us very much.

We need a way around that problem. Recall we do tasks to meet our needs. It seems reasonable to assume meeting our needs is part of living the good life. Since tasks and task sequences are goal directed, once the goals are stated, we can define objectives. Once the objectives are defined, anyone can assess how well a tool, method, material, etc. contributes to attaining the objective(s). More contribution equals more utility. Technologies have utility if they are used in tasks that someone believes facilitates living a good life.

Not surprisingly, just what makes a good "*better*" is an empirical question. We cannot know what "*better*" means until we look at what specific people want to accomplish. Better measures the incremental utility that the technology provides. This incremental contribution is measured on some dimension relevant to that end user who defines the goals and objectives of the task.

We can summarize our discussion as follows: If we want to know if a technology is commercializable, we ask how it helps conduct one or more tasks that satisfy particular needs for specific end users. Deals are made where technology creates superior net utility for buyers.

People almost always assess utility on just a few criteria. The trick is to identify just what those criteria are and to be better than them. For the rest of the potential evaluation criteria it is usually sufficient to be as good as the competitors. An example is a non-skid surface for aircraft carrier landing decks. On a key criterion, resistance to tail hook strikes, a new technology for these surfaces underperformed. When struck, it created a shower of splinters that could endanger the eyes of unprotected sailors, and aircraft if sucked into engines. Nothing else mattered with that technology unless tailhook strike could be endured. The solution for commercialization was to shift the technology to an application in which the strike impacts were not important. We thus focused on ships with helicopter pads, where the key issues are durability and time to apply; secondary criteria for aircraft carrier landing strips. On these criteria the technology shined.[9]

Again just *what is* superior utility is an empirical question. The metrics measuring better can be classified into two broad categories: performance and ease-of-use.

Performance is a measure of functionality. It addresses how the end user actually completes the task with the aid of this technology. Performance is usually measured on interval scales in standard international units (SIUs) and key units outside the SIUs.[10] The battery in my laptop provides so much power at such a rate and weighs so much. That means it is useful for working at the beach.

Ease-of-use is a measure of the difficulty an end user will experience when using the technology to attain the promised performance. It is usually measured in ordinal or cardinal scales using characteristics and features of the technology. Ease-of-use is determined with the aid of two sets of criteria: characteristics and features.

Characteristics measure how well our technology maps to the skills, capabilities, and resources of, or available to, end users. Adaptability is an example of a characteristic. Because I can stick a CD into my laptop and

---

[9] For an analysis of why people use limited criteria, see Legrenzi, Girotto, and Johnson-Laird, "Focusing in Reasoning and Decision Making," in *Reasoning and Decision Making, Cognition Special Issue* (New York: Elsevier Science, 1993). For evidence this is the case in purchasing decisions see Ozanne, Brucks, and Grewal, "A Study of Information Search Behavior during Categorization of New Products," *Journal of Consumer Research* 18 (March 1992).

[10] For these units, see the descriptions at the National Institute for Standards and Technology at http://physics.nist.gov/cuu/Units/index.html and http://physics.nist.gov/cuu/Units/outside.html (accessed September 25, 2004).

load a new software program, my laptop can be a publishing system, a word processor, an Internet telephone, a DVD player, or any number of other things. My laptop is a lot more adaptable than my cell phone, say, for sake of argument, five levels higher on a scale of one to ten.

Features refer to the interfaces end users utilize to access and manipulate the technology. Mismatch between characteristics and end-users are barriers to entry. Features can be used to mitigate these barriers. The fact I can load software does me little good if I cannot figure out how to use it. But if the desktop publishing software can be accessed through the same drop-down menu structure as my word processor, I probably can figure it out.

Together these metrics define the utility of a technology. Ideally, for both performance and ease-of-use, we would weight the specific metrics to reflect their importance to end users.

Better does not always mean more. Over-performing can be as bad as under-performing, especially when there is a cost penalty to get the performance. Many years ago I supported commercialization of a new magnet technology for magnetic resonance imaging (MRI) machines. The inventor's father had been a grain farmer. His preferred application for his technology was in high throughput machines for measuring moisture in grain. The grain would be measured as it ran along the conveyer into the grain elevator, providing a precise measure for the amount of crop versus water. Unfortunately, precision came at a significant cost increment. Market research established that moisture was currently determined by using low cost capacitance probes that were stuck several places into a truck load of grain before loading it into the elevator. Sometimes you won, sometimes you lost, when the money paid for your grain was determined by the weight of product going into the elevator. Overall people believed it averaged out even though moisture measurement could be more accurate, but both farmers and elevator operators felt the current technology created fair results. They had no incentive to pay a premium for a high precision system and the technology could not be commercialized in that application.

OK, lets return to equations and see if we can describe a fair deal. My buyer wants:

$$\text{Performance } (\Sigma p_{1 \ldots n} \times w_{1 \ldots n}) + \text{Ease of Use } (\Sigma e_{1 \ldots n} \times w_{1 \ldots n})$$
$$= \text{Utility } (u)$$

where w is the weighting, and there can be multiple metrics.

Obviously, if we can put a price on utility, we have a basis for doing deals:

$$\text{Performance } (\Sigma p_{1\ldots n} \times w_{1\ldots n}) + \text{Ease of Use } (\Sigma e_{1\ldots n} \times w_{1\ldots n})$$
$$= \text{Utility } (u) \approx \text{Value } (v)$$

Value is just the expression of utility in money. Note that in the above equation we use an approximately equal sign rather than an equal sign. Value, an objective metric, is never a perfect substitute for utility, a subjective one. But we can ask a person to set a dollar value on the utility, establishing a rough correspondence.

Note that once we know what end users want in terms of performance and ease of use we can predict the utility of different technologies and thus we can compare them and determine who has a competitive advantage. Competitive advantage means your technology meets end-user needs better than any substitute. That makes it more desirable, and thus worth more to the end user.

Using value, which is expressed in dollars, also allows us to compare the relative utility of different technologies for widely divergent tasks. For example, we can compare the relative advantage for any individual of a new biocide for drug resistant staff infections in hospitals with the relative advantage of a new way to stop spam in email. All we need to do is ask that person to express the utility in dollars, that is, to define each technology's value to them.

We cannot, however establish value by asking someone, "What will you pay for it?" Value only exists where benefits are obtained, that is, to be useful a technology has to lead us to the task *"better"* than we did before. We want some improvement net utility. Charlie trades because he thinks "This year I am going to be a babe magnet" so he trades his Dodge truck for Harry's classic Harley motorcycle.

$$\text{Value} \approx \text{Net Utility } (nu) \approx \text{Benefits } (b) - \text{Costs (Price (\$) - Other Costs } (c))$$

What goes in other costs? Other costs include the costs of acquiring, implementing, and using a new technology. You buy your son his first two-wheel bike for Christmas and next thing you know you are putting up with your husband's grumbling while he reads the instructions and puts the darn thing together. And then "Ouch" that was his finger he squished and now you are running upstairs to get him a bandage. But there are none so you have to run out to the store while he holds a tissue against the wound to keep from dripping blood on the living room carpet.

Usually when a new technology is implemented there is a need for training, some revisions to procedures, maybe improvements in physical plant, etc. All of this takes time and money to accomplish. These labor and other expenses are called *"changeover costs."* There are always changeover costs; the question is: When can we assume they are insignificant enough to be set to zero?

Large change-over costs make it more difficult to make the case for a deal because the changeover costs for the current technology, having been spent in the past, are now sunk costs. That means they are not included in calculations comparing the value from implementing the new technology to continued use of the current technology. For this reason, new technology is often readily adopted after the current technology has been fully, or sufficiently depreciated.

To highlight the significance of sunk costs: Changeover costs are a major factor in the continued dominance of Microsoft operating systems for servers. At the heart of these costs is the client-server model built into the Microsoft architecture. In the Microsoft world, the client is often a key processing center. In the Unix world, the server is the key processing center. Thus, changing over is not simply a matter of swapping operating systems on the server but of rethinking the functionality across the network, rebuilding the client-server relationships to reflect the new architecture, and learning how to manage and support a new set of interfaces.

In *Productivity Dilemma: Roadblock to Innovation in the Automobile Industry*, William Abernathy examined why the U.S. auto manufacturers took so long to respond to the Japanese import threat during the 1973 oil crisis.[11] He found that the American automobile manufacturers were locked into a dominant design in which cars kept getting bigger. That made it difficult to see the impending collapse of the large car market. To make matters worse, they had just invested in new factories to build larger cars. So they were locked in, having spent their cash, and could not reinvest in designs and factories for fuel efficient cars. They had to tough it out till large car sales recouped the costs of building and operating the factories. By that time, the Japanese were able to establish a firm beachhead in the U.S. market.

---

[11] William Abernathy, *The Productivity Dilemma* (Baltimore: Johns Hopkins University Press, 1978). For more on the oil crisis see Wikipedia, "1973 Oil Crisis," n.d., http://en.wikipedia.org/wiki/1973_energy_crisis (accessed July 18, 2005).

How much net benefit or profit is required to make a deal happen is another one of those empirical questions. All our model says is that:

$$\text{Net Utility } (nu) \approx \text{Net Value } (nv) \approx \text{Net Benefits} = (\text{Performance } (p)$$
$$+ \text{ Ease of Use } (e)) - (\text{Price } (\$) - \text{Change over Costs } (cc)$$
$$- \text{ Operating Costs } (oc))$$

where **Net Benefits$_{t1}$ > Net Benefits$_{t0}$.**

Where economic transactions like most technology transfer are involved, we can simplify the net benefit calculation by simply measuring the profit.

$$\text{Net Utility } (nu) \approx \text{Net Value } (nv) \approx \text{Price } (\$) + \text{Profit } (p)$$

Bottom line: Technologies suitable for deals have to offer net utility for the end users that acquire them and net value is never a perfect substitute for net utility. Let's return to the guy putting together his son's bicycle. Suppose he is a professor of theoretical particle physics. Now suppose he is an auto mechanic. The professor probably does not spend most days taking apart and assembling machinery. The auto mechanic probably does. When the professor squishes his finger, he may think, "dang bike." The auto mechanic is more likely to think, "that was silly of me." The out of pocket costs are the same whether a professor or mechanic buys the bike. But the hassle factor is probably different, and thus the value of a self-assembly bike will differ when these guys go shopping for bikes for their younger children.

Of course, deals are more than just equations. The deal is a social relationship. On the one hand, the establishment of an enduring relationship (a pipeline) is often part of the motivation for doing a deal to move technology. On the other hand, since all people are not of noble character, you have to worry about being ripped off.

If you want to sell technology, you must be able to stop people from just taking them for free or they have no economic incentive to deal with you. Like any other kind of property, intellectual property is a social artifact. Once an idea becomes property, one party can exclude others from accessing or using it, that is, the rights to use become attributes of the technology. In market economies, technologies are associated with a bundle of rights related to control of the object(s), which is (are) the goods that constitute the technology. What deals do is transfer part or all of these rights from one party to another in exchange for consideration. The value of that consideration is defined by the equations underlying the deal.

PRACTICES

The context in which utility is determined is a practice. Practices are structured sets of activities that are repeated in order attain some end (see Exhibit 1.3). Practice makes perfect: the practice of law; medical practice; baseball practice.

Understanding practices is critical in our model of technology transfer so let's be sure we understand what we mean by the term. Let's say I want to shoe a horse in the era before the industrial production of horseshoes. I measure the horse's hoof. Then I make the horseshoe.

1. I buy an iron bar with the holes already punched in it. *Task.*
2. I build a very hot fire. *Task.*
3. I heat the bar in the fire to make it malleable. *Task.*
4. I take a hammer and pound the bar into the right shape on an anvil. *Task.*
5. Iterate 3 and 4. *Task*
6. Quench the metal. *Task.*[12]

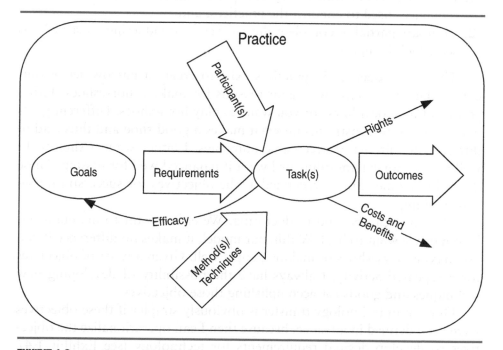

EXHIBIT 1.3 Attributes of a Practice

---

[12] Adapted from *Fremline's Forgery,* "Tutorial: Constructing A Fullered Straight Bar Shoe," 1996, http://www.horseshoes.com/advice/fremlin1/cnastbrf.htm (accessed September 18, 2004).

The specific procedure for making horseshoes listed above is a *task sequence*. There is a separate task sequence for measuring hoofs. Shoeing horses is a *practice*.

Note that practices are not dependent on any specific task or task sequence. Prior to 1857, when the first machine for making horseshoes was patented, I only had the option of making them myself. When the Civil War broke out, demand for machine made horseshoes skyrocketed as horseshoes were needed for the Union Army. By the 1870's, H. Burden and Sons had forging machines that produced six shoes per second.[13] In less than 20 years, the task sequence for making horseshoes went from artisan production to mechanized batch production to mass production. But I can still hand make a shoe if I choose.

I want to highlight four aspects of practices important for technology transfer: goals, outcomes, dominant designs, and participants.

Because practices are repeated sets of structured activities, the goals of, or motivations for, each practice can be described. As we have indicated, given any specific set of goals I can:

1. Define what constitutes acceptable performance for the tasks and task sequences used to conduct the practices, and
2. Compare partial or complete alternatives for conducting those tasks to see which is superior.

The task sequences in practices exist to create a narrow set of outcomes. There are only two major reasons for making horseshoes: Either you want to shoe a horse or you want to play horseshoes. Different goals will set different constraints on what makes a good shoe and thus lead to different definitions of acceptable outcomes. I either want a shoe to fit well for the horse I am riding or I want it balanced well for tossing. These desired outcomes can be redefined as the objectives for successful horseshoe making.

The same can be said of doctoring. We either want to maintain our health or we want to heal. Within our model, it makes no difference if you are making horseshoes or making people well. Given any set of objectives for a repeated activity, I always have the possibility of developing new techniques and goods for accomplishing those objectives.

Our job in technology transfer is obviously simpler if these objectives have been defined in advance, because then I can operationalize the objectives to develop desired requirements for technology (see Exhibit 1.4). These requirements provide a baseline against which I can compare my

---

[13] Pacific Horseshoeing Company, "Trivia," n.d., http://www.farrierschool.com/trivia .shtml (accessed September 18, 2004).

technology's functionalities and interfaces. I can also compare how well my technology performs with substitutes for meeting the requirements. I can rapidly determine if I have a competitive advantage. Exhibit 1.4 provides an example. It is based on data I collected during a project for General Dynamics on electronic controllers for electric motors. (Because almost everything we do in technology transfer involves proprietary data, what you see is dummied data.)

Over time, as people opt for better ways of conducting practices, one (or no more than a small number) of combinations of labor, techniques, and goods emerge as the dominant way for conducting each task within that practice.[14] The result is that after a period of product innovation and experimentation by end users, their expectations for goods tend to coalesce around a set of functionalities and features. The result is the emergence of a dominant design for that good.

Once a dominant design does emerge, there are sound reasons to figure out how to make it as efficiently and effectively as possible. The reason has to do with the advantages of attaining economies of scale and scope and with the benefits of moving down the learning curve. In economies of scale and scope, the average cost of production decreases as

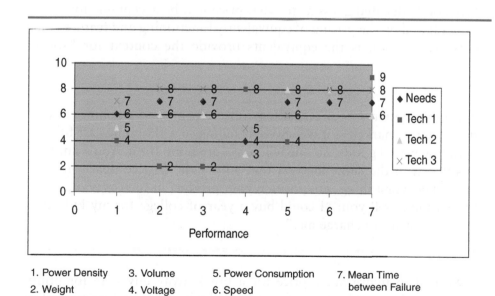

| 1. Power Density | 3. Volume | 5. Power Consumption | 7. Mean Time |
| 2. Weight | 4. Voltage | 6. Speed | between Failure |

EXHIBIT 1.4 Competing Technologies

---

[14] I first ran across the concept of a dominant design in Abernathy's *The Productivity Dilemma*. The concept of dominant design has been explored in James Utterback's *Mastering the Dynamics of Innovation* (Boston: Harvard Business School Press, 1996).

output increases, thereby cutting unit costs. In economies of scale this occurs by doing or making the same thing many times, allowing specialized equipment and techniques to be used. The higher the rate of production, up to some limit, the more efficient the operation. In economies of scope, the benefit comes from using the same equipment and techniques to make a family of related products or services. Again, up to some limit, cost per unit is reduced as the number of units increases. Learning curves operate differently. Here know-how and expertise is gained as a process is repeated. Thus, productivity grows over time, again to some limit. Other learning curve advantages come as systems are debugged and optimized.

Where a dominant design does exist, by definition end users expect vendors will sell them a specific bundle of functionalities and features (see Exhibit 1.5). The functionalities constrain the performance expectations. The features constrain the end-user interfaces used in the good, and thus its ease of use. When these expectations are rigid enough, the constraints can be codified as standards. The result is, where dominant designs exist, we can quickly determine if a technology likely will have utility in the eyes of end users by comparing the technology's performance and ease of use with the likely feature and functionality expectations of participants in the relevant task(s) given the dominant designs in place. We can even make a pretty good educated guess as to what price will be acceptable for a new product based on the pricing of equivalently functioning and feature laden goods. The reason is the equivalents provide the context for "sticker shock."

It doesn't matter if your technology outperforms and outshines anything on the market; if it is viewed as falling in a shopping cart filled with low priced goods, no one will pay a premium for it. You want to position it in the shopping cart that allows the best comparison on price. The worst thing is to position your product in such as way as to have a buyer tell you: "I could buy a year of college for my kid for what you want to charge me."

We had to figure out a price for a break-away guy wire for utility poles. Guy wires can be a significant hazard when drivers lose control as cars frequently run up them and flip over, causing death and injury. We concluded that $200 was a feasible price, as follows. Our analysis suggested that a breakaway base ($120) made the cost of a wooden pole about 160% more expensive than a basic pole ($200). We believed that this technology would be viewed by end-users as a similar safety improvement for the standard wooden pole. Since it fell in the same shopping cart,

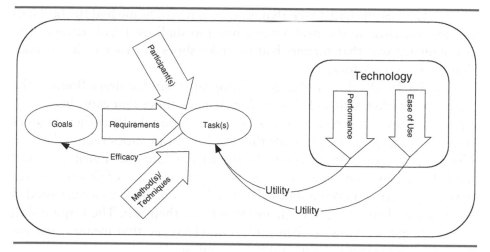

EXHIBIT 1.5   Practice with a Dominant Design

a similar price incremental should be seen as reasonable. So we set the price 200% over standard guy wire pricing. To confirm potential reasonableness, we made another comparison to breakaway metal poles (which do not require guy wires). The least expensive breakaway metal pole at that time was $1260, an increase of 630% over the standard wood pole. Using this technology with a breakaway base provided a much less expensive alternative to a breakaway pole, while providing the same safety benefit. Our analysis further suggests that labor costs are smaller when using this technology on breakaway base wood poles and for installing breakaway poles. So we could ignore that cost. By putting our solution in the same shopping chart as the breakaway poles we ended up with very favorable pricing—$520 for a wood pole modified to breakaway to $1260. We now had a starting point for surveying end users to see if they agreed $200 was a reasonable price, which they did.

The more a dominant design is solidified, the more likely it is that the current task sequence for accomplishing the objectives has been documented and thus the easier it is to assess our competitive advantage. We now have a more solid set of outcome requirements (performance). We also a have pretty good idea of the skills, habitual behavior, and expectations participants will bring to the task, and thus can better understand what constitutes ease-of-use.

The people who shoe horses are called farriers. That person has a skill set. This skill set changes over time and sets constraints on what is and is not an easy to use method/technique or tool. Go back several decades and there was no source for high quality manufactured horseshoes in the United States. The general used steel shoes that were sold had a variety of design flaws. Some had a web that was too narrow. Some had the heel nail located too close to the heel. Others had too shallow a nail pattern. The consequence was that farriers had to make shoes in order to have shoes that fit the horse's foot.

By the 1980's things changed. European manufacturers flooded the American market with well designed, well made shoes that came in enough sizes to fit most horses. As the shoes gained popularity, other vendors began to supply the E-type nails that the European shoes required. Then North American manufacturers began to emulate the Europeans and made better shoes. A core task sequence for the practice of shoeing horses was disappearing: making shoes. The result was farriers no longer needed to lug around coal forges, coal, and iron to do their job. The forging skill was no longer essential for being a farrier. However, that meant a generation of farriers emerged with a different skill set.[15]

Now, let's return to the reason for shoeing horses. Let's say our goal is to give a horse a well-fitting shoe. Because switching to manufactured shoes enables getting rid of the forge, hot shoeing has been generally replaced by cold shoeing. However, there are situations where hot-fit shoes are better. One situation is where clips are used.

Clips are the flat projections that extend upward from the outer edge of a horseshoe. They are usually round or triangular. They create a small lip at the edge or wall of the hoof.[16] A hot-fit shoe fits better and is more stable than a cold-fit shoe so long as it is nailed on where the shoe was originally fit for the same reason that a custom tailored suit will almost always fit better than a manufactured one bought in a department store.

Although hot-fit horseshoes have higher utility than cold-fit shoes in certain circumstances, like perhaps horse racing, in general cold-fit shoes are just as good. So now a farrier has a choice to make. Should she learn how to run a forge and make shoes with it, buy a coal forge, and lug it around for those limited situations where a hot-fit is better or should the farrier leave those jobs to a "specialist?"

It is situations like this that are the necessity which mothers invention. Ken Mankel invents the portable liquid propane fired forge. This product greatly simplifies the decision because the LP forge is cheaper to operate, lighter and smaller, and easier to use as it does not require the skills for tending the coal fire.

As we saw earlier, we can ask people or we can examine what they do

---

[15] The example is based on Stovall, "Hot Shoeing: Pros and Cons," n.d., http://www.horseshoes.com/advice/stovall5/hotshoeing.htm (accessed September 18, 2004).

[16] See Pollett, "Anatomy of the Inner Hoof Wall," n.d., http://www.horseshoes.com/advice/anatomyandfunction/anatomyofinnerhoofwall/anatomyofinnerhoofwall.htm for a discussion of hoof walls and related graphics (accessed September 18, 2004).

when we try to understand their behavior. The first method taps subjective insights. The latter is based on objective observations. By focusing on the practice, that is, on the goals, outcomes, tasks done, and participants, we can define what is "better" without relying on the subjective opinions of people. We really can explain why Mankel's LP forge is better than a coal forge. The practice provides an objective basis for predicting whether a technology will create net utility for participants in that practice.

I would be remiss if I did not mention the horseshoe nail. "For want of a nail, the shoe was lost. For want of a shoe, the horse was lost. For want of a horse, the battle was lost. From loss of the battle, a war was lost." The nail is actually more complicated to manufacture than the shoe. For around 3000 years, nails were made by hand. In the mid-1800s Daniel Dodge, Silas Putnam, and George Capewell each patented nail-making machines to mass-produce horseshoe nails.[17] The Putnam Nail Company began to manufacture nails in the 1860s, By the 1890s the firm had 400 to 500 workers who each produced around ten tons of nails per day.[18] In other words, it was once again the creative burst created by Civil War demand that spurred innovation. As the adage goes: "Necessity is the mother of invention." In our terms, understand what people need to do their jobs better and you can have a pretty good idea as to what technologies you can sell them.

This ability to predict utility on the basis of observation is found wherever thought precedes action. By definition, thought-based activities presume thought can be used to make the activity better. Practices provide a context in which to apply relevant scientific/engineering knowledge and experiential know-how. For such practices we can manipulate syllogisms like:

No germs no bad breath
Swish with hydrogen peroxide no germs
Therefore swish with hydrogen peroxide and no bad breath

Implicit in the ability to make the syllogism is the ability to compare mouthwashes, toothpastes, peroxide, etc. on the dimensions of (1) number

---

[17] Breninstall, "Horseshoe Nails," *Rural Heritage,* n.d. found at http://inventors.about.com/gi/dynamic/offsite.htm?site=http://www.horseshoes.com/advice/nails/horseshoenails.htm, accessed December 18, 2005.
[18] Taylor, "Town History, Dorchester Athenium, December 7, 2004, http://www.dorchesteratheneum.org/page.php?id=52, accessed December 18, 2005.

of germs or nastiness of breath, and/or (2) cost to obtain some threshold of germ reduction or nastiness reduction. We can always ask: "How I can improve efficiency or efficacy?" "How can we cut the cost per unit or improve the utility per unit?"

Our ability to use this kind of analysis is limited wherever taste or lifestyle considerations enter as a major criterion. As another old adage goes, there is no accounting for taste. Sometimes people even seem to act stupid. For example, cigarette sales in the U.S. are estimated to be at about $81 billion in 2004, despite the fact that cigarettes are dangerous, addictive, and likely to kill you. They are sold by tobacco companies that, under the 1998 $206 billion Master Settlement Agreement, all but admitted they knowingly sold products with these traits. So why do hip young college students smoke?[19]

Let's look at one more example. Suppose my practice is cooking. Suppose I want to cook Toll House cookies. I look up a recipe and find the oven has to be preheated to 375 degrees Fahrenheit. Depending on whether I sit the cookies on baking sheets or in pans, I need the oven to hold that temperature from 9 to 11 or 20 to 25 minutes.[20] Because I just looked up this information, I am engaged in a practice in which thought precedes action. Bingo!

I have two parameters on which technologies may be evaluated for suitability: temperature and time. The parameters define efficacy, the performance I need to attain outcomes.

I can compare ovens on these parameters to see how well they can do the job. Clearly the acceptable ovens will have performance at or above my requirements. If an oven performs more poorly than I desire, the only question is can it be adapted somehow to make it acceptable. If not, it is not a candidate for baking my cookies.

In general, the ovens whose performance clusters most tightly to my requirements will be most attractive. Why? Because I am looking for a particular outcome: cookies. Attaining that outcome creates a benefit for me: the satisfaction you get from eating chocolate chip cookies still warm

---

[19] See Mintel International Group, "Cigarettes—US—April 2004," http://www.the-infoshop.com/study/mt19265_cigarettes.html (accessed September 18, 2004).
[20] Well.com, "The Real, the Original, the Authentic Nestle Toll House Chocolate Chip Cookie Recipe," n.d., http://www.well.com/user/vard/cookierecipe.html (accessed September 18, 2004).

from the oven. At the same time, as we saw, there will be costs. Not only must I buy the oven and the ingredients; there also is time it takes to cook the cookies. If my son or daughter is in the house, they may want cookies too. Then I have to decide whether to share or not. That increases the costs for me as I have to make even more cookies or eat less.

(Of course, being kids, for them, however, the cost-benefit calculus is different. They are just eating cookies. The point is that both cost and benefit can only be calculated with reference to some player or situation. They are intrinsically referential.)

Now I am writing this book and I am getting hungry. I want some cookies. I want to bake about 3 or 4 cookies on a 10" x 8" sheet. (Don't want to pig out too much or I will spend all my time eating rather than writing and besides the Surgeon General is warning us about how Americans are getting too fat. Fat is associated with higher risk of diabetes. Get diabetes and you can kiss your cookie eating days good-bye. More thought-preceding action. See, it is a very common experience which helps explain why technology is so ubiquitous in today's world.)

Now I am torn. I am hungry but I have to finish this book. Because I have a deadline for the manuscript, I do not want to sit by the oven. I now have additional criteria. I have the size of the oven and a yes/no (10 or 0) parameter called automatic timer. Let's say I am only going to use this oven to make cookies when I am writing. In that case I have yet another criterion: cheap. I want the cheapest oven that will hold a temperature of 375 degrees Fahrenheit for 11 minutes and turn off after that.

No matter how low or high tech the application, the process is the same. We look at the 5 W's:

1. Who puts their hands on the technology?
2. What are they doing with it?
3. Where are they doing it?
4. Why are they doing it?
5. When are they doing it (including how often)?

The 5 W's tease out metrics we can use to compare solutions. For baking my cookies the metrics are things like temperature, time, automatic shut-off, and cost. Once I have the metrics, I can hop on the Web, call my best friend, drop by the appliance store, or collect data in any other way I choose.

In technology transfer market research, our practice is to start with the Web. A quick search reveals all I need is a toaster oven, so I can narrow my search. I find some units, like Cuisinart TOB-175, that have more bells and whistles than I need, but clearly will make great cookies. Unfortunately it costs around $180 (or did at the time I am writing this).

Over performance usually carries cost penalties. Ever hear about the Boeing B-52 $640 toilet seat? Boeing took a lot of flack for that one. But then it was milspec'ed for B-52s intended to be in use more than 40 additional years. So over-performance can only be defined with reference to a requirement or baseline.

Other units, like the Panasonic FlashXpress NB-G100P, cost less but do not have automatic shut-off. Then I find the Sanyo Space Saving Toasty Oven. Bingo! That's my ticket to cookie happiness. It is only $50 and has a 15 minute timer with an automatic shut-off.[21] My choice is clear. All I need to do is to check reviews to confirm the Sanyo unit is a suitable tool given my cookie cooking criteria.[22]

One caution: Be aware that within practices, there are divisions of labor. These are important. Although end-user needs determine adoption opportunities, and resistance from end users can kill a transfer, the people who actually use a technology are not normally the folks who make the decisions about acquiring new technology. That decision is usually determined by managers farther up the organizational hierarchy. The oft-cited golden rule is: (S)He who has the gold, rules. A key challenge is determining the various players in the decision process and their roles and responsibilities.

To conclude: Insofar as people engage in practices, the goals of those practices set constraints on the techniques and goods that can be used in each practice. Why? Because the techniques and goods have to allow the people engaged in the practice to attain their goals or it is pointless to use them. These constraints can be operationalized into some range of acceptability for metrics determining competitive advantage.

Needs –> Functionality –> Performance

where a –> b means a constrains b

We can say more. Since each task or task sequence is conducted by someone, there is a participant. As noted, that player enters into the practice with some skills and knowledge. Sometimes the skill sets and knowledge

---

[21] Data from Consumersearch.com, "Toaster Ovens," 2002, http://www.consumer search.com/www/kitchen/toaster_ovens/comparisonchart.html (accessed September 18, 2004).

[22] See Amazon.com, "Reviews Written by J. Manly 'healthychoices,'" n.d., http://www .amazon.com/gp/cdp/member-reviews/A1B4917VQ36TVX/104–5562854–0551143 ?display=public&page=3 (accessed September 18, 2004).

vary widely among players. Other times they are uniform, particularly where certification or licensing is required to engage in the practice. Regardless, once we know the skill set and knowledge of the participant we can say whether we are likely to find on hand the know-how and other capabilities to use a technique or to use a tool or material. If the know-how and capabilities are there, the technique or tool or material is likely to be easier to use.

$$\text{Knowledge} + \text{Know-How} + \text{Skills} \rightarrow \text{Ease of Use}$$

PLAYERS

To do a deal, there must be parties. To conduct a practice, there must be participants. Even technologies cannot exist without inventors. So the last construct we need to model technology transfer is players (see Exhibit 1.6).

Needs are an attribute of players. As we have seen, needs are imperatives rooted in the fact that outside some range of conditions we cease to exist. Don't eat. Die. Freeze. Die. Pretty simple.

Abraham Maslow argued that humans need more than basic survival imperatives. He proposed a hierarchy of needs. He argued first we meet

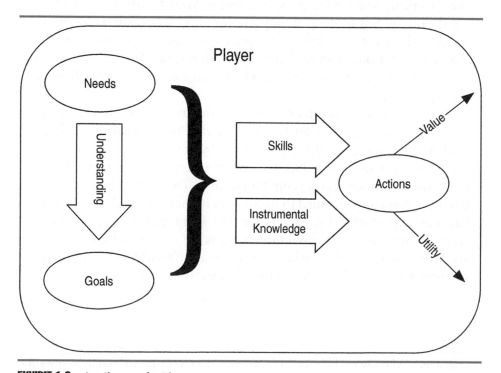

EXHIBIT 1.6 Attributes of a Player

physiological needs, then safety needs, then love and esteem needs, and finally self-actualization needs.[23] Physiological needs address what we need to survive. We die if we do not take in food, air, water. Safety needs address avoiding bodily and psychological harm. They include things like home, family, and as September 11th pointed out, prevention of attack. Love needs address community and belonging. If the prior two sets keep us alive and functioning, love needs acknowledge we are social creatures and that sociability creates needs for companionship and ways to facilitate making and keeping friends. Esteem needs are both self- and other-directed. These needs address the human tendency to seek admiration and power. Finally, self-actualizing needs reflect the inner beauty of people— that something that leads to art, philosophy, charity, and the like. These needs are the ones that emerge when one's life allows leisure time.

For our purposes, it is irrelevant whether Maslow is right or not. It is irrelevant if his categorization makes sense. It does not even matter if the needs he describes are not rooted in humanity as animals but rather are some social creation that varies by time in history and geographic region. All that matters is needs exist and they must, by definition, be satisfied.

Ask yourself, what is the price of a suit in your favorite store? Odds are if you are not looking to buy a suit you will not know. No need, no sale. Have you ever known the prices for suits? If you were ever in the market for one, you probably did at that time. The lesson: Needs are temporal. You have to move when your customers have them or they go away.

As always, an example. We assessed an advanced tunable IR-laser based spectrometer in order to find a market niche where it could be sold. We found significant interest in the laser within the semiconductor industry. Companies like Intel were interested due to problems with contamination during chip fabrication. Two years later, the spectrometer company returned to us for help in making the deal. The firm had never contacted the targets we had identified during our prior work. When we re-contacted those targets we were told they had subsequently found a solution last year from a different vendor and were no longer interested in our customer's spectrometer.

---

[23] Gwynne, "Maslow's Hierarchy of Needs," 1997, http://web.utk.edu/~gwynne/ maslow.htm (accessed September 18, 2004).

The way players meet needs is by applying skills, knowledge, and know-how in order to manipulate tools, techniques, and materials.

Skills are capabilities for accomplishing tasks, which is to say skills are ways of shaping ourselves as tools for meeting our own needs. I can bake cookies. I can toss the ball through the hoop from the free throw line. Skills encompass both the manual dexterity and mental aptitude to do a task or ability repeatedly over time.

Sometimes a skill is innate rather than developed. You can be at the carnival and see this kid walk up and start knocking down the dolls with a baseball even though he never threw one before. The kid is just a *"natural."*

Knowledge is an organized set of information (data and analysis) that can be used to make conclusions about facts not in the original data set. I can add and subtract numbers I have never seen before. I am confident that I will be able to comprehend and analyze poems that will be written tomorrow.

Knowledge can be categorized into two types: instrumental knowledge and understanding.

The first type of knowledge relates to perceptual experience, to *"what is."* It is this kind of knowledge, to use an example from Umberto Eco's *Kant and the Platypus,* that allows us to say "this is my wife and not a hat" when confronted by an object of perception.[24]

Perceptual knowledge contains an inter-subjective organizing scheme for the raw data of perception. It can be formalized and codified, in which case we talk about a field of knowledge or body of knowledge, or it can remain tacit and implicit. One way to formalize and codify knowledge is to filter perception through explicit sequences of behavior designed to ensure the conclusions about what is being perceived are recreated reliably across observers. Science, from this perspective, is a way of creating formalized perceptual knowledge.

As we have seen, knowing "what is" allows us to create "how to's." We call this kind of formal knowledge instrumental knowledge, in recognition of its utility for inventing "how to's."[25]

Instrumental knowledge underlies technology. If I can calculate trajectories and I know the weight of a ball, I can adjust the force I apply when

---

[24] Umberto Eco, *Kant and the Platypus: Essays on Language and Cognition* (New York: Harcourt, 1999). The issue addressed in the book is how we construct, and what is, "intersubjectivity." Eco explores how one goes from the awareness of sensation to what is unique and individual to each of us, the subjective, to labeling something part of that hard, rap your fist against it, knock knock on the door, stuff of the world called objectivity.

[25] Instrumental knowledge is, in the German philosophical tradition, *verstand.* See Wikipedia,"Verstand," September 12, 2004, http://de.wikipedia.org/wiki/Verstand (in German, accessed September 18, 2004).

throwing it to improve my odds of knocking down enough dolls to win that Kewpie doll at the carnival. I can use that same knowledge to design a machine that will throw the ball for me. Since there is not a big market for machines to knock down carnival Kewpie dolls, I can reposition it as a baseball pitching machine so I can get out of playing catch with those dumb boys on the little league team my parents made me join. But those dumb boys grow up and go to war and so I turn my machine into an artillery gun in the hopes of keeping my friends out of harm's way. (As William Tecumseh Sherman said: "A battery of field artillery is worth a thousand muskets."[26]) From there it is not far to launching rockets that put men on the moon or making toys that toss little basketballs into hoops when you put a quarter in the slot at the carnival arcade.

Stepping back for a moment, consider that the same instrumental knowledge can be applied to help satisfy a wide range of needs. Of course, as the example above suggests, as the knowledge is applied in different contexts, it needs to be adapted. Tossing artillery shells requires considering the effects of chemical combustion whereas tossing a baseball with a pitching machine does not. But there is little doubt that the underlying knowledge for making pitching machines can provide a jumping off point for making howitzers.

Should we make howitzers? We pause here for a moment because, like all human activity, technology transfer does have a moral dimension. If you want to make deals, you should always be asking is this specific deal the right thing to do?

There are actually two ethical dilemmas here: one about ends and one about means. The first dilemma is whether we want to make weapons at all. It cannot be answered with instrumental knowledge because it is about goals, about the ends of the human activity called deal making. The second dilemma is different; it can be answered with instrumental knowledge. It presumes the answer to the first question is yes and asks two further questions. The first question is which weapon works best, given the goals of the practice. Are we safer making howitzers than exploring some other alternative, such as making directed energy weapons or increasing foreign aid for humanitarian purposes? The second question addresses the moral integrity

---

[26] CWArtillery.org, "The Civil War Artillery Page," October 31, 2000, http://www .cwartillery.org/artillery.html (accessed September 18, 2004).

of the party to whom we are transferring the technology. Should we do this deal if it licenses military technology to the Iranian government? Should we do it if the license goes to a terrorist cell?

We cannot avoid the moral responsibility we all bear for the fate of humanity, our planet, and with the move into space, the cosmos. We must always ask should the technology be transitioned to anyone and if so, can the party we are dealing with be trusted with it? Last year we assessed a technology for looking through walls in order to watch the activity of the people inside. One potential market is police and intelligence agencies. Anti-terrorism? Of course. Meth labs? Yes. Sex between consenting adults? Whoops. Political dissidents? No way. If you license it for police use globally can you control which police forces or internal security agencies get their hands on the technology?

Understanding is the second type of knowledge. It addresses meaning. Understanding results from contemplation rather than perception, from reflection on imagination.

The German word for this kind of knowledge is *verstehen. Stehen* is to stand, to become, to face. *Ver* gives us motion, action, a *"to do."* If perceptual knowledge is objective, understanding is subjective. What you see depends on where you stand and where you are going. For our purposes, it is relevant because the *"might be"* can spring from it. That *"might be"* constrains the goals for a practice.[27] It provides the meaning and motivation for undertaking the practice. Knowing meaning and intention allows us to understand *"why."*

Understanding *"why"* is critical for determining whether the outcome of action is successful or not *for the player who conducts it.* That suggests any technology is actually meeting two sets of criteria: One which reflects the demands of the practice, the other which reflects the demands of the participants. The extent to which these demands can be expressed as measurable criteria we can improve our ability to determine competitive advantage. But we must define *which* player's goals when making the determination.

Know-how is unorganized procedural data and analysis. It is fragments of technique that can be articulated or documented, but which have not yet been systematized into knowledge. As I type this, I set my notebook computer on a portable Instand™, but have my mouse on the pull out shelf of my roll top desk. I find this a very comfortable configuration. I know the

---

[27] Wikipedia, "Verstehen," July 29, 2004, http://de.wikipedia.org/wiki/Verstehen (accessed September 18, 2004).

stand is adjusted to be an inch or two above my thigh and the mouse is about a half inch to an inch above the computer. Now by telling you this, you can figure out how to replicate it. I could come over to your house, sit you down at a table, and figure out how to set up a workspace you might find comfortable. But to say that is very different than saying the Center for Disease Control's ergonomic position for computers has the keyboard at a 90 degree angle at the elbow, the mouse at the same level, etc.[28] Similarly, I had a discussion the other day with a chemist and manager at a pigment company. He told me that the industry was slowing moving overseas to places like China, but one factor slowing the move was that there was still a bit of art in running the formulations. Art in this context is know-how that is transmitted through apprenticeship.

CONCLUSION

Technology transfer occurs where people do deals in order to obtain better tools, techniques, materials, etc. for conducting practices. It is a transaction in which each side gives something to the other, usually money in exchange for technology.

End users evaluate potential technology on the basis of its net utility for them. This utility is constrained by the tasks and task sequences being conducted in the practice and by the skills, knowledge, and capabilities or the people who do the practice. Where the net utility is large enough, the end user may become a buyer.

The utility of a technology can be described in terms of three sets of criteria: performance, ease-of-use, and aesthetics. At least the first two of these can usually be discovered by examining the dominant design for the core technology used in a practice. The dominant design also provides a reference point for what will constitute sticker shock.

When utility is expressed as money, net utility is roughly equal to value. Value is more than purchase price. Value has to take into account all the costs of acquiring, implementing, and using the technology, as well as some marginal utility that the buyer seeks in order that it is worthwhile for her or him to engage in a transaction with the seller of the technology.

Where each party believes the deal is fair and that they will be better off by doing the deal than waiting or abandoning the deal, a transfer occurs.

---

[28] "Computer Workstation Ergonomics," August 11, 2000, http://www.cdc.gov/od/ohs/Ergonomics/compergo.htm, accessed December 18, 2005.

CHAPTER 2

The Board

INTRODUCTION

In Chapter 1, we focused on the deal and what was necessary to have a deal. In this chapter we introduce a second set of concepts you will need to understand technology transfer deals: the context. To do so, we must pull back from the micro-level to the macro-level.

The macro-level is the game board on which the players do deals. The board is predominately influenced by the context in which the technology is put to use, which we call the arena. The reason is simple. Technology transfer is usually a *"push"* game—you are pushing a solution looking for a problem. Thus, finding buyers is the core challenge.

In today's global economy, the arena is made up of organizations. We shall briefly discuss how the structure and operation of organizations constrains which technologies are of interest to potential buyers. We shall see that technology transfer is a way for organizations to have access to knowledge and know-how without having to pay for the development or storage of technology they might not need. In a manner analogous to just-in-time inventory, technology transfer provides access to "just-in-time knowledge™."

Of course, deals happen somewhere. That somewhere is called a market. So markets are another part of the context for our game.

Finally, we shall see there are all kinds of other players with a stake in whether our technology makes it into the market successfully or not.

ARENAS

Arenas, to continue our metaphor, are the stadiums in which the game of technology transfer is played. They are defined as the set of organizations in which a technology can be applied plus those organizations that want to influence who uses a technology.

There are five major categories of organizations in arenas: *users, buyers, competitors, markets,* and *stakeholders.*

Buyers are the organizations that procure the technology for people who will literally touch and use it. If we have a better catalytic converter for automobiles, by looking at who might put their hands on the technology and understanding why they might touch a catalytic converter, we can find the end users. The organizations in which the end users work or apply the technology are the users.

Sometimes the organizations developing technologies are also users. Many drugs and biological innovations have their initial use as a tool, technique, or material for additional research.

> Materials transfer agreements (MTAs) are used to structure the loan of a technology for research use. They are not usually considered deals as normally no consideration other than reporting of research results is provided. As the U.S. National Institutes of Health Technology Transfer Office notes: "An MTA generally is utilized when any proprietary material and/or information is exchanged, when the receiving party intends to use it for his/her own research purposes, and when no research collaboration between scientists is planned. Neither rights in intellectual property nor rights for commercial purposes may be granted under this type of agreement. MTAs define the terms and conditions under which the recipients of materials . . . may use the materials."[1]

Some organizations in the arena do not contain people who actually touch the technology. Take the catalytic converter as an example. At the time of its initial introduction it was a superior way of reducing emissions. Its use has led to less pollution related illness and a score of other social impacts. Even though EPA regulators and the Sierra Club activists may never touch a catalytic converter as part of their day-to-day work, they are still active in the arena and affect the adoption of catalytic converter technology. We call such organizations *stakeholders*.

Not all organizations that address a technology are in the arena. For example, if you go to "How Stuff Works" on the Web, you can find a description of catalytic converters.[2] The site is not part of the arena as it's function is strictly educational. It is not an advocate for or against the adoption or use of converters.

---

[1] National Institutes of Health, "Material Transfer Agreement: Overview," n.d., http://ott.od.nih.gov/MTA_over.html (accessed July 24, 2005).
[2] Nice, "How Catalytic Converters Work," http://auto.howstuffworks.com/catalytic-converter.htm, (accessed July 20, 2005).

If you are confused about who is in the arena, ask someone likely to be a stakeholder. Call them, and while talking to them ask who else is a stakeholder. Knowledgeable people can be found in relevant associations, university/industry centers, and government agencies. The stakeholders can indicate the other organizations where the technology will be used, be procured, be sold, etc. Keep talking to people till the information you receive is repetitive. Usually after five to seven calls you will have a fair idea of who is in the arena

A few years ago, we were tasked with moving a polyurethane shock and vibration mount into the Navy. We searched on the Web and discovered that someone was testing mounts at the Naval Surface Warfare Center, Carderock Division. A few calls identified that person. He helped us map out the rest of the arena by identifying other stakeholders, users, and buyers. It turned out there was another test facility that ensured when something was subject to fire or explosion it did not outgas toxics, there was someone in a NAVSEA maintenance code who set the specifications for mounts and approved them, there were a set of engineers in various program executive offices (that buy ships) who approve mounts for their vessels, there were design engineers at prime contractors who would spec the mount as equipment, there were a bunch of competitors, there were shipyards that installed mounts, there were the crews that maintained them and replaced them at sea, there were a group of guys who hung on the periphery who were looking for new technology for commercial ships.

Markets are places where buyers and sellers come together to conduct transactions, that is, to make and close deals. Where markets are institutionalized, they may be fixed, like the NY Stock Exchange, or they may float, as is the case with many industry trade shows. While markets can exist as discrete organizations, there is no need that they do.

You are driving along a rural highway in Pennsylvania. You pass an Amish couple in a horse drawn wagon. In the wagon are five beautiful rocking chairs. A little while later you stop for lunch in a little roadside park. Sitting at a table under a large maple, you listen to the brook singing. You turn your head and see the Amish couple pull in to a table nearby. They nod hello. You nod back. They ask where you are from. You reply and ask where they are going with those beautiful chairs. "Why, to market," the man replies. "Today is the farmers' market." "Can I buy one here?" you ask. "Sure," he says. A non-organizational marketplace has emerged.

Hopefully this story reminds you that arenas are no different than every other construct in our model. Arenas are physical. They exist at specific points in time and space. Ford, Engelhard, and Joe's Gas and Garage all have coordinates in longitude and latitude. They can be located on a map and, if we animate the map as a time series, we can watch them appear or disappear as the timeline runs from the Big Bang through the end of the universe. Further, it is not necessary that arenas be physically continuous. For example, Ford has manufacturing facilities in the United States, Thailand, Portugal, Spain, Mexico, France, etc.[3]

CHANNELS AND MESSAGES

Channels are physical paths that link players within the same organization or in different organizations. There are two kinds of channels in our model: communication channels and distribution channels. Some channels are both. Messages are passed in the communication channels and goods in distribution channels. Money used to pass in distribution channels, when it consisted of species and coin, but in today's world it also passes through message channels. When you pay your electric bill by logging onto your account at the bank, you send a message through a message channel to the bank that cuts a check and mails it through a different message channel, the U.S. Mail, which also serves as a distribution channel.

A simple channel is two paper cups and a string. Talk into one cup and the message comes out the other cup. But no matter how simple, channels take energy to set-up and maintain. Some organizations (FedEx, Verizon, etc.) specialize in this activity. Others specialize in regulating them (e.g. the Federal Communication Commission).

Messages consist of information transmitted from one player to another. Goods are objects with physical dimensions. A story is a message. A book is a good.

If we are interested in information, we may monitor the messages in a relevant channel. You wake up in the morning, a bit groggy from last night's party. You drag yourself to the kitchen, put on a pot of coffee and while it brews slog over to the front door, open it, and pick up the paper. You are channel monitoring.

Note that message-passing channels always involve transmissions of embodied expressions. We can track the flow of electrons through the wires and airwaves of the Internet just like we can track the flow of a letter

---

[3] Wikipedia, "List of Ford Factories," June 15, 2005, http://en.wikipedia.org/wiki/List_of_Ford_factories (accessed July 20, 2005).

through the post. For this reason, their content is protected by copyright unless the creator of the message chooses to relinquish copyright.

> The easiest channels to use to make people aware of your technology are the channels they already monitor. In a project involving DNA microarrays for forensic science, we needed a weeding methodology because, quite frankly, there was a lot of junk on the Web. What we did was the Web equivalent of building a panel of experts. In traditional panel studies, you build an expert panel by calling experts and asking them whom they would call if they had a question like yours. The method we used mimicked that approach. Technically it can be considered a form of influence diagramming.[4] The method is robust and can be used for any kind of exploratory market research where statistical validity is not important. As a starting point, we went to Yahoo. (*http://dir.yahoo.com/science/forensics/*) a stop on the Internet as a communication channel. That led us to the FBI (not surprising) and Forensic Science International (*http://www.elsevier.com/wps/find/journaldescription.cws_home/505512/description#description*), a journal referenced on many other sites. These are more stops in the communication channels. We also went to Forensic Science.com, itself not critical, but its links (*http://www.forensic-evidence.com/site/Link_wo.html*) were more helpful as it was a university site with links to the professional associations. By now we had plenty of people to call to confirm the structure of the arena. We quickly got an idea of which people were likely to be most helpful by tossing forensic science and their name in Google. We got a number of pages, like Zeno's Forensic Science site (*http://forensic.to/forensic.html*) and Forensic Science Resources (*http://www.tncrimlaw.com/forensic/*) There are, of course, other websites. But no matter how many times a page is linked, the only way to know if it is monitored is to ask someone or to examine blogs, chat rooms, list servers, and the like to see who is on them. For example, if you want to reach people in the aerospace industry, you get your information into *Aviation Week and Space Technology* by sending an article, writing a letter, or taking out an ad.

In deal making, what is being passed is messages concerning rights. In one direction, proposals for transfer of ownership rights to the technology are being offered. In the other direction, rights to money or other

---

[4] For a description of influencing diagramming and other helpful tools, see Bureau of Reclamation, *Decision Process Guidebook,* n.d., http://www.usbr.gov/pmts/guide/ (accessed September 26, 2004).

consideration (value) is being offered. The channels through which deal information passes are called sales channels. Indeed, the whole negotiation may be simply passing messages back and forth through a phone and/or Internet channel. Even the deal may just be message passing. You fax or mail a contract, they tell the bank to transfer money into your account.

When the object being moved is something that can be sold in commerce, the channel is called a distribution channel. Distribution channels involve getting the product or service from one player to another. Usually we think of this as moving it from the seller's hands into the hands of the buyer, but channels can also exist inside organizations. Where software, documents, and other expressions are involved, the channel may be the Internet. Otherwise a distribution channel requires more traditional transportation options (trucks, trains, airplanes, and ships) and the geophysical routes (roads, tracks, airways, sea lanes) they use to move from point A to point B.

Both communication and distribution channels can be described in terms of the contents they carry, the players they carry them between, the directions they carry the content, the parties who can access them, the parties who monitor them, their carrying capacity, cost, security, and so forth. If a channel does not exist, it can be created.

SUPPLY CHAINS

Sellers, buyers, and users are linked in supply chains. The farm delivers its milk to the cooperative that processes it and ships it to the stores where we shop. A professor takes a leave of absence for a year, hires a few former graduate students, and spins out of the university to further develop a technology she invented in order to license it. All of these are segments of a supply chain (see Exhibit 2.1).

Just who is in a supply chain and what they do depends on what is being made. High-tech goods typically involve supply chains containing process equipment vendors selling tools and machines for making the good and/or its components; vendors selling software; vendors with equipment and devices to integrated into the good; vendors providing raw or

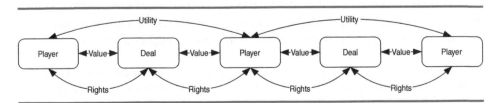

EXHIBIT 2.1 Supply Chain

semi-processed materials; and a range of infrastructure vendors (facilities, utilities, training, accounting, legal, knowledge and know-how, etc.) selling things required to support core value chain practices and ancillary ones. If arenas are the stadium, knowledge and know-how supply chains are the playing field for technology transfer. In this case, the *"raw material"* is ideas being extracted from the heads of clever people.

What makes technology transfer interesting from a supply chain perspective is that it enables organizations farther up in the chain (e.g. businesses, government agencies, non-profit public service organizations) to avoid the necessity of maintaining inventories of ideas and technologies in order to gain access to the "how to" they may need. Just-in-time systems for technology can be build which are analogous to just-in-time systems for products. As in product supply chains, there can be pre-qualified vendors who make their living by stockpiling tools, techniques, materials, and products for customers to use to exploit changing marketing opportunities. For example, CM2h Hill is a multinational firm providing engineering, construction, operations, communications, security, environmental, and related services to public and private clients in numerous industries on six continents. A customer of ours, they offer non-exclusively in-license technologies for solving problems in fields such as environmental remediation in order to have methods in their toolkit to bid on projects. Most repeat players in technology transfer seek to build these kinds of trust relationships with their licensors and alliance partners in order to have pipelines through which they pull innovations related to core customer segments. Similarly, developers of technology seek to build pipelines with licensees to have a pipeline to monetarize the inventions their staff develops.

Viewing technology transfer as a supply chain problem fits well with the emerging structure of the global economy. Michael Guralnick and Vincent Eavis of Citigroup argue supply chain consolidation is an effective means for achieving global organizational agility.[5] The RAND Corporation reports that global competition in the commercial aircraft industry means increased downward cost pressures, leading companies to seek ways of reducing overhead.[6] Cost pressures and the need for agility are major factors behind the push by the airframe manufacturers to shift the locus of R&D down to their suppliers. Similar trends are seen in pharmaceuticals, automobiles, and other R&D intensive sectors.[7]

[5] GTNews.com, "Commercial Cards: Logic and Control in the Supply Chain," July 11, 2005, http://www.gtnews.com/article/6024.cfm (accessed July 21, 2005).
[6] Lance Sherry and Liam Sarsfield, "Redirecting R&D in the Commercial Aircraft Supply Chain, *RAND Corporation* (2002), http://www.rand.org/publications/IP/IP212/IP212.pdf (accessed July 21, 2005).
[7] See UPS, "Building Supply Chain Capabilities in the Pharmaceutical Industry; Part One: Trends Impacting the Supply Chain," 2005, http://www.ups-scs.com/solutions/white_papers/wp_pharma1.pdf (accessed July 21, 2005).

As major firms set and manage R&D agendas for their contractors and subcontractors, these firms must respond or they are replaced in increasing consolidated supply chains. One consequence is that technology transfer within the supply chain increasingly takes on the dynamic of transitioning a technology from one part of an organization into another part of that same organization. Long term supply-sale contracts (that is, strategic alliances) are used to move away from the more arms-length dynamic of traditional technology transfer. A project we did for Boeing is a good example.

Boeing had developed an algorithm for predicting crack propagation in composites. It wanted to have their algorithm integrated into the finite element analysis software it was using. We developed a *"fair deal"* term sheet that was used by Boeing to negotiate a license with that vendor.

Be aware at the platform integrator level the issue is often not which technology will be used but what performance must be provided. Increasingly the platform integrators are setting requirements to be met, but not specifying how they should be met.[8] When looking to do a deal with a supplier of a major integrator, it helps to go to the platform integrator to get their blessing and to find out who in their supply chain they think would be a good target for commercialization.

Another Boeing project can be used an example here. We were tasked with assessing need for a portfolio of noise and vibration technologies into the ground transportation sector. We rapidly determined that the criteria for acquisition were dramatically different in aviation than in automobiles. In commercial aviation, a major objective is to eliminate noise and vibration. In automobiles, the goal is to tune the noise and vibration. A luxury car should sound and feel differently than a sports car. But just how auto firms want their cars tuned, and how much they will pay to attain that tuning, changes over time. We were told repeatedly by firms supplying auto companies, "We explore, we consider, we propose, but what we buy and make is set by what our customer specifies. What we try to have is a portfolio of options on hand that we can propose to meet changing needs." We found a lot of interest in what Boeing had to offer, but little willingness to engage in substantive discussions until we ran the trap lines with the auto companies to clarify what they saw as high priority problems for the next generation of cars, what technologies seemed interesting to them, and the price range of solutions that would interest them.

---

[8] Jos Jans, "Turning NVH into a Competitive Advantage," *Sound and Vibration,* September, 2004, http://www.findarticles.com/p/articles/mi_qa4075/is_200409/ai_n9458492#continue, (accessed July 21, 2005).

In highly consolidated supply chains, first you have to ensure that the top level system integrator (1) sees a problem and (2) sees your technology as a potential solution. They define if technology is potentially timely and useful. Only after gaining their endorsement does it make sense to go to work down the chain until you reach a contractor or subcontractor interested in doing a deal to gain competitive advantage over other vendors in the chain.

Where stable supply chains exist, it is an empirical question just where the best target for transfer is found. Sometimes it makes more sense to transition a technology to an organization further up the chain, which will retain the right to use and sell but sublicense its vendors to make. Sometimes, when the technology can provide a de facto standard, it may make sense to work through an association or consortium which in turn makes it available to all its members. It may even make sense to given the technology away as a way of leveraging first mover advantages for product sales implementing equipment.

Xerox's Ethernet is an example of using a technology to create a standard that can then be leveraged to exploit the original technology. Ethernet was invented by two employees, Bob Metcalf and Dave Boggs, in 1973, as a way of networking computers. Xerox partnered with Digital Equipment Corporation to build equipment for Ethernet and Intel to provide the chips. Faced with potential competition from IBM, the team elected to license Ethernet to anyone interested in building hardware for only $1,000 and to work through Institute of Electoral and Electronics Engineering (IEEE) to develop standards. The strategy worked. As PC sales exploded, so did the use of Ethernet. Unfortunately Xerox never really reaped the fruits of its labor. Metcalf did. He left Xerox and formed 3Com, which rapidly leaped to over $45 million in sales.[9]

A literature review by two business school professors, Tatikonda and Stock, found a variety of differences between knowledge supply chains and traditional product supply chains, at least for now.[10] Traditional product

---

[9] Economist.com, "Out of the Ether," *The Economist* (September 4, 2003), http://economist.com/science/tq/displayStory.cfm?story_id=2019967 (accessed July 21, 2005).
[10] Mohan Tatikona and Gregory Stock, "Product Transfer in the Upstream Supply Chain," *Journal of Product Innovation Management* (November 2003): 447. This article is part of a very stimulating two volume series on product development and the supply chain.

supply chains involved a regular and continuous flow of materials. Knowledge supply chains are still far more episodic. Traditional supply chains are built to sustain high volumes of parts and materials, which are normally delivered in batches. Whereas products are procured primarily for manufacturing or ramp up to manufacturing; technology is procured far earlier in the product development cycle, usually at the design stage. This difference means the specifications for product supply chain goods can be far more rigorously defined. Correspondingly, the risk of not getting what you want is much higher with technology than products. A factor in the risk is the difficulty that sometimes occurs when you adapt a new product or process technology into a company. There is typically very little integration or adaptation risk involved with traditional parts or materials supply chains. Finally, the professors found management objectives for using traditional supply chains is almost entirely tactical: Get component cost down, cut inventory cost, improve quality, etc. In technology supply chains, both tactical and strategic concerns are motivations. Tactical concerns include cutting time to market, keeping within budget, and enhancing performance. Strategic concerns include competence and scientific, engineering, and technical capacity building with respect to new areas of technology.

The utility of knowledge and know-how supply chains, like any supply chain, cannot be taken for granted. A study on 115 R&D alliances by David Deeds of Case Western and Frank Rothaermel of the University of Washington found a U-shape to the performance of, and value from, such alliances. After an initial honeymoon period, the performance dissolves as the divergent interests of the parties come into play. Only if pro-active efforts are conducted is this downward slide reversed. Such efforts can include assigning gatekeepers and champions to projects, holding frequent joint planning sessions, and monitoring and providing feedback to partners about the performance of the alliance. As cross-organizational social and functional ties are built, the performance and value curves back upward. Thus, building successful knowledge and know-how supply chains take around five to eight years.[11]

USERS AND BUYERS

The organizations within the arena are not monolithic. They can be studied to discover their formal and informal structure and how they use this structure to control and conduct practices. As most technology transfer

---

[11] David Deeds and Frank Rothaermel, "Honeymoon and Liabilities: The Relationship between Agenda Performance in Research and Development Alliances," *Journal of Product Innovation Management* (November 2003): 472–482.

involves moving technology into businesses, we focus our discussion on them. The general principles, however, apply to any type of organization. Although our focus here is on businesses, an equivalent analysis could be made for a government agency, non-profit service provider, or other kind of organization.

Successful organizations align their operation structure, control systems, and strategies with each other. We will use a user/buyer organization as an example, If this organization is a company, it will acquire technology that helps it meet its goal of returning value to its shareholders.

The following table illustrates how three different strategic approaches to the market and value creation will affect the kind of technology being sought. Cost leadership involves selling at rock bottom prices. Differentiation involves selling a wide range of products so you have something for every customer segment. Focus emphasizes listening closely to customers and then providing the precise product and service package customers want.[12] For each strategic orientation we provided the strategy, structure, and control systems alignment and then indicate what kinds of technologies are likely to be deemed interesting acquisition candidates.

Market Strategy	Cost Leadership	Differentiation	Focus
Organizational Structure	Functional	Product team or matrix	Functional
Procedural Controls on Practices	Budgets and standardized processes (financial and managerial accounting controls)	Rules and budgets (bureaucratic controls)	Budgets
Outputs Metrics for Practices	Cost, efficiency, productivity	Quality and efficiency metrics	Mixed cost, efficiency, and quality with strong emphasis on customer satisfaction
Key Practices for Value Creation	Manufacturing	R&D and marketing	Product development and customer service
Internal R&D Emphasis	Product and process improvements	Innovation and speeding product development	Rapid response to customer expressions of need

(Continued)

---

[12] The chart grew out of discussions with Charles Hill at the University of Washington in the late 1970s (http://bschool.washington.edu/faculty/faculty_detail.asp?ID=13). See also his book *Strategic Management: An Integrated Approach,* with G.R. Jones, 6th ed. (Boston: Houghton Mifflin, 2004).

Market Strategy	Cost Leadership	Differentiation	Focus
Technologies of Interest	Incremental product and manufacturing process enhancements that have working prototypes	Mature extensions for, and adaptations to, product families and methods and techniques for practices	Prototyped or mature products

Often there are subsets of organizations in arenas with common reasons for using the technology. These subsets are called customer segments. A catalytic converter could affect a wide range of practices in the automobile sector of the economy. Depending on how it is attached to the car, it may affect automobile manufacturers. Companies like Ford, GM, and Toyota will also be looking at how this technology affects fuel consumption, safety, and interacts with other automotive systems. The technology could also affect some of their subcontractors, such as Engelhard who make converters. We also will find people who touch them in dealerships, gas stations, and collision and repair shops. At the very least, these people will have to maintain our catalytic converter and probably need training to do that.

For example, a few years ago, we did the market section for a business plan involving a real-time, highly sensitive nitrogen oxide (NO_x) sensor. One use we found was real time engine optimization for automobiles and light trucks, where the sensor was part of suite of sensors for monitoring emissions. At that time, the likely end users included engineers at engine and automobile companies and technicians at state certified emissions test centers. Each set of users had specific reasons for wanting to measure NO_x emissions. The engineers at the engine companies wanted the sensor to determine how best to design and operate fossil fuel engines. They wanted a small number of highly accurate sensors for lab use. The automobile production engineers wanted mass-produced sensors that cost a fraction of a penny apiece. They were willing to accept lower sensitivity so long as the sensor was robust enough to last the life of the engine, reducing maintenance problems when deployed on hundreds of thousands of cars. The emissions testing firms had yet different criteria. They wanted their technicians to have cheap sensors whose accuracy was defined by state and federal emissions standards, which at the time were below what was needed for engine optimization. Plus, they wanted the sensor robust enough for repeated handling as in one scenario the sensor would be stuck in each vehicle's tail pipe. We ended up with three distinct customer segments: research engineers, production engineers, and emissions technicians.

Usually one reason for the different buying criteria is that dominant designs vary somewhat depending on the organizational affiliation of the end user and the specific practices in which she or he is engaged. The task sequence for emissions testing is different from the task sequence for engine research, which in turn is different from that for keeping an engine in tune. Our market research found that these differences did not mean different dominant designs, just variations on a theme. We concluded we could use one sensor with different packaging and software to address all the customer segments.

As we cross organizational settings, we usually are also crossing industrial sectors. Crossing sectors increases the likelihood of finding different dominant designs. Using the U.S. Census' North American Industrial Classifications, we can see the engine manufacturers will be in NAIC 33631, Motor Vehicle Gasoline Engine and Engine Parts Manufacturing; the auto makers in 33611, Automobile and Light Duty Motor Vehicle Manufacturing; and the emissions stations in 811198, All Other Automotive Repair and Maintenance.[13] The higher the NAIC classification, that is, the fewer digits, the more likely this is to be the case.

To find the buyers, we simply have to figure out who procures this kind of technology for the end users we have identified. Typically buyers and users are the same organization, but not always. For example, in Britain, the Defense Procurement Agency is an executive agency of the Ministry of Defense that buys equipment for the individual armed forces.

We can view organizations as comprised of a set of practices that are used to create outputs. When the organization is a business, the outputs are goods that can be sold.[14] Because businesses seek to create value, following Michael Porter we can call the core practices of a business its *value chain*. He identifies five main practices, each of which contains several task sequences:

1. Inbound logistics—receiving, warehousing, inventory management, and other activities necessary to get the materials, equipment, and supplies required for operations.

---

[13] For a listing of NAICs, go to http://www.census.gov/epcd/naics02/naicod02.htm.
[14] The Internet is full of discussion of Porter's value chain. See Institute of Management, Cambridge University, "Porter's Value Chain," n.d., http://www.ifm.eng.cam.ac.uk/dstools/paradigm/valuch.html (accessed September 19, 2004).

2. Operations—production and the other activities needed to produce products and services. In regulatory agencies, enforcement is included in operations.
3. Outbound logistics—warehousing, shipping, order fulfillment, and other activities needed to get the product or service to the customer.
4. Marketing and sales—market research, strategy and tactics formulation, advertising, sales, and other activities needed to get the orders and obtain payment. In non-market organizations, outreach, dissemination, and adoption can be substituted, as here the activity is focused on creating awareness and adoption.
5. Service—customer support, repair, training, and other activities required for enabling the customer to realize the value sought when the purchase was made.

In addition, Porter saw four overhead or support practices as important for value creation:

1. Procurement—the activities required to buy or obtain the inputs and infrastructure used by the organization
2. Technology development—R&D, product design and development, process development, test and evaluation, and the other activities needed to create the intellectual assets used by the organization to conduct the five main value chain practices above
3. Human resource management—recruitment, training and education, pay and benefits, and other activities associated with finding and retaining labor
4. Infrastructure—finance and accounting, legal, quality control and assurance, and other activities that ensure the main and support value chain activities are tied together and perform as anticipated and desired[15]

> In most organizations, technology transfer is an infrastructure activity. But the real decision power is usually not there. The decision power typically lies either in marketing and sales (for product technology) or in the relevant practice (for process technologies).
>
> If you are trying to commercialize a technology and get shunted to legal, hang up and call back in and ask for a senior manager in the relevant value chain activity. Similarly, if they want you to talk with someone in R&D, if possible, decline. The person in R&D is usually

---

[15] Adelakun, Enterprise Information I, Lecture 1, Winter 2004–2005, http://facweb.cs.depaul.edu/yele/Course/IS425/425Lect1.ppt#257,23,Slide23 (accessed September 25, 2005).

a researcher whose job it is to come up with new technology. So you are a threat. After all, they should have thought of what you have invented. On the other hand, the job of someone in sales and marketing is to make money for the company. If you have something better or easier to sell, you just helped them do their job. That is the trick, of course. Finding the person for whom your technology helps them do their job.

The classic example of R&D turning down an invention that turned out to be a big money maker is 3M's Post-It notes. The adhesive for the notes was invented in 1968 by Spence Silver. Because it was a weak adhesive at a time that 3M was emphasizing finding stronger ones, it was seen as useless. Spence continued to promote his invention however and in 1974 Art Fry, another 3M researcher, applied the adhesive to slips of paper he used as bookmarks for his hymnal during choir. Fry was sold. He too became an advocate. After repeated attempts, Fry convinced senior people at 3M to give the "temporarily permanent bookmarks" a try. In 1977 they sent pads out to secretaries to do with as they pleased. A wide range of uses emerged because secretaries or their bosses were always taking notes that contained comments or information related to documents. By 1990, Post-It notes were one of the top five selling office goods products in America.[16]

Organizations take the output of one practice and use it as the input to the next practice. This input is reworked at each step in the chain until something useful for someone outside of the organization is created. Exhibit 2.2 depicts this process using Porter's value chain.

Note that each practice has an internal "*customer*" for whom its output has utility. Although the work product is transitioned between these internal units, technology transitioning is different from technology transfer.

Getting an organization interested in doing a deal often involves building consensus inside the organization across multiple players in multiple practices. I once helped put a development contract in place

(Continued)

---

[16] Snopes.com, "Sticking with It," http://www.snopes.com/business/origins/post-it.asp, November 10, 2000 (accessed July 21, 2005).

> with Apple for a 3-dimensional scientific visualization software program. At the time the Mac was just being introduced. In addition to working with the product line manager for university and research sales and legal, we had to coordinate with the public relations folks because the pretty pictures the software provided was seen as critical *"show ware"* for positioning the Mac as a graphics platform in distinction to the DOS-based IBM machines and clones. It was the advertising potential that led the PR people to provide the funds necessary to make the deal happen.

In our model, technology transfer only occurs when you move a good across the external boundaries of two organizations. Transitioning is a different, but closely related activity that involves moving a technology across boundaries between practices in the same organization.

The distinction is important. To see why, we will briefly digress to explain the difference between cooperative and non-cooperative games in game theory.

A dominant strategy is one that yields a higher payoff than others, regardless of what strategies everyone else in the game chooses. In cooperative games, the participants can make use of binding commitments to be sure that everyone will honor an agreement to coordinate their strategies. The ability to use commitments means coordination can be used to rule

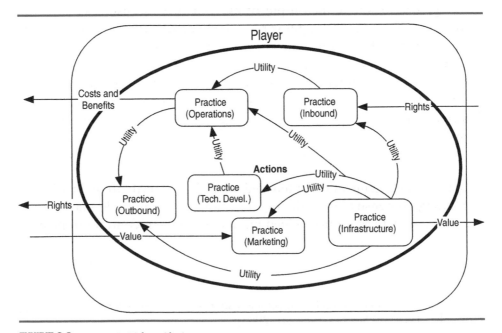

EXHIBIT 2.2   Porter's Value Chain

out potentially very adverse outcomes of the game, helping transform zero sum games into win-win games.

Inside an organization, the movement of technology can be a cooperative game. By definition an organization has a decision and command structure. So the participants in one practice can go to the boss for a ruling that provides everyone an incentive to coordinate their efforts. (Even bureaucratic infighting does not negate that assumption. There is infighting over what the coordinated strategy should be and how various factions will seek to maximize benefits, power, etc. But when the boss says that's enough, that's enough or you get fired or transferred to an outpost in Nome, Alaska.)

Cooperative settings always have a solution for barriers. When transitioning of an organization's high priority technologies is blocked, the organization's decision and command structure can use side payments (subsidies, pay-offs) to balance the equation and make transitioning attractive for all its members. Such side payments ensure everyone is better off cooperating than they would be from not cooperating.[17]

External transactions are different. Here we are in a non-cooperative game until the deal is signed. Without a legally binding agreement, there is no enforceable agreement or common decision and command structure for the nascent partners to call upon. That means each party is self-interested only. Although a deal may be in everyone's best interest, it still may not happen because the parties cannot come to agreement on the precise terms. For example, entrepreneurs can be curiously risk adverse when it comes to deals because they fear a big company will run away with ("steal") their technology. From their perspective, control is a key issue and maintaining full control is a strategy that dominates giving up partial control. So they can end up with no deal at all because deals always involving relinquishing some control over the underlying knowledge and/or its use.

COMPETITORS

There are two sets of competitors for any technology. There are competitors relevant when selling goods embodying or made with the technology to end users and there are competitors relevant when determining who is developing substitute technologies. In either case, just as we saw segmentation with respect to customers, we can find segmentation in competitors. These segments are typically called sectors. Sectors are a set of competitors who pursue similar strategies.

---

[17] See Roger McCain, *Game Theory* (Mason, OH: Thomson South-Western, 2004), chap. 12.

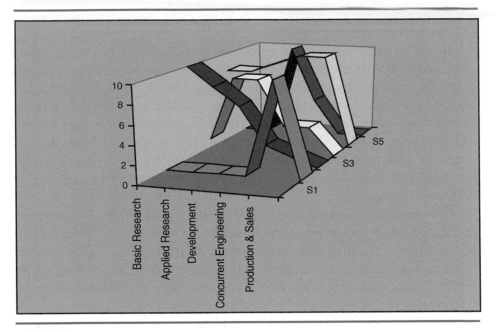

EXHIBIT 2.3   Practices Conducted by Competitors

In our discussion here, we will focus on competitors who are developing substitutable technology. We define these competitors as players who can introduce a technology that can sell within the five-year window after introduction of your technology. In other words, depending on the capabilities of an organization they may not be a threat even if they are working in a related scientific or engineering field. The difference in strategy between R&D performing sectors will relate to the practices they conduct and what else, other than R&D, they do. We can examine the various sectors in terms of the kinds of practices they conduct, as Exhibit 2.3 suggests.

Another factor is how far along the potential competitor is in their R&D and technology development. Our experience, which maps pretty well to studies we have read, is that acquirers of technology want to see a return on investment within five years of market introduction. Thus we use five years from the date of earliest possible introduction as a default to see if there is a window of opportunity in which we can sustain a competitive advantage over competitors who are chasing for market share.[18] After that we can accept being technologically obsolete and irrelevant.

---

[18] See Louise Joselyn, "Picking the IP Winners," *Scottish Technology News* (August 2004), http://www.scottish-enterprise.com/sedotcom_home/stn/scottishtechnology/ scottishtechnologynews-backissues-2004/scottishtechnology_aug04/scottishtechnology news-industrynews_aug04.htm (accessed July 24, 2005).

We often can use the Census Bureau's North American Industrial Classifications to get a quick idea of the ways our competitors will pursue market opportunities.

One of the sectors is NAIC 611310, a school industry sector, contains colleges, universities, and professional schools. Census informs us that for them income may be a secondary consideration, as they have an educational mission. In fact, we know that most university technology transfer offices emphasize faculty service and public service in their licensing programs, with cost recovery replacing income maximizing as the revenue metric. Our experience at Foresight indicates that university licensing executives tend to see industry average royalty rates below those of their industry counterparts—even for technologies at the same level of maturity.

Another sector is small firms. These fall across a range of NAICs. That suggests that internal use is often as important as external use. The data supports this conclusion. In a study of over 100 small firms with awards from the U.S. Department of Agriculture Small Business Innovation Research Program for whom we provided commercialization support, we found roughly 50% had signed, or were in the process of signing, a deal for external commercialization but over 70% were already using their USDA supported technology as the basis for at least one product or product line.

The use of R&D for internal purposes suggests some technology development is strategic, designed to provide defensive hedges against patenting by others or stake out turf for later exploitation. As Robert Cooper of McMaster University notes, R&D and product development can serve at least three strategic functions: development of new product families, development of new platforms that change the company's basis of competition, and support of current product families (extensions, modifications, improvements, cost reductions and the like).[19]

R&D also provides a tool for securing market share by making the small firm a collection point for knowledge in an industry. This cross-organizational collection enhances its position as vendor for customers as it can carry solutions from one venue to another. In two case studies on co-development projects involving chip manufacturers and their equipment suppliers, Melissa Appleyard of the Darden Graduate School of Business at the University of Virginia found knowledge accumulation at the supplier has contributed to a growth of supplier power within that arena.[20]

---

[19] Robert Cooper, "Your NDP Portfolio May Be Harmful to Your Businesses Health," *PDMA Visions,* (April 2005): 26.
[20] Melissa Appleyard, "The Influence of Knowledge Accumulation on Buyer-Supplier Codevelopment Projects," *Journal of Product Innovation Management* (September 2003): 371.

The bottom line is small firms are likely to use R&D to maximize income. By embedding their knowledge and know-how in products and services, they capture a larger share of the value than if they had merely licensed the innovations.

Examples of sectors these firms may fall into are NAIC 541710, "establishments primarily engaged in conducting research and experimental development in the physical, engineering, and life sciences, such as agriculture, electronics, environmental, biology, botany, biotechnology, computers, chemistry, food, fisheries, forests, geology, health, mathematics, medicine, oceanography, pharmacy, physics, veterinary, and other allied subjects" and 541720 which contains "establishments primarily engaged in conducting research and analyses in cognitive development, sociology, psychology, language, behavior, economic, and other social science and humanities research." Note that in this segment, the primary mission is the creation of knowledge and know-how. Note that in this sector will also be large competitors like SRI International or Battelle, who emphasize income maximizing as their ability to create knowledge and know-how is their primary means of making money.

Similarly, there is no single NIAC for larger firms. We would expect the same considerations that motivate strategy at small firms to motivate it at larger firms. But we also would expect additional factors to come into play, as we saw in our discussion of supply chains. Larger firms need to conduct a certain amount of R&D just to stay abreast of developments sufficiently to manage their contractor and subcontractor pool. Our experience suggests that while income maximizing is always of interest, the primary concern is for internal use, where technology can be used to fence competitors away from business opportunities. Only after the strategic value is dissipated by advances elsewhere does its potential for external licensing or other revenue generation become of interest.

Contract manufacturers will cut across a range of NAICs as well. Here there is almost no capability outside production and concurrent engineering.

Other sectors could be added. NAIC 541380 contains testing laboratories and 62151 which is medical and diagnostic laboratories. Work by Eric von Hipple and others found that end users often develop new process technology, which is then licensed to their vendors, who in turn sell it to others in the field.[21] This suggests that they will not be excessively

---

[21] Cf. Postrel, "Innovation Moves from the Laboratory to the Bike Trail and the Kitchen," *The New York Times,* April 21, 2005, http://dynamist.com/articles-speeches/nyt/innovation.html, (accessed July 24, 2005).

aggressive and will be willing to sign less than optimal deals in order to get lower cost access to needed equipment, plus a royalty revenue stream. In fact, this is what we find at Foresight. Licensing revenues are seen as icing on the cake. Indeed, we have found many customers simply want to transfer their technology in order to obtain it from a vendor more cheaply than they can produce it in-house.

To conclude, the strategies competitors follow, and the aggressiveness with which they implement them, reflect the general mission of the organization. Ultimately, sellers of technology are constrained by organizational goals and objectives. In the short term, however, it is once more one of those empirical questions just how important those constraints are.

MARKETS

Where communication and distribution channels cross, there are nodes at which markets can arise. Like everything else in our model, markets have a physical reality. They exist at certain points in time/space and the trades that occur in them are made by people, even if they may be playing on behalf of their organization (see Exhibit 2.4).

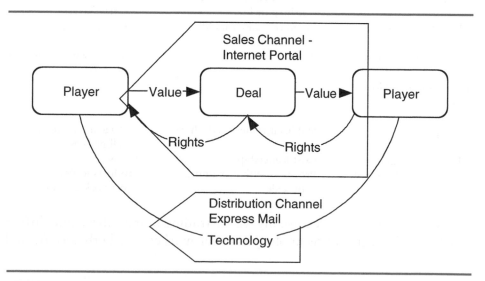

EXHIBIT 2.4   Sales and Distribution Channels

Four dimensions are particularly useful for classifying markets. First, we can classify markets on whether they are general or specialized with respect to the goods being traded. In specialized markets only one type of good is traded. Industry specific trade shows are an example. The second dimension is location. Some markets are centralized, others are diffuse. Diffuse markets can be ad hoc creations developed as buyers and sellers seek each other with the aid of websites, articles in trade publications, telephones, email, mail, or just chance meetings. Indeed, they may be so diffuse that the entire transaction can never involve a face-to-face meeting. The final dimension is the number of buyers and the number of sellers.

The variety of goods being offered in a market, and the rate of change in what is offered, places pressures on other competitors.[22] The larger the variety (the more generalized the market) and the more rapid the rate of change, the more pressure there is on competitors to come up with new product offerings. That in turn affects their interest in various kinds of product or process technology. The following table depicts this situation and highlights the market strategy and kinds of technology likely to be of the most interest to buyers.

	Fast Rate of Change in Goods Offered	Slow Rate of Change in Goods Offered
High Variety of Goods Offered in Product Families		
Example	Dynamic customer needs–fishing tackle	Variety intensive needs–screwdrivers
Market Strategy	Rapid response (muddling through)	Differentiation
Technology of Interest	Product	Processes with economies of scope
Low Variety of Goods Offered in Product Families		
Example	Stable customer needs–hoes	Change intensive needs–cell phones
Market Strategy	Cost leadership	Focus
Technology of Interest	Processes with economies of scale	Products leveraging network economies

In technology transfer, usually we are trading in specialized and diffuse markets. The fact that technology transfer markets are both specific and

---

[22] See Susan Sanderson and Mustafa Uzumeri, *Managing Product Families* (Scarborough, Ontario: Irwin, 1997).

diffuse means that buyers and sellers may have trouble finding each other. Because the market is specific, sellers have a harder time building awareness of their technology. Advertising in newspapers and business publications to make people aware of what you are offering is not cost effective. It is better to place articles in trade publications, which leverages a specialized channel reaching out to that diffuse population, or even creating a website and making sure the metadata facilitates indexing by the search engine crawlers. Most effective however, is targeted market research, followed by picking up the telephone and calling.

> In technology transfer, we always are concerned with two markets. One market is our market: that is the market for licensing, joint venturing, raising capital, or otherwise commercializing our technology. The other market is the market of our targets, that is, the market in which our potential commercialization partners sell something with the aid of our technology to their customers: the end users.

> Harvard Medical School's technology transfer office conducted a focus group with some of its major licensees. One of the topics explored was how they preferred to find out about technology available for licensing. The response was overwhelmingly in favor of being telephoned. It turned out in-licensing executives, like the rest of us, received so much junk virus loaded email, their instinct was to delete material they were not expecting. Phone calls also allowed for a level of interaction that quickly determined whether there was likely to be interest in the technology being offered.[23]

Another consequence of ad hoc diffuse markets is that it is often difficult to identify and track the competition. At a centralized market, like a trade show, you can walk around and see who is offering what. Where you cannot do that, it is far more important to aggressively pursue opportunities lest the window of opportunity close before you are even aware there is competition.

Location affects the costs of, and constraints on, doing transactions. If we have to travel, it costs more to do a deal. Similarly, if translation is

---

[23] Private communication with Kenneth Levin, who at that time was at the office, sometime in 2004.

needed, costs rise. Location also affects the cultural and legal framework we use when developing negotiating strategies.

Let's use language as an example of costs and ease of dealing. Type "define: love" in Google. The first definition from Princeton's WordNet is "a strong positive emotion with affection and regard." Now take the French word for love and see how it gets used in English. Type "define: amour" in Google. The first definition from Princeton's Wordnet is "a secretive and illicit affair." That definition never shows up in the listing in Wordnet under love. Now let's see what happens when we type "define: deal" in Google: We think we are asking "Do you want a deal for this parallel processing computer?" meaning do you want to "engage in a transaction" for a specialized piece of computer hardware. Our counterpart, for whom English is a second or third language thinks we are asking about block cipher derived from the Data Encryption Standard (DES) and are asking if he wants to buy code to run on a parallel processing machine.

We will use the legal system as an example of constraints associated with location. Since transactions require the transfer of rights, the rules concerning creation and transfer are critical for deals. Be aware there are different rules as you cross national borders, and often even within a country. For example, in the United States, the first to invent is the only one who can obtain a patent. In other jurisdictions it is the first to file. Other differences relate to remedies in case a deal goes bad. In the Common Law countries, like the United States, a party to a lawsuit can ask for decisions based on equity if the law suggests a solution that is unfair. Equity has its roots in the King's ability to overrule a court of law to fix decisions that were unjust. In Civil Code countries, however, there is no appeal to equity. There is only codified law.[24]

The number of players in the marketplace in light of the goods being sold is another constraint on strategies for marketing. In the following table, the columns reflect the goods being sold and the rows are the number of buyers. Note that with more buyers, it becomes harder and harder to customize your offering to meet individual idiosyncrasies. Thus, cost or differential strategies tend to make the most sense, depending on whether the buyer wants a standardized or more specialized good. If there are only a few buyers, it makes sense to shape the offerings to better meet needs. If the product is a commodity, you can tailor the financing, warranty, service, training, or other aspects to attain a unique positioning.

---

[24] See Wikipedia, "Common Law," July 20, 2005, http://en.wikipedia.org/wiki/Common_law (accessed July 24, 2005).

	Many Buyers	Few Buyers
Commodity Goods (Fixed Standards for Performance and Ease-of-Use)	Cost leadership	Focus
Specialized Goods (Partial or No Fixed Standards)	Differentiation	Focus

Markets involving end users can be very different than the market for commercialization partners. The markets of classical theory, which are assumed to have large numbers of buyers and sellers all of whom have perfect information, are an example. In this situation, the law of supply and demand governs the price of goods.

In the real world these assumptions obviously do not hold for any market. What we can assume is that for any given buyer there will be a probability distribution for the likelihood of a deal. In the absence of any data, this distribution can be any shape we want, but we normally consider it Gaussian out of a certain laziness that leads to reliance on habitual behavior when drawing curves.

The distribution of buying behavior is shaped by the attributes of the buyers and the constraints placed on them. For example, we did a market study on residential elevators for a company that was using lift technology (the technology for fork lifts) rather than traditional elevator technology (pulleys and cables). This innovation allowed for a relative inexpensive home elevator. (Our study focused on home elevators because of building code considerations.) The price for the lift at that time was around $10,000.

To sell an elevator you need at least two things: a building with more than one floor, and people who do not want to walk stairs. To use lift technology, you need a building with only a couple of floors, as it cannot carry a load higher than that. So the question became, Who wants a lift in a two or three story home? Actually, the question is a bit more complicated because of the cost of the shaft. What we really wanted to know is who either wants a lift in a two or three story home that already has a shaft or wants to install a lift and is willing to build a shaft? This question became: Who wants to live in a two or three story building and is either retrofitting a home with a shaft or buying a new home?

Some common sense with a bit of Web searching suggested the people who do not walk stairs in their home are either old or infirm. Where do we find old or infirm people buying new or retrofitted two or three story homes? Again common sense came to our aid. Usually old folks buy single floor homes when they retire, so they only are going to buy a multi-floor home, if land is expensive, such as at higher-end southern coastal waterfront communities. Going to the Web confirmed that townhouse communities were being built in the South for retirees.

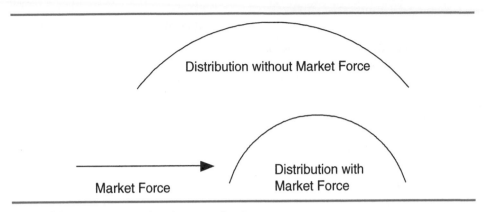

EXHIBIT 2.5 Sales with and without Market Force

Now we had a potential arena. We did more market research and determined that given the economic profile of the likely buyers of a new townhouse, another $10,000 was not likely to be a showstopper. We talked to developers and found out the idea of putting lifts into townhouses was desirable. It turns out, many of the developers already were thinking of adding elevators, but the cost was an issue.

Did the market drivers support entry? Drivers are statistical tendencies that influence the shape of the probability distribution of buying behavior. We looked at population statistics and found an aging population. The direction and magnitude of this force meant the probability distribution was skewed towards higher sales of townhouses with elevators to retirees (see Exhibit 2.5). Of course, we needed to take into account whether these retirees were moving to southern coastal communities. Trends for mortgage and land costs also had to be considered. At the time of this analysis, land costs were favorable, mortgage trends were not. Although the direction for mortgages was negative, sensitivity analysis suggested the magnitude of the impact was only slight. Bottom line: After addition, the vectors of the market forces still left a positive imprint on the outcome distribution.

STAKEHOLDERS

There is one other group of players in arenas we need to discuss, even though they are not directly involved in deals. These are the stakeholders. Stakeholders are anyone or any organization interested in shaping behavior in an arena. Examples include standards bodies, regulators, publishers, university/industry centers, advocacy groups, consultants, and, of course, competitors. Any of these can be proponents or opponents of deals and the adoption of technology.

Information channels can be used to shift behavior by making people aware of new goods, changes in constraints on practices, etc. For example, if the EPA promulgates a new regulation on mercury emissions for coal fired power plants, a message must be sent from the regulators to the plant operators for behavior to shift. (Part of the content of this message is the description of what is changing, such as the permissible emission levels of power plants. The other part is information on penalties for failing to comply. Both parts are necessary for changing how players view their strategic options.)

Legally, these changes are published in special government channels: the Federal Register and updates to the Code of Federal Regulations. But commonly it is through supplemental channels, such as the web sites of power plant trade associations or their newsletters, that news of new regulations initially reaches plant operators.

Messages sent by regulatory agencies and standards bodies are usually significant in arenas. Such messages create frameworks for cooperative games involving parties in different organizations. In Exhibit 2.6, the imposition of a regulation shifts the cost and benefit calculation for the player affected. That impact may be (1) a change in the utility of goods being used in a practice, thereby affecting their value or (2) a more dramatic shift to set of requirements that in turn sets minimum acceptable performance/ease-of-use thresholds for goods, thereby eliminating some goods from the market. These impacts can affect goods used as inputs for practices or created as outputs of practices. They may also affect how goods can be handled and processed during practices.

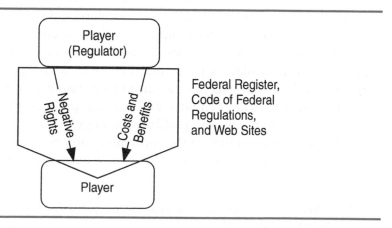

EXHIBIT 2.6 Regulation as a Constraint

Regulation per se has little impact on markets. What counts is the intent and commitment to enforce regulations. Increased enactment of regulations is a market force, as it makes prosecution of violations possible. Increased enforcement is an even stronger market force as it means violations will have real costs. But jawboning without intent scares no one into compliance.

In an assessment of a mercury recovery system for dental use, conducted in 1999, we concluded there were over a half a dozen technologies (filtration, sedimentation, centrifuge, chelation, electrolysis, water vortex, ionization) that had already been applied to the removal of particulate and soluble heavy metals from dental wastewater. There was no shortage of technology to solve this problem; the key issue was getting regulation enacted and enforced by the EPA. If that happened, it would force every dental clinic to be "green," creating a hundred million dollar plus national market virtually overnight. Another environmental example: A State of Rhode Island plan notes that in FY '04, they will not prosecute egregious air pollution violators criminally. In FY '05 they plan to. A violator will have a much stronger incentive to stop polluting in FY '05 than in FY '04.[25]

What stakeholders attempt to do is skew behavior in the supply chain in order to attain their own objectives. In Exhibit 2.7, by prohibiting certain behavior (taking away the right to do), a regulator changes the utility of a good for a member of a supply chain and thus the value it has for that entity.

We note in passing that vigorous enforcement, which increases the costs of current behavior, is often associated with increased adoption of new technology. Organizations violating clean air and water regulations have to pay fines as well as come into compliance. The EPA realized that dual necessity—pay fine; come into compliance—could be leveraged to push the state of the art in environmental technology. They have a program that allows violators to devote their fines to adopting and testing better technology that exceeds the current minimum compliance levels.[26] As such technologies are validated and put into practice; they push up the bar for what is minimally acceptable technology.

Other stakeholders lurk in the communication channels monitored by the organizations in an arena. Once channels exist, all sorts of things can

---

[25] "Clean Air," 2003, http://www.state.ri.us/dem/pubs/plan2003/pdf/criminvs.pdf, accessed September 26, 2004.

[26] Beth Termini, "EPA and State Innovative Settlements," 2002, http://www.epa.gov/opei/symposium/e-settl2.htm (accessed July 22, 2005).

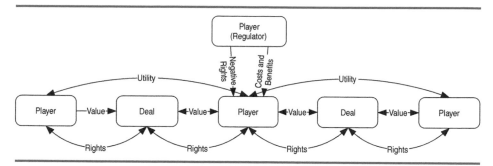

EXHIBIT 2.7   Regulation Affecting a Supply Chain

flow by them. The same FedEx truck that takes a part to the company over in the industrial district can carry your birthday present for Aunt Nellie. The same communication channel that carries news about new product announcements can carry news about consultants' views on where the market is going. Further, any organization or individual can set up their own channels.

CONCLUSION

In this chapter we have hopefully expanded our understanding of our model by focusing on the macro-level context within which people do deals. We have seen these people work in organizations. The goals and other activities of those organizations act as motivations and constraints for people when looking for technology to acquire and during its adoption.

Arenas are comprised of a set of organizations using, or interested in the use of, technology. The organizations are linked by communication and distribution channels. Channels can be used to form supply chains. For us, technology transfer is a solution to a supply chain problem, having access to knowledge and know-how when you need it without having to pay for its development and storage when you do not need it.

We then briefly looked at different kinds of organizations active in arenas: users, buyers, sellers, markets, and stakeholders. Users are where end users work. Usually buyers and users are the same or units within a larger organization. Competitors are the organizations developing and/or selling substitutable technology. Markets are organizations whose mission is to be a venue for deals. We have seen that technology transfer tends to take place in ad hoc, specialized, diffuse markets and the character of these markets influences the strategies that can succeed. Finally, we have briefly discussed stakeholders as they can be advocates for or against deals and adoption of technology.

CHAPTER 3

Strategies

INTRODUCTION

If there is a secret to the art of technology transfer, this is it: Sell customers, not technology. Whatever legal vehicle we want to use for the deal, we need to be able to demonstrate that our technology can win customers and be sold profitably. If we can do that, we can always find a commercialization partner because there is always someone who wants to make money.

In this chapter we take a bird's eye view of how to use the model to do deals. So far our model is descriptive. It helps us understand what factors are important for understanding technology transfer. Strategy adds a prescriptive element.

We introduce the concepts of objectives, strategy, and tactics.

- Objectives operationalize goals so we can measure progress toward our goals. Without objectives we would never know if we reached our goals or have failed.
- Strategy is the plan for attaining our objectives. Strategies are just a special kind of decision tree. At each node there are options, which have a greater or lower probability of leading to success. If you take this path, then you have a greater likelihood of reaching your objectives.
- Tactics are the techniques we use to implement the plan. Tactics are the way we move from node to node.

We also shall introduce two other critical concepts: *technology niches* and *Nash Equilibriums*.

- Technology niches are sets of applications for specific technologies. Despite the different focus of the activities involved in the various applications, the end users require technology that has similar performance functionality and ease-of use features.
- Nash Equilibriums exist where each player adopts a strategy which, given the options for strategies that other players have, is the best choice for that player. When all the players adopt their best possible choice, none of them should have an incentive to change strategies so long as all other things remain constant.

I have always found market research to be much like putting together a jig saw puzzle. Each piece of data has "edges" that point you towards the next piece, because the first piece constrains what will fit. In Chapter 2, we laid the theoretical framework for market research, which involves identifying the pieces and how they can fit with each other. Our goal there was to make a picture.

Strategy is different. It is more like playing Clue (called Cluedo in Europe). Like jigsaw puzzles, Clue is a game based on finding coherences. But making a jigsaw puzzle is not a competitive activity. You and your friends sit around a table and work the puzzle together. Clue is different. It is about winning. You want to be the first one to say it was Doctor Mustard in the kitchen with a rope. So let's look at how to win.

We shall see that to develop a winning strategy we have to be able to answer three critical questions. The first one is can we find at least one application for the technology. The second one is can we find a deal vehicle that will work for us. The third one is can we can find a player who might be interested in a deal and for whom that vehicle is desirable enough that they actually do a deal.

In this chapter we lay out the questions and our general approach for answering them. In the rest of this book we focus on how to use this approach to actually answer them.

TECHNOLOGY NICHES

Face it, we are people. Tuesday we wanted oatmeal for breakfast. Thursday we want pancakes. Over time, people want different things.

Change breeds change. As the goods being produced change, the techniques and goods based on dominant designs are extended to include new functionalities and features.

These enhancements often suggest other goods that can be made. Once I dehydrate oatmeal, I can dehydrate chicken and I am in the backpacking food business.

Sometimes extensions in functionality or feature suggest other practices in which the technology can be used. If I can dehydrate oatmeal, maybe I dehydrate beverages. Bingo: Tang. Suddenly I am in sports and spacecraft. If I can make Tang, I can make dehydrated blood. Suddenly I find I can sell to hospitals, the military, missionaries, etc.

Science Applications International Corporation put a laser range finder on a spinning base, added some software, and developed a way of mapping features or terrain and structures for creating virtual reality environments. The same laser range finder used to find the distance to the enemy in times of war now could be used to measure the distance to a wall or window or whatever could be detected with the aid of an infrared beam. We found a rich and diverse technology niche for the technology.

There was a demand for laser mappers for use in recording the architectural features of historic buildings. Contractors wanted a tool that could be used in factories and refineries to update original construction blueprints when preparing for renovations. My favorite, however, was an application in automated construction. Machines are now being developed that will use computer aided design/computer aided manufacturing (CAD/CAM) approaches to build structures. One machine reads the CAD drawing. The next machine picks up the appropriate size of I-beam from a trailer and lifts it into place. A third machine bolts or welds it into place. Only one problem: If the picker/placer is a little off, its arm can knock down whatever has been built so far or it may just be positioning a beam in free space with nothing to attach it to. Something is needed to track what has just been done and update the specs of the building as is, rather than as it is in the CAD drawing.

We have only scratched the surface. For example, in the military, range finders have been adapted to paint targets with a spot that infra-red missile seekers use as a beacon. Painting suggests that once I have digitized these images, I can paint them on real objects. By using IR photo-curing, I can now take my laser mapper outside, make an image of the Iwo Jima memorial and then use the same tool with a special plastic formulation to cut out miniature versions of the statue to sell to tourists. I can send that file over the Internet and have that memento knocked out in Bangladesh. And since I can modify the digitized image, I also have a rapid prototyping tool.

Of course the classic example is the personal computer. It's origin was when Ed Roberts of Micro Instrumentation and Telemetry Systems (MITS) developed a do-it-yourself kit based on Intel's 8080 chip because his company needed a new product. It was named Altair after a planet in a StarTrek episode (itself a sign something more than mere instrumentality was at play) and was introduced as a way for engineers to free themselves from the central computing facility and the mainframe bureaucrats.[1] Today it is ubiquitous.

---

[1] Thayer Watkins, "Early History of the Personal Computer," n.d., http://www2.sjsu .edu/faculty/watkins/pc.htm (accessed September 26, 2004).

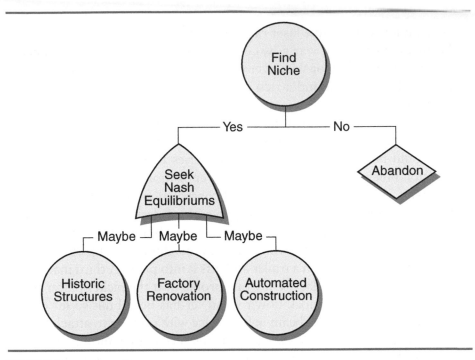

EXHIBIT 3.1 Decision Tree

Note that technologies can get applied in practices from across widely divergent markets and market niches. That is why we use the term technology niche, to highlight we are not dealing with traditional market niches.

Strategy formulation can be viewed as making decision trees. The first step in strategy formulation is to find the end users. Find the technology niche and you find the end users. Find the end users and you find the niche. It's reciprocal (see Exhibit 3.1).

Of course, we will usually see different customer segments within the niche, depending on the precise way the technology is likely to be used. The customer segments are end-user communities with similar buying criteria. That means our commercialization strategy has to consider whether we want to just choose one customer segment and focus on it, or select multiple ones to penetrate simultaneously. Because of the difficulties associated with product introduction, almost always it makes sense to choose one. But which one?

NASH EQUILIBRIUMS

The short answer is the one in which it is easiest to sell the technology. Since we cannot, by definition, have perfect knowledge of each player's

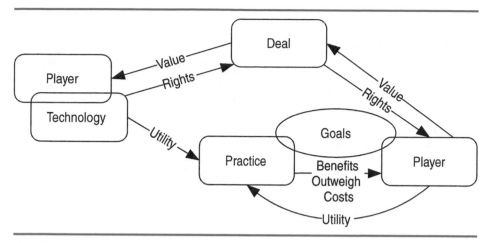

EXHIBIT 3.2 Deal as a Nash Equilibrium

motivations, we cannot even be sure we would recognize in which application sales will be easiest. The nice thing is we do not really care. We just want easy, so we can seek any application in which the end users are likely to be better off in their own eyes by buying our technology than by not doing it.

What we are seeking is called a Nash Equilibrium in game theory (see Exhibit 3.2). Nash Equilibriums occur where there is a set of strategies that have the property that no player benefits by changing their strategy unless one or more other players also change their strategies.[2] Obviously, it makes sense to opt for Nash Equilibriums, because we all want to be better off rather than worse off. Because sometimes there are several ways in which we can be better off, more than one Nash Equilibrium can exist.

Remember when we said our job is to create acceptable equations. We now know how to recognize one. Acceptable equations are Nash Equilibriums. Any application where buying our technology is part of a Nash Equilibrium is a candidate for market entry. So we follow the maxim: *Seek applications where we can create Nash Equilibriums.*

To create a Nash Equilibrium, what we want to do is figure out how to make it attractive for end users to adopt our technology into a practice. As Exhibit 3.3 suggests, there are three likely ways to make our technology

---

[2] See Roger A. McCain, "Solutions' to Nonconstant Sum Games," in *Strategy and Conflict: An Introductory Sketch of Game Theory,* n.d., http://william-king.www.drexel .edu/top/eco/game/nash.html (accessed September 19, 2004). For the entire text, begin at http://william-king.www.drexel.edu/top/eco/game/game.html. For a great explanation of Nash Equilibriums, see the movie, *A Beautiful Mind,* which is well worth seeing for Russell Crowe's performance, anyway.

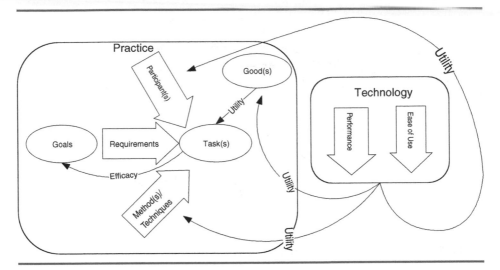

EXHIBIT 3.3   Making the Technology Attractive

attractive. We can make it desirable as a product, a service, or a process that will be used in the practice.

But why should anyone find it attractive? To rehash what we have discussed before, we want to find applications where the performance and ease of use of our technology maps to the requirements and skill/knowledge set of the participants in the practice in light of what that product, service, or process costs. All other things being equal, the better the fit and the lower the cost, the greater the utility and thus the greater the likelihood our technology will be found attractive.

Technology transfer deals seek to freeze Nash Equilibriums for the length of time anticipated by the parties to the agreement. The parties seek to implement this freeze by relying on legally enforceable exchanges of rights to constrain each other from changing strategies. Break the agreement and the other party can use a lawsuit to make you pay. They can be angry enough to seek the full measure of legal damages. Payback can be a bitch.

Making Technology Conducive for Nash Equilibriums

If we want to encourage creation of an Equilibrium, we need to position our technology so that it is attractive to the buyer. Since a dominant design "*encapsulates*" a set of expectations on performance, ease of use, and price, we can use dominant design to help us determine where our technology might have competitive advantages, and thus be viewed as attractive.

We can distinguish three logically distinct alternatives for what might make our technology attractive. Our technology can sustain, extend, or disrupt the dominant designs in a practice.[3]

From a theoretical standpoint, our technology may be capable of being positioned in any of these roles. Whether it actually can be any one of these is an empirical question, of course. We have to go out and look at the technology, kick the tires, rattle its chips, or do whatever it is you are supposed to do with the dang thing and see what folks think that's pretty cool and buy one.

Now, let us examine each of these options in more detail because our goal is to figure out which application we want to select. As we shall see, usually we give preference to applications where we can be positioned as a sustaining or extending innovation. The reason is simple. These kinds of innovation fit well enough with the current dominant design that we only need minimal education and awareness building for end users before they can recognize the utility of the benefits we are touting.

The first option is to position the technology as a sustaining innovation. This positioning is feasible if (1) the technology's utility can be measured using buying criteria currently invoked by participants in the relevant tasks and (2) the technology can be deployed without any significant restructuring of the task sequence in a practice. An example is automatic egg candling.

Egg candling involves holding the egg up to a light to see if there is an embryo inside, in which case you really do not want that egg being sold on a supermarket shelf. The U.S. Department of Agriculture's Small Business Innovation Research Program funded a machine that can do egg candling. It replaced manual labor. Yet although the machine replaced workers, it did not really change the way eggs are examined or the metrics for a good egg candler. The sequence is still hold the egg up to a light, look at the egg to see if the light is blocked by an embryo. The metric is still, no embryos.

In cases like this one, the new technology fits with the current methods and techniques for the task (see Exhibit 3.4). We demonstrate utility by comparing the functionality and features of the new technology against current methods and techniques using the same criteria that are currently used to measure utility. Mary is a better candler than John because she is faster and more accurate. The metrics come from the requirements driving the tasks. The best functionality and features of the current technology substitutes are the benchmark to beat.

---

[3] The concept of sustaining and disruptive technologies was coined by Clayton Christensen. For an overview on Christensen, see Wikipedia, "Disruptive Technology," September 25, 2004, http://en.wikipedia.org/wiki/Disruptive_technology (accessed September 26, 2004).

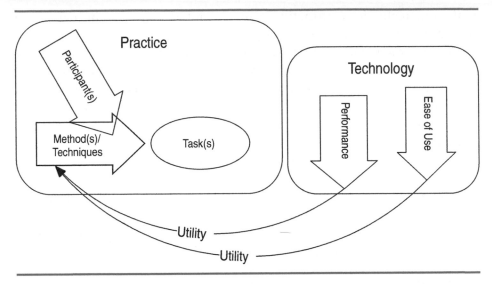

EXHIBIT 3.4   A Technology that Sustains a Dominant Design

With sustaining innovations, the buying decision is strictly instrumental—does a sufficient improvement occur when measured using current criteria to justify the cost? Ma and Pa Kettle, with their four chickens, will probably continue to manually candle. Purdue with its industrial production will buy a machine. The technology with the greatest net utility wins.

If the sustaining technology we are positioning is based upon current technological approaches deployed in the practice, we call it an incremental innovation. "Improved" is our mantra. It's this year's *Motor Trend*'s SUV of the Year.

If it is based on a different scientific and engineering domain, we call it radical. "Next generation" is the mantra. It's this year's *Motor Trend*'s Hybrid of the Year.

Incremental innovations are things like replacing a 1000 hour incandescent light bulb with a 2000 hour one. They tend to be easy to adopt because they require minimal reeducation of participants and probably can be used with the existing infrastructure. If you know how to use a yardstick, it is not hard to figure out how to use a tape measure. Radical innovations, like the automatic egg candler usually are harder to adopt because end users typically need to learn new skills. Our egg inspector has become a machine tender. Just because you can use a tape measure does not mean you can measure the distance to a wall with a laser range finder. Further, new infrastructure likely will be required. The range finder or the candling machine needs a power source. We caution, however, not all radical innovations call for training or infrastructure. Consider the energy-saving fluorescents that just screw into the socket on the lamp.

One of the fascinating things about radical technologies is that once they are incorporated into the dominant design they tend to be adapted for new uses. These adaptations often provide functionalities and features not foreseen when originally introduced into a practice. For example, in 1969, Intel had been hired to design and fabricate a chip for a calculator. It was made like other silicon chips. What was different was that the gates and circuits were laid out to allow the chip to be programmed differently. Instead of "hardwiring" the processing instructions for the calculator into the chip, the logic was now a function of the software. The personal computer has its roots in the decision by Ted Hoff of Intel to make an *"extended"* chip, which he called a microprocessor.[4] He certainly never thought he was launching a new industrial revolution.

In 1963, the U.S. government began research to develop lighting for military applications that did not generate heat or require electricity. The result was chemiluminescence—light created by mixing chemicals. This was radically different than the flashlight, which required batteries, although both are portable lighting. It extended the functionality of the gas discharge bulbs (e.g., neon) by providing a new way of starting the chemical reactions that generated photons. Today glowsticks are used for toys, novelty jewelry, camping, emergency lighting, making landing zones, and a variety of other purposes.[5]

Our laser mapper is a way of updating blueprints. But by creating a virtual environment, we can also see the output to architects as CAD files, which provide a starting point for working with customers to design renovations. The created image or mapper creates and provides the baseline against which to compare various renovation options. And that opens up new possibilities. For example, an interior designer can go into a mansion, quickly image what is there, and then show how changing the colors, the couch, or the curtains will look just lovely for the next time your business associates or up-scale neighbors visit. Since we can do that, why not take the mapper outside. Now it is a tool for landscape architects. Too cutesy? How about using it for land management to document forests prior to logging or cutting roads? What about bridge inspection?

This discussion helps explain why it might make sense to position your technology as sustaining. You position as sustaining when you have to get

---

[4] Watkins, "Early History of the Personal Computer," http://www2.sjsu.edu/faculty/watkins/pc.htm, accessed September 26, 2004.
[5] OmniGlow, "About OmniGlow," n.d., http://www.omniglow.com/omniglow/about.shtml (accessed September 26, 2004).

Note that the education/training and infrastructure differences affect change-over costs and thus net utility calculations. For that reason, we would expect radical sustaining innovations to require greater utility in order to be adopted as there are higher costs in the net utility calculation. One way to compensate for that is to introduce our technology as a service, thereby reducing the changeover costs. For example, we looked at an ozone replacement for methyl bromide as a poison for nematodes. Nematodes kill crops like strawberries by getting into the roots. Methyl bromide is an environmentally nasty pesticide. The new technology worked by hooking an ozone generator to the drip irrigation system and flooding the roots for a day when the nematodes were young. The rest of the time the drip irrigation system carried water just like before. Simple and elegant but for one thing. You had to have a pretty large and expensive ozone generator. Payback took a long time because methyl bromide was cheap. Our solution: Franchise existing vendors of leased equipment, who in turn will provide ozone treatments as a service. The grower gets access at a price equal to or below methyl bromide. The vendor has a new service to sell. We focused on organic strawberry growers as the initial customer base because for them methyl bromide was by definition unacceptable, plus there is a premium price charged for organic produce which means reduced damage by nematodes would pay off quickly.

We supported commercialization of software for optimizing fluid flows within municipal water systems. The system combined optimization techniques with an artificial intelligence (AI) method that provided the data to be optimized. The AI method was able to adapt the system to different customer demands and different water sources (which in turn required different flow rates through the system to handle their filtering and sterilization). Although a software solution that was easy to use once installed, setting up the software was difficult. It was easier to introduce the software as a turn-key result of a service contract to design optimization routines rather than through a site license to be set up by the utility engineers on their own since AI had not yet penetrated that sector.

Radical innovations like the ozone example are easiest to introduce when they are based on technologies already known to the end users. Here the drip irrigation system is in place. In our horseshoe example, the liquid propane forge is a radical innovation. Since liquid propane (LP) barbeques were already in widespread use, you could assume the farriers would require little or no training on how to start or maintain LP forges.

into the market fast to make money. There are all sorts of reasons you have to get in fast. Maybe you are a *"me too"* technology in a niche capable of sustaining two or three vendors. For example, you might have a better mousetrap . . . literally. Or maybe you are simply selling into an innovation resistant customer segment and such a positioning helps minimizes market barriers.

The second option is to position the technology as an extension to a current dominant design (see Exhibit 3.5). In this case, by definition, we are no longer accepting the requirements for the task *"as is."* (If we did accept the requirements "as is," there would be no reason to adopt our technology unless it outperformed on functionality or had superior ease of use. But in that case, we would be positioning it as a sustaining innovation.)

Extending technologies require more awareness building and education to help end users understand their potential benefits. So why make our job harder and argue a change in the metrics is needed unless:

- We can only meet the current benchmarks for features and functionality without any significant price advantage, or,
- The buyer's requirements are changing (or likely to change) so that using the current ones will lead us astray.

But now we have a problem! If we cannot define utility in terms of "what is," we need to define it in terms of *"what should be."* What we need to do is appeal to the objectives or guiding the practice so we can argue that the current methods and techniques or goods are inadequate, thereby justifying change.

From the buyer's perspective, the acquisition decision is once again instrumental. The technology with the greatest net utility wins. What is

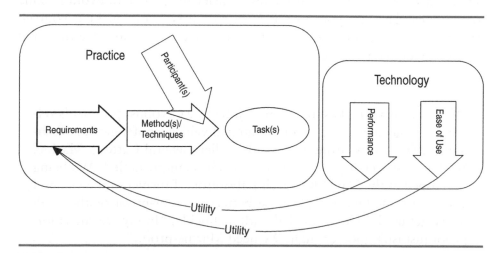

EXHIBIT 3.5 A Technology that Extends a Dominant Design

different is that we are not using the existing operations within the practice as a benchmark. This time we are saying to the buyer:

> *"If you really are serious about meeting your goals and objectives, it is time to revise your requirements. But to do so, you have to change your activities. This is how to do it and these are the metrics to use."*

What we are doing is positioning our technology for an emerging intersection between its performance, ease of use, and price on the one hand and the evolving requirements of our end users on the other. We are like the hunter in a duck blind waiting for the birds to fly by on their migration. If they fly the path we anticipate we have duck for dinner. If not, we go hungry.

Consider the razor. The goal here is to leave the face (or leg) without hair. So the objective is "clean shaven."

In 1170, Jean-Jacques Perret developed the concept of the safety razor—in his case an L-shaped wooden guard that surrounded the blade and prevented it from penetrating the skin too deeply. At the time, if you wanted to be clean shaven, you went to the barber. The barber used a razor made of forged steel and wood. Perret's invention required no new technological approaches—merely a rethinking of how to apply the existing technologies for forging and wood working. Yet without industrial production razors were specialty items. Since barbers were "trained professionals" the safety feature, while nice, was not essential.

Notice that the core attribute offered by the safety razor is a better user interface. The more complex the user interface, the more likely education and training of end users will be required to use it. So a simple interface is helpful for early acceptance of extending innovations. The safety razor works because it makes it easier for people to avoid nicking themselves. The fact you do not need to worry about nicking yourself means you can rethink how to get clean shaven. You can save time and money by doing it yourself.

> Of course, what makes for a simple interface or robust product is relative. I remember being at an unmanned vehicle conference in Washington, DC. I was sitting next to Brigadier General Catto, a Marine. We had just seen a presentation on small, man-portable UAVs being developed at the Naval Research Laboratory. I turned to the General and said something like, "Those better be sailor-proof or they will never get used." He responded with a chuckle, "In my world, sailor-proof just isn't good enough. We need Marine-proof."

It took until 1880 to change that economic configuration, when the Kampfe brothers filed a U.S. patent for the safety razor as we know it today. In their patent a blade is inserted into a protective mechanism that allows only the edge to protrude.[6] More important, this razor could be industrially produced, driving the cost down to make it affordable for a new customer segment, family men and their sons. (The disposable blade, in contrast, is a radical sustaining innovation as it was made by cutting the blade from a template, rather than forging it. Prior to its invention by Gillette in 1901, all blades were sharpened and reused.)

> We did an assessment on a natural language processing based on an efficient algorithm that determines the meaning of words by examining co-occurrence of referential terms. The term skunk means one thing if it appears in a discussion of forest mammals and another thing if it appears in a discussion of swindlers. The problem with the technology was that at the time of our assessment, it was just a "me-too" technology. The trick for getting it into the market was to build a customized application of the technology focused on pharmaceutical discovery. By providing a customized set of co-references and a subroutine for determining the analogs for acronyms and chemical symbols, the technology was positioned as an extension or add-on for Internet and database search engines.

Positioning a technology as extending is my preference. Extending technologies can bring new benefits to customers, which, if end users really want them, allows you to grab market share from competitors. Since the benefits are new to the market, you may also be able to attract new customer segments for which the old features and functionality mix just did not provide enough net utility to result in buying behavior. At the same time, at least some of the features and functionality will be familiar to buyers and end users, reducing barriers to adoption to due difficulty in appreciating the benefits or understanding how to use the technology.

Price an extending technology at or below current substitutes and you can pitch them as getting something for nothing. "More" is the mantra.

The final option is to seek opportunities where the goals of end users are changing (see Exhibit 3.6). Where goals change, the door is open for a ground-up rethinking. Everything is now up for grabs.

---

[6] Marco Migliari, "Shaving with a Hoe: Evolution of the Razor," *Stileindustria* (May 1995), http://mywebpages.comcast.net/steelbeard1/hoe1.htm (accessed September 26, 2004).

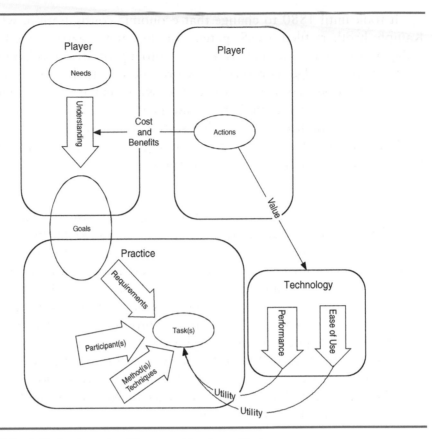

EXHIBIT 3.6   A Technology that Disrupts a Dominant Design

Unfortunately—at least from the perspective of doing deals—goal changes open a Pandora's Box. Discussions of goals inevitably point towards moral/ethical issues. Should the need even be satisfied? Should it be satisfied now? If yes, how should it be satisfied? Can the ends justify the means? Can we afford to drive electric cars if we have to make power with coal-fired plants? What if you learn that in 280 years, if we continue on the path we are, global warming will make the Northern Hemisphere uninhabitable and the Southern Hemisphere 40 degrees warmer?

Disruptive innovations involve new mixes of functionalities and features than are deployed in the practice today. These inevitably require changes in the conduct of the practice and new skills or education for the participants. Viagra is an example. Call it sildenafil citrate or 1-[4-ethoxy-3-(6,7-dihydro- 1-methyl- 7-oxo- 3-propyl- 1*H*-pyrazolo [4,3-*d*]pyrimidin-5-yl) phenylsulfonyl]- 4-methylpiperazine citrate and most people have never heard of it. It was originally developed to treat angina (lack of oxygen in the heart muscle), but its other functionality made it a higher performance replacement for traditional erectile dysfunction remedies like tiger penises and rhinoceros horns.

What interests us here is that Viagra is not sold on the grounds of performance comparison. It is sold on the basis that sex is a good and therefore Viagra is a good. In other words, if you accept the need should be met, then you should adopt this technology if you have erection problems because it eliminates them. There is an emotive connection established that says if you should want these benefits and because you should want them then you will want this technology. It is fundamentally *not* an instrumental calculation.

Clearly what we are doing is appealing to "what should be." But in distinction to extending innovations, this time we are offering our vision of the "good life" to the buyer. We are offering an alternative vision of how their world can be. "Dream" is our mantra.

> OZ is a display format for aircraft control panels invented by David Still and Leonard Temme of the University of West Florida. OZ is a radically redesigned display based on the way we use our peripheral vision. Simulations have established it dramatically cuts the time needed to learn how to fly with instruments while improving pilot performance and thus safety. It has been called perhaps the most significant development for instrument flight since the artificial horizon.[7] We were hired to help commercialize OZ. We discovered that professional pilots did not like OZ, because it required fighting the training they had received in the current display interface. It was too disruptive.
>
> Our solution was to bring OZ in as a display technology for a new customer segment in private aviation, built around experimental plane enthusiasts. The Federal Aviation Administration (FAA) was introducing a new class of private aircraft certification (sport aircraft) and pilot licensing (sport pilot) aimed at making flying almost as ubiquitous as driving.[8] The FAA notes that more than 15,000 people who will now earn FAA certificates to operate more than 15,000 existing uncertificated ultralight-like aircraft. Another 12,000 pilots and new aircraft will be certificated over the next 10 years. Key features of the sport pilot license are reduced training requirements and no necessity for a

(Continued)

---

[7] Adrian Gerold, "OZ: A Revolution in Cockpit Display," n.d., http://www.aviationtoday.com/cgi/av/show_mag.cgi?pub=av&mon=1003&file=1003tech_focus.htm (accessed September 26, 2004).
[8] For more on sport piloting, see http://www.faa.gov/avr/afs/sportpilot/index.cfm. The sport pilot regulations went into effect September 1, 2004.

medical certificate. Associated is a new certificate for currently uncer-
tificated aircraft. So this segment should experience rapid growth,
meaning we did not have to worry about overcoming ingrained training. The limited nature of the sport pilot license means these newcom-
ers would not worry about switching between old and new screens as
they will not be flying traditional aircraft. By positioning the technology as a disruptive one for sport aircraft, we were able to find manufactures of avionics interested in licensing it.

Let's step back and look at what is involved in positioning a technology as disruptive. Dominant designs are part of the structure of practices.
When we use techniques, tools, materials, etc. we grow accustomed to
the functionality and features of these designs and thus we come to
expect them.

When disruptive technologies are successfully introduced we experience the analog of what Thomas Kuhn calls a paradigm shift in science.[9]
For Kuhn, normal science is a relatively routine, day-to-day activity in
which scientists replicate work patterns they learned as students. These
work patterns involve using tools to examine natural phenomenon that
are significant in intellectual frameworks that not only suggest how to test
theories but also constrain what is considered a theory. In normal science,
the labor of theorists, experimenters, and tool makers coheres with each
other and the intellectual constructs that guide their activity. This pattern
of coherence is called a paradigm.

Over time, the work of experimenters results in findings that cannot
be easily incorporated into the theories. This leads theorists to propose
new ideas, which in turn leads tool makers to create new tools. Or tool
makers may create new instruments that lead experimenters to find data
that does not fit current theories, leading theorists to put on their thinking
caps. Obviously, the order is irrelevant. What counts is that at some point
facts emerge that cannot be incorporated at all in the theories, leading
them to collapse.

At this point a scientific revolution occurs. Everyone scrambles around
until some genius points the way towards a new pattern of coherence and
normal science reasserts itself. An example is science during the Renais-
sance. The work of Kepler, Galileo and others revised our understanding
of the heavens. The Earth was no longer the center of the universe. By the
end of the revolution, the observation-based theories of Aristotle had been

---

[9] See Thomas Kuhn, *The Structure of Scientific Revolutions* (Chicago: University of
Chicago Press, 1962).

replaced by the mathematical mechanics-based schema of Newton and the science had adopted a paradigm of empirical experimentation.

Our problem is, of course, not science but technology transfer strategy. So why position a technology as disruptive? Simple: If the technology cannot meet any currently articulated requirements or goals, you have to look at it differently. We need to look at it as a means to realize dreams.

We have entered the amorphous world of less well articulated needs. To tell someone they have a goal they do not yet recognize is bogus. What we can tell them is that there are goals that make sense for them, given needs they recognize, but have not fully explored. These goals may appear non-intuitive, but they can make sense. Gutenberg's printing press was introduced as a way of bringing Luther's German translation of the Bible to the masses. But at the time the Bible was first printed, very few lay people could read German. But people who felt the need to be closer to God understood why they might want to have a goal of reading what they saw as the word of God.

By positioning our technology as disruptive, we are seeking to endow it with sufficient emotive appeal to overcome the changeover costs inherent in abandoning the current dominant design. Making the net utility case is hard because abandoning the dominant design means, by definition, there are no objective (and thus consensual) criteria to use for calculating net utility. The good news is we just do not care if we can tap into an inter-subjective (shared) image of the "good life." If sex is a good, then having the little feller flaccid is not good. Whomp: Viagra is an instrumental good. If knowing the Bible is a good, then being unable to understand the Bible when read in Latin is not good. Gott sei Dank: Printing the Bible in German is an instrumental good.

Stepping back, we can see that the utility of disruptive technologies presupposes some imperative that makes that technology useful in the first place. Without that imperative, there can be no utility and the technology is economically a disaster (see Exhibit 3.7).

Objectives

Why do we care? The motivation for commercialization points towards the positioning and thus the feasible applications.

We can offer no advice on motivations or criteria for commercialization. Those are up to the owner of the technology. However, once the motivations or criteria are defined, we can use them to determine which applications should be preferred and what kinds of deal vehicles are desirable.

Usually there are multiple motivations or criteria. In that case it is

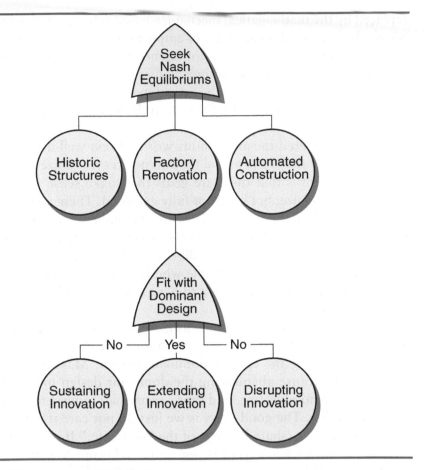

EXHIBIT 3.7 Motivation and Objectives

necessary to figure out how to reconcile and combine them. One technique for doing so is the multiattribute utility technique (MAUT). Essentially MAUT is like a decision tree in which various criteria are laid out, each with its own branch. Each branch has a weighting. Each option is assessed to see how well it does on each criterion. If the performances can be measured on a cardinal scale, various options can be ranked by multiplying each score by a weight reflecting the importance of the criterion and adding them up. The problem is that utility is not always additive. Recalling our bowls of cereal from Chapter 1, we can rapidly see that after eating several bowls the marginal utility of the next bowl starts to drop rapidly.

SMART, or the simple multi-attribute rating technique, is a variant of MAUT that is relatively easy to use. A SMART is simply a subset of nodes in our decision tree. It is built through eight steps:

1. Identify the decision maker(s) who will set the criteria.
2. Identify their specific criteria or objectives.
3. Identify the relevant scales for determining utility, desirability, goal attainment, objective stratification, etc. for each criterion.
4. Have them rank the criteria in the order of their importance.
5. Have them rate each criteria or objective preserving the order of the ranking.
6. Sum the ratings and divide each rating by that sum to give a weight for the criteria.
7. Now measure how well each alternative does on each criterion and multiply that value by the weight for the criterion.
8. Add up the results for each option to determine which one should be preferred.

Since most people want money (at least as one objective), let's focus on it as one criterion for purposes of our discussion. If we want quick money, we select an application where we can position ourselves as an incremental innovation. If we can be a bit more patient, we can play for larger, but longer-term income, and position ourselves as an extending innovation. If we want to gamble on a big hit, or just do not have other choices, we seek an application with a large market potential where we can position as a disruptive application.

We may have other criteria. For example, we might want to select as a lead entry application one which will be a good springboard into other parts of the technology niche. Continuing with our laser rangefinder example, let's take the extending application where we can profitably gain market share and then use the application to leapfrog into other parts of the niche. Factory renovation meets these criteria.

Before leaving application selection, we need to briefly address the situation where there are several possible applications that might work. In that case we commonly use two supplemental criteria to choose between them. The first criterion is to choose the application that is likely to provide the highest payoff, however we calculate that. The second criterion is to choose that application that is likely to be easiest to enter, that is, the one which has the lowest risk of failure and loss. If we use the first criterion we shall say we are choosing the payoff dominant option. In the latter case, the risk dominant option.

It seems obvious that an application that is both payoff and risk dominant should be selected. In the jargon of game theory, we would say that such applications may be Schelling points or focal points, that is, where more than two Nash Equilibriums exist, they are the likely choice because of the clues that suggest to the players in a game they are more likely to be realized. So where it may be possible to find or create multiple equilibriums, we look for Schelling points.

Now that we have our objectives: make money, springboard into other applications, and the initial market entry application. The next question is: What kind of a deal are we looking for? We could license, joint venture, get an investor, do cooperative R&D or for that matter sell contract R&D or other services. We can do product sales. The possibilities seem almost endless. Again we can use SMART to evaluate options, so long as we know what criteria to use when evaluating the options.

Here we can offer some advice. We have moved out of the realm of motivations and into the realm of realizing goals and objectives (see Exhibit 3.8).

Ideally the commercialization vehicle should lend itself to creation of a Nash Equilibrium. Deals occur where at least each party feels it will better off after the deal than before and the other party feels it at least will not be worse off. So the first question is what do we want to trade that will not make us feel worse off?

Let's do a mind experiment. Suppose we are a firm like Science Applications International Corporation (SAIC) and have a laser mapper. We recognize its commercial utility and are faced with the question of how we

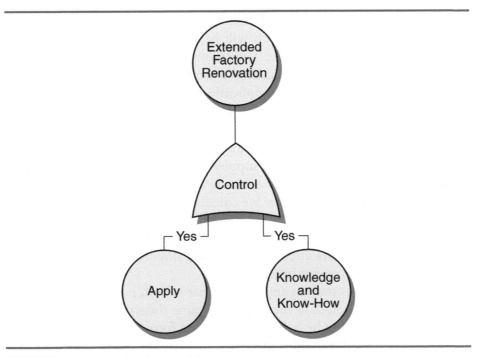

EXHIBIT 3.8   Realizing Goals and Objectives

should go about extracting money from this situation. Our ownership of the intellectual property in the mapper (the patents and possibly also trade secrets) gives us the right to exclude others from our turf. This turf consists of the right to make, use, offer for sale, or sell the technology. What we are trading then is a bundle of rights to make, use, offer for sale or sell to some extent. By transferring any or all of these rights, we also transfer part or all of the right to exclude others from the turf transferred in the deal.

What is at stake in the deal is the transfer of some degree of control over the technology. This control falls into two categories or bins. The first is control over application of the technology, the "make, use, offer for sale, or sale" of it. The second is access to, and control over, the knowledge and know-how underlying the technology—the intellectual in the intellectual property. Clearly, for the other party to a deal to realize value, we need to transfer enough intangible assets (knowledge and know-how) and rights (legal permission to apply) that the buyer can realize the value proposition we assert for the technology when declaring its fair market value.

Often a firm will want to retain control in its markets, but give it up elsewhere if it makes business sense to do that. Indeed, when we were tasked to find markets for the laser mapper, SAIC told us to only look at commercial applications. The company was retaining control of how the technology might be applied in the military and the knowledge/know-how specific for those applications.

Building on work by V.K. Jolly,[10] we can arrange potential deal vehicles by the kind and amount of control they transfer.

So, we can start determining what deal vehicle we want by asking ourselves how much control are we willing to give up to get a deal?

Note that the increments on the axis of Exhibit 3.9 are not precise in an interval or cardinal sense. We cannot say I want to give up 3% of control over application, look at the graph, and conclude we should have a cooperative research and development agreement (CRADA) rather than a strategic alliance. All it does is suggest ordinal relationships, that is, the likelihood of losing all control is greater with an assignment or sale of all rights than it is in an exclusive license or it is with a joint venture and so forth.

Fortunately, we can use other criteria to help us hone in on the deal vehicle. Recall we want to find the easiest deal we can. The concept of

[10] V.K. Jolly, *Commercializing New Technologies: Getting from Mind to Market,* Harvard Business School Press, 1997.

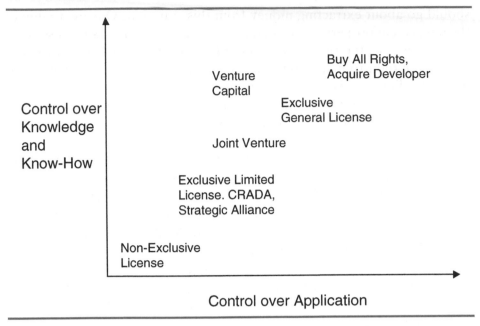

EXHIBIT 3.9   Control and Deal Vehicle

absorptive capacity, that is our familiarity with to the fields of science and/or engineering that underlie the technology and our familiarity with the markets we wish to enter. Here we apply this concept to our ability to conduct commercialization.

Let's look at how this works. It is obvious that deal-making is easier where you know what you are doing than not. Domain expertise refers to knowledge and know-how concerning technical fields. Here the focus is the fields needed to complete R&D and product development. Context expertise has to do with knowledge and know-how related to where technologies are applied. Here the focus for context expertise is the application we have selected for market entry.

Now, suppose we have strong domain expertise. Resource issues aside, (and we shall look at them next), if we want to maximize revenue, we will want to enhance our share of the downstream revenue flow by carrying the technology as close to maturity as we can. Of course, as we move from R&D into product development, the more important context expertise becomes because we want to end up with a product that really does meet end-user needs and thus has an attractive value proposition (see Exhibit 3.10).

We can use our mind experiment to illustrate. This time, let's pretend we have a friend, whom we will call Fred. Fred is a university professor who has developed a set of fractal equations that allows us to better display

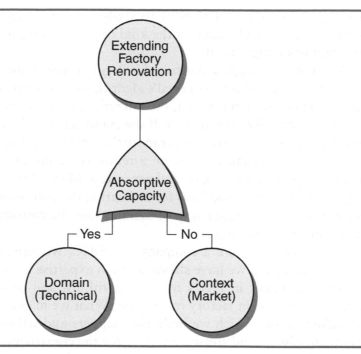

EXHIBIT 3.10 Absorptive Capacity

virtual reality images. We can use Fred's advance to create better 3-D images. The computer game guys love him.

Fred considers himself lucky. He wasn't trying to figure out how to make better computer games. He was just doing fundamental research on fractals. But now our friend is developing context expertise, because he is starting to rub shoulders with his colleagues in the gaming industry. The university technology transfer office is happy too because software companies that build development environments for gamers are interested in licensing Fred's algorithm.

Licensing makes sense where there is high technical expertise, but low market expertise. Not surprising, most university technology hits the market via that path. But other vehicles may also make sense. Suppose Fred is willing to go to trade shows and potential lead customers to talk about their needs. Consulting is certainly an option. Suppose he realizes through one of these meetings that he can make better simulations for training pilots. Now the military and the flight simulator folks are interested. Suppose he wants to stay involved with our technology through product development. Now a joint venture makes more sense. (A joint venture is a company in which each party to the deal owns equity. A technology developer may receive equity in exchange for a license or complete assignment of all rights in the technology.) He might even consider spinning out and forming a company as the ability to apply his technology in a variety of rapidly growing fields makes it the kind of platform technology that venture capitalists might fund.

Alternatively, suppose our friend is Peggy, a contractor. One day Peggy gets this idea that if she uses Fred's algorithms to post-process data from our revolving laser range finder, she can reduce the amount of time it takes to generate virtual reality images. If she could generate images in near real time, she can use laser mapper for more than planning. Every time the customer requests a change order on a renovation, she can take a mapper on-site, map the work to date, and generate a 3-D CAD file and associated images which provide the basis for estimating the cost of the change order and also provides a better way of making sure the customer understands what they are requesting.

Of course, if we are a company like SAIC, we represent yet a third player. In this case, we have strong domain expertise in the laser mapper, but not necessarily in Fred's fractal algorithms, and probably even less (context) expertise in factory renovation. What we might want is a strategic alliance under which we build the mappers and sell them to a fourth party, a hardware and software vendor for the construction industry who has the domain expertise to integrate Fred's algorithm and the context expertise to optimize the product for folks like Peggy. Alternatively, we end up licensing our technology to the construction industry vendor, who in turn sublicenses a contract manufacturing firm that makes the hardware for them.

I am making no attempt to accurately reflect the historical project for SAIC in this scenario. Historical accuracy is not the point here; pedagogy is. What is important is once again we can arrange deal vehicles along ordinal scales of domain and context capacity in order to select those that are most appropriate for us given our objectives. Exhibit 3.11 does just that. It is based on the Familiarity Matrix developed by Edwards and Berry.[11]

Now we have two criteria. We know what we are willing to trade away and we know what we are likely capable of pulling off. But within those constraints one other question remains: Do we have the resources? These resources fall into two major bins: tangible and intangible assets (see Exhibit 3.12). Tangible assets are factories, equipment, land, bank accounts, and the other things you can pick up or touch. Intangible assets are things you cannot "touch" like intellectual property, goodwill, and know-how.

Once again, we can use our mind experiment to illustrate. Suppose

---

[11] Roberts and Berry, "Entering New Business: Selecting Strategies for Success," *Sloan Management Review* (Spring 1985).

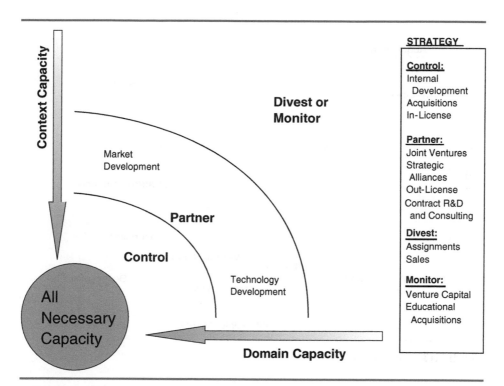

EXHIBIT 3.11 A Familiarity Matrix

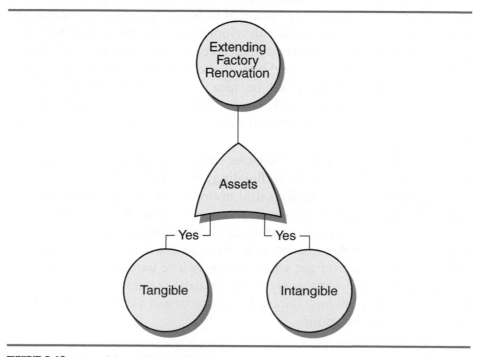

EXHIBIT 3.12 Tangible and Intangible Resources

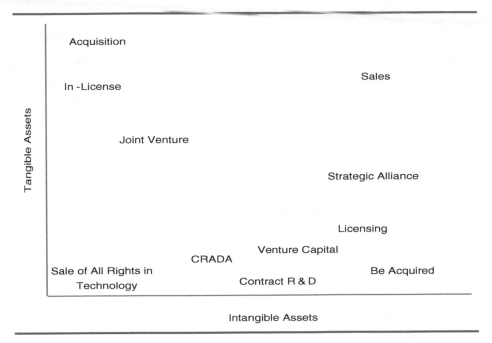

EXHIBIT 3.13   Deal Vehicles

Peggy works for CM2Hill, a major consulting engineering firm. She is likely to have very substantial tangible assets and pretty good intangible ones. That means she has the option of in-licensing Fred's algorithms and using them in-house to complete development of her invention. Now suppose she and her husband have a small construction company called Peggy and Bill's Factory Renovation Shop. If she wants an easy route to commercialization, she likely will sell her idea to one of her hardware/software vendors or to a firm who sells laser mappers. That firm will complete product development and sell an off-the-shelf piece of software to Peggy and her competitors.

As before we can plot deal vehicles on a chart with ordinal scales from low to high (see Exhibit 3.13). Building on work by Megantz,[12] we can once again look at how various deal options arrange themselves depending on the asset mix of the developer. Clearly if we have everything we need, there is no reason to partner at all in commercialization. Alternatively, as our example suggests, if we have no assets at all, we should just sell the technology and get what we can before we lose our shirt. Even contract R&D (including government awards), assumes we have enough knowledge and know-how (intangible assets) to win a contract. In between, there are a range of options.

---

[12] Megantz, *How to License Technology* (Hoboken, NJ: Wiley, 1996).

We now have three criteria to use when selecting the commercialization vehicle for our technology in factory renovation: control, absorptive capacity, and assets. In our mind experiment example, the SMART that the major company that developed the technology might use to choose its deal vehicle, ends up looking something like Exhibit 3.14.

We already elected to have an objective of seeking to maximize income through positioning our laser mapper as an extending innovation. Now we can present several deal vehicle options to management, such as licensing, joint venturing, or a strategic alliance. If we only want one vehicle, we

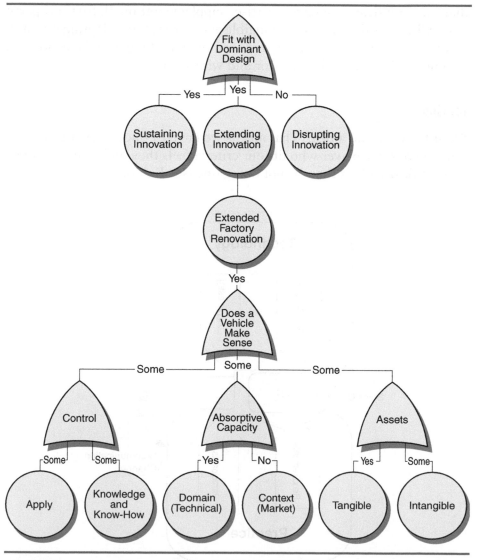

EXHIBIT 3.14 SMART Deal Vehicles

can once again examine each option to see which are likely to be payoff or risk dominant to help us down select.

Note that our work in objective setting has taken us farther than just the application and deal vehicle. By identifying how our technology relates to the dominant design of the practice, we have a pretty good idea of how much education and awareness building we will have to conduct to make end users appreciate our value proposition. By identifying our strengths and weaknesses on absorptive capacity and assets, we define capacity and assets that we need to find in our partner. Further, our partner should find our control preferences acceptable. In the case of the laser mapper mind experiment, what we want is to do a deal with a player that has strengths that has significant context expertise, supplemental intellectual property, goodwill, and other relevant intangible assets useful for adapting our laser mapper for customers in factory renovation and selling it to them. So, now we know what we are looking for and with whom.

Tactics

We still have to do a deal. That means we have to find, or create, a situation where some player who fits our criteria feels they will be better off by doing a deal with us than by not doing one (see Exhibit 3.15).

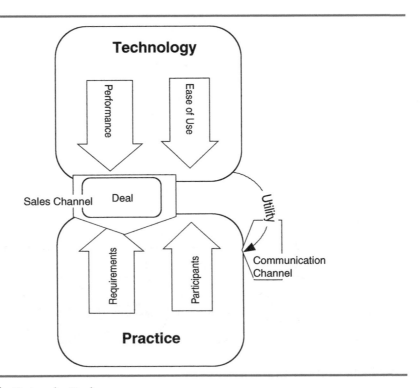

EXHIBIT 3.15   Doing the Deal

To do the deal you need to create a situation where:

- The performance and ease of use of the technology coheres with the requirements of the practice and the expectations of participants;
- A communication channel exists and the buyers become aware of this coherence;
- The coherence has either:
  - Greater net utility for the buyers than any other option or
  - Is weighted so heavily that they are not comparing net utilities;
- A sales channel exists through which the deal can be consummated; and
- All the parties want to, and are able, to do the deal.

What we need are ways to lock the constructs of the deal together and find leverage points to push them into place. Suppose you are doing a jigsaw puzzle. The way you lock the pieces is to look at how they fit and then match up the peninsulas that stick out with the indentation bays. In our model, fit occurs through relationships like utility, value, costs and benefits. Relationships fit constructs together because they share attributes or have interlocking attributes.

In distinction to a jigsaw puzzle, in commercialization we can alter the shape of the peninsulas and bays. If relationships are how we link the pieces together, then one way we can implement strategy is to change the relationships under our control. A few examples: We can do additional R&D to enhance utility of our technology. We can change the costs and benefits of our technology for its users by implementing or rescinding regulations that mandate functionalities we provide or prohibit them. We can increase its net utility by building partnerships with upstream and downstream vendors in the supply chain, so the infrastructure to use it is readily available. We can change its value by manipulating its price. We can affect the cost/benefit of a practice by educating end users as to their options and the costs and benefits of these options, thereby building pull-through for our technology (see Exhibit 3.16).

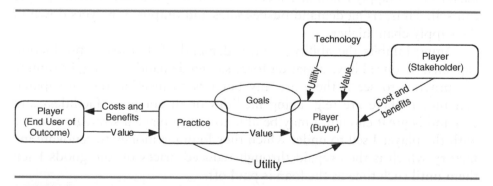

EXHIBIT 3.16 Educating End Users about Options

But where are the leverage points so we know where to intervene? The leverage points are market forces. Metaphorically, market forces push constructs toward each other. More precisely market forces are simply trends in one or more attributes of one or more constructs.

Forces can be statistical tendencies reflecting either micro or macro-level social trends. By micro-level we refer to forces that affect attributes of practices. Macro level forces affect attributes of arenas and markets. These trends appear in our model as probabilities for the instantiation of attributes. For example, recall the example about the elevator lift for retiree homes in southern coastal communities. In that example, wealth is an attribute of the player buyer, as is age. Land is a good, with the attribute of price, which reflects market value and the price of another good, called a mortgage.

Market forces are either opportunities to exploit or threats to neutralize or irrelevant. They are relevant when they affect the probability of a deal occurring by affecting the likely number of buyers and sellers and what they probably want. The impact on number is the magnitude of the force. The direction is whether they are more or less likely to help you commercialize. A strong positive force means lots more sales are likely to happen. You are happy and taking the family to Tahiti. A weak positive force means a few more sales are likely to happen. OK, so it's Disney Land. A weak negative force means some falling off in sales is likely. It means more headaches and probably some aspirin in the morning. A strong negative force means serious heartburn and you're grabbing for the antacid.

Once again, an example: If I know that the general factory inventory in the United States is aging and I also know that demand for factory capacity is rising, I can conclude there is likely to be a better opportunity for my laser mapper than in the absence of these forces. What are the forces? They are statistical trends in attributes. Age is an attribute of the infrastructure used in a practice. Demand is an attribute of markets. Demand links players within a supply chain. The demand of the upstream player in the supply chain interlocks with the supply a downstream player can sell. Thus, rising demand pushes sales and output of players down in the supply chain higher.

Aging inhibits the ability to meet demand, if it restricts production capacity. So once I have a market force saying demand is rising, I examine my practice to see if there are any barriers to meeting the anticipated demand. If there are (e.g. aging facilities or in adequate facilities) and demand is great enough, I may be able to put in place a strategic alliance with the player I sell to under which they loan me money to renovate my factory which is then repaid through reduced prices on the goods I sell them until such time as the loan is paid off.

We helped put a deal together like this several years ago for a small company, manufacturing a polymer that was an electrically switchable coating for glass which would control the light transmitted. The military wanted electrically switchable glass for aircraft instrument display panels. A prime contractor was interested in our customer's solution, but at that time, the company was still young and lacked the resources to rapidly scale their factory to meet the demand. The solution was for the prime contractor to loan money as a prepayment on part of the purchase price. As the product was delivered the principle and interest was paid down through prime's withholding of part of the sales price for the polymers until the loan was paid off.

Now, if we are going to leverage a market force, we need two things. First, we need a relationship where a relevant force is changing the attribute that is the basis of that relationship. Second, we need a channel to exercise the influence. If channels already exist, we need to gain access. If not, we need to build them before we can access them.

To use market forces to our advantage, what we need to do is design our relationships in such a way as to make the vector mathematics of market forces work in our favor. We want to use relationships that are likely to occur and avoid those that are unlikely. Alternatively, we want to make the relationships sought by our competitors unlikely and those which disadvantage them more likely. We do this by positioning our technology in such a way as to make us the beneficiary of positive forces and to avoid damage from negative ones.

Competition

Of course, as we are developing our strategy, there probably are others developing theirs. So part of the challenge is to design our tactics in such a way as to neutralize the threat from competition.

Clearly the best way to neutralize is to have a superior product. There is an oft-told story concerning Betamax and VHS formats for video tape. It highlights that *superior* has to be defined in terms of what customers want. Technically, Betamax had a higher yield on video bandwidth. None the less, Betamax was a market disaster. Akio Morita, who founded Sony, attributed that loss to Sony's somewhat restrictive licensing program. By comparison, VHS was widely licensed.[13] But this viewpoint ignores a

---

[13] Wikipedia, "Betamax," August 2005, http://en.wikipedia.org/wiki/Betamax (accessed September 11, 2005).

critical factor: No one cared about the higher yield. As Jack Schofield correctly argues, at least in my opinion, the key factor in the market failure was that Betamax initially could only record one hour and that was too short to record a movie. So, why get a Betamax when you could get a VHS that recorded much longer, especially since the image quality difference was not really noticeable.[14]

Having said that, it is true that who sells a product can make a difference. This is called brand loyalty. You want to sell to people who have customers already. It simplifies your market entry if you can leverage their access to their customers. For example, suppose you have a new disk drive for cheap notebooks. You want to make and sell it. You want to sell it to companies who will sell their notebooks so you can make money. After all a disk drive in a machine that does not sell is not a great money maker. So you go to *PC Magazine,* read a bunch of other publications and visit websites to see what shows up.[15] If a company does not show up in multiple places, they are not in your initial target list.

Windows of Opportunity or Being Just-in-Time

The market is never static. It is always changing because the players involved are always seeking to gain advantage over each other. Deals are about being fair, but they also are about gaining advantage over competitors.

From a buyer's perspective, acquiring a technology is driven by either offensive or defensive considerations. Offensive considerations are things like gaining first mover advantage by being first to market with a new generation of product, catching up with a competitor who has already introduced a next generation technology, or rounding out a product line to pick up a new customer segment. Defensive considerations are things like removing a potentially competing technology prior to its introduction, hedging your bets by acquiring a technology that can be used to make products if your current technology bombs, or gaining rights that extend your intellectual property further, making it harder for competitors to enter your space.

Whether offensive or defensive, acquiring a technology has costs. Even if you pick it up for a song, it costs money to negotiate the deal and comply with any reporting requirements. So the optimal thing is to only buy it when you need it or, sometimes even better if you are hedging, to acquire an option that allows you to acquire it should you need it.

---

[14] Jack Schofield, "Why VHS Was Better Than Betamax," *Guardian Unlimited* (January 25, 2003), http://www.guardian.co.uk/online/comment/story/0,12449,881780,00.html (accessed September 11, 2005).

[15] For example, see *PCMag.com,* http://www.pcmag.com/products/0,,qn=Laptops+Notebooks+Value,00.asp (accessed September 11, 2005).

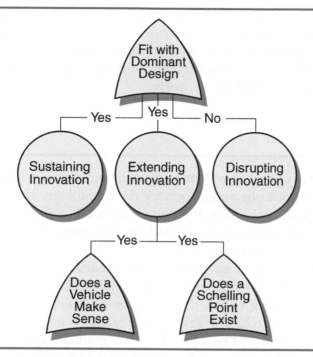

EXHIBIT 3.17   Developing Strategies

In other words, there is a window of opportunity for deal making, just as there are windows of opportunity for introducing new products into the market. We can never ignore the time dimension when commercializing technology. If we try to do a deal too early, no one wants it. If we are too late, we miss the boat. The trick is to be just-in-time. If you are, a Schelling Point likely exists. (See Exhibit 3.17.)

According to Gary Cohen, President BD Medical, they have already spent over $600 million in R&D and acquisition related to safety syringes since the 1980s.[16] The reason why funding flowed to create safety syringes in the 1980s is simple. In June of 1981, the first AIDS patient seen at the National Institutes of Health was admitted. By August, the Centers for Disease Control reported 108 cases of the "new disease" in the United States.[17]

---

[16] Phone interview with the author, December 14, 2004.
[17] "Timeline, 1981–1988," June 4, 2001, http://aidshistory.nih.gov/timeline/index.html, accessed December 18, 2005.

The easiest way to be in-time is to build a relationship with the down stream acquirer in which they provide you a heads up about what they will be looking for and when. For this reason, initial deals with a party are often as much or more about relationship building than they are about discrete pieces of intellectual property.

CONCLUSION

There are three critical questions for developing strategies. The first one is can we find at least one application for the technology. The second one is can we find a deal vehicle that will work for us. The third one is whether we can find a way to make that vehicle in that application appear to be a Schelling point for another player.

The first question is answered through market research. The second question is answered by developing our objectives. The third one is answered by developing tactics that allow us to leverage what we learned during market research. The key to these tactics is understanding how to leverage market forces. I recall reading as a graduate student somewhere in the works of Hungarian philosopher Georg Lukács that what business people do is try to figure out where the rainbow will strike the earth so they can position themselves to receive the pot of gold when it does.[18]

With this chapter, we complete our overview of the model. The next chapter begins Part Two: Market Research.

---

[18] I think the passage is in Lukács, *Zur Ontologie des gesellschaftlichen Sein—Die Arbeit,* (Luchterhand, Darmstadt, Germany, 1973).

Market Research

CHAPTER 4

Finding the Customer

INTRODUCTION

Market research is conducted to find answers to questions. The question usually is: "How can I make money off this technology?"

Our model tells us how to make money. First, find a positioning with competitive advantage. Then have good launch tactics. The market research we conduct to answer "How do I make money?" begins by asking where to find customers who will want to buy the technology.

In this chapter we explore how to find customers because if you can find them, you almost always can make money if only because there is usually someone who will help you take a technology to the market for a piece of the action.

Finding customers is a four-step process. The first step is to get our arms around the technology: What do we have to sell? Once we have determined what it is we are trying to commercialize, we determine what practices may provide applications. Next we figure out who in those practices will be the end user for our technology. The fourth and final step is discovering who might buy our technology for them. One two, who needs a shoe, three four, open the door. If a door doesn't exist, we build one.

WHAT WE HAVE TO SELL

A technology can be considered a bundle of functionality, characteristics, and features. We shall examine each of these in more detail.

Functionality

Functionality is context bound. Look down at your shoes. Go ahead; look at them. If it is summer, you probably have on a shoe that breathes. It probably is able to protect your feet from rocks and glass and the ooze of squished bugs and worms between your toes. Basically, all you need is a comfortable pad under your feet and way to keep that pad on your feet—in other words, sandals.

The context is different in winter. When there is snow on the ground, you probably want something else. You want to keep your feet warm and dry. You want the shoe warm enough for going outside but not too hot inside. And you want that comfortable pad.

Now, think about your winter shoes. Let's say they are leather. Since the moisture in the snow and slush can soak the leather, you either have to coat the leather or insert a moisture barrier that keeps the water out but has enough "breathability" to keep your feet from sweating.

A semipermeable barrier that blocks moisture, retains heat, but lets water vapor pass might help. Gore-tex® does just that. Not surprisingly, it is now used in shoes.[1]

What our quick example demonstrates is that functionality only counts when it can be linked to end-user requirements. The end user's performance requirements define what things meet our needs. Say we want our shoe to insulate. Then Gore-tex® is not enough. We need a way to get a better R-value.

R-values are measures of thermal resistance. To be precise, it is a measure of resistance to heat flow calculated in Fahrenheit degrees times hours times square feet per Btu or Kelvin degrees times square meters per watt.[2] The higher the R-value, the better the insulation. Loose fiberglass insulation has an average R-value around 2.7 per inch while polystyrene boards have an R-value of 4 per inch.[3] The point being we can set a requirement (an R-value) for insulation for shoes and evaluate potential materials in terms of how closely they hit that value.

Of course, what we usually have is a solution looking for a problem. So, how can we take what we have and find it a home? The first thing is

---

[1] For a picture, toss the string, "how Gore-tex works," into Google or another search engine. For example, there is an illustration at http://www.aabjornsson.se/ARCHIVE/Page_01/archive03.page01/page01.design/design3old.html (accessed October 10, 2004) and a video at http://www.tvo.org/iqm/site_contents.html (accessed October 10, 2004). Actually, you can pretty much learn about how anything works by tossing the string, "how things work," into a search engine. One of my favorite sites is *How Things Work* at http://howthingswork.virginia.edu/. Another helpful site is *Science, Technology and How Things Work* at http://www.academic-genealogy.com/science.htm, which is a catalog of links.

[2] Thus another insight: The measures you use depend on whether you are in the United States or if you are anywhere else in the world.

[3] Wisconsin K–12 Energy Education Program, "Energy Use Investigation," n.d., www.uwsp.edu/cnr/wcee/keep/Audit/glossary-r-s.htm (accessed October 10, 2004).

to forget about what we think we have. We do not have a technology but rather a bundle of functionality, that is, of performances. The second we put a label on our technology, we tend to restrict what we will consider as an application. A digression helps.

> Although you want your feet warm, you do not want them hot. More is not always better—even if it does not cost anything extra to get more. Get your feet too hot and they will sweat and end up stinking. Better to focus on what end users want rather than what you think they should want, so your end users do not conclude your technology stinks.

Years ago, we were asked by the U.S. Navy Undersea Warfare Center, Division Keyport: "What do you do outside the military with a torpedo range now that the cold war is over?" Now, even back then there were not a lot of uses for torpedoes in non-military applications. So, what we quickly realized was that we were not commercializing a torpedo range, but floating and fixed fiber optic arrays to which sensors could be attached. It did not matter what sensors were attached nor did it matter what depth below water or how far above the surface. What we were looking for were people who wanted sensors in or on or above the water.

At that time there was a problem in Glacier Bay National Park in Alaska. I remember reading in the Seattle paper about how tour boats would come into the Bay and the whales and other marine life would leave. Noise was destroying their habitat. The article said the Park Service was looking for ideas to solve the problem other than just banning everyone from entering, which was counter to the principle of having a park.

We did a bit of research. It turned out that the tour boats ran the coast of Mexico in the winter and in the summer sailed up to Alaska. On the way north, they steamed past the base with the torpedo ranges. Bingo! Application. We could take a Navy floating torpedo range up to Glacier Bay, monitor noise levels, and determine at what threshold an impact on marine life occurred. The Park Service could require that any ship or tour boat entering the bay sail through the Navy's fixed ranges so their noise generation could be profiled. We could also use the fixed array or the floating one to get profiles for various small craft. In short, we could have a pretty good idea of what level of underwater noise to expect for each type of pleasure craft and each ship.

If that was done, the Park Service could stack the profiles as each ship or boat entered the bay. As the threshold was approached, all new boats and ships could be banned until someone left and the noise levels dropped, after which the next ship or boat in line could enter so long as their profile, when added in, was still under the threshold.

But there were other applications. My favorite involved America's Cup racing yachts. It turns out that under some conditions, some of the assumptions in the Navier-Stokes equations for computational fluid dynamics break down. That means you have to do physical testing on top of simulations to validate what you have when you design a surface in a flow is what you want. Further, the equations are computationally intensive and difficult to use. For that reason, and because of small variances in manufacturing, physical model testing is used to supplement the use of models and simulations when making America's Cup racers. Indeed, at the time of this project, competitors always built two boats and down selected to the best. Optimizing was critical as there is usually only one to two percent difference in the speed of the winning and losing boats.[4]

We started thinking about how we could use a torpedo range to test America's Cup racers. With a bit more research we discovered we could listen to the flow of bubbles moving and popping around the hulls of boats. The sounds were correlated to the performance of the boats, providing a way to scientifically select a superior hull. In other words, what a torpedo range could be is a test site for full sized vessels.

Just as an FYI, by hanging pressure rather than acoustic sensors, our torpedo range became a way of measuring the wake impact of various ferry designs. Wakes are important because they damage break walls and impact unprotected shoreline along ferry routes. So, when buying a new generation of ferries, minimizing the impact on communities is a consideration.

What the example indicates is that to cross walk from a technology to its applications, we can use its performances to see who might want those performances. In order to facilitate this process, I recommend measuring these performances on Standard International Units (SIU).

Exhibit 4.1 presents the SIUs and their relationships.[5]

Two data points are useful to determine. First, what is the technology's *potential,* that is, its maximum feasible performance on any metric. Obviously, this potential is limited by the fundamental physical laws applying to metric. Refrigeration technology, for example, cannot have a cooling potential lower than absolute zero. But more relevant is the state of the art

---

[4] See Giovanni Ceccarelli, "On the Approach to Designing an IAAC Yacht," *MDY'04,* (n.d.), http://www.etsin.upm.es/Noticias/mdy06/mdy_04/ponencias/Papers/01-Ceccarelli/BN%20(1).pdf (accessed September 4, 2005).
[5] The NIST Reference on Constants, Units, and Uncertainty, "Relationships of the SI Derived Units with Special Names and Symbols and the SI Base Units," n.d., http://physics.nist.gov/cuu/Units/SIdiagram.html (accessed October 5, 2004).

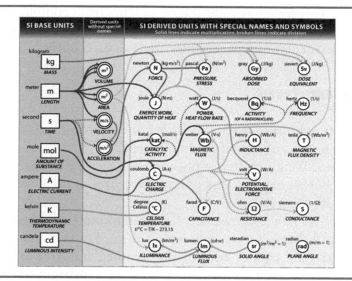

EXHIBIT 4.1   SIUs and Their Relationships

and science underlying the technology, as what we know and can do limits what we can attain.

The second data point is *yield*. Yield is the currently accomplished performance on the metric.[6]

Given yield and potential, we end up with a range between the two. This range, which represents how well our technology can perform on the metric if we sought to optimize performance through R&D is called *stretch*. We can ask, how far we can stretch the performance of our technology.

Of course, yield and potential can be more or less attainable. Because technologies are ideally proven solutions that can be repeatedly applied, we also need to determine with what degree of confidence we can repeatedly attain a performance. We want to know: Can we repeatedly measure bubbles around a hull with a torpedo range with a high confidence in the replicability of our results?

The way we get confidence is to have control over relevant physical phenomena. Confidence is a function of the scientific and engineering knowledge and of the artisan know-how we possess. In a 1994 article "Measuring and Managing Technical Knowledge," Roger Bohn provided an ordinal scale for measuring certainty of results in terms of the underlying control over the phenomena being manipulated in, or through, a

---

[6] Marco Iansiti, *Technology Integration* (Boston: Harvard Business School Press, 1998), 31.

technology.[7] This scale has eight stages, ranging from complete ignorance to complete understanding. The stages vary in terms of how our knowledge about particular inputs variables affect desired outputs.

Bohn Knowledge Levels

1. *Complete ignorance.* Even though we are aware a phenomenon exists we have no idea of how it might be useful.
2. *Awareness.* We know that a phenomenon exists and that it might be relevant but we have no idea of how to control or use it. All we can do is begin studying it.
3. *Measure.* We now can measure variables accurately, although we cannot control them. But we can exploit them. For example, there is an adage that you cannot control the weather. But you can move the party inside when it rains. At this level we can begin to experiment with variables, changing them to see their control implications.
4. *Control of the mean.* We can now control variables accurately across a range of levels, even if not precisely. So, we can control the mean level, while accepting variance around that level. This allows us to stabilize processes, with respect to the mean of the variables we can control. We are starting to do controlled experiments on variables to precisely measure their impacts on our process.
5. *Control of variance.* Now we have enough control to peg the variables with precision where we want them across a range of values. We are at the level of "cookbook" production, that is, having the ability to follow a consistent recipe—even if we can precisely ensure output quality at all times. Our focus is shifting from controlling key variables to how to control environmental factors and interactions of variables.
6. *Process characterization.* Once we know how the interactions of variables and environments affect outcomes, we can start fine-tuning our processes in order to reduce costs and to change the characteristics of what we produce. Feedback control for output quality is possible. This reduces the variability of outcomes, ensuring more consistent quality. By knowledge engineering the know-how we are accumulating, and combining that with what we have learned about the empirical relationship of variables and environments, we can start modeling our process.
7. *Scientific model of the process.* We have reached the stage of a nonlinear and interaction model in which the effects of this variable can be known with respect to other variables of interest. Optimizing the

---

[7] Roger E. Bohn, "Highbeam Research," *Sloan Management Review* (September 22, 1994), http://www.highbeam.com/library/doc3.asp?DOCID=1P1:29037540&num=1&ctrlInfo=Round8b%3AProd%3ASR%3AResult&ao= (accessed October 4, 2004).

process using feedback and some feed-forward control becomes feasible. Implementing control via the model means ultimately we can turn it over to a computer. We become the controller of the model rather than of the actual process. Simulations allow for studies that are too expensive or dangerous to conduct using the actual process. We can now begin to anticipate problems that we have never faced.

8. *Complete knowledge.* We have complete control over a process. We understand exactly how to produce what we want when we want it. In short, something impossible to attain. The best we can hope for is to approach it asymptotically by more and more detailed study of the process.

Note that the difference between yield and potential need not mean the technology is still in R&D or immature. If I am interested in keeping the milk for my cereal cold, I do not care about reaching zero Celsius, let alone absolute zero. But I am interested in how close your technology is to be able to keep my milk cold.

In evaluating potential applications, we do, however, want to consider maturity. It means little to say there is an application *today* if we cannot provide a product, process, or service that people will buy *now*. What we really are looking for is an application *tomorrow* when we will have something to sell.

We can measure the maturity of a technology with the aid of technology readiness levels (TRLs).[8] TRLs help us get a handle on how far away from market introduction we are. The lower the readiness levels on an ordinal scale of one to nine the further the technology is from practical use and thus the less mature it is.

Technology Readiness Levels (TRLs)[9]

1. *Basic principles observed and reported.* At this lowest level of technology readiness, ideas are transitioning out of fundamental research into applied research and development. This transitioning occurs in paper studies of a technology's basic properties.

---

[8] For a crossover from TRLs to traditional terms for progress from basic research, see Houston Advanced Research Center, "Definitions of TRLs for Components and Subsystems/Systems," n.d., http://www.harc.edu/harc/Projects/BlueWater/About/Files/ TRLDefinitions.pdf (accessed October 4, 2004). This PDF also provides examples. For complete definitions of each level in the military context, see Acq.osd.mil, "Appendix 6, Technology Readiness Levels and their Definitions," *DOD Deskbook 5000.2-R,* n.d., http://www.acq.osd.mil/actd/FY04/TRL%2050002R.doc (accessed October 4, 2004.)

[9] Adapted from the Technical Support Working Group, "Technology Readiness Levels," n.d., www.tswg.gov/tswg/techtrans/TRLDefinitions.pdf (accessed October 5, 2004).

2. *Technology concept formulated.* This level is where research gives way to invention. The application may be speculative, in the sense that no proof or detailed analysis exists to support the assumption the invention will work as promised. Paper studies are still occurring.

3. *Analytical and experimental critical function proof of concept.* Now formal analytical (including simulations) and laboratory studies are conducted to evaluate the performance predictions that have been made. The emphasis is on proof of concept, that is, critical but separate elements of the technology.

4. *Component and/or breadboard validation in a laboratory environment.* By integrating several technological components, a bread board or brass board is created that establishes that the pieces will work together. This bench top crude prototype validates the utility of the knowledge underlying the technology

5. *Component and/or breadboard validation in a relevant environment.* Now a prototype with key functionality exists that provides a *"high fidelity"* laboratory integration of the components. The prototype, in turn, enables more testing, such as testing in a simulated environment like determining the impact of moisture by using a spray jar and soaking the prototype. The testing may involve validating thresholds that suggest the technology will operate acceptably in a relevant environment.

6. *System/subsystem model or prototype demonstration in a relevant environment.* The prototype now is a fully functioning prototype or computer model that enables testing performance yields in a "high fidelity" laboratory environment or in simulated operational environment, like a compression or environmental chamber. This level involves alpha testing.

7. *System prototype demonstration in an operational environment.* The prototype is now taken out of the lab and put in the hands of end users in their actual working conditions. This is beta testing. By the end of beta testing, the technology has been proven to work in its final form and under expected operational conditions. Ideally, what is being tested is the intended or pre-production configuration to determine that the technology does meet the design specifications and has operational utility. This testing is the basis of acceptance testing.

8. *Actual system completed and operationally qualified through test and demonstration.* The technology has been proven to work in beta testing and has been tweaked to address any issues that emerged there. In almost all cases, this TRL represents the end of the development process.

9. *Actual system, proven through successful practical use.* The technology is now transitioned and in the hands of the end users. It may still

involve beta testing, as the last "bug fixing" occurs. Sometimes this bug fixing endures forever.

> There is an old joke about a physicist, a chemist, and an economist who are stranded on a desert island. A case of canned food washes ashore. They are ecstatic until they realize they do not have a can opener. The physicist says, don't worry, I will find a rock and figure out the price force and spot to hit the can and the lip will pop open. The chemist says, why bother, I can just build a fire, heat the can, and the resulting energy will generate such a pressure that the can will explode. The economist scratches his head in amazement. Why worry, he says, let us consider the can opened. End users, like the economist in the joke, want to assume a technology works, that is, is at TRL 8 or 9.

Without test results, it is meaningless to claim a TRL level. For example, the U.S. Army is a major consumer of boots. Suppose we have a new kind of material we think is great for very high performance athletic shoes and boots. We could make a set of boots and take them to the Army for testing.

> *"We beat up boots here. We beat the heck out of them," said Michael Holthe, lead project engineer for footwear programs at the U.S. Army Soldier Systems Center here. "They have to be durable, but also help the person do their job. You could make a boot that lasts forever, but you really couldn't use it. It wouldn't be functional for the soldier." ... Equipment in the lab was assembled to create a specialized ability to test and evaluate footwear and check heat insulation, shock attenuation, pressure distribution, water penetration, flex resistance and dynamic stiffness. "None of this replaces field testing, but it helps us know if an item is going in the right direction. We can do the pre-testing here so we don't waste time," Holthe said.*[10]

If the U.S. Army Soldier Systems Center-Natick agrees to test our material, they will do a battery of tests that establish our materials suitability for the anticipated environments in, and conditions under, the boots will be used. Some examples are:

- To test flexing, a machine is used that pivots up and down along the boot's natural flexing line for a 12-hour test, cycling 140 repetitions per minute. To test flexing and leaking when wet, the boot is positioned

---

[10] U.S. Army Soldier Systems Center-Natick, "Boots Take a Beating," April 2, 2003, http://www.natick.army.mil/about/pao/2003/03–11.htm (accessed October 11, 2004).

inside a stainless steel tank filled with enough water to cover up to the ankle. A piece of paper is put inside the boot. If it ends up wet, the design fails.

- To test impact, another machine slams a steel piston onto either a separate midsole or the entire manufactured boot sole system. This shock allows assessing shock attenuation, energy return, and material deformation. These measurements allow calculating deceleration, which is a measurement of how of the impact is absorbed and how long it takes to stop deforming and rebound to its original shape.
- In-shoe pressure is measured by embedding sensors in the insoles of footwear worn by a human research volunteer. Data is logged onto a portable recorder worn by the volunteer.
- Insulation is measured by placing the boot in a metal tray that contains a hotplate filled with sand. The entire sole is covered in the sand. It is heated to 150 degrees C. By placing a probe inside the boot, the temperature is measured over time. The criterion, by the way, is an increase of no more than 22 degrees C over a 30 minute period.

After completing such a battery of tests, our material will be at TRL 6: system/subsystem model or prototype demonstration in a relevant environment.

We shall see later in this book that maturity and confidence play into the level of technical risk borne when transitioning a technology out of the lab and into practical use. Knowing this risk is important because risk is a key factor in valuating technology, The allocation of risk to the party able to best control it is critical for doing a successful deal. What concerns us here, however, is not that but simply whether we even have the stretch to fit within the performances desired by players in a specific application.

Characteristics

As we saw in Part One, performance is not enough to establish utility and thus competitive advantage. The technology must also be easy to use. Characteristics are objective factors on which we can measure ease of use. They address the likely comfort levels people will have with our technology within an application.

Following Tornatzki and Fleischer, we can identify several characteristics with broad applicability across technologies.[11]

- **Complexity** measures the number of "*layers*" of technology that must be integrated into this technology. The technology being transitioned

---

[11] The discussion here draws on Louis Tornatzky and Mitchell Fleischer, *The Process of Technological Innovation,* (Lanham, MD: Lexington Books, 1990), 165 ff.

may be a material, component, subsystem, system, or platform. Often the lower the complexity, the easier it is to transition the technology.

- **Scalability** measures how easy it is to duplicate the technology to meet market demand. Highly scalable technologies are easily replicated (i.e., software or plastic cups). Technologies whose scalability is compatible with the number of units that need to be produced to meet market demand are easier to transition.

- **Adaptability** measures how easily end users can tweak the technology to meet their specific needs. Typically, greater adaptability is an advantage when transitioning a technology.

- **Packaging** measures how much special infrastructure must be provided with the technology in order for the end user to capture its utility. Training, no harmonics power, and a vibration free floor are examples of packaging that a technology may require. Substantial packaging may or may not be a problem for transitioning, depending on the capabilities and resources of the end user and the in-place infrastructure. A problem does exist when a technology does not always come with all or part of the packaging, and the packaging is not readily available.

- **Fragility** measures how robust the technology is once it moves outside the lab. Limits on acceptable environmental operating conditions, susceptibility to damage, or embedded software that crashes are examples of factors contributing to fragility.

- **Trialability** measures how easily the end user can test a technology to determine whether or not to acquire it. Two factors are important: how convenient it is for the end user to test the technology, and how large the set of activities is that must be affected to conduct the test. The most trialable technologies are those that can be shipped to end users with minimal instructions and that end users can test with no or minimal impact on their current activities.

- **Platform relationships** measure how tightly integrated the technology is with a second product (i.e., cameras and film or computers and software).

Let's use shoes as an example again. Recall the discussion on what makes a good winter boot. We need something to waterproof our shoes against the slush but that does not make our feet hot. Thomas Frey of the DaVinci Institute suggests gel-cells can provide performances superior to breathable membranes like Gore-tex®.[12] Gel-cells are an expansive polymer gel technology that uses microvoltage to expand or contract the gel. By making shoes with hundreds of gel-cells, each slaved to a temperature

---

[12] Adapted from Thomas Frey, "Smart Shoes," *Da Vinci Institute* (2004), http://www .davinciinstitute.com/page.php?ID=29 (accessed October 10, 2004).

sensor that is in turn controlled by an embedded microprocessor, pores can be opened or closed to maintain a desired temperature. By only partially opening a pore, we can let vapor out from inside the shoe while keeping water from diffusing into the shoe. An added benefit is that the gel-cells can also be used to maintain an even pressure by expanding or contracting them as appropriate for the use going on. For example, we might increase the pressure to keep our foot from slipping in a boot when going downhill rather than tightening the laces. The result could be a very comfortable shoe.

But wait, think of all the packaging that gel-cells require. Not only do we need the gel-cell membrane, we need the microprocessor and a power source. If the battery fails when backpacking, we'd better have a spare or we will miss our old Gore-tex® boots. This is a packaging issue. Also, how do we program the gel-cell for our preferences? Suddenly I realize this is adding a level or two of complexity to my shoes that I am not sure I want. I am pretty clear on how to tighten and loosen my laces. And I do not need a manual for that.

Compare the shoes with my Vespa® motorscooter. I bought one this year to get around town as I really do not need a car. I ride a bicycle so I know how to use the brakes. I owned a car so I know how to put in gas and oil and check the water level in the battery. I had to learn to twist the handhold on the right to throttle the gas. That's it though. The scooter is less complex than my car was. And I need no training even though I have never owned one before. No wonder scooter sales are climbing as gas prices soar.[13]

Note that characteristics, like yields, can be measured. A technology can be more or less fragile or require greater or lesser packaging. But whereas yields are usually measured on interval scales, characteristics are measured on ordinal scales.

We can use characteristics to eliminate some of those applications from further consideration. What we are looking for is mismatches between the values of our characteristics with those usually found in an application, where the mismatch is in a less desirable direction. As we move more and more in less desirable directions, we are likely to move outside the comfort range of people in that application. The result is a barrier to market entry may emerge—and why try to enter into an application where barriers exist so long as you have applications where they do not, assuming all potential applications provide sufficient revenues and profits.

[13] Balde, "Scooter sales soar in 2004," *Columbia Chronicle Online,* May 17, 2004, http://www.ccchronicle.com/back/2004_spring/2004–05–17/arts5.html, accessed December 18, 2005.

We did a project for the U.S. Department of Agriculture involving the use of water from coal-bed methane production for fish farming. The water was a by-product of pumping out the methane from below ground. At that time, the water was a waste product because it was not economically viable to clean it up for agricultural or other use. The idea was to clean up the water and use it to grow arctic char. Selling the char would provide the value-add needed to make the clean-up viable. Plus, once cleaned and loaded with fish poop, the nutrient rich water would be great for crop irrigation and fertilization.

The end users were to be the ranchers on whose land the methane was found. Our analysis found, however, that the operation of fish farms was far more complex than normal ranch operations. Further, disease could decimate the output if not promptly addressed, yet ranchers had little familiarity with char so the training (packaging) required was steep.

Our solution was to change the end user. Instead of the rancher, the end user was a fish farm operation that leased land and water for their facilities from the ranchers The Northern Cheyenne Tribe was one of the groups potentially interested in being the operator of the fish farms as they were looking for higher wage jobs for their people.

Features

Features are the way we, as users, interact with the technology to obtain the performance. They are what makes a technology more or less easy for an end user to adopt and use. If we want to wear a shoe, we need a way to put it on our foot and hold it there. Shoelaces, zippers, Velcro®, snaps, and buttons are some of the alternative ways of providing that feature. If our end user is a four year old, Velcro® or a zipper may be a more attractive feature than shoelaces.

Feature desirability depends on the end user. That Microsoft® Windows® GUI (graphical user interface) that you find so intuitive and easy to use is a mystery to your 80 year old grandmother. Suppose we use that GUI interface as the read out for our CO_2 sensor and then we give the sensor (with a small display screen) to people out in fields to measure plant respiration. If the end user is a graduate from Texas A&M, he/she will probably find the interface intuitive and easy to use. It he or she is a migrant laborer without a high school education, it will likely be less intuitive and much harder to use. For this reason, before we finish determining suitability of a technology for an application, we have to look at who will be using it. Only then can we determine the desirability of the technologies features.

We can use features to compensate for mismatch on characteristics. In another agriculture technology project, our customer had invented a way of bonding a pheromone to a pesticide, making a highly specific way of killing predators such as the pine boring beetle. The problem was the bonding involved making a bead that was very sticky. So, it required manual application to trees and other crops, which made it prohibitive to scale its use for large tree farms. The solution the customer realized was to design a special nozzle for spray applicators already in use for applying other pesticides. This innovation gave their bead the feature of being able to be applied with existing equipment. The scaling issue was solved by designing around it.

> We were hired to help find designs for the nozzle. We also developed a way of applying the beads from the air using the technology for dropping propaganda leaflets in war and other technology used for making candy buttons.[14] The pesticide beads were applied to strips of biodegradable paper that was caught on the branches of the trees as they floated toward the ground. The point is that characteristics mismatches should be viewed as design problems rather than showstoppers. As we shall see later, the trick is to use a concurrent engineering approach during R&D that teases out the mismatches early so they can be solved in a timely manner.

Product, Process, or Service

From our standpoint it is irrelevant when searching for applications for a technology whether we conceptualize it is a product, process or service. Usually it is best to remain open. An example can clarify this.

Suppose I invent a new way to micro-machine an optical array for the infrared (IR) sensors. Process technology is a set of functionalities and features that affects the way that goods are created, produced, distributed, sold, and disposed of. Whether the good—for example a CO_2 sensor based on IR scanning for a signature spectrographic line—performs better because of the process technology is relevant only if that is the benefit promised by the product, the sensor. If cheap is a benefit we want from the sensor, then the fact our way of making it offers reduced labor and/or materials costs is of interest. Otherwise, it is not.

---

[14] See Hans Moonen, "Propaganda Leaflets of the Second World War," 2005, http://members.home.nl/ww2propaganda/spread5.htm (accessed September 4, 2005) and Old Time Candy Company, "Candy Buttons on Paper Tape," 2005, http://www.oldtimecandy.com/candy-buttons.htm, (accessed September 4, 2005).

Now, if I am in the business of making machines, I may sell this process technology. But I do have another option. Suppose I am in the business of making sensors. Now I have the option to keep it proprietary and use it internally to improve my own product offerings. Now my process technology is being integrated into a new product, which could not previously be manufactured because I could not make the array without a micro-machine. If we are TSI, a small firm, this sensor consists of an IR light-emitting source tuned to emit at 4.26 µm with a known intensity, a sensing chamber into which the CO_2 can enter, an IR array detector, a filter in front of the IR detector to eliminate all light from entering the detector except for light at 4.26 µm, a DSP (digital signal processing) chip with the software on it that takes the intensity of light at the sensor and calculates the amount of CO_2 using Beer's law and outputs that result to a computer. By using a tunable laser as the IR source, we can shift the wavelength of the IR source to range around 2 microns, enabling us to detect H_2O, NH_3, NO_2, and N_2O as well.[15]

What makes our sensor unique is its detector, that is, a component of the sensor. So if we wanted we could just sell that component to others to integrate into their sensors.

Product and process technology exist in a dynamic tension. Often advances in product technology cannot occur without advances in process technology. Alternatively, new product technology often demands new process technology. Alpaca sweaters are an example. Alpaca fiber has microscopic air filled cells, which provide for thermal insulation and also aids wicking moisture away from the skin. It has only minimal natural lanolin content, so it resists solar radiation while its bulk makes it moisture resistant. The use of alpaca for clothing highlights the interaction of product and process technology. Alpaca wool was manufactured into cloth by the Incas, who called it "the fiber of the Gods." Yet it was not used commercially in any significant quantities in Europe until the mid-1800s. The reason was the difficulty of spinning the alpaca yarn. It does not appear to have been done in England till 1808. It was disparaged as an unworkable fiber. The problem, it turns out, was the kind of yarn people were trying to make: camlet, an Asian fabric originally made by combining silk and camel's hair. With the introduction of cotton warps, things changed. In a cotton warp, when the fabric is woven, some yarns run lengthwise

(Continued)

---

[15] See "NDIR CO2 Sensing Technology," *TSI,* 2004, http://www.tsi.com/exposure/appnote/ndir_co2.shtml for an example. Accessed October 11, 2004.

and are interwoven with the fill yarns (called weft yards). As this technology was adopted in the British town of Bradford, it was adapted around 1936 for weaving alpaca. The adaptation was popularized by Titus Salt, a young Bradford manufacturer, and as the saying goes: "The rest is history." The moral: Product technology without the process technology to produce the products cost-efficiently is of only limited utility.[16]

We also could run a service. To say a technology is a service is simply to say it is being transitioned with a lot of labor content bundled to it (see Exhibit 4.2). Following our example, I can start a company that takes the sensors I make and leases, installs, and maintains the CO_2 sensors as a service. Now, there is billable labor provided to a customer. (In this light, a service simply is a practice that has been contracted out.) While not hard and fast, the rule of thumb is that services require more labor content to be successfully transitioned than processes which require more than products. The critical factor is how much undocumented know-how has to accompany the transfer to make it possible to use the technology as intended.

From the standpoint of defining our technology, the way of making the sensor, it is irrelevant if we position that technology as a product, process, or service vis-a-vis our end users. All that concerns us here is that depending on (1) the functionalities provided and (2) the characteristics and (3) features desired, we have more or less flexibility on how we position our technology. So long as the functionalities involve transforming the physical world, the technology can be positioned as a process, embedded in a product (something transformed) or sold as a service (in which we do the transforming for someone else).

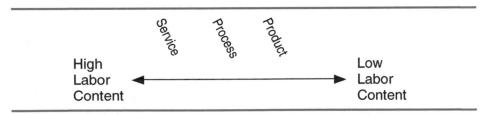

EXHIBIT 4.2   High versus Low Labor

[16] Discussion draws from Wikipedia, "Alpaca," n.d., http://www.fact-index.com/a/al/ alpaca.html; Kelowna Alpaca Farm, "Fibre History," n.d., http://www.kelownaalpaca .com/FibreHistory.htm; and Rocky Bay Alpacas, "Alpaca Fiber," n.d., http://www .alpacas.co.nz/Fibre.htm (accessed October 10, 2004).

Many years ago, I won a Phase I and II USDA SBIR grant to develop an expert system that would enable rural economic development officials to locate and support adoption of new technology by local manufacturers. The expert system, not surprisingly in retrospect, required a wieldy amount of data for a pre-Internet period. During beta testing, economic development agents told us that it was too complicated for them to gather all that data. OK: That is why you beta test—to get the bad news before you enter the market. We made the decision to use the algorithms internally and sell a service. Bottom line: Difficult-to-use products often are better sold as services.

FINDING THE APPLICATION

Technologies get applied in practices. Go into a shoe store and you quickly realize there are dress shoes, walking shoes, running shoes, hiking boots, snow boots, and a host of other categories. These categories reflect the practices where the shoes are usually worn.

We can use functionality to find potential practices where our technology might fit. All we need do is throw the functionality provided by a technology into a web browser, like Google™ and then add a word like "problem," "need," or "requirement." We scan what comes back for problems we can solve.

Practices tend to have a dominant design. Thus, for most technologies, finding an application is finding a way the technology can improve or extend a dominant design. Ideally, we would like to find a practice in which our technology not only is better than existing or emerging alternatives but can be applied *"as is."*[17] After all, if we can sell what we have today, that simplifies deal making. But suppose we cannot do that. No worries. Technologies need not map to applications "as is."

Recall the distinction between yield and potential yield. What is important when looking for applications is the range of possible yields we can attain without too much headache (that is, as a "simple matter of engineering"). Stretch allows us to see our technology as a dynamic set of features and functionalities that can evolve over time (see Exhibit 4.3). We can even measure stretch through the trajectory of the yield. These can be defined in terms of their direction, magnitude, and rate of change (slope). That allows us to look for emerging applications as well as existing ones,

---

[17] Competing technology is addressed later in this book.

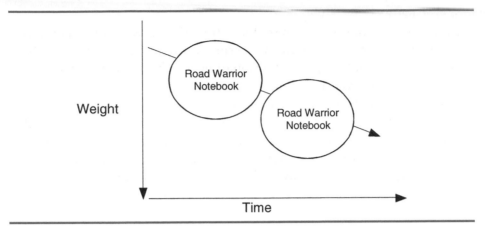

EXHIBIT 4.3 Direction, Magnitude, and Rate of Change

so long as the relevant trajectories of our technology will intersect end-user needs at some time.

An example: Suppose you are a traveling salesman for gel-cell membrane shoes. You are on the road traveling from shoe store to shoe store. You buy a lightweight laptop so you can keep up with your work while on the road. When you went to buy it, a key criterion was weight. Lighter is better for "road warriors" as there is less weight to lug around. That creates a trajectory in your needs that maps to a performance trajectory. (Of course, in our example we are only looking at one requirement: weight. In real life, we usually have to consider all the critical requirements as, given the end users' needs, there often is an interplay and trade-off between the yields sought.)

Over time, the market place changes. Consolidation hits the shoe business. Now its chain stores in malls and though you are still traveling, you are only going to corporate headquarters in Chicago or New York or wherever and pitching a buyer who controls purchasing for 500 stores across the United States. You like portability but your job now requires you to spend more time in the home office than on the road. Because you do not travel as much, you want a machine more like a desk top so it is suited to the activities you do at your home office, but you still can take it on the road when needed. Besides, it sure helps if you can take it back and forth to home when you have to work evenings to coordinate with that customer in Hawaii, who is on a different time zone than Maine, where your factory is located. Weight now is a less important factor (see Exhibit 4.4). What you want is portability without sacrificing processing power, file storage space, displays, and other features you have become accustomed to.

Different criteria lead to different trajectories being relevant. In marketing lingo, what we are seeing is a split into two customer segments for laptop computers. The people who travel all the time want light. The

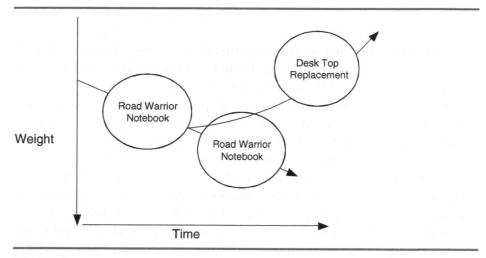

EXHIBIT 4.4 Weight and Time

people who travel rarely want a desk top replacement. Change the practice, the yield requirement changes.

Now business is good and you are traveling internationally to open up Europe and Asia. As with your U.S. travels, these are short trips to buyers at corporate headquarters. You need to stay in touch with the office, but you are not living on the road. You realize you do not need a full function computer. Word processing, spreadsheet, presentation capabilities, email, web, data base are all the functionality you need (see Exhibit 4.5). You think to yourself, "Why am I lugging that desk top replacement?" Heck,

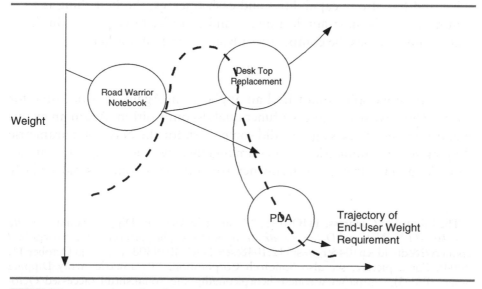

EXHIBIT 4.5 Trajectory of End-User Weight Requirement

you do not even want your old road warrior unit back in light of the fact that since the 9/11 terrorist attack you have to dig it out and open it for scanning at every dang airport security check point. A high end PDA makes more sense as it gives you all the functionality you need at a light weight—and PDAs can be scanned in your purse.

What the example highlights is that both changes in practices and potential for changes in yield trajectories need to be considered when looking for applications. A change in the practice changes the yields sought on requirements, and that in turn means either a shift in the relevant technology trajectories is required or a branching into multiple trajectories, in the case of emerging customer segmentation. Alternatively, changes in technology trajectories can open up new possibilities for the conduct of practices, although in this case we may have to "build" the market through extensive end-user awareness building and education.

> Even when you find a potential application, you may not be able to exploit it. Years ago I did some market research on a sapphire liquid crystal display. It was very robust, and you could pump lots of power through it. We came across a great application: projectors for computer-generated images. Back then, there was a limit on how much power you could pump through a projector, and thus they could not be used where there was any light in the room. A bit more research revealed that Texas Instruments has just introduced silicon etched mirrors as a competing approach. The TI solution was regrettably superior. Sometimes an application dies because you cannot figure out how to be better or less expensive. When faced by a competitor who is established in the market and has strong capabilities and cash reserves, the best thing is to move on to the next application . . . and consider buying stock in the company that has the competitive advantage in that market.

Suppose we still cannot find an application. Again, it is not time for panic. The next step is to do a functional decomposition. Again an example: A number of years ago we did some work for the Navy on parametric dipping sonar. Parametric sonars slam together two high frequency pitches to make a very strong low frequency sound.[18] This sound is particularly

---

[18] The Library of Congress, THOMAS, "Parametric Airborne Dipping Sonar," *Senate Rpt.104–112—National Defense Authorization* (1996), http://thomas.loc.gov/cgi-bin/cpquery/?&db_id=cp104&r_n=sr112.104&sel=TOC_307930& (accessed October 11, 2004). For a picture, see also Sonotech Corporation, "Parametric Array Dipping Sonar (PADS)," http://www.sonetechcorp.com/dipping_sonar.shtml (accessed October 11, 2004).

useful for detecting small submarines and mines in littoral regions, like the coast of Iran and Iraq.

Now who cares? Clearly the Navy does. If you are going to sail into harm's way, it is nice to know where the bad guys are and where they have left surprises for you. But who else might care? There is not really a big demand for parametric dipping sonars. You are not going to use them for fishing. When you go boom and the fish float up to the surface stunned, the whales and other marine life get headaches. That gets the environmental lobby mad. Besides, it is not a very resource-responsible way to fish. So, scratch that. Nor are you going to use it to look for pipes or other outflows from municipal utilities because you can just look on a map and find them. You might use it to hunt for sunken shipwrecks, but then that is a tiny market. So where do you go with it?

We did a functional decomposition, ending up with a casing, some transmit electronics, some receive electronics, and a way to get the received signal back to a ship or helicopter. When we look at these in more detail, we realize the only unique and interesting thing about parametric sonars is their transmit electronics—that is, how you take two high frequency noises, slam them together, and make a very focused powerful low frequency noise.

We now have a different question. We want to know who needs a very powerful low frequency noise. It turns out, there is a field of chemistry called sonochemistry.[19] It uses sound to drive chemical reactions. So our ability to make a very powerful low frequency noise (functionality) may have utility for folks who need very powerful low frequency noises.

Most inventions can be transitioned into a variety of applications. In other words, innovation involves making an invention useful in a practice. However, without market research, we can say little about end users so we initially define the technology in terms of its functionalities and then go fishing around for relevant practices where it can be applied.

Where fundamental scientific or engineering breakthroughs are involved, the application may be hard to find, even with tossing terms into search engines. Brainstorming is helpful whenever you are having problem finding applications. Two tools are Marioni Matrices™ and Contradiction Matrices.

The Marioni Matrix™ was invented by Don Marioni, a systems engineer and principal at Foresight Science & Technology. The Matrix has two dimensions. Along the top of the matrix is a list of needs, based on Maslow's hierarchy discussed in Chapter 1. Along the vertical dimension is a generic set of value-creating supply chain activities running from raw

---

[19] See American Chemical Society, "Sonochemistry," *Chemistry* (2000, Summer), http://www.scs.uiuc.edu/suslick/pdf/chemistry.summer00.sonochem.pdf (accessed September 4, 2005).

material extraction through design and manufacturing to ultimate disposal of a product. To brainstorm, you look at each of the cells resulting for the interaction of the two axes and ask yourself "How could my technology be used here?"[20]

	Food	Shelter	Clothing	Health	Power	Transportation	Communication	Security	Finance	Education	Science	Entertainment	Art/Philosophy
Raw Materials Extraction													
Processing Tools and Techniques													
R&D													
Design and Product Development													
Test, Evaluation Measurement and Calibration													
Manufacturing													
Packaging, Distribution, and Logistics													
Marketing, Sales, and Promotion													
Operations and Maintenance													
Disposal and Recycling													

Contradiction Matrices are a tool in TRIZ, a Russian acronym for Theory of Inventive Problem Solving (Teoriya Resheniya Izobreatatel-skikh Zadatch). Invented by Genrich S. Altshuller, TRIZ is a tool for

---

[20] The matrix is named after its creator, Don Marioni, a board member of Foresight Science & Technology (See Darrell Mann and Simon DeWulf, "Updating the Contradiction Matrix." Paper presented at TRIZCON2003: Fifth Annual International Conference of Altshuller Institute for TRIZ Studies, Philadelphia, PA, March 16–18, 2003, http://www.osaka-gu.ac.jp/php/nakagawa/TRIZ/eTRIZ/epapers/e2003Papers/eMannDeWulf0303/eMannMatrix030316.html [accessed October 4, 2004], for a discussion of the matrix). For more information and examples, see the *TRIZ Journal* at http://www.triz-journal.com/matrix/ (accessed October 4, 2004).

making inventions. It is based on the premise that most inventions address ways to improve parameters, such as speed, accuracy, weight, and the like. (these are similar to SUIs), despite the fact that there were reasons why the improvement could not be easily obtained and thus was not intuitive to a practitioner of the field.

Altshuller called a demand for performance improvement that butts up against a physical barrier that suggests the only way to improve performance is to go in another direction, a technical contraction. An often used example is the light bulb. Filaments needed to burn hot to produce light, but not so hot as to burn up themselves. Another example is pouring filling into chocolate candy shells. The filling should be hot as then it pours fast, but it should not be too hot or it will melt the chocolate. The goal is to resolve the contradiction. Altshuller proposed 40 principles for making such resolutions. In the case of the light bulb, the solution to the contradiction was to encase the filament in a vacuum.

The principles are:[21]

- *Segmentation.* Divide the object, make it easier to take apart, or increase the degree of segmentation.
- *Taking out.* Separate a problematic part or property from the rest of the object.
- *Local quality.* Change the structure from uniform to non-uniform, institute a division of labor in the parts, or create special environments/conditions that are optimized for the operation of each part.
- *Asymmetry.* Make symmetrical objects asymmetrical and vice versa.
- *Merging.* Bring parts closer together or merge them, make them together or in parallel, or bring operations closer together or make then occur simultaneously (in parallel).
- *Universality.* Eliminate parts by making others perform their function.
- *Nested doll.* Place parts inside each other or have them pass through each other.
- *Anti-weight.* Merge heavy objects with things that lift them or compensate for weight by shaping it to interact with the environment in such a way as to mitigate the impact of its weight.
- *Preliminary anti-action.* Create conditions where harmful acts are neutralized or mitigated when they occur, or create stresses early that will counteract harmful stress to occur later.
- *Preliminary action.* Perform acts to change objects before that change is required in a process, or prearrange them to come into the process from a convenient place and at the right time.

---

[21] Based on Ellen Domb, "40 Inventive Principles with Examples," *TRIZ Journal* (1996), http://www.triz-journal.com/archives/1997/07/b/index.html (accessed October 11, 2004).

- *Beforehand cushioning.* Prepare solutions beforehand for unreliable performance of objects.
- *Equipotentiality.* In potential fields, limit the possible position changes, or eliminate the need to move the objects.
- *The other way round.* Invert actions used to solve problems (movements, temperature changes, etc.), make fixed parts movable and vice versa, or turn upside down objects or processes.
- *Spheroidality and curvature.* Instead of rectangular forms, surfaces or parts use curved ones; move from flat surfaces to spheres; shift from cubes to balls; use rollers, domes, etc.; or shift from linear to rotary motion and forces.
- *Dynamics.* Allow designs or processes to change on the fly to be more optimal, divide parts so they can move relative to each other, make rigid objects or processes movable and adaptive.
- *Partial or excessive actions.* Use slightly less or slight more of the same.
- *Another dimension.* Add degrees of freedom or more dimensions, use multi-story arrangements for objects rather than single story, tilt or otherwise reorient objects, use another side of an area to enhance capability or functionality.
- *Mechanical vibration.* Make objects vibrate or oscillate, increase frequency, use resonate frequencies, combine different field oscillations (e.g., acoustic and electromagnetic); or use piezoelectric vibrators rather than mechanical ones.
- *Periodic action.* Shift from continuous to pulsed or periodic, change the period amplitude or frequency for periodic actions, introduce pauses between impulses.
- *Continuity of useful action.* Work all parts at full load at all times, eliminate down time or intermittency of action.
- *Skipping.* Conduct processes or actions (especially harmful or dangerous ones) at high speed.
- *Blessing in disguise.* Use harmful factors to generate desired and positive effects, counteract one harmful factor by another one, amplify or decrease a harmful factor until it is no longer harmful.
- *Feedback.* Introduce feedback loops for processes or actions, change the loop's magnitude or influence.
- *Intermediary.* Introduce intermediary carriers or processes or merge objects or processes temporarily with each other.
- *Self-service.* Have objects or processes perform auxiliary functions that help it attain its purpose and that are desired in their own right; find uses for waste resources or scrap.
- *Copying.* Make simple and inexpensive copies of hard to get or expensive objects, replace real objects with reproductions or optical copies, shift the wavelength used to make optical copies.

- *Cheap short-living objects.* Replace one unit with a bunch of less expensive shorter-lived ones.
- *Mechanical substitution.* Use sensory means to replace mechanical means of defining boundaries or objects, use force fields to replace mechanical manipulations, shift from static to movable fields or from unstructured to structured fields, use field-activated particles or objects.
- *Pneumatics and hydraulics.* Use fluids rather than solid parts.
- *Flexible shells and thin films.* Use shells and films to isolate objects from the environment.
- *Porous materials.* Make objects porous or add porous elements or, where pores exist, use them to introduce new substances or functions.
- *Color change.* Change color or the transparency of an object or its environment.
- *Homogeneity.* Make two (or more) objects interacting with a common third object out of the same material or out of materials with the same properties.
- *Discarding and recovering.* Restore consumable parts of objects, a feature of the objects operation, or make objects that have fulfilled their function disappear or go away on their own.
- *Parameter changes.* Change physical states, change concentration or consistence, change degree of flexibility, change temperature.
- *Phase transitions.* Leverage the way materials shift phase to accomplish objectives.
- *Thermal expansion.* Shift to materials with different coefficients of thermal expansion, or revise procedures to leverage the thermal properties or current materials.
- *Strong oxidants.* Replace normal air with oxygen-enriched air or pure oxygen, leverage oxidation, use ozone or expose air or oxygen to radiation.
- *Inert atmosphere.* Introduce inert environments, or add inert materials or parts to objects.
- *Composite materials.* Change from uniform to composite materials.

In TRIZ, you look at the intersections between the conflicting performance metrics, and then apply the principles until you figure out a solution. In our context, what you do is look at the intersection of the performances of your technology, and ask what advantages you can create by applying the principles, and thus the kinds of problems you can solve. This insight, in turn, provides new search terms for seeking applications.

Suppose we still cannot find an application. There is one final fall back position. We look at the knowledge domain that underlies the technology. We have a set of skills and capabilities with respect to that field of science and/or engineering. In our IR sensor, one aspect of this domain is spectroscopy; another is the design and fabrication of electro-optical devices. Tossing "spectroscopy and electro-optic and need" into a search engine returns a series of articles about ultrafast spectroscopy, a fast growing field of physical chemistry. The reason for the growth is we can now use very fast lasers to observe and control chemical reactions in real time. We can watch the position of atoms as a function of time as reactants move products through transition states. We can track the flow of vibrational energy through molecules. These capabilities, in turn have application in a wide range of fields from medicine to micromachining. The lesson? If nothing else works, use what you have learned to find a pressing problem in a hot field for your next R&D proposal.

Let's recap where we are. In the first section we saw how to define our technology. Now we have taken that definition and looked for relevant practices where it might be applied to real problems people want solved or opportunities they want to exploit.

Consider our IR sensor. We search for practices where people might need it. Along the way we find an article by David Sundersingh and David W. Bearg from July 2003 entitled "Indoor Air Quality in Schools (IAQ): The Importance of Monitoring Carbon Dioxide Levels."[22] They point out that exposure pollutant levels outside those accepted by EPA's National Ambient Air Quality Standards is a particular concern for children. There are several reasons: Children breathe a larger volume of air per unit of body weight than adults; the impact of pollutants is usually greater on small children and pollutants often settle so they are more often found down where children breathe than up where we grown-ups do. The solution, of course, is to minimize pollutants and one way to do that is to maintain adequate ventilation. Just what is adequate is defined by Standard 62–1999 Ventilation for Acceptable Indoor Air Quality of the American Society of Heating, Refrigerating and Air-conditioning Engineers. But to know if ventilation is occurring we have to measure it. Carbon dioxide monitoring performed in accordance with the sampling guidelines of ASTM D6245, Standard Guide for Using Indoor Carbon Dioxide Concentrations to Evaluate Indoor Air Quality and Ventilation is one way of doing just that.

We have found a potential application. Now we only have to match-up the demands of the practice with our definition of the technology to see if it works. Can we measure CO_2? Yep. Can we do it cheaply enough to install enough sensors to cover all the necessary sampling points? Yep. Is

[22] David Sundersingh and David Bearg, "Indoor Air Quality in Schools (IAQ): The Importance of Monitoring Carbon Dioxide Levels," *Design Share* (n.d.), http://www.designshare.com/Research/Sundersingh/IAQ_Monitoring.htm (accessed October 11, 2004).

the technology mature enough to meet an existing need? Yep. Good, we have an application: HVAC in schools and indoor air quality in general.

But why stop there? Since the application is monitoring for HVAC systems, how can we enhance functionality. There is a principle in TRIZ called *"preliminary anti-action."* By hooking our sensor up in a feedback loop, we can increase ventilation when the air starts getting sour. Applying *"self-service"* suggests we can adapt our sensor to also monitor for specific pollutants or perhaps even toxins and chemicals potentially released by terrorists. In other words, once we find an application, we can look at trends in that practice in order to figure out how to enhance the competitiveness of our technology. If it is not immediately obvious what these trends are, we can use TRIZ to brainstorm possible enhancements and then search the web to sustain or falsify their desirability. Doing this leads us to an article in *Sensors Online,* "Improving Indoor Weather with Carbon Dioxide Sensors," which discusses IR sensors and their utility.[23] It and other sources confirm that an application exists.

Our performance specifications fit well with the needs of the commercial heating, ventilation and air conditioning (HVAC) industries, specifically in demand controlled ventilation (DCV) systems. The CO_2-sensor's application will be to activate fresh air intake in HVAC systems when CO_2 levels are too high. Everyone has a financial incentive to use the technology—the HVAC manufacturer can make money selling this product enhancement to their system, while the building owner can decrease energy expenses by infusing fresh air into the system only when necessary, making this a very attractive application, and driving demand for the technology, *if it is price competitive.*

How can we tell if it is price competitive?

First, given the ASTM standard, we know there are competing CO_2 sensors already on the market. We can benchmark against them. A quick search on HVAC and CO2 reveals Honeywell and Texas Instruments are among the competitors. So we can find prices for their devices. Second, we can look at the price of various sensors (or other equivalent technology) used in practice in the context of the relevant dominant to determine typical price given performance. For example, here the issue is what other sensors are hooked up as feedback subsystems for school and other non-residential building HVAC systems. The obvious choice is the thermostat. As a first approximation, we can use the price/performance ratio for sophisticated thermostats as a benchmark to figure out above what order of magnitude sticker shock is likely to kick in.

---

[23] Scoot Lindblom, "Improving Indoor Weather with Carbon Dioxide Sensors," *Sensors* (July 2004), http://www.sensorsmag.com/articles/0704/35/main.shtml (accessed October 11, 2004).

Next, assuming sufficient data, we can plot the price/performance of competing solutions, we can get a pretty good idea as to whether there is unoccupied space where we might attain product advantage.

In Exhibit 4.6, Product 1 provides a modest level of performance at a modest price; Product 2 gives a higher level of performance at a higher price. The circular region between Product 1 and Product 2 represents an un-served product region; buyers might need a technology with better performance than Product 1, but do not require the high performance of Product 2. Thus, they are not willing to pay Product 2's price.

We have indicated some of the areas that represent possible product placement by using circles. Entering into any of these regions provides some advantage, whether price, performance, or both, over Product 1 or Product 2. Although it is not always feasible for technology to enter into unserved regions, you want to stay out of very crowded regions where you

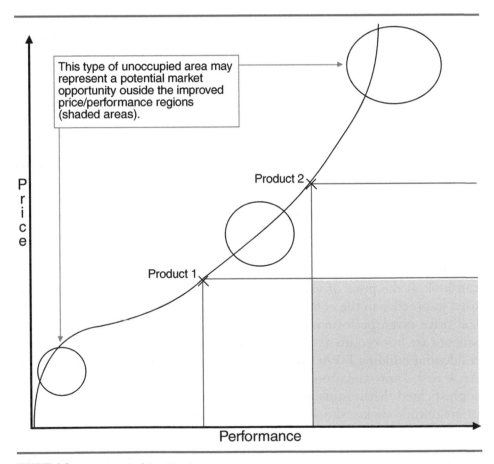

EXHIBIT 4.6   Unoccupied Positioning

have no competitive advantage, such as the crosshatched rectangle which both Product 1 and Product 2 serve.

All of which is to say, once we find an application, we want to focus on what makes the participants of that practice happy so they will want our technology. We want to revise our technology to re-calibrate its yields to improve our ability to meet the precise requirements (or anticipated trajectory of requirements) of end users. If possible, we also want to offer some extension of functionality or improve the features of the technology to increase ease-of-use. In marketing lingo, what we have done is gone from a situation of technology push to building market pull. We have attained market orientation.

But there is more. As cash flow builds from penetrating this application, we can penetrate others. So now we want to know where else we can use our CO_2 sensor. Entering the string "CO_2 sensor" in Google™ returns approximately 42,000 hits. A scan of the first 20 hits reveals a slew of potential applications, including combustion byproduct monitoring in vehicles; environmental monitoring for ambient air quality; personnel safety monitoring; fire suppression systems monitoring; biomedical respiration monitoring; (and our new friend CO_2 sensing in HVAC systems.) Our sensor technology can potentially provide advantages in all these applications.

FINDING THE CUSTOMER

The customer is whoever literally buys the technology. Usually this player is an organization. Within that organization there are two key roles that concern us here. The first is the end user, the second is the buyer.

The End User

The people who put their hands on our technology and use it are our end users. These people are participants in the practices we have found. By determining those roles, we can get a pretty good idea of who they are, and thus further refine our definition of what we are selling.

We identify the end users by looking at precisely how our technology might be used, why it would be used, how often, and thus who is putting their hands on it. What we want to know is, will the folks with their hands on it view adoption of our technology as a priority? If they do, we have pull-through. If not a priority, we at least hope they will view it as desirable.

Pull-through is a clear sign of product advantage. It exists where end users like a product, process, or service so much that they demand a good,

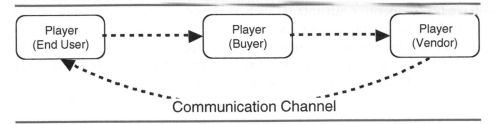

EXHIBIT 4.7 Pull-Through

creating pressure on buyers to procure it. I once came across this great example, which, of course, now that I want to write about it, I cannot find. So I will just tell you the story. We shall take poetic license as, regardless of whether the story is true or not, it illustrates the point I want to make.

A truck manufacturer saw its market share and sales declining. It looked at market data and trends and made a startling discovery. A lot of truck drivers were women. Now, you stand up any female friend next to any male friend and you can see at a moment that women's bodies are different then men's. That was the key to inspiration, because up until then, trucks were designed for male bodies. Truck drivers work long and brutal hours so comfort is important. Anyway, the truck manufacturer redesigned the seats, changed the height of steering wheels, and made a host of other changes in the cab to end up with a "woman's truck." They drove it around the country, parking it for a few days at every truck stop. Pretty soon all the lady drivers were talking about it. Then, as trucking firms went to buy new vehicles for their fleets, these ladies encouraged their companies to buy vehicles more comfortable and productive for them. They pressured their employees who then buy.

That is pull-through. The end users pull through goods by pressuring the buyers (see Exhibit 4.7). It works when communication channels exist, or are built, that can be used to create demand for a product among end users and then convey that demand from end users to the buyers.

Another example: McDonald's sells hamburgers, fries, and drinks just like other burger chains. But what gave it edge in the market was the early realization by management that their best customers were children. Get the children to ask for McDonald's and it's hard for parents to say no. So McDonald's bundled products together as Happy Meals and put toys in them to draw children in. The kids want the Happy Meal. The parents want the kids to stop whining. Pull-through.[24]

---

[24] Described in Nahas, "Mid Market Strategies," *Trailer Body Builder* (March 1, 2001), http://trailer-bodybuilders.com/mag/trucks_mid_market_strategies/ (accessed October 11, 2004).

Now, to go from market orientation to pull through, we need to understand what end users want. For our purposes here, what end users want resolves into two things. First, the technology must do the job. Second, it needs to be perceived as desirable and worth having. All other things being equal, for end users desirability is created where technologies that work (i.e. have the necessary functionality) are easy-to-use (i.e. have good characteristics and features) and do not threaten their jobs. Easy-to-use usually is a matter of how closely a technology aligns with the skills and capabilities of the users.

This time, let's use an agricultural example. White mold is a problem for soy farmers. It kills crop, leading to losses of 15 bushels/acre or more. The mold can be controlled by a fungicide, but the chemical drives costs up. Fortunately, fungicide is often unnecessary. The fungus *Sclerotinia sclerotiorium,* which causes the mold, only occurs in years of excessive moisture. In general, an average of three inches of rain over during a two-week period between late June to mid-July is when sclerotia germinates. So, it usually can be avoided in dry seasons or by planting late.

"Usually" only goes so far. We assessed the commercial potential for a computer program that incorporated remote sensing data, weather analysis and forecasting, and crop and canopy modeling to create an economic tool for in-field assessment of sclerotinia spore concentrations and thus more precise guidance on when to apply the fungicide. Such programs fit within a movement called precision agriculture. Precision agriculture involves using high tech to precisely control agricultural inputs in order to improve productivity, lower adverse environmental impacts, and reduce costs.

It is clear that if you do not have the training and computer and sensor infrastructure for precision agriculture, this software program is not very easy to use. Fortunately for the developer, at the time we did our assessment, agriculture was changing rapidly. Farmers were increasingly college educated, with two or four year degrees becoming the norm, especially on large farms, which were the ones most likely to adopt this program as its benefits were greater where economies of scale existed. Also at that time, according to the National Agricultural Statistics Service, the number of farmers who owned or leased computers was 50% and growing. The number of farms with Internet access was 43% and growing. In other words, where as a generation ago this technology would have been hard to use for most farmers, today the skills, capabilities, and infrastructure were in place. But although 50% of the farms had computers, at that time, only 29% used them for farm business.

What could be done to improve ease-of-use? As we have seen, one answer is to focus on features. Clearly a Windows®-like screen would help make operation of the software intuitive. The reason is that the dominant design for farm business software is the personal use software. Such de facto designs for user interface are sometimes called interface standards, in acknowledgment of the analogy to standards that make it possible to connect one device to another.

By understanding what end users currently do, and what training, education, and experience they have, we gain insights into their comfort zones when adopting and adapting a new technology to meet their needs. This ability to adapt technology is called absorptive capacity, briefly introduced in the last chapter. Absorptive capacity is to end users as stretch is to technology.

Absorptive capacity falls into two sets. The first set is capabilities with respect to specific fields of science, engineering, and technology. To install a sensor into a HVAC system, the end user needs to know something about electronics, something about HVAC systems, etc. This category of absorptive capacity is called domain capacity, as it refers to domains of knowledge. The other set relates to knowledge, know-how, and skills concerning the arena in which the end user works and is called context absorptive capacity.

Arenas are the socio-economic settings where the practices occur. Let us assume the sensor's functionality maps well to air circulation needs in multi-zone large buildings. There are many arenas where our CO_2 sensor could be applied, including hospitals, factories, homes, universities, hotels, schools, and office buildings, to mention only a few. Even if a dominant design for a HVAC system applies to all of them, there are likely variants unique to each setting. For example, hospitals may need to filter air in some wards to prevent diseases from spreading. The principal of a school may want higher air flow during the cold and flu season than at other times. The end user's understanding of these unique aspects may be important for adapting the technology for use. Arena influences may be micro-level (tied to the specific hospital in this example) or macro-level (tied to hospital buildings in general). Both can influence functionality and feature preferences of end users in a manner analogous to the way that market forces operate.

Knowing the arena allows us to make a rough estimate of the market size. The seat sales for a baseball game are limited by the size of the stadium. Similarly, we can estimate the size of a market for technology by the size of the arena. If we can determine how many buildings are in the arena, what proportion are likely to be multi-zone, their average size, and the number of sensors per so much square feet or meters, we can estimate the total addressable market. By looking at arena trends, such as retrofitting of older buildings or the rate at which new buildings are going up, we also have a preliminary idea as to the penetration rates for the market. If we want to base the market size on number of establishments, we can find this data in the U.S. Census Bureau's Census of Manufacturers and annual surveys.

So much for the overview, now let's see how this works when we have a deal to do. Continuing with our IR sensor, since the sensor is used to monitor the circulation of fresh air in the multi-zoned building to assure air quality, heating, air-conditioning, and refrigeration mechanics and installers are our end users. They are the people installing, operating, and maintaining the HVAC system. If we switch to the shoe lasting machine, our end users would be production workers in cut and sew operations.

To find out more about our end users we can search the U.S. Department of Labor's *Occupational Outlook Handbook.* (There are analogs in other industrialized countries.) Talk about your tax dollars at work! This on-line resource tells us all about our end users, including nature of their work; working conditions; employment; training, other qualifications, and advancement; job outlook; earnings; related occupations; and, sources of additional information.

Looking to our end users for a HVAC CO_2 sensor, we find these folks tend to be well educated. They increasingly graduate from 6-month to 2-year programs in which they study theory, design, equipment construction, and electronics while also learning how to install, maintain, and repair equipment. These courses are taught at secondary and postsecondary technical and trade schools, junior and community colleges, and in the armed forces. An alternative path is apprenticeship training. So, we can conclude that the end users have good domain absorptive capacity and should be capable of using our technology—especially in light of the fact that the Department of Labor notes, HVAC equipment is becoming increasingly sophisticated.[25]

Equally important is that the Department of Labor sees arena trends encouraging HVAC mechanics and installers to look favorably on our technology. For example, our end users increasingly work for larger

---

[25] U.S. Department of Labor, Bureau of Labor Statistics, "Heating, Air-Conditioning, and Refrigeration Mechanics and Installers," *Occupational Outlook Handbook, 2004–05 Edition* (March 21, 2004), http://www.bls.gov/oco/ocos192.htm (accessed October 11, 2004).

organizations as in-house staff or staff for vendors operating under service contracts that involve heating, air-conditioning, and refrigeration work for particular customers on a regular basis. This long-term relationship encourages them to think about improving the efficiency of the HVAC system.

Employment is expected to grow faster than the average for all occupations through the year 2012 due to economic growth spurring demand for new residential, commercial, and industrial climate-control systems in the context of rising energy prices that stimulates demand for cost savings from energy conservation devices. So no one is worrying about working themselves out of a job by installing these. Instead, use of more sophisticated control systems should increasingly be a normal part of the job. (Energy costs also encourage retrofitting or replacing older systems to be more efficient.) Thus, context absorptive capacity should make end users receptive to energy saving devices like this. Since our technology creates more work for these folks and their training in electronics enables them to easily install and maintain these sensors, pull-though may emerge.

> If we are selling something for individual use by end users, like safety goggles, the data on numbers of workers in a career in the *Occupational Outlook Handbook* provides us a market size estimate.

Compare these end users to those for a next generation shoe lasting machine. The Department of Labor notes that in the apparel industry, which for our purposes includes shoes: "Most production workers are trained on the job. Although a high school diploma is not required, some employers prefer it. Basic math and computer skills are important for computer-controlled machine operators."[26] In other words, this is a work force not generally well prepared for new high-tech equipment. Further, at least for the apparel industry in general, sewing is one of the last remaining functions that has not been automated. Domain capacity is probably lacking in the work force. Fortunately, a technical training infrastructure does exist at vocational schools, but going through it may require educational skills long rusty. So there may be a mismatch between new technology and the capabilities of end users, and this mismatch raises the costs of adoption. In this context the user interface is critical. If it is designed to be

---

[26] Bureau of Labor Statistics, "Apparel Manufacturing," *Career Guide to Industries, 2004–05 Edition* (February 27, 2004), http://www.bls.gov/oco/cg/cgs007.htm (accessed October 11, 2004).

simple and fool-proof, some of the packaging adoption costs (training) can be mitigated.

Again, we can get some insight into trends encouraging or discouraging adoption. It turns out advanced technology is a way to stave off outsourcing, since apparel remains labor-intensive on the one hand and the industry is increasingly taking factories to countries with lower labor costs on the other. (One implication is that this technology should be focused on a global market more than a domestic one. That means, among other things, training needs to be in more languages than English.) The factories that do remain are being pushed to higher and higher levels of automation in order to compete. Thus, other workers can be expected to be ambivalent at best towards new technology, as it is likely to take some jobs away but may be the only way to keep others.

Buyers

End users put their hands on a technology. What they seek is utility. Buyers purchase technology. What they seek is value. As we have seen, net utility is roughly equivalent to the net value of a technology.

Once we have found the end users, it is relatively straightforward to find the buyers. Either it is the end user, or it is someone whose job it is to buy for them. Especially in larger organizations, those who buy are usually not those that use. Rather they have formal titles like "*buyer*" or "*contracting officer*" or "*procurement specialist.*" Further, there may be multiple people and roles involved in purchasing, such as gatekeepers whose job it is to moniter the environment outside the organization for goods of interest. For our purposes, however, we usually want the decision maker who pulls the strings for the buyer and gatekeeper. This individual carries a title like CEO, vice president for business development or marketing, or product line manager.

Years ago, I had an ex-CIA agent working for me. He told me that he was taught waiters and secretaries are among the most useful people for gaining information. Now I have yet to figure out how to learn useful things about high technology customers from waiters, but secretaries are great. To find the right person to talk with in a company or government agency, pick up the phone, call, ask for secretary of the boss, say hello nicely and explain you are doing some market research, and ask with whom you should speak.

We can distinguish four "ideal types" or constructs of buyers.[27]

- *Price buyers.* Price and delivery time are the only criteria, so there is a premium placed on a low price quote. Since price and delivery are the criteria, buying decision can be made by purchase managers, a central buying department, or other non-technical people

- *Value buyers.* Best value for total lifetime cost is the key criterion, so a premium is placed on optimizing a value function that includes features, quality, supply conditions, safety, purchase price and cost in use, regulatory exposure, etc. Since a number of factors are involved in decisions, a team often advises on purchasing decisions. The members of the team represent technical, financial, quality assurance, logistics, and other buyer organizations responsible for managing the business areas reflected in the purchasing decision function.

- *Availability buyers.* Familiarity and immediate availability are key criteria, so there is a premium placed on buying known products or buying from known vendors. Here, price (and sometimes lifetime cost) is a threshold issue, that is, there is a price ceiling that cannot be exceeded or a cost reduction floor that must at least be met. Because the product installer (a formal, support contractor, value-add reseller, or distributor) knows both the operation and what is available, he or she heavily influences the buying decision.

- *Technical performance buyers.* Performance and technical image are key criteria, so there is a premium placed on service and technical support in buying decisions. Price and/or lifetime cost is a "fuzzy" constraint. At some point, technical performance can cost too much, but in general, "more bang" is better. Because engineers or installers of the product are most familiar with performances of substitutable products, they influence the buying decision.

Which type of buyers are relevant tends to reflect the strategy of the organization in which they work:

- Commodity firms tend to compete on price leadership, as there is not really any difference between one company's offering and the next competitor's. Their primary emphasis is on manufacturing and operations. They usually are price buyers. Examples are Phelps Dodge and Weyerhauser. Retail firms like Staples and Sears also are examples.

---

[27] The types draw heavily from Jolly's discussion of the work of Pascal Lecordier, 139. Again, we are following Max Weber's usage, in which *ideal types* or constructs are conceptualizations based on observation but are designed to emphasize features that make comparisons possible.

- Diversified product companies tend to compete on differentiation, that is, supplying variants of their product families targeted towards each customer segment. Because of their wide range of offerings, they tend to emphasize marketing and R&D to sustain product flow. They tend to be value buyers. Examples are P&G and General Motors.
- Niche players tend to compete on focus strategies, that is, they try to be very responsive of customer needs. Their motto is "love the customer" because they survive by providing just what customers are seeking. They tend to be technical performance buyers. Examples are General Dynamics and Delphi. Service firms, like my own company, Foresight Science & Technology, which specializes in technology transfer, or RotoRooter are also examples.
- Performance players are specialized companies selling on the basis of pushing the state of the art. Usually these firms are component or subsystem suppliers, but sometimes they show up in consumer niches. Wherever they compete they are looking for techno-junkies receptive to the next greatest thing. In distinction to companies pursuing focus strategies, which are market driven, these companies are the "if we build it, they will come" folks who are making inventions and building markets by leveraging niche communication channels. Performance drives premium pricing. Examples of such firms and products are Dean Kamen's Segway™ and Apple's IPod™.[28]
- Some service firms supporting equipment also compete on access, that is, on their ability to get to the customer. They show up and solve the problem with minimal headache for their customer (or you go carry the equipment in and they fix it). For this reason they tend to be availability buyers as supply problems mean a delay that means headaches for their customers. Examples of service firms are Unisys and Midas.

The types of strategies are not hard and fast. Hybrids also exist. For example, electronic commerce firms tend to compete on both access and differentiation, that is, on the ease of conducting business with them to obtain a wide range of goods. They usually are availability buyers, because the key to operations is efficiency in the pipeline from orders to delivery. Examples are Amazon and eBay.

We can summarize this discussion in two tables. The first table indicates the kind of strategy that is likely given what is being sold to what size of a customer base.

---

[28] See the Segway scooters at Segway Inc., http://www.segway.com/. For how to build your own, see Trevor Blackwell, "Building a Balancing Scooter," n.d., http://www.tlb .org/scooter.html.

	Commodity Like Products	Specialized Products
Diversified Customer Base	Price Leadership	Diversification
Narrow Customer Base	Access	Focus

The second table indicates the kind of buying we expect from firms, given their strategy.

Strategy	Buyer Type
Price Leadership	Price
Diversification	Value
Access	Availability
Focus	Technical Performance

We can also classify buyers in terms of when they are likely to make their purchase. Different groups of buyers enter the market at different stages in the product live cycle of a technology. (Note this classification has ramifications for launch tactics as it points out that each group of buyers may monitor different communication channels and be influenced by different message contents.)

Everett Rogers, in his seminal work *Diffusion of Innovations,* distinguished between five categories of buyers: innovators, early adopters, early majority, late majority, and laggards and provided estimates for their distribution (see Exhibit 4.8).[29] These categories are described as ideal types. From the standpoint of commercialization or other transitioning, Rogers' first two ideal types contain the buyers of interest for market entry.

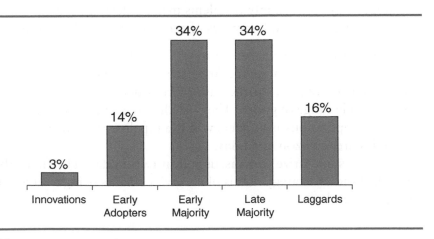

EXHIBIT 4.8 Five Categories of Buyers

[29] Everett Rogers, *Diffusion of Innovations,* 4th ed. (Free Press, 1995), 262.

Innovators are technology junkies who are open to trying anything that seems useful, says Rogers.[30] They typically are the first people to try out a new innovation. Their communication patterns and friendships involve a clique of similarly oriented innovators. They must have sufficient financial resources to absorb losses from technology not working. They must also have the ability to understand and apply complex technical knowledge as, by being the first to adopt, they often try innovations that are not quite ready for general commercial introduction. They are cosmopolitan in the sense they monitor a wide range of developments from around the world and communicate with like-minded people located in geographically widely dispersed areas. The drawback to such buyers is they are not well respected in the market, since they are known for trying almost anything (i.e. will take crazy risks in the eyes of others) and thus, their adoption of a technology does not necessary encourage others to adopt.

Early adopters are the users who have operational strategies that include using "cutting-edge" technology to be leaders in their sector. For deal-making purposes, this group is critical. In distinction to the techno-weenies just discussed, these folks are well respected and often serve as opinion leaders.[31] They are less cosmopolitan and more like other downstream buyers in the early and late majorities. They have judicious decision-making procedures for making adoption decisions that balances risk and uncertainty with anticipated benefits. Thus, their adoption reduces uncertainty about an innovation's utility. Potential adopters look to early adopters for advice, information, and/or role models about innovation adoption.

For our purposes here it suffices to note that if our technology sustains or extends a dominant design, we want to target early adopters. What that means is we want to target buying organizations whose buyers have the traits of early adopters. The reason is we can move into take-off more rapidly. Take-off occurs where the slope of the cumulative sales S-curve suddenly ramps up (see Exhibit 4.9). In my experience, take-off usually occurs with a market penetration of 5 to 10 percent, although some research pushes the upper limit back to 20 percent. The reason for targeting early adopters is that they are opinion leaders. On the other hand, if the technology disrupts a dominant design, the best shot for sales is usually with innovators.

There is coherence between buying criteria and where a buyer is on the adoption sequence. Innovators tend to focus on technical performance and early adopters on best value. Those later in the sequence tend to focus on price and availability.

---

[30] Ibid., 263.
[31] Ibid., 264.

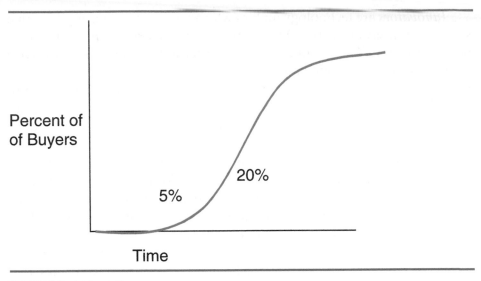

EXHIBIT 4.9   Take-Off

CONCLUSION

We know people tend to buy goods that provide net value. That means our technology has to offer one of four things:

- Better performance—the performance exceeds the capabilities of current offerings and this creates better outcomes given some level of resource use.
- Lower costs—there is a reduction of labor, energy, resources, and other consumables; in the purchase price; or in both.
- Easier use—there is a simpler user interface so less skill or training is required to use the innovation.
- Some combination of these.

We can use the functionality our technology offers to help us seek our practices where we may have an application. By examining characteristics of our technology and its features, we can gain insight into whether what we can offer is what potential end users are seeking.

Assuming we can provide benefits people want, there should be at least a potential interest in buying our technology. Whether this interest is acted upon reflects the priority of the practice and the importance of solving the problem or exploiting the opportunity for the end users and their bosses.

Buying depends on one other thing. It depends on the buyers' comfort with the claims of the technology and estimation of their ability to bear the costs associated with purchase and implementation of the technology.

As Eric Viardot notes, the key to success with high technology is to understand customer values. He elaborates that value reflects: (1) socio-cultural, psychological, personal and sociological factors; (2) environmental factors such as political context, economic situation, demand level, competition; (3) personal factors, such as risk tolerance, fascination with technology, prestige; and (4) most importantly for non-consumer goods, the economic benefits generated from their use. [32]

Bottom line: There is a bottom line and if you want to sell technology, speak to it.

---

[32] Eric Viardot, *Successful Marketing Strategy for High Tech Firms,* 2nd ed. (Boston: Artech House Publishers, 1998), 63.

Intellectual Property

No book on technology transfer would be complete without the obligatory discussion of intellectual property. So, here we go.

Intellectual property (IP) is composed of creative ideas and expressions that have commercial value and can be protected legally as a property right. IP is distinguished from the tangible and physical embodiments that represent the IP. For example, the musical arrangement in a song (the expression) is the IP. Copyright is the legal means for protecting this expression. A consumer purchases a band's CD containing that song; in other words, they purchase an embodiment of the protected expression. Protection means no one can record the song unless the composer (the copyright owner) agrees.

IP includes patents, trademarks, copyrights, masks, and trade secrets. In the United States, patents and trademarks are handled by the U.S. Patent and Trademark Office, part of the Department of Commerce. Copyrights and masks are handled by the Copyright Office of the Library of Congress. Trade secrets are not registered and are protected through litigation.

Intellectual property is an important aspect of commercializing technology since it legally protects your property for sale, licensing, joint ventures or other deal making. Legal protection means you have turf. It gives you a de jure monopoly that enables you to prevent others from using or practicing your invention or creation. Turf gives you a competitive advantage in the market because you can now price your goods according to a monopoly position (and thus extract premium prices).

The grant of patents, trade marks, or copyright secures your monopoly against all others for the period that the right is in force. Trade secrets are different. They protect you against someone stealing your idea or creation, but they do not protect you against independent invention of it.

This appendix is designed to walk you through various forms of intellectual property and IP protection.

PATENTS

A patent is a grant by the federal government or a foreign government that gives the patent holder the right to exclude others from making, using or selling the holder's invention in the country granting the patent. Generally, a patent lasts for 20 years from when it is first filed.

In the United States, before a patent can be issued, the inventor must demonstrate his/her invention is new (unique) and non-obvious.

- To be *new*, an invention must neither have been known nor made by others in the United States. The invention can also not have been previously patented or presented in a publication prior to the claimed date on which the invention was made.
- The fact of being *non-obvious* is established with reference to what would be obvious to a person of ordinary skill in a relevant technology area at the time of the invention. "Ordinary skill" can vary across technology areas. For example, for a more complicated technology developing at a great rate in a specialized industry, the skill-level of a person would be considered high in everyday life but still considered "ordinary" in the technology area. Non-obviousness is determined by examining prior patents, technical publications, and non-secret work being conducted.

So what is patentable? The landmark 1980 Supreme Court case *Diamond v. Chakrabarty* upheld claims to a genetically engineered bacterium. In support of its holding, the Supreme Court interpreted 35 U.S.C. 101 to "Whoever invents or discovers any new and useful process, machine, manufacture, or composition of matter, or any new and useful improvement thereof, may obtain a patent therefore, subject to the conditions and requirements of this title."[33]

It is important to recognize that different rules apply in different countries. In the United States, you have one year from the time of first disclosure, use, publication, or sale of an invention to file a patent application (it usually takes 18–24 months for a patent to be granted after an application has been filed). Where more than one person or group makes a claim to be the inventor, the patent goes to the person or group that can demonstrate they were first to come up with the idea. Overseas, the rules are different. Usually, the invention must be patented before any public disclosure, use, publication, or sale. In case of a dispute, priority goes to the first person or group to apply for a patent, regardless of who may actually be the inventor.

---

[33] *Diamond v. Chakrabarty*, 447 U.S. 303 (1980), http://www.cs.virginia.edu/~jones/tmp352/projects98/group13/genelegal2.html (accessed October 11, 2004).

There are three distinct types of patents in the United States: utility, design, and plant. Utility and design patents are the most common. According to the USPTO:

- *Utility patents* are "issued for the invention of a new and useful process, machine, manufacture, or composition of matter, or a new and useful improvement thereof, it generally permits its owner to exclude others from making, using, or selling the invention for a period of up to twenty years from the date of patent application filing, subject to the payment of maintenance fees. Approximately 90% of the patent documents issued by the PTO in recent years have been utility patents, also referred to as patents for invention."[34]

- *Design patents:* "A design consists of the visual ornamental characteristics embodied in, or applied to, an article of manufacture. Since a design is manifested in appearance, the subject matter of a design patent application may relate to the configuration or shape of an article, to the surface ornamentation applied to an article, or to the combination of configuration and surface ornamentation. A design for surface ornamentation is inseparable from the article to which it is applied and cannot exist alone. It must be a definite pattern of surface ornamentation, applied to an article of manufacture."[35]

- *Plant patents* are "issued for a new and distinct, invented or discovered asexually reproduced plant including cultivated sports [sic], mutants, hybrids, and newly found seedlings, other than a tuber propagated plant or a plant found in an uncultivated state, it permits its owner to exclude others from making, using, or selling the plant for a period of up to twenty years from the date of patent application filing. Plant patents are not subject to the payment of maintenance fees."[36]

Note that software can be protected by both utility and design patents. A utility patent can protect a software *"machine,"* which is code that functions as part of a hardware/software system to do something. Mathematical formulas (algorithms) per se are seen as part of nature and therefore not patentable since they are not invented but discovered. Design

[34] U.S. Patent and Trademark Office, "Types of Patents," June 1, 2000, http://www.uspto.gov/go/taf/patdesc.htm (accessed October 11, 2004).
[35] U.S. Patent and Trademark Office, "A Guide to Filing a Design Patent Application," October 11, 2004, http://www.uspto.gov/web/offices/pac/design/definition.html#difference (accessed October 11, 2004).
[36] U.S. Patent and Trademark Office, "Types of Patents," June 1, 2000 http://www.uspto.gov/go/taf/patdesc.htm (accessed October 11, 2004).

patents can protect the visual features, such as look of the screen or monitor (as in the case of a GUI).

TRADE SECRETS

A *trade secret* is a plan, process, tool, mechanism, or compound that is known only to its owner and to the employees in whom it is necessary to confide. With a trade secret, there are no forms to fill out or registration required. So long as it is kept secret, it is a form of protected property, and the owner may sue those who steal it for damages.

You cannot have both a patent and a trade secret on the same invention, for they are mutually exclusive. Patents, once issued, are published and accessible for anyone to examine. Trade secret protection is preferred when no public disclosure is desired. The most famous trade secret in the United States is probably the formula for Coca Cola.

TRADEMARKS

Trademarks can be used to protect words, names, symbols, devices, or any combination of these that are used to identify your technology or other products or services. The trademarked identifier distinguishes them from similar goods sold by others. Trademarks protect product identifiers, and service marks protect service identifiers. If the trademark is registered with the USPTO, you will see the symbol®; if it is not registered, the symbol ™ is used. Trademark protection can be maintained as long as the mark is in active use in commerce.

While a trademark does not protect the underlying technology, owning a federal trademark registration on the Principal Register provides several advantages. The most important advantages are:

- Giving constructive notice to the public of your claim of ownership of the mark
- Creating a legal presumption of your ownership of the mark and the registrant's exclusive right to use the mark nationwide on or in connection with the goods and/or services listed in the registration (important if there is a lawsuit)
- Giving you the ability to bring an action to enforce your rights with respect to the mark in federal court
- Giving you a basis to obtain registration in foreign countries (if it is a U.S. registration)
- Preventing importation of infringing foreign goods (if it is a U.S. registration and filed with the U.S. Customs Service)

COPYRIGHTS AND MASKS

Copyright is a right to something that is written or composed, which can include a software code as well as books and music. It gives the holder an exclusive right to make copies of the literary items, publish them, and sell them for the author's life plus 70 years. What is protected is the form of the expression of the idea, not the underlying idea. In the United States, a copyright is automatically granted when an embodiment of an idea is made if the symbol ©, the name of the owner, and the year of first publication are added to the expression (e.g., "© Foresight Science & Technology, 2004"). Titles, short phrases and slogans are not protected under copyright law, but they may be protected under trademark law (e.g., "Avis: We Try Harder"®).

Enforcing the right in court against infringers requires registration with the U.S. Copyright Office, which is part of the Library of Congress. If the registration is made within three months of the first publication date, rights to statutory damages and attorney's fees in suits against infringers can be obtained.

Masks are a form of copyright protection for semiconductor products, established through the Semiconductor Protection Act of 1984. Masks or *"mask work"* refers to a series of related images that define the three-dimensional pattern of metallic, insulating or semiconductor material on or removed from semiconductor chips. The term of protection for a mask work extends for a maximum of ten years from the earliest date that the mask work is either (1) registered, or (2) exploited commercially anywhere in the world.

(A good source of additional information on masks comes from the Stanford Copyright & Fair Use informational site from the Stanford University Libraries. Please see *http://fairuse.stanford.edu/primary_materials/codes/92chap9.html*).

IP CONTROL

Now that we have discussed the basic forms of intellectual property, let's go over IP protection. Securing your IP portfolio is critical in order to safeguard your technology for commercialization; intellectual property audits can be an effective tactic to use toward this end.

A comprehensive *intellectual property audit* involves examining the systems by which your company tracks ideas generated by its employees, determining which ones to protect, selecting appropriate legal protection, and implementing that protection. It also examines the company's portfolio of intellectual property to make sure that all important ideas are adequately protected and that resources are not wasted protecting unimportant ideas. These audits are almost always conducted with the aid of a qualified lawyer.

The three rules of thumb are:

1. Examine all files, applications, and registrations associated with existing intellectual property. This examination should assess the adequacy of documentation, including the stories of the ideas' creation and testing, accuracy of all formal filings, records of maintenance payments, records of actual and attempted licenses, and any litigation.

2. Assess the operation of systems throughout the entire company to make sure new ideas/inventions are documented and protected. Inadequate or nonexistent protection can exist in accounting or marketing as well as in the R&D lab. Thus, a complete audit will examine company operations such as handling of employee hiring and firing or exiting, publication, incentive procedures, and vendor agreements as well as procedures for keeping lab notebooks, establishing confidentiality agreements and covenants not to compete, and the process for designing new products.

3. Examine the company's relationship with its environment, particularly with suppliers, customers, consultants, outside research sponsors, universities, investors, and competitors. By including these groups in addition to licensees or licensors and research partners, areas of potentially damaging leaks or failures to establish company claims to property can be identified.

During normal operations, a formal disclosure document should be prepared for each potential invention. During an audit, these disclosures should be reviewed and, as appropriate, updated. A careful check should be made to ensure each invention has adequate documentation.

For each invention, a basic audit format would include a description of the following:

- The technology and its potential uses
- The underlying science and engineering knowledge and the know-how on which it is based
- Current owner(s), their shares in the property, and the basis of their claims
- A brief history of the technology establishing relevant dates in its creation and development
- A notebook detailing the invention (including drawings, designs, or results of experiments) and the relevant dates
- Current and desired intellectual property protection
- Steps required to move from current to desired protection, including tasks, timing, resources, and costs

We recommend consulting your IP counsel to ensure your disclosure documentation is adequate for your needs.

Audits need to be done periodically to ensure that these practices remain in place. Once every five years is often suggested. Furthermore, audits should be prepared by, involve, or be reviewed by an intellectual property lawyer with experience in the relevant technical area(s).

In addition to your intellectual property portfolio, you need to protect your documents as well. In this section, we identify three means of doing so: disclosure, material transfer agreements, and confidentiality agreements.

Disclosures are comprehensive, proprietary documentations of the invention and why it is significant. A good disclosure collects data that will support patenting or copyrighting the invention. It clarifies who the inventors are, when the invention or creation occurred, what was invented or created, and what proof exists for the act of original invention or creation.

Many universities and federal labs put their disclosure forms on the web, providing templates for developing your own.[37] However, we caution that any draft you prepare should be reviewed by your IP counsel before use.

The transfer of research materials from you to another institute or vice versa is a legally significant event that should be accompanied by a *materials transfer agreement* (MTA). MTAs clarify who owns both the materials and any research results obtained through use of the material. As with disclosure documents, university and federal lab examples provide guidance.[38] However, we once again caution that any draft you prepare should be reviewed by your IP counsel before use.

Confidentiality agreements are used to maintain control over confidential information or inventions while permitting limited access to others so they may determine whether they are interested in the technology. Confidentiality agreements protect trade secrets. Accordingly, they only protect the specified information and technology against use by the recipient. They do not protect the information or technology from use or discovery by others who have not signed the agreements.

The agreements may be stand-alone legal documents or incorporated as clauses in other agreements, such as licenses, sales, employment or

---

[37] Some examples are: Temple University (http://www.patents.temple.edu/docs/ID_guidelines.doc) and the University of Wisconsin at Madison (http://www.warf.ws/uploads/media/20011128124730196_Microsoft_Word_-_IDR2001final.pdf).

[38] One example is the MTA of the Mouse Genetic Research Facility located at the Oak Ridge National Laboratory (http://lsd.ornl.gov/mouse/mta.htmlx) and the MTA of the National Institutes for Standards and Technology (http://patapsco.nist.gov/ts/220/external/forms/incomingmta.pdf).

consulting agreements and options. Confidentiality agreements should be legally binding, which means they need to be signed. Paper works best for this reason, though faxes are also common. The agreement is typically not long. It may be only one page, though many use multiple page formal documents.

The prospective receivers, of course, are under no obligation to sign a confidentiality agreement. If this occurs, there are alternatives. A telephone call to the legal department, in-licensing office, merger and acquisitions office, or president's office might result in directions to a person who has authority to waive a "no confidentiality" policy. You can also disclose what it does without revealing how it does it. But a warning: Do not disclose any details of how your technology works without a confidentiality agreement unless a patent has been issued.

Confidentiality agreements, also called non-disclosure agreements, offer a precise form of protection for technology and information.[39] The protection is not against appropriation in general but is effective in preventing misappropriation by the receiver of property that has signed an agreement. The particular confidentiality agreement should be tailored for the specific technology that is disclosed, the receiver's organization and business ownership, and the nature and extent of the necessary evaluation, testing and dissemination. Specific steps should be stated in the event that the evaluation results in an indication of lack of interest by the receiver.

One of the most important points to remember is never to disclose the "secret sauce" behind a technology, detailed performance data, or other similar information before having a signed confidentiality agreement. To generate interest in technology or information before an agreement is signed, say what it does but not how it does it.

We reiterate that any draft you prepare of this or other legal documents should be reviewed by your IP counsel.

Forming and safeguarding your IP portfolio are fundamental components to the successful commercialization of your technology. By doing so, you secure your rights to dispose of IP and prevent others from using it, which can provide a significant competitive advantage in the market.

---

[39] Once again, university and federal lab examples are easy to find. For example, the University of Oregon's is at http://www.uoregon.edu/~techtran/docs/CONFAGMT.pdf; Kansas State's is at http://www.ksu.edu/research/forms/preaward/confidential.pdf. In addition, a number of commercial examples can be found on the web from law firms and other vendors.

CHAPTER 5

Competing Technology

INTRODUCTION

Recall that in the introduction to this book we said the most important factor in the success of a new product, process, or service is competitive advantage. Competitive advantage means one technology meets end-user needs better than the others. Ideally you want this to be your technology. You want this so badly that it pays to redesign your technology to gain it, and if you cannot, to look for another niche for market entry.

No matter how brilliant your technology, there is going to be competition. Sooner or later everyone has competition, and usually it is sooner rather than later: The more brilliant your invention, the more it stimulates imitators. Someone figures out how to design around the patent. Someone else reverse engineers it and starts making knock-offs in China or some other country where IP enforcement is not rigorous. Someone figures out how to adapt other technical approaches to provide equivalent performance. Competition is so ubiquitous that I used to play a game when I lectured. I would challenge people to give me a technology without competition. Made for a great teachable moment. . . .

In this chapter we learn how to do market research on competition. We are concerned with four questions:

- Are we redundant? Is this technology just a reinvention of what someone has already invented? What other technologies can compete with this technology? That is, how else can the mix of performance, ease-of-use, and price that end users want be created?
- Is the competing technology positioned vis-à-vis the dominant design as we are? Is it incremental, radical, adaptive, or disruptive innovations? If it is disruptive, how stable is the dominant design? What are the trends in end-user needs which may help or hinder various substitutes?
- Who is selling those substitutes? Is our competition an established player in the market or a new entrant? Is our competition a big company or one with deep pockets or is it a small, resource limited firm or some company on the verge of bankruptcy?

- The final question is: Who else might emerge as competitors? Who else is out there developing relevant technology? Is the locus of competing R&D in universities and government labs? Is it in small firms or companies outside the industry? Or is it in well established players?

REDUNDANCY

The analysis of competition begins with end-user needs. The same end-user needs that drive the requirements for our technology drive the requirements for our competition. So, the first thing we have to do is revisit our price, performance, and ease-of-use metrics and use those as a baseline for finding competitors.

We shall discuss where to find competing technology. Here it suffices to say we search patents, R&D data bases, referred journals, gray literature, trade literature, business press, etc. (gray literature refers to government R&D reports, old dissertations, and the like. It is called gray because this is not peer-reviewed literature that shows up in print. Rather it was the stuff that was submitted on paper, photographed, and stored on microfiche. When you printed a report off the fiche, it had this gray background. Hence, the name.)

In general we are concerned about two types of competition: four square identical and other ways of accomplishing what we are doing.

The first focuses on who else is pursing similar requirements with a similar technical approach. It is critical because if we find it, either we or the competitor is infringing if any of us was able to secure a patent or copyright.

Recall that the party that owns a patent for a technology can exclude others from making, using, selling, or offering it for sale without a license. In the United States, patent law protects the first to invent. So, if we find patents that are just like our technology, but we can prove that we invented the technology first, we can sue for infringement. In Europe and the rest of the world, it is different. There it is first to file. So, regardless of when we invented, if we did not file in the relevant country in a timely manner, we could be infringing. Of course, if we are not the first to invent, we might be infringing in the United States as well.

The financial impact is substantial. If we have the patent, we can go after all the infringers and demand they take licenses from us. This approach is called assertion licensing. Jerome Lemelson, who claimed he was the inventor of machine vision, made millions this way as company after company settled out of court until Cognex went to court and the judge found 14 critical patent claims were unenforceable under the defense of prosecution laches, which means there was an unreasonable delay or negligence in pursuing a right.[1]

Just because you have a patent does not mean you can practice it. Suppose you have the patent for a drop leaf table. Now, suppose someone else has a patent for a table. You cannot make drop-leaf tables without making tables, so you need to license or sublicense the table patent in order to practice yours. This is called stacking.

Royalty stacking occurs when you have to license other people's patents to do licensing deals for yours. The more there is a multiplicity of overlapping patents, the harder it is to make a profit as more of the royalty is going to others. Some argue that stacking discourages technical innovation for this reason. It is often an issue in pharmaceuticals and biotech, where companies cross-license to avoid infringement fights.[2] On the other hand, stacking can be used to your advantage if you are a patent holder.

> In a project for a small company a few years ago, we examined all the patents that cited the company's patents as prior art. Then we examined the products of the firms citing our client's patents as prior art to determine which ones required a license to practice their own technology. It led to a series of assertion licensing deals.

Once we figure out who, if anyone is pursuing the same technical approach, we can determine, with the aid of patent counsel, just what IP we own. For example, we have countless times found university and federal lab invention disclosures commercially worthless because, unbeknownst to the inventor, someone else already has published the invention.

> My favorite example of already invented technology involved an algorithm that used geometric formulas to figure out the optimal placement of multiple video cameras for security applications so you get

(Continued)

---

[1] Goodman, "Legal Machine Helped Inventor Gain Wealth," *Red Nova* (August 23, 2005), http://www.rednova.com/news/science/216929/legal_machine_helped_inventor_gain_wealth/ (accessed September 14, 2005).
[2] See News-medical.net, "Solutions to Royalty Stacking Issues a Top Priority in Pharmaceutical and Biotechnology Sectors," *Pharmaceutical News* (January 31, 2005), http://www.news-medical.net/?id=7570 (accessed September 14, 2005).

the best coverage with the fewest number of cameras. The inventor, a professor, argued there were no other such algorithms for cameras. He was right. We could not find any. But we did find the same formulas used to solve a problem called the Art Gallery Guard Problem. This problem asks how you place guards in an art gallery to have optimal coverage with the fewest possible guards. Sound familiar? Sound obvious? Not much difference between placing a guard and a video camera for security. Makes sense that as you replace guards with cameras you would use the same algorithms for placement. Funny thing was, our professor had never heard of the Art Gallery Guard Problem. He had invented the algorithm on his own—an impressive technical feat, but commercially irrelevant. (This, of course, points out that just because a technology is commercially worthless, does not mean it is bad science or engineering.)

Note that just because someone is pursuing a similar technical approach does not necessarily mean we or they are infringing. Nonetheless, these competitors are still potential threats. For example, is the other technology easier to use or cheaper? If so, it may have a competitive advantage over us.

A great way to understand this principle is to go to the U.S. Patent Office's patent server at *www.uspto.gov* and search on the term "*spork.*" Sporks are spoon-forks. The have a concave section like a spoon, but on the end are tines. Sporks are usually covered by design patents. There are a lot of them. Now put in "tunable IR diode." These are utility patents, but there are a lot of these too. You have to read claims closely to differentiate. (It is the claims that count in patents. That defines what you own.)

We also are interested in other ways of accomplishing the same thing because these technologies are also potential threats. What we want to know is the range of other ways similar performance can be obtained, and then what is the likely ease-of-use and price of those ways.

We can plot the performance, ease of use, and price of our technology and its competitors on a chart with normalized values. We can also plot the baseline, which is the end user needs. In the following chart we have seven performance metrics. What they are is irrelevant right now.

Exhibit 5.1 replicates part of a graphic from Chapter 1. In this graphic, on metric 4, the number 7 represents the baseline. By looking at how closely our technology, and its competitors, are positioned to number 7 we get an idea of how competitive we are. Of course, if we are below the baseline we are out of luck unless we can somehow stretch the performance of our technology to hit the baseline. If we are above the baseline,

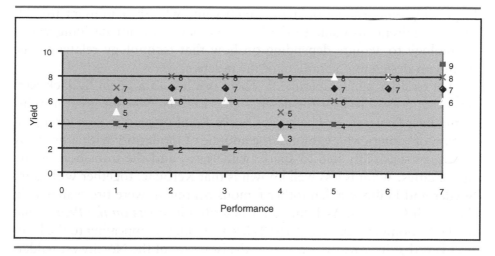

EXHIBIT 5.1   End-User Needs

the question becomes what are the trade-offs. Are we more expensive, harder to use, or do we just deliver a lot more value?

All things being equal, we find initial competitive advantage in three steps. First, we determine out who is at or above the baseline. Next, we determine who clusters most tightly with the baseline, because they have the best fit with the requirements. Finally, we determine if anyone is "leaving value on the table" by over-performing on some metrics without any penalties on other ones.

With this analysis we can now determine if we are redundant or not. If we end up below the "*competitive range,*" that is, the set of competitors who are either at or above the baseline, we are redundant. (If we can improve our technology we can still compete.) If there are competitors who are leaving value on the table and we are not, that is another way we can end up redundant.

RELATION TO THE DOMINANT DESIGN

It is wrong to assume there is always just one set of requirements for any set of end users. The requirements for a specific technology are influenced by the full range of relevant needs of real living people, not just a small set of abstract criteria, As we have seen, the relevant needs tend to reflect the practices in which the technology is to be deployed, and that means the motivations for engaging in those practices, the paradigm for the conduct of the practice, the dominant designs for technology in the practice, and the skills and capacities people bring to, and develop in, those practices.

Depending on the situation in the practice and who the end users are, different requirements come to the forefront as criteria for deciding which technology to acquire depending on how that technology relates to the dominant design and paradigm of the practice.

Let us do a mind experiment. There is a line in a poem by Jack Kerouac that goes, "To hear the desert sigh." Kerouac was the great novelist of the Beat Generation. His book *On the Road* opened a door for a generation of writers who explored the anomie of modernity with a uniquely American sensibility tied to space, wilderness, and the transition in and out of cities. What is less well known is that Kerouac, together with Gary Snyder and Philip Whalen (other famous beatniks), were fire watchers in the North Cascades. As John Suiter describes in *Poets on the Peak,* what made the dominant design of 1950s fire watching so appealing to the beatniks was that it provided a way into the isolation of the Northwest wilderness. It offered an opportunity to experience both themselves and the world in the absolute terms. In the isolation of a fire-tower hut in the mountains, one hears the sound of one hand clapping and the desert sigh.

Now, suppose we are the National Forest Service, and our mission is to find and control fires as rapidly as possible. Suppose our goal for the year is to have quicker reporting of potential fires because of an organizational mandate and motivation for the practice of fire watching. But, the mandate is only one factor in the requirements of the actual end users. Now, toss Kerouac, Snyder, and Whalen into the picture. We are the Forest Service management, and we go to out to the field and say to the Beats, "Hey guys, we've just heard the CIA has these things called sitcoms, and we're thinking of buying some for you to use. It will let you call us whether you are in the hut or on the trail. That's a big improvement over the telephones we use now because now you can run around on the trail to check things out as well as sit in the hut and still be in communication."

For the Beats, the radio likely would be a mixed blessing. On the one hand, it is a better way to report fires than the telephone and loving the wilderness they probably had no desire to see it burn. Plus they have a job to do and they signed on to do it. On the other hand, a field portable sitcom radio makes you pretty much accessible anywhere, meaning the jerks in management can reach you whenever they want and order you to carry out all sorts of silly make work, which certainly takes something away from your Zen meditation and poetry writing time. So, we suspect their end-user requirements for a sitcom radio probably would include the ability to control when the transmissions can occur.

Suppose we come to them and instead say, "Hey guys, we've just heard the Air Force is developing this doohickey called a forward looking infrared (FLIR) system. What it does is scan the horizon for heat. If it sees heat, it automatically radios in a potential hazards warning and sounds an alarm in the hut as well so you can pull out the binoculars and check it out. Pretty cool ehh?"

Note that the FLIR system probably does not need the requirement that the fire watcher have control over when transmissions can occur. Zen meditation is great, but the forest burning down is a good reason to break into the meditative moment. Plus as the system is always on, you can slack off a bit more, making more rather than less opportunity for writing poetry.

In other words, depending on motivations and paradigms of end users, and the way they develop behavior patterns given the interaction of these with the dominant design, the priority of requirements for buying goods differs depending on the way technical approaches operate differently. Here we have two very different ways to solve a common problem— speeding discovery and reporting of fires. Let's take the argument a step further.

America is far too dependent on foreign oil. The end-user requirement is to reduce dependency. One way to do that is solar, wind, tidal, and other kinds of renewable energy. Another way to do that is to build nuclear plants. Unfortunately, it is intrinsic in nuclear power generation that there will be very high radiation materials required and disposal of these needs to be taken very seriously. Security becomes a priority for end-user needs whereas for renewable energy it is not because the devices do not intrinsically have mass destructive potential.

What we see are two ways in which requirements can differ across technologies, given the same set of needs.

In the first way, how the technologies operate differ and this difference has an unequal impact on *"latent"* needs of end users. By latent needs we mean needs that were not articulated in the original set of requirements set by whomever. In our mind experiment it was management. Not surprisingly, this phenomenon is most often seen where one person buys for another, as when a corporate or government procurement activity is a separate part of the bureaucracy from the end users.

The other way is when there is something intrinsic to a technology that makes it riskier or more difficult to adopt than its competitors because it requires a change in the dominant design for technology and/or the paradigm for behavior in the practice. In this case, we are not talking about latent needs and requirements. The need for risk mitigation in nuclear power plants is definitely articulated as requirement. In fact, in the United States we have a special agency, the Nuclear Regulatory Commission, that exists precisely because the risk is unusually high and cannot be ignored.

Let's go back to the kinds of innovations, given an existing dominant design. Suppose our technology is an incremental innovation, but all the other ones are adaptive. The sitcom radio is an adaptive innovation. A better telephone would be incremental. The new functionality of the adaptive innovation raises the possibility of latent needs being triggered and new requirements emerging. Tell me you can bug me whenever you want and if I am a Beat poet my Zen retreat to the mountains is harder to accomplish. I am thinking, "Why did I take this job?"

Now, suppose I have a radical technology like nuclear power or tidal power generation. The very fact it is a different technical approach means I have to ask, "What is necessary to make this work in my practice?" because I cannot simply assume it will. I have to think about different packaging, like training or new infrastructure. In other words, ease of use concerns cannot be avoided.

Finally, let's look at the FLIR. This technology is disruptive. It is changing the dominant design for technology and the paradigm for behavior. Where before the human fire watcher was the primary resource for finding a fire, the fire watcher's job now is to make sure the FLIR is working and then to confirm its findings. The man (Kerouac, Snyder, Whalen) is now an adjunct to the machine—ironically, this would be fine with them given their motivation for being there in the first place.

What does this discussion tell us about competitive advantage? Competitive advantage is likely greater where the technology does not raise barriers to entry. In our examples, the barrier was intentionally always poised as involving ease-of-use. There is seldom such a barrier for an incremental innovation. It does not require us to change our behavior as practitioners, nor does it require us to learn how to work with new technology. Adaptive and radical innovations do present some ease-of-use issues, because to leverage the new functionality or operate the new technical approach means something is changing and change means we, the practitioners, have to learn to do something differently. Disruptive innovations are a wild card. If they cause a shift to a new dominant design and paradigm for behavior that better fits our motivations, great. All for it! If they make us shift in ways that are contrary to our motivations for doing or participating the practice, not so great.

We can now further our analysis. We take all the technologies in the competitive range and see which ones are likely to be the easiest to adopt. Those are now the contenders for the holder of competitive advantage.

Once we say "focus on the ones easiest to adopt," two other factors related to dominant designs come into play: infrastructure and supply chains.

Infrastructure is required to use a technology. We cannot put a nuclear power plant in the middle of a desert unless we can find water, because without water we cannot cool the reactor. If we already are pumping water out of a river or from an aquifer, adoption is easier. Similarly, if we cannot find anywhere to store the waste, after a while it gets harder and harder to build new reactors.[3]

Supply chains are needed to make technologies into products, processes, and services. I used to have a fellow, Stan Goddard, who worked for me. Stan was a retired engineer who had spent his career at Battelle, where his job was to pretend he was a Soviet engineer and figure out ways to kill U.S. tanks. Stan used to say, "It's hard to commercialize a technology that relies on strategic materials." It reflected his Cold War orientation.

What Stan was referring to was materials managed by the Defense National Stockpile Center. The center is part of the Defense Logistics Agency. Its mission is to ensure safe, secure and environmentally sound stewardship of strategic and critical materials that come from foreign sources, but which would be needed to fight a war.[4] Stan's point was that if your technology required one of those materials, if war broke out, you could be out of business because your supply chain would dry up.

Now-a-days we do not worry quite so much about foreign dependency . . . until we think about access to cheap oil, which in term affects the prices of a lot chemicals, plastics, etc. So if your technology is heading to market in a very price sensitive sector of the economy and you have no control over the costs of some of your supplies, well, time to think about options or hedge contracts. For example, hedge contracts are commonly used by financially strong airlines to provide some mitigation of the impact of shifts in fuel prices.[5]

WHO IS SELLING?

Yet another factor is who is selling the technology, the goods that embody the technology, or the goods made with it. At the heart of this issue is brand loyalty and how you build and maintain it. Brand loyalty refers to a buyer's tendency to repurchase a brand. Clearly, repeatedly providing products with competitive advantages is one way to build brand loyalty. To the extent a buyer can assume a vendor will provide competitive products,

[3] See Wald, "A New Vision for Nuclear Waste," *Technology Review* (December 2004), www.technologyreview.com/articles/04/12/wald1204.asp?p=0 (accessed September 15, 2005).
[4] See https://www.dnsc.dla.mil/default.asp (accessed September 15, 2005).
[5] Alexander, "Fuel Prices Have Airlines Watching Their Weight," *Washington Post*, September 10, 2005, www.washingtonpost.com/wp-dyn/content/article/2005/09/09/AR2005090902018.html (accessed September 15, 2005); and Ang, "Aviation Sector's Grapple with Soaring Fuel Prices," *The Star* (September 12, 2005 (accessed September 15, 2005).

it simplifies buying decisions. In order to create brand loyalty, vendors focus on making buyers aware of their goods and educating them as to its superior value proposition. Brand name advertising is used to reinforce positive associations from the past.

For our purposes here, how you create brand loyalty is less important than determining whether it exists. Obviously, surveys or interviews with experts can be used to determine who has it, but other indicators are favorable appearance of company names and product names in trade press and general media articles; in newsgroups, blogs, and listservers; and presence in focused review articles and "editor's choice" picks.

John Ellis provides a good metaphor for understanding brand loyalty. He points out that it is analogous to being on a computer network, arguing what a competitor wants to do is to stay connected and to be connected at all times with the customer. The reason is simple. Purchasing should be a repeat, habitual activity, like getting the newspaper each morning, rather than a ground-up sale each time.[6]

Exceptional brand loyalty leads to goodwill. Goodwill is an intangible asset that represents the premium a vendor can charge above the market price due to the advantage or reputation a business has acquired. The premium represents the incremental value of a company over and above the value of its tangible assets and other intangible assets. Where brand loyalty is strong, not only does buying continue, but goods can be sold with a "surcharge."

Sometimes advertising can create goodwill even if there is substantive basis for competitive advantage. If you are unclear about this phenomenon, go into any supermarket or drugstore and look at the toothpaste. Read the ingredients and who makes it. You will find the same ingredients in different brands sold at different prices by the same company. They have their premium brands and their discount brands. It's no different than why people buy Hummers, which you do if you want a 4×4 that always has to be polished and spotless. (Try finding one of those spotless Hummers in Iraq. The only reason to buy a Hummer for consumer use is to say you can afford to pay a premium so you can have a Hummer. Wow, advertising can be used to create goodwill even where there is no substance. Ouch!)

Deep pockets are important because money can be used to buy brand loyalty. It not only buys advertising. it also buys better market research and product development, plus superior marketing, manufacturing, and customer support.

Size is important because it provides momentum, which can be used to

---

[6] Ellis, "Customers Expect More Than a Coupon from P&G," *Fast Company* (April 2001), http://www.fastcompany.com/magazine/45/jellis.html (accessed September 15, 2005).

overwhelm, at least for a time, the impact of actions that destroy brand loyalty. (OK, so size is not important. What counts is how you use it.) For example, even though Dell retains the reputation of a high service company, a number of articles point out that Dell planned its technical support outsourcing so poorly that it has received so many complaints about bad customer service along with rude comments it decided to move technical support back to the United States. Despite that fact, the way it unbundled the practice of customer support continues to cripple the company and at some point, unless fixed, will destroy its reputation and thus brand loyalty.[7]

What brand loyalty indicates is that customer/vendor interaction has managed to increase the net utility of one vendor's goods due to factors extrinsic to the specific price, performance, and ease-of-use metrics for the technology per se. It points out there are costs and ease-of-use factors associated with the buying transaction and its aftermath that affect a competitor's ability to shape perceptions concerning the merit of its products. A product for which service is easy to obtain, does perform better than one for which service is a nightmare. Thus, when competitive advantage is difficult to determine, secondary factors associated with the vendors will come to the fore to determine who has competitive advantage.

WHO IS EMERGING?

Because technology changes over time, we cannot only look at current substitutes, we also have to consider future ones. There are a variety of sources for finding data on emerging technologies and the players creating and developing them. By categorizing the hits from these sources in terms of the TRL or development process stage they reflect, we can use bibliometric analysis of past and current information to project what competition we might face in the future.

Consider a simple linear process running from basic research through applied research to early stage engineering development, concurrent engineering, and on to production and sales. Data sources on basic research include resources like Current Contents, scholarly journals, professional society presentations, dissertation abstracts, and other databases on fundamental research. Applied research data sources include data bases of

---

[7] Bizbrim, "Dell Outsourcing—Latest News," n.d., www.bizbrim.com/outsourcing/dell-outsourcing.htm (accessed September 15, 2005); and Comment.CIO.com, "Dell Outsourcing," *CIO* (June 1, 2003), http://comment.cio.com/comments/19119.html (accessed September 15, 2005); Kouviles, "How Not to Outsource Global Business Processes," *Olin School of Business* (Spring 2005), http://www.olin.wustl.edu/discovery/feature.cfm?sid=545&pg=1 (accessed September 15, 2005).

government R&D (although some basic research can also be found there), patent data bases, and the like. As we move into early engineering development we get more patenting, plus applied tracks at scholarly meetings and the like. Concurrent engineering resources include articles in trade publications, newsletters focused on markets or industrial sectors, and sometimes the business press. Product and sales articles show up in trade publications, the business press, and general media.

Now, these sources are illustrative. There is no hard and fast rule here. But we can say that different sectors have different time frames for moving technology out of people's heads and into the market and by looking at when information starts appearing and what stage in technology development is presented, we can get some idea of how far away a technology is from market entry.

Exhibit 5.2 reflects bibliometric analysis from three hypothetical competitive intelligence projects. In each case we are counting hits relating to a technology and mentioning a specific company as the affiliation of the

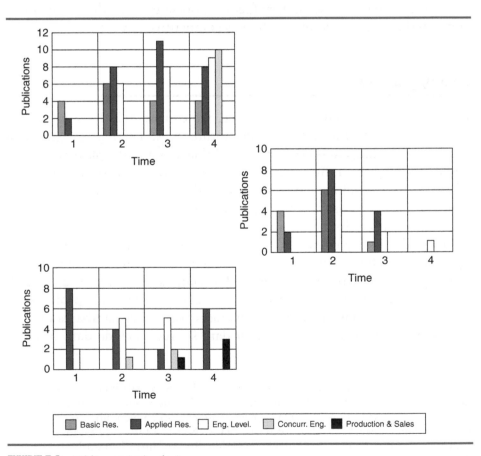

EXHIBIT 5.2 Bibliometric Analysis

author, the assignee on a patent, the awardee of a government grant, etc. The first chart, in the upper right hand, depicts a technology moving to market. We see references to work taking place in a university/industry center, as indicated by co-authored articles by employees of the firm of interest and the university running the center. Later we see patenting and papers at technical society meetings, plus a federal R&D award. Yet later we find articles in the trade press and many more presentations. Finally, we find articles in newsletters and the business press. It appears, a technology is heading for market.

The pattern is dramatically different in the next chart. In this case what we see is a project start to move forward, then die. Actually, that last little bit of engineering development suggests it is one of these projects that hang on and refuse to die.

The final chart suggests a technology already moving to the market. The product was introduced and we can track a shift in the R&D program to a next generation.

TIME

For a company or other party to invest in a technology, they will want a return-on-investment (ROI). Just how much return they will want is an empirical question. Because the return-on-investment is a threshold criteria for buying, licensing, or otherwise acquiring a technology, the ROI rate is called a hurdle rate. If you cannot jump over it, no deal.

The ROI needs to be obtained in some period of time. As noted, my experience suggests 5 years is usually a reasonable period, but again this is an empirical question. To find out what the period is for a company or an industry, you ask experts and other knowledgeable people.

From the standpoint of competitive advantage, we need to recognize that we are only interested in substitutes that can take away business or swamp our product life cycle, thereby destroying our ability to attain the necessary ROI. Exhibit 5.3 depicts a product life cycle[8] As the graphic indicates, at some point in the cycle, a new product or product extension is needed because market saturation occurs and buying declines to replacement levels.

A substitute which takes away business reduces the amount of product we can sell. It affects the area under the curve, but we still have a curve. A product that swamps us, cuts off the curve at some point. It means our good does not make it through the product life cycle.

---

[8] Lynn Ellis, *Evaluation of R&D Processes* (Norwood, MA: Artech House, 1997), 30.

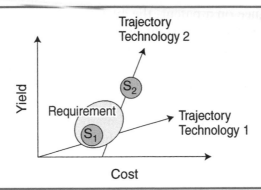

EXHIBIT 5.3   End-User Requirements

In order to understand how a technology can reduce our sales, we have to remember that both the development of technology and markets are dynamic. End-user needs shift over time as do the yields of various competitors.

In Exhibit 5.4, the circle represents end-user requirements. S1 and S2 are two technologies. Note that although S1 and S2 are both originally in the competitive range, over time, their trajectories on cost, if development continues, will make them too costly for the end users. S2 is already outside the cost requirements for this customer segment. An example is the U.S. Navy's new DD(x) destroyer. High capability; too expensive. As former Navy Chief of Staff Vern Clark told Congress in April 2005, shipbuilding expenses spiraled out of control. The Navy has gone from expecting to buy 24 DD(x)s to five.[9]

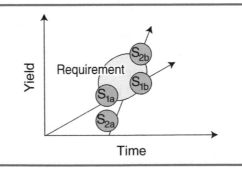

EXHIBIT 5.4   Radical Technology Becomes Competitive

---

[9] Arabe, "Can Plans for a 21st Century Navy Remain Afloat?" *Industrial Market Trends* (April 26, 2005), http://news.thomasnet.com/IMT/archives/2005/04/can_plans_for_a .html (accessed September 15, 2005).

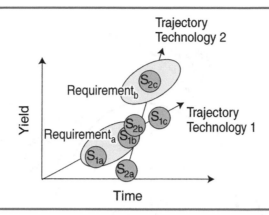

Trajectory
Technology 2

Requirement_b

Requirement_a

Yield

Trajectory
Technology 1

Time

EXHIBIT 5.5 Technologies No Longer Competitive

The situation is different in Exhibit 5.5. Here S1 is originally competitive, but S2 is not. Over time, however, S2 becomes more competitive, surpassing the yield of S1. The pattern is often seen with radical technologies. Another military example can be used. As large aircraft enter the airspace in Iraq, they can come under attack from heat seeking missiles using infrared sensors. Countermeasures originally involved shooting out flares to spoof the missiles. Now a new generation of much more capable technology is being introduced based on using lasers to blind the heat seekers.[10]

The final example in Exhibit 5.6 portrays yet another situation. Here the end-user requirements shift, making technologies that used to be competitive, no longer competitive. The space shuttle is a good example. Originally it was designed to be a low cost reusable system for access to space. As Robert Zubrin of Pioneer Astronautics argues, it was built in a pre-space station era when the United States needed a Winnebago—essentially a space station that could move itself in and out of orbit. Now that we have a station, we need something else. On the one hand, we need heavy lift. On the other hand, we need a small crew transfer vehicle. The shuttle is too small for the former and too large for the latter.[11] It no longer is a viable system given the Bush administration's announced goals of building bases on the Moon and Mars.

In each case, where competitive advantage lies is a function of the interaction between yields, cost, or ease-of-use and requirements over

[10] Pike, "Large Aircraft Infrared Countermeasures (LAIRCM)," April 27, 2005, http://www.globalsecurity.org/military/systems/aircraft/systems/laircm.htm, (accessed September 15, 2005).

[11] Zubin, "No Time to Cut and Run," *St. Petersburg Times,* February 9, 2003, http://chapters.marssociety.org/usa/il/no%20time%20to%20cut%20and%20run.doc (accessed September 15, 2005).

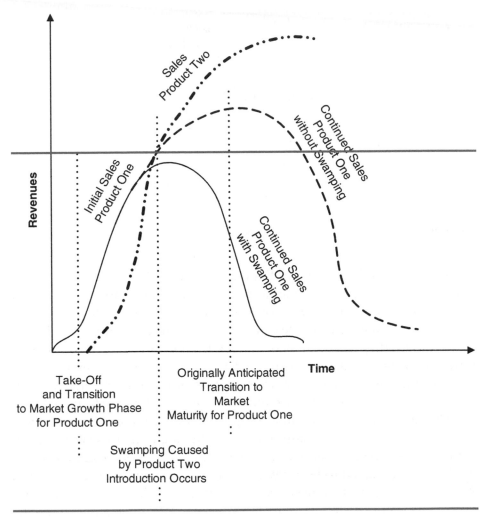

EXHIBIT 5.6 Swamping

time. Time is critical because to succeed in the market, a technology cannot be a short-term wonder. It has to be sold long enough to make enough profit to justify the cost of developing and commercializing it.

As noted, swamping is another threat to having sufficient duration to reap ROI from a good over its life cycle. There are a variety of reasons for swamping. Sometimes, a new technology is introduced that obsoletes the good we are selling. Other times other factors may emerge, as discussed previously in the context of militarily critical strategic materials. Regardless, what counts is that we cannot ride out the life cycle because it is cut short before its time. It is analogous to being in a canoe cutting across a lake when some jerk in a high-speed powerboat races up to you and cuts by you, tossing you into his wake and filling the canoe with water. You probably do not die, but you sure have to work hard to get to shore in a swamped canoe.

Note that swamping is not a function of short life cycles per se. The computer chip industry has short life cycles, but has adapted to them. Swamping is a problem because it is an unforeseen shortening of the time in which a good can be sold.

CONCLUSION

Competition exists where substitutes can be found that can reduce or swamp sales of goods based on, made with, or embodying your technology. To impact sales, these substitutes must be able to meet end-user needs. Usually, they will leverage existing infrastructure, but a technology may be so attractive as to pull investments in infrastructure along. Substitutes also have to be capable of having supply chains, or they will not be made.

We can compare substitutes in light of end-user needs to discover which goods or technologies have competitive advantages. Where multiple competitors are in the competitive range, secondary concerns, such as brand loyalty, increase in importance.

It is important to always remember both technology and markets are dynamic. Thus, we always are looking out over some time period to determine if our technology can hold a competitive advantage long enough to meet our objectives, the objectives of the people who buy it, and the objectives of the people who license, joint venture, invest in, or otherwise partner with us to commercialize the technology.

CHAPTER **6**

Markets

INTRODUCTION

Markets are where buyers and sellers meet to do transactions. In this chapter we will focus on two particular aspects of markets: market barriers and market forces. Barriers add stability to markets. They help us understand how customers and their buying preferences get locked in and become resistant to change. Forces add dynamics to markets. They help us understand how customers and their buying preferences shift over time, thus providing clues as to how we can position our technology today to sell in the future.

Barriers and forces are adaptations based on a bastardization of Newton's Laws of Motion. Newton's Laws of Motion rest on two concepts: objects with mass and forces. The laws describe their interaction. These laws were designed for physical objects, not social ones, hence our use of the phrase bastardization.

Newton's First Law states that if the net forces on an object are balanced, then that object will stay at rest if it is resting, or in constant motion, if it is moving. Net force is the vector sum of all the forces. This law is called the Law of Inertia.

Following the Newtonian model, barriers are the analog of mass. Barriers make it difficult for forces to change market behavior, the object. More precisely, patterns of buying are objects. Barriers are an attribute of these patterns that can lock us out of the market for some specified period of time with part or all of a specified customer segment. These barriers consist of factors that support those patterns and give them "*mass.*" Unlike forces, which are tendencies, barriers are facts. They either are or are not there. Only after confirming a barrier exists does it makes sense to talk about how substantial is that barrier.

Newton's Second Law states that if the forces are not in balance then the acceleration of the object is dependent on the net force acting upon it and the mass of the object. This law states: The acceleration of an object due to a set of forces is directly in the direction of the net force and proportional to the magnitude of that net force and inversely proportional to the mass of the object.

$$\text{Force (net)} = \text{mass} \times \text{acceleration}$$

Given that, what is a market force? As with most other social phenomenon, in commercialization it is very hard to find empirical causal relationships. What we do find are statistical tendencies that we can describe with greater or lesser degrees of confidence. Market forces are simply social statistical tendencies that affect economic transactions. Like an electron wave heading for a sensor, market forces are the statistical probability of a collision with buying behavior in a direction and magnitude, which for our purposes we can treat as a vector so long as we recognize that both the magnitude and direction may vary over time. Need a reality check as to what is a market force? If you can't measure it, it ain't a force.

Recall that in the last chapter we discussed that it is not enough to say there are customers for a technology. These customers must be willing to buy at the time the technology is mature enough to be sold. Yet too often when people study markets, they are not rigorous about whether and how these markets will evolve and change. The analysis of market barriers and forces is the key to rigor when predicting buying behavior in the future and an extrapolation of current behavior. As in Newtonian physics, an object at rest (here a buying pattern) can be put into motion, but it requires the application of enough force (here market forces) to overcome the inertia of the mass (the barriers which sustain the buying pattern).

With a handle on barriers and forces, we can now estimate total addressable market size and the share we might capture. The share estimate is preliminary as we still need to factor in specific competitors and whom we might partner with in more detail, but insofar as we have examined competition as a barrier, it will get us into the general ball park.

In this Chapter we seek to understand just what market forces and barriers are, so we can identify, study, and quantify them. We use this information to help us make our initial estimate of market size and the share we can capture. In Part Three of this book we will explore how to leverage market forces to overcome barriers.

MARKET BARRIERS

What barriers do is ensure that the probability of successful market entry or expansion is less than 50%. This result can be attained in three fundamental ways: either access to the good can be prohibited, the net utility calculation can be made to come out negative with respect to adoption by the

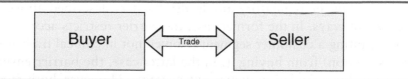

EXHIBIT 6.1   Components of a Market Transaction

buyer, or sellers can be prevented from entering the market. Where net utility is involved, there are two possibilities. Either the good may be viewed as undesirable, or it is viewed as less desirable than one or more substitutes.

We can categorize barriers in terms of how they limit market entry or expansion. Obviously, to be a barrier, the factor must affect one of the three components in a market transaction: buyers, sellers, or what is being traded (see Exhibit 6.1). We will use breast augmentation technology to illustrate some of the ways in which barriers can operate.

Breast implants were first marketed in the United States around 1960, prior to Amendments to the 1976 amendments to the Food, Drug and Cosmetic Act that added the requirement medical devices be shown to be safe and effective. Silicone had been assumed to be biologically inactive and was assumed to have no harmful effects. However, as cases of connective tissue disorders and cancers were reported in several studies, in 1992, the Food and Drug Administration (FDA) restricted the use of silicone gel breast implants to controlled clinical trials involving breast reconstruction.[1] By this action, the FDA dramatically curtailed who was allowed to be a buyer.

Adverse health impacts make implants unbearable or less desirable than alternatives for many women. The early history of breast implants involved the use of a variety of materials. Paraffin injected into the breast caused a range of complications. It was replaced by the use of glass and ivory balls.[2] These caused infections. Today, there is solid data that silicone is correlated with increased health hazards such as respiratory and brain cancer—certainly something to give one pause to reconsider.[3] The FDA also lists other impacts.[4]

---

[1] National Cancer Institute, "National Cancer Institute Breast Implant Study," September 22, 2004, http://www.nci.nih.gov/newscenter/siliconefactsheet (accessed September 5, 2005).

[2] A Board Certified Plastic Surgeon Resource, "History of Breast Implants," 2005, http://www.aboardcertifiedplasticsurgeonresource.com/breast_implants/history.html (accessed September 5, 2005).

[3] National Cancer Institute, "Breast Implant Study."

[4] U.S. Food and Drug Administration, "FDA Breast Implant Handbook," 2004, http://www.fda.gov/cdrh/breastimplants/handbook2004/specificissues.htmlm (accessed September 6, 2005).

Note that the regulatory and health barriers described above operate in different ways. In the former case, the barrier restricts access to a good by prohibiting a customer segment (women not in clinical trails for breast reconstruction) from buying it. In the latter case, the barrier ensures that the net utility calculation comes out negative. However, both factors are barriers because they constrain who will be a buyer,

A third mode of operation for barriers is also common. The barrier may ensure that any net utility calculation comes out unfavorable. This mode is the basis for hypercompetition, in which one competitor raises barriers for others by drastically cutting prices or engaging in other predatory behavior. (Microsoft was notorious for hypercompetition for years.) Consider that the United States accounts for an estimated 350,000 implants a year, about 60 per cent of global demand. According to Silimed, a Brazilian manufacturer of silicone implants, the industry is fraught with cut-throat competition.[5] Hypercompetition is also seen in a July 2005 contest held by a bar in Penticton, British Columbia. Seeking to pull in more business, the bar held a contest during which 36 contestants sought a free set of breast implants, including surgery.[6] (If this sounds weird and a bit deranged, think about extreme make-over reality TV.)

Note that a fourth mode of operation is to limit what can be sold or offered for sale to anyone. Intellectual property (IP) rights are one way to raise such barriers, as they restrict what other players can make, use, offer for sale, or sell. Brava is a breast enhancement system based on the regular and extended use of gentle suction.[7] The suction is supplied by a microprocessor controlled unit in a special bra. Eleven patents and one patent pending are used to protect the IP and limit competition. Thus, for a competitor to sell a similar product, they would have to find a way to circumvent the patents or have them declared invalid.

Obviously, regulations and standards can also operate in this mode. For example, the FDA prevents medical devices for breast enlargement from being sold that cannot sustain the claims being made for them.

Barriers limiting what can be sold can emerge in other ways. Competition can be a barrier if the competition meets end-user needs better than your technology. Indeed, sometimes it is not even necessary that the competition actually is superior, so long as it is perceived to be superior. Brand

---

[5] Chinadaily.com, "Boom in Busts," *Shanghi Star,* April 10, 2003, http://app1.chinadaily.com.cn/star/2003/0410/fe21–1.html (accessed September 5, 2005).
[6] Amy Carmichael, "Women Spin Wheel for Free Breast Implants at B.C. Nightclub," *The Cannon* (July 25, 2005), http://www.thecannon.ca/news_details.php?id=2167 (accessed September 5, 2005).
[7] See the Brava web site at http://www.brava.com/home.asp (accessed September 5, 2005).

loyalty and goodwill towards a particular company can contribute to such perceptions—so can the opinion of respected people or publications.

Prescription estrogen-based hormone therapy can be used for breast enlargement. Of course, high doses of estrogen can be cancer causing. Thus, there is an industrial segment of herbal product companies that claim they get estrogen-like results without the risk by using phytoestrogens, which are non-hormonal plant estrogens that stimulate new breast tissue growth.

A variety of plant extracts are mixed in the pills. Several sites claim to have survey data on effectiveness that provide objective comparisons (for example, *http://www.mdbreast.com/pill_reviews.htm*). Of course, these studies are likely bogus as Consumer Labs found no scientific evidence to support breast enhancement through use of dietary supplements.[8] The FDA concluded that effectiveness of these products is unlikely. Further, if they were to work, then they would have likely caused breast cancer as factors that cause proliferation in the breast, like estrogen, are linked to an increase in risk of breast cancer.[9] Nonetheless, they likely affect what is bought by people willing to buy the supplements.

If comparison of herbal mixtures of phytoestrogens seems too esoteric, consider the editor's choices on computer hardware and software from sources like *PC Magazine* or CNET. The basic principle is the same. Poorly rated competitors should have a harder time selling their products as the low rating constitutes a barrier to entry.

A fifth mode of operation is limiting who can sell. In the case of Brava, sales are conducted through authorized Brava system physicians, which in plain English means people who have a license to sell it. In most jurisdictions, where public health and safety is involved, licenses are required to sell. For example, the State of Michigan requires almost every food establishment to obtain a license prior to commercially handling, serving, or even giving food to the general public.[10]

What our review confirms is that barriers can be categorized by the component of a transaction that they affect. It really does not matter what kind of technology we are researching. Computer software can be

---

[8] Consumer Labs, "Review Article: Breast Enhancement Supplements," April 16, 2002, http://www.consumerlab.com/results/besupp.asp (accessed September 6, 2005).
[9] U.S. Food and Drug Administration, "Herbal Medicines and Breast Cancer Risk," updated May 26, 2005, http://envirocancer.cornell.edu/factsheet/diet/fs53.herbal.cfm (accessed September 6, 2005). See also Sorokin, "Clinical Trials of Phytoestrogens for Breast Cancer," February 5, 2004, http://nccam.nih.gov/research/concepts/consider/phytoestrogen.htm, (accessed December 19, 2005).
[10] Michigan Department of Agriculture, "Who Needs a License to Sell Food?," 2005, http://www.michigan.gov/mda/0,1607,7–125–1569–11869—,00.html (accessed September 5, 2005).

examined using the same approach as breast augmentation. What counts is finding out if, and when (and how long), various factors may inhibit your ability to sell your technology to the customers you have identified.

Often identifying barriers facing adoption of existing technology can point towards factors that will make your technology attractive.

In 2000, we were tasked by the EPA with finding an application for a method of formulating replacement adhesives that replace volatile organic compounds (VOCs) and hazardous air pollutants (HAPs) based adhesives, caulks and sealants. The method used commercially available monomers to formulate monomer/polymer mixtures into two-component adhesives. Viscosity, working time, bond strength, and cost were critical parameters. The R&D to date suggested that the adhesives resulting from the proposed work would be cost-competitive with solvent-based adhesives because of less shrinkage than those containing water or solvent; better thermal and flow resistance than hot melts; and an ability to be used on heat-sensitive substrates. The formulations all involved a system in which a nonvolatile monomer served as both a vehicle (replacing solvents) and a binder. Polymerization occurred through a variety of curing methods, including UV, visible light, epoxy-amine cure, and redox reactions. We found an application in secondary wood processing. That industry is a major user of adhesives, consuming around $1.6 billion worth at the time. The secondary wood processing industry consists of cabinet-making, office and kitchen furniture, foam, and lamination industries. Manufactures still continue to use a large amount of solvent-base adhesives for performance reasons.

What was critical for our analysis is that there was no market force favoring adoption of "*green*" adhesives. The adhesives industry, as a whole, had already adopted a "green" solvent-free approach. Thus, we had to find a place where superior properties to those out there already were needed.

A member of our staff spoke with the chair of the Forest Products Society's Adhesive Group. He agreed the solvent problem had been largely addressed by technology (water-solubles and hot melts) yet the performance of "green" adhesives remained an issue. We also found a number of anecdotal communications from sources such as wood industry newsgroups and listservers that stated the same. Speed was an issue frequently mentioned. Given this data, and the fact the EPA technology could be stretched to provide fast-curing, we were able to find concurrent engineering partners in the wood products sector willing to participate as test sites and advisors. With their help we identified 23 design parameters to guide subsequent R&D. While there are many environmentally friendly adhesives in the forest industries, there are problems with the newly introduced aqueous and hot-melt adhesives. These parameters were technical barriers to adoption of existing "green" adhesives: (1) slow curing, (2) warping, (3) instability in freeze/thaw conditions, (4) delamination, (5) misting, (6) adhesive breakdown in pumps and regulators, (7) the need for additional equipment, such as backer sheets, to absorb excess water, and (8) extra heat or evaporative aids. In addition, where furniture is sent through an oven to speed up evaporation, additional production considerations may be disadvantages: (9) the retrofit of existing equipment, (10) increasing oven capacity because of water's ability to trap heat, (11) slowing ovens because of longer evaporation times, (12) damage to the substrate by oven drying, (13) extra energy costs, (14) production of sludge instead of VOCs or HAPs, (15) more time required to clean ovens, (16) more labor for maintenance, (17) constant monitoring of adhesive mixtures for viscosity. Additionally, (18) water-solubles may not pass flammability testing. Hot melts, adhesives that are heated prior to use, are also used extensively since the elevated heat increases viscosity and eliminates or reduces the need for solvents. Again, as with water-based adhesives, some of the disadvantages are: (19) lower shear strength at higher temperatures, (20) gelling may occur, (21) workers may literally be burned, (22) short shelf or pot life, and (23) the need for specialized hot-melt equipment. These limitations to competing technology all represent excellent opportunities for adhesive formulations that require neither heat nor water to cure.

Usually putting the name of the application and the string "barriers to entry" in a web search engine is sufficient to get your started. For example, tossing breast augmentation and barriers to entry into Google turns up an article by David Tarantino.[11] The article discusses breast augmentation in the context of marketing strategies and barriers to entry for cosmetic surgery. Tarantino uses Michael Porter's Five Forces analysis to tease out barriers and strategies for overcoming them. (Porter's forces are threat of new entrants; threat of substitute services; bargaining power of buyers; bargaining power of suppliers, and rivalry between competitors.)

---

[11] David Tarantino, "Developing a Marketing Strategy—Nuts and Bolts of Business," *Physician Executive* (January-February 2003), www.findarticles.com/p/articles/mi_m0843/is_1_29/ai_96500904.

A submittal to the Committee on Technology of the National Science and Technology Council by the president of the Health Industry Manufacturers Association in 1999 highlights litigation worries as a barrier to entry for breast and other medical implants.[12]

As barriers are found, I find it useful to enter them in a table like the following. The data is initial impressions of barriers for silicon breast implants based on initial web searching.

Barriers to Implant Market Entry	Affect Buyer	Affect Seller	Affect Goods Sold	Period of Applicability	Weight
IP		X	X	Until 2020	High
Regulations	X	X	X	1992 (ongoing)	High
Standards		X	X	Uncertain	Low
Competition	X	X		2000 forward	Medium
Authoritative views			X	Indefinite	High
Adverse impacts	X			Indefinite	Medium
Liability	X	X	X	Indefinite	Low (once FDA approved)

Note that the last column in the table is the weight of the factor on an ordinal scale of high, medium, and low. The weight represents how much impact we feel the barrier is likely to have on our ability to enter the market with our own silicone breast implant. The higher the weight (mass), the stronger the net market forces needed to overcome the barrier.

Also note that because this is initial data, it is important to check it. Usually if data is from secondary sources, it makes sense to check it with primary sources, such as a few experts from the FDA, NIH, university, or private sector. (As with most of our examples, you do not have to agree with the data entries. What counts is understanding the approach used.)

Market Forces

We can categorize market forces by how they will affect market transactions. Recall the basic structure of a transaction: We have a buyer, a seller, and a trade. So as with barriers, to impact the transaction, a force has to affect either the buyer or seller, or what is being traded. Market forces of interest will affect one of these components or elements to a transaction.

---

[12] Pamela Bailey, "Priorities for Federal Innovation Reform," September 17, 1999, http://www.ostp.gov/html/rand/summit/MedicalReformHIMA.doc (accessed September 5, 2005).

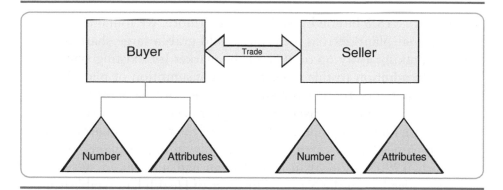

EXHIBIT 6.2   Quantifying Players

We shall start by looking at forces that affect who are the players in a market transaction and how many of them there are (see Exhibit 6.2). On the one hand player forces are macro-level drivers in that they affect how many people engage in a practice. At this level, the market force drives or draws people into or out of an arena. In other word, macro-level forces affect market size. On the other hand, depending on which attributes are affected, player market forces may be micro-level drivers as shifts in skills and absorptive capacity can affect willingness to use, and interest in using, one technology rather than another in the conduct of a specific practice. Micro-level forces thus affect market share.

For the Centers for Disease Control, we assessed whether a new drug for cancer prevention should be patented. The compound was naturally occurring and extracted from plants. In studies, it prevented the expansion and spread of neoplastic progressions. It inhibited the growth of cancer cells and reduced the size and incidence of chemically-induced skin tumors. Furthermore, in vivo studies using nude mice suggested that it significantly inhibited malignant invasion and metastasis. The problem was a market barrier due to competition. The market space was crowded with chemically related compounds.

Despite this barrier, we recommended patenting the compound. The reason was dramatic growth in consumer demand for plant-based drugs. The market for plant-derived drugs is growing. According to a 2003 Business Communications Company report worldwide sales of plant-derived drugs were expected to soar from $13.7 billion

(Continued)

in 2001 to $18.8 billion by 2007.[13] Furthermore, we found data suggesting that plant-derived medicines could grab a large share of the market, taking away up to 30% of the market for existing synthetic drugs. In addition to this trend toward consumption of plant-based drugs by patients, there was a strong market force supporting active development of plant-derived drugs by pharmaceutical companies. We found data indicating that in 1980 none of the top 250 pharmaceutical companies had research activities involving higher plants, but by the early 1990's, more than half of them had introduced such programs. Indeed, even the National Institute of Health had established a natural products branch in the National Cancer Institute. Bottom line: These market forces supported adoption of a plant-derived substitute for existing synthetic substitutes if it could deliver on treatment and low secondary impact promises. The market forces suggested the barrier due to competition could be overcome, making patenting justified.

We shall simplify our discussion in this chapter by referring to buyers and sellers as the players. It is important to remember, however, that buyers and sellers may be organizations that are themselves comprised of multiple players. So far, we have touched on three roles in buyers: the end user, the person who actually does the procurement, and the ultimate decision-maker. Our discussion applies to all of these roles. Similarly, in the seller there is the marketer or deal-maker, and developer, and a decision-maker. Again, our discussion is intended to be generic. So, now that the qualifiers are out of the way, let's see how this works.

In our discussion of market forces, we will introduce a new example: tires. The pneumatic tire consists of a rubber or other elastomer in which air is enclosed air to improve traction and reduce vibration. It was invented by Robert W. Thomson, a Scottish engineer, in 1845. But as with the zipper, the original invention did not catch on. At that time, wheels were made out of solid rubber, prepared with the aid of Charles Goodyear's vulcanization process, invented only nine years earlier. Solid rubber tires were able to absorb shocks, resist cuts and abrasions—important for the quality of the dirt roads over which goods moved at the time and they were strong enough to bear heavy loads.[14] Solid rubber tires were a vast

---

[13] Nutrasolutions.com, "Plant-Derived Drug Sales Climbing," March 1, 2003, http://www.nutrasolutions.com/CDA/ArticleInformation/news/news_item/0,1273,112869,00.html.

[14] Mary Bellis, "History of Tires," *About* (2005), http://inventors.about.com/library/inventors/bltires.htm (accessed September 5, 2005).

improvement over traditional wagon wheels made out of wood or metal. So, the early pneumatic tires were a solution looking for a problem.

Around 30 years later, in 1888 John Boyd Dunlop of Scotland reinvented the pneumatic tire. (Dunlop claimed not to know of Thomson's invention.) This time the pneumatic tire did catch on. Why?[15]

What was different was the bicycle—a different use for tires. For bicycles, solid rubber tires are heavy and give a poor ride. Pneumatics are clearly superior. Since the modern bicycle was only invented in 1861 by Ernest Michaux, who invented the pedal and cranks still the basis for what we use today, there were few bicyclists in 1845. Indeed, the name bicycle only came into use in 1869.[16]

In other words, we can trace the rise in the number of bicyclists, an attribute of the buyers (being a bicyclist) as a market force driving the rise in demand for a better tire, where better means lighter and more shock absorbing and smoother riding. Increasing numbers of bicyclists is a market force in a positive direction for pneumatic tire sales with a magnitude equal to the increase in the number of bicycles sold. The more bicyclists, the more pneumatic tires we can expect to sell.

Over time, other market forces come into play. In 1908, Henry Ford introduced the Model T. Clearly the rise in automobiles was a driver for more tire sales. But the impact on pneumatic tire sales was not there. Indeed, André Michelin had already put pneumatic tires on an automobile in 1895, but the innovation did not catch on until 1911 when Philip Strauss invented a tire, which was a combination of a solid rubber outer tire and air filled inner tube. (The tubeless tire was invented in 1903 by P.W. Litchfield of Goodyear Tire Company, but it was not successfully sold until 1954.)[17]

Under U.S. Department of Agriculture funding we supported commercialization of a simple, cost-effective, deacidification method for preserving library and archive materials. Manuscripts could be treated at the storage point, be it a library, archive, or storage facility. The key innovation was developing a process that did not involve the use of liquids or complex mechanical equipment and could be conducted in

(Continued)

---

[15] Ibid.
[16] Ibid.
[17] Continental AG, "The History of General Tire from 1915 Up to Now," 2005, www.conti-online.com/generator/www/com/en/generaltire/automobile/themes/history/ctwl_history_en.html (accessed September 5, 2005).

normal office workroom environments without specially trained personnel.

There was a clear infrastructural driver for this technology. According to the U.S. Library of Congress, the older a book or manuscript usually the better it survives. Paper-based materials older than 150 years are in many cases in better shape than those less than 50 years old. The reason is that longer cellulose chains in paper are stronger and more supple than shorter ones. The longer the chains, the more a piece of paper is able to withstand degradation by acids and other abuse without showing visible signs of wear and tear. Early papers, such as those made up to the middle of the 19th century, were made from cotton and linen rags, making them still strong and durable, especially if they were stored properly under conditions that were not overly warm or humid. Most modern papers are based on newsprint, which have a relatively short life span due to short fibers. Further, in the presence of moisture, the alum used in the manufacturing process generates sulfuric acid. Acid also is absorbed from pollution. Newsprint is particularly vulnerable, which is seen in the brown and brittle edges of old newspapers and books.[18]

We can see there are several infrastructural drivers for adoption of this technology. The shift in paper fibers, the shift in how paper is made, and increasing pollution all make deacidification necessary for long-term storage. Further, the amount of paper used soared in the middle of the century, creating a body of material increasingly needing treatment as it ages. We also can guess that these drivers operate only over a limited time frame as by now paper-based documentation is almost entirely replaced by electronic storage.

What was needed to allow sales of pneumatic tires to soar were paved roads. Dirt roads were the norm until the turn of the century. The absence of paved roads was a market barrier to adoption of pneumatic tires. A barrier to paving roads with asphalt use was material supply and cost (see Exhibit 6.3). Almost all asphalt used in the United States was coming from the natural sources of Lake Trinidad and Bermudez Lake in Venezuela. By 1907, however, production of refined asphalt surpassed importation of natural asphalt. Rising domestic production of asphalt was a market force that helped overcome the lack of roads. With domestically produced asphalt,

---

[18] Library of Congress, "The Deterioration and Preservation of Paper: Some Essential Facts," *Preservation* (July 19, 2002), www.loc.gov/preserv/deterioratebrochure.html (accessed September 6, 2005).

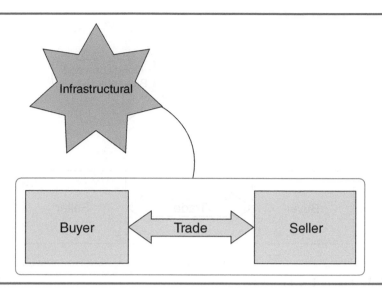

EXHIBIT 6.3   Barrier to Trade

this barrier was removed, highway construction soared (the rising rate of construction being a market force), and pneumatic tires on cars become standard equipment.[19]

As more asphalt highways were built, demand for increased asphalt highway building grew. Congress enacted the Federal-Aid Road Act until 1916, which made funding for highway improvement in order to get "farmers out of the mud." The Federal Highway Act of 1921 was passed which provided the funding to build paved highways, creating the Federal Highway System. That bill meant even more roads suitable for pneumatic tires. (Later, a similar dynamic was involved in adoption of tubeless tires.) Eisenhower's signing of the Federal-Aid Highway Act of 1956 built the interstate freeways, which, together with improvements in automobile technology affecting speed, drove sales of tubeless tires.[20]

What this discussion adds is another type of market forces— infrastructure forces. Infrastructural forces ease or increase constraints on sales of goods being offered in the market, by facilitating or hindering a buyer's ability to garner net utility through their acquisition. They are important as they help overcome barriers to adoption of technology. As such they can affect the macro-level, that is the number of people active in

---

[19] National Asphalt Paving Association,"History of Asphalt," 2004, http://www.hot-mix.org/history.php (accessed September 5, 2005).
[20] About, "How the Wheels Got Turning," *A Historical Perspective on American Roads* (2005), http://inventors.about.com/library/inventors/blcar3.htm (accessed September 5, 2005).

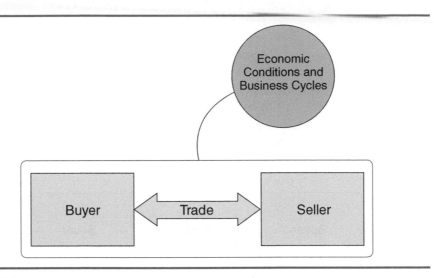

EXHIBIT 6.4   Macro-Level Forces

an arena, or the micro-level, what options people will select to conduct specific practices in that arena. Indeed, a factor for bringing rural buyers into the bicycle market was that in 1893, the Federal Government established an Office of Road Inquiry with a budget of $10,000 and the job of encouraging rural road development to improve travel of wagons, coaches, and bicycles on dirt roads.[21]

The Federal-Aid Road Act did not have a large magnitude of impact. The reason is the country entered World War I shortly after its enactment. Thus federal largess had to wait for better times, which arrived with the Roaring Twenties. The wealth being generated enabled allocating funding to the Bureau of Public Roads (the old Office of Road Inquiry renamed) to build the two-lane paved highways called for by the Federal Highway Act.

The discussion highlights that forces influencing money are another category of driver. Shifts in economic conditions and business cycles affect how much of it is around and available for purchasing.

Note that infrastructural and economic forces have another impact on markets (see Exhibit 6.4). They can also stimulate new sellers to enter the market. For example, by the time General Tire was founded in 1915, over 300 companies were making tires,[22] a testimony to the rapid rise in

---

[21] Ibid.
[22] Continental AG, "The History of General Tire from 1915 Up to Now." http://www.conti-online.com/generator/www/com/en/generaltire/automobile/themes/history/ctwl_history_en.html, (accessed September 5, 2005).

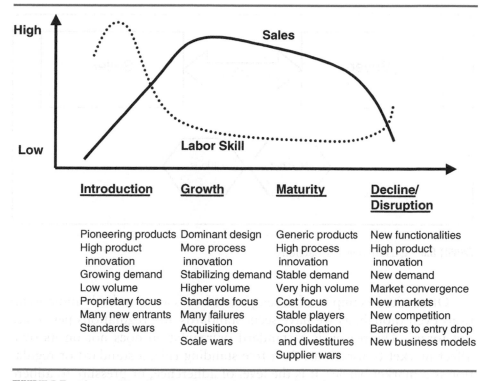

EXHIBIT 6.5   Phase of Product Family Development and Exploitation

Introduction	Growth	Maturity	Decline/ Disruption
Pioneering products	Dominant design	Generic products	New functionalities
High product innovation	More process innovation	High process innovation	High product innovation
Growing demand	Stabilizing demand	Stable demand	New demand
Low volume	Higher volume	Very high volume	Market convergence
Proprietary focus	Standards focus	Cost focus	New markets
Many new entrants	Many failures	Stable players	New competition
Standards wars	Acquisitions	Consolidation and divestitures	Barriers to entry drop
	Scale wars	Supplier wars	New business models

automobile sales—automobiles being a key part of the infrastructure needed to sustain the demand for tires.

As industries grow, buyers tend to seek different kinds of technology to address market needs on the one hand, and cut labor and other costs on the other.[23] Exhibit 6.5 depicts these relationships as industries move through phases of product family development and exploitation. (Examples of product families include solid rubber tires, pneumatic tires, and radial tires.)

Clearly another category of market forces are those affecting the number and kinds of substitutes being sold in the market. By kinds we refer to both trends in technology and trends in industrial sectors with respect to pricing and the bundle of functionality, characteristics, and features offered. As these forces relate to the development of substitute goods, we shall call them development forces (see Exhibit 6.6).

---

[23] The discussion draws on the work of Abernathy and Utterback. For a good overview, see Utterback, *Mastering the Dynamics of Innovation* (Boston: Harvard Business School Press, 1994).

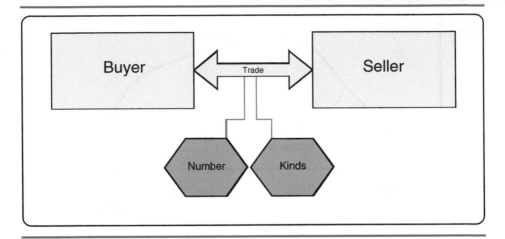

EXHIBIT 6.6   Quantifying Transactions

Often-cited examples of development forces are standards and regulations even though, as we have seen, standards and regulations per se are not forces. The reason is a standard or regulation does not on its own affect market transactions. As a free-standing rule, a standard or regulation is a market barrier. It is the level of adherence, or pressure to adhere to standards which actually is the force. This need for an action or behavior is even clearer with respect to regulations, as we are used to saying some regulations are *en-forced* and others are not, meaning they can be safely ignored. What we measure is the increase in promulgation or some other indicator that this standard or regulation should be taken seriously when describing or projecting market dynamics.

The emergence of flat-run tires illustrate this point. Flat-run tires can be used at zero-pressure when driving at normal speeds for enough distance to get to a repair station in the event of a puncture, deep cut or other damage to the tire. "Anti-*puncture*" tires have been patented since at least 1892. By 1934, Goodyear had an inner tube that deflated progressively rather than blowing out. Goodyear's self-supporting tire was introduced in 1978. In 1996, Michelin introduced a tire using a solid inner wheel support on which a pressure-less tire could run safely for some distance. But such tires never became mainstream.

In 2001, Firestone, a unit of Bridgewater, suffered through a series of blowouts and related deaths that brought tire safety to the forefront of public awareness. The company's tire recall was perhaps the largest recall in U.S. history. This increase in tire recalls was a significant market force leading to expansion of market offerings of self-supporting tires as well as other tire technology.

Responding to the public uproar, Congress passed the Transportation Recall Enhancement, Accountability and Documentation (TREAD) Act in 2000.[24] That law and the associated public pressure, in turn, spurred further innovation in tire technology given the substantial likelihood of enforcement. For example, TREAD mandates installation of tire pressure monitoring systems (TPMS) in all U.S. automobiles and light trucks by 2006.[25] The uproar over the safety of tires also provided the impetus needed to spur widespread commercial introduction of flat-run tires. BF Goodrich, Bridgestone, Dunlop, Firestone, Goodyear, Kumho, Michelin, Pirelli, and Yokohama all now sell self-supporting run flat tires.[26]

As with barriers, we can create a simple table for recording data on market forces collected during market research. We want to know what the force is, in what direction it operates, how strong it is, and over what period it operates.

ESTIMATING MARKET SIZE

We can estimate total addressable market size in four ways: finding hard data on sales, using comparables, building up sales from the number of users and frequency of purchasing, or parsing down from aggregate market size data.

The easiest way to figure out a market size is to find data giving you the market size. According to the FDA, breast implants were on the rise throughout the 1990s, despite the acknowledged dangers. Exhibit 6.7 provides information on the number of implant surgeries in the United States between 1992 and 1999.[27] If we were interested in the market for that period for surgeries, we need not look further. If we want more recent data, we can look at the website of the Food and Drug Administration which reports American Society of Plastic Surgeons data indicating there were nearly 255,000 breast enhancement implant surgeries in 2003, nearly twice the number done in 1998. Another 68,000 women received

---

[24] CBS News, "Yet Another Recall For Firestone," January 2, 2001, http://www.cbsnews.com/stories/2001/01/02/national/main260774.shtml (accessed September 5, 2005).
[25] Desai, Chance, and Ozawa, "Steering Safer Wheels for America's Motorists," *RFDesign* (2004), http://rfdesign.com/mag/406rfdf4.pdf (accessed September 5, 2005).
[26] Tire Track, "Flat-Run Tires," 2005, http://www.tirerack.com/tires/tiretech/techpage.jsp?techid=56 (accessed September 5, 2005).
[27] "Making an Informed Decision about Breast Implants," *FDA Consumer Magazine*, September-October 2004, http://www.fda.gov/fdac/features/2004/504_implants.html, (accessed September 7, 2005).

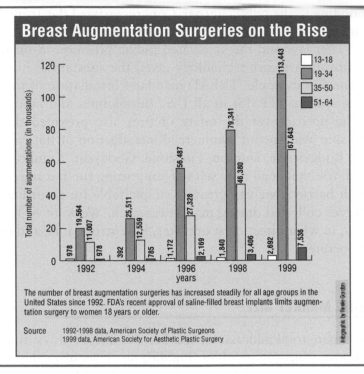

The number of breast augmentation surgeries has increased steadily for all age groups in the United States since 1992. FDA's recent approval of saline-filled breast implants limits augmentation surgery to women 18 years or older.

Source   1992-1998 data, American Society of Plastic Surgeons
          1999 data, American Society for Aesthetic Plastic Surgery

EXHIBIT 6.7   Breast Augmentation Surgeries on the Rise

breast implants for reconstruction following mastectomy due to cancer or other disease.

We can use this data to extrapolate into the future. The rule of thumb is you can go as many periods forward as you have going back. We draw our curve (which can be a straight line) and then adjust it to take into account market barriers and forces. For example, in 1992 the FDA called for a moratorium on silicone implants, except for certain circumstances. Thus, if we are projecting their sales, we have to account for the fact that the FDA's action constituted a barrier that skewed buying in favor of saline-based implants.

Of course, in order to project market size over multiple years on the basis of data from the past,, we need a growth rate. The compound annual growth rate (CAGR) is often used to estimate growth. It is a smoothed rate, meaning it assumes the year over year growth rate is constant. It is calculated as follows:

$$\text{CAGR} = (\text{ending value/beginning value})^{(1/\# \text{ of years})} - 1$$

In other words, we take the nth root of the total percentage growth rate. Here n is the number of years in the period for which we are calculating growth.[28] If the projection is in currency rather than units, be aware that inflation can create to misleading results.

The next easiest way is to find a comparable. For example, if we know how many tires are sold for automobiles in the United States, and we have developed a tire pressure monitoring gauge that goes in an automobile tire, then the number of car tires sold represents the total number of gauges that can sold by ourselves and all of our competitors. Similarly, if we want to know the market size for a new farmed fish, such as arctic char, we can benchmark against another similar farm raised fish, say tilapia, and then adjust those numbers to take into account the difference between char and tilapia.

Once again, we have to take into account barriers and forces. According to the U.S. Department of Transportation, looking only at commercial fleets, around 7.08% of all tires are underinflated by 20 psi or more while only 44.15% of all tires are within ±5 psi of their target pressure. The primary consequences are increased tire wear, shorter tire life, poorer fuel economy, and more road calls. After examining the economic impacts of these consequences, the DoT concluded that "For a typical TL or LTL operator, improper tire inflation increases the total operating costs by about $750 annually per tractor-trailer combination. Cost penalties for other types of fleets are similar and range from about $600 to $800."[29] So, clearly cost is a force encouraging adoption of tire air pressure systems. Indeed, the DoT found that "Tire inflation maintenance practices correlate closely with the size of the fleet,"[30] leading us to expect that larger fleets, where the savings impacts are more readily apparent, will be among the early adopters of tire air pressure monitoring systems even if there are no regulations mandating them.

Also pretty straight forward is building up from the number of users. According to the EPA, there are about 195 million cars on roads in the U.S. today. Four tires per car gives us a market size of 780 million tires.[31] But this size is low as it does not take into account replacement buying as tires wear out. The EPA tells us that U.S. drivers drive 6.3 billion miles every single day, but what we really need to estimate market size is the

---

[28] Answers.com, "Compound Average Growth Rate," n.d., http://www.answers.com/topic/compound-annual-growth-rate-cagr (accessed September 6, 2005).

[29] Lang, "Tech Brief: Commercial Motor Vehicle Tire Pressure Sensors," July, 2005, http://www.fmcsa.dot.gov/facts-research/briefs/tire-pressure-sensors.htm (accessed September 7, 2005).

[30] Ibid.

[31] U.S. Environmental Protection Agency, "A Consumer Guide to Auto Emission Inspection and Maintenance Programs," updated February 1, 2005, www.epa.gov/otaq/cfa-air.htm (accessed September 6, 2005).

average mileage per car per some period of time to estimate replacement purchasing due to wear. Another way to get replacement is to track sales of autos per year, assume the tires are new, and then assume they need replacing about five to seven years later, which is a common estimate of when tires need replacing.[32]

When building up, the protocol is to find a solid number you can use, be it a component, subsystem, system, or platform. Estimate the number of units you will sell per unit of the known item. Do the math. In other words, if I need an average of three sensors per floor, the average number of floors in a commercial building is four, and there are one-half kazillion commercial buildings, the number of sensors (excluding replacement units) is calculated as follows.

$$3 \times 4 \times \tfrac{1}{2} \text{ kazillion}$$

Often when building up a market estimate, it is difficult to get good data on all customer segments. For example, we know tractor trailer fleets have pretty good track records at maintaining tire pressure and are likely to have strong economic benefit from adoption of a system that improves pressure control. Any fan of country music knows the big trucks are the semis, the 18 wheelers. (Semi tractors commonly have 3 axles. The front, or "*steer*" axle has two wheels, the two rear drive axles have double wheels, making a total of 10. The remaining 8 are on the trailer.)

Using data from the U.S. Census, we find there were around 9 million tractors on the road with three or more axles in 2002, up about 24% from the number in 1997.[33] Some of these pull one trailer, some two, some three. Now suppose we simply assume that no matter how many trailers there is only one Tire Pressure Monitoring Systems (TPMS) per semi. That means that if we are selling TPMSs there was a potential market for 90 million units in 2002 just assuming each truck is retrofitted. Clearly we have underestimated the market. We have not accounted for new trucks entering the fleet. Nor can we assume, barring federal regulation, that all trucks will have TPMS. So let's be conservative. Let's say for sake of argument only one-quarter will get one in the next five years. That is about 22.5 million units that can be sold. Still pretty good.

Now TPMSs range in price from $20 to several hundred dollars,

[32] Eckert, "When Are Tires Too Old?" *InService* (March 8, 2005), http://inserviceextra .firechief.com/ar/firefighting_tires_old/ (accessed September 6, 2005).

[33] U.S. Census, "*Vehicle Inventory and Use Survey,*" Table 2a., *2002 Economic Census* (December 2004), http://www.census.gov/prod/ec02/ec02tv-us.pdf (accessed September 7, 2005).

> It is always wise to check your market size estimate with a second source. According to *Sensors Magazine,* once Federal regulations kick in (estimated in 2006), TPMS sales will explode to around 100–150 million units annually.[34] So 22.5 million TPMS units for U.S. semis seems plausible.

depending on how sophisticated is the system.[35] In a cost-benefit analysis, the U.S. National Highway Transportation Safety Administration used a price of around $48 to $69 per unit. So, let's take $50 per unit to make the math easy. That means we have an initial estimate of the total addressable market for TPMSs for domestic semis over the next five years of around $1.125 billion. Ohhhhh. Suppose we are licensing our TPMS technology. (Actually, if the market explodes in 2006, we are late for licensing, but we will stick with the example having come this far. Let's say the royalty is between 2 and 5 percent. Let's use 2%. Do the math. Still pretty good, eh?

This kind of analysis is called a threshold analysis. What we are looking for is a threshold level above which market entry is worthwhile. Once we have it, anything more is gravy. We can do a threshold analysis with any of the methods for calculating a market size.

The final way to get a market size is to find a known market size and parse down. This method is fraught with dangers as you have to be very careful not to count apples when you are doing market research on oranges.

Suppose we are at a university and Professor Smith has just developed a new digital X-ray image analysis algorithm that can dramatically improve the results of mammography. We are looking for a threshold market analysis as we need some idea of market size to determine whether it makes sense to apply for a patent or copyright on the invention.

We recall we have market data on the number of women with breast implants. The National Cancer Institute estimates there are between 1.5 million and 2 million women in the United States that have had breast implants since they first appeared on the market in 1962.[36] A study reported in 2004 found the screening mammography missed 55% of breast

[34] Mnif, "A Smart Tire Pressure Monitoring System," *Sensors Magazine* (November 2001), http://www.sensorsmag.com/articles/1101/index.htm (accessed September 7, 2005).
[35] Truckworld.com, "Pressure Eyes," *Truck World Online* (July 23, 2003), http://www.truckworld.com/How-To-Tech/03-tire_pressure/03-pressure_2.html (accessed September 7, 2005).
[36] National Cancer Institute, "National Cancer Institute Breast Implant Study." http://www.nci.nih.gov/newscenter/siliconefactsheet.

cancers in women who had undergone breast augmentation.[37] That means there is on the order of 80 thousand women who would benefit from this invention, assuming it can detect cancers behind implants. (We say on the order as we have not taken into account deaths that have already occurred or the number of women who have removed their implants.) Since the same study reports cancers are missed in 37% of the women who do not have implants, the market is likely larger.

The cost of a screening mammography in the United States is around $100.[38] Again for sake of argument, let's say a royalty rate for Smith's algorithm is 1% of the price for patients with whom it is used. Taking the implant patients and assuming one screening every other year, we have a two year average of $40,000 in revenues per year. Enough to put a child through a high-end private college for that year or hire a post doc and a part-time work study student for the lab. Plus it may save lives. All good things.

Of course, we have to adjust the total addressable market by who is buying. In Chapter 5, we saw that different groups of buyers will enter the market at different times. If there is no dominant design for our technology and the market is immature, perhaps only innovators have entered, limiting the total addressable market at this time to perhaps 3% of what cumulative sales might end up being. (The actual percentage is an empirical question, but the work done by Everett Rodgers and others allows us to make an initial guess.) Furthermore, market barriers may reduce that number further while market forces may add or subtract buyers at any given point in time depending on the net direction and magnitude of the forces.

We also have to adjust the total addressable market in light of the kind of innovation we are introducing. Recall that in Chapter Three we distinguished between different types of innovations. By looking at whether the innovation introduces new features or functionalities and whether it uses a technology approach known in the market or new to the market, we can create a four-cell matrix.

	Better Yields on Existing Functionalities	New Functionalities
Builds on Existing Technical Approaches	Incremental innovation	Adaptive innovation
New Technical Approaches	Radical innovation	Disruptive innovation

---

[37] Gardner, "Breast Implants Can Mar Mammo Detection," January 27, 2004, http://www.hon.ch/News/HSN/517133.html (accessed September 7, 2005).
[38] Imaginis: The Breast Health Resource, "Mammographic Screening is Key to the Early Detection of Breast Cancer," September 2004, http://imaginis.com/breasthealth/screening.asp#cost (accessed September 7, 2005).

The type of innovation influences whether new buyers will enter the market or not, and thus the size of the total addressable market.

	Reallocate Customers	Bring in New Customers
Incremental	X	
Adaptive	X	X
Radical	X	
Disruptive		X

Finally, we noted that adaptive and radical innovations tend to require greater awareness building and education to make their benefits clear, so takeoff of sales is later than with incremental innovations. Disruptive innovations, because they require a shift in the way practices are conducted, usually present the greatest market entry challenge, and take even longer to take off. Whether a radical or adaptive technology experiences delay is an effect of player-based market forces. The delay usually experienced by disruptive technologies is a consequence of the market barrier created by abandoning the dominant design.

Exhibit 6.8 is simply illustrative of this phenomenon and not intended to reflect real data.

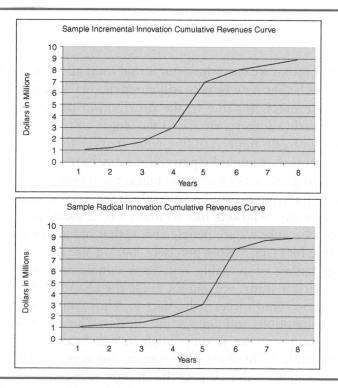

EXHIBIT 6.8 Innovation Type and Revenue Projections

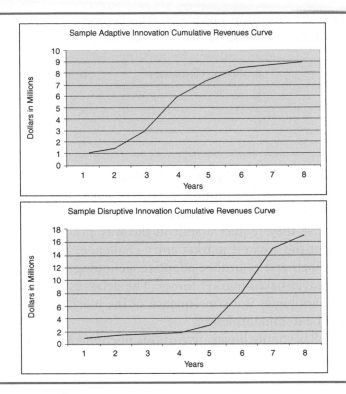

EXHIBIT 6.8   *(Continued)*

The point is that we can adjust our initial total addressable market size estimates by whether new buyers will enter the market, when buyers are likely to make purchases due to the distribution of customer segments (innovators, early adopters, etc.), and the length of time it likely will take to attain take-off. By understanding what market forces are likely to be relevant and how they might help overcome any barriers that exist, we can make educated guesses as to how the market will build.

It is, regrettably, impossible to provide any hard and fast rules for estimating market size. Markets like so many other social phenomena have contingencies because we are people and as that old adage goes: "There is no accounting for taste." More precisely, market size is a matter of a probability distribution of possible outcomes concerning buying behavior. Without empirical study, we cannot guess the shape of that distribution nor what barriers and forces will affect it. With empirical study, we can define our assumptions and make some guesses. These guesses can then be provided to others to see if they laugh in our faces or say, "Yep, that sounds reasonable." This kind of testing, by the way, is what social scientists call face validity—does it pass the straight face test?

Now I am sure there will be folks out there who say, "Whoa! This is a pretty quick and dirty approach to estimating market size." They are of course right. But to do a market size estimate in great detail is costly and in commercialization we have to think about the cost-benefit ratio of the market research as well as the technology. For a low value technology, like Smith's algorithm, it is not worth spending $5,000 to $10,000 to estimate the market size. It is not worth spending $4,000 or $5,000 to buy a Freedonia or Gartner or Frost and Sullivan market study. What is needed is just enough depth to justify going forward and to explain to a potential commercialization partner (licensee, alliance partner, venture capitalist, etc.) what kind of money they can expect to make. Then, if there is interest, you can make the decision as to whether to invest in a detailed market estimate in support of a more detailed valuation. (We shall discuss valuations in Chapter 10.)

To gain confidence in a total addressable market size, we can use an expert panel to formalize our straight face test. We take our best guess and call between three and seven experts. We ask them if the estimate sounds reasonable and if so, why, or if not, why not. We ask them to give us their estimate. Usually by the time you call three people, you are starting to see a pattern in the answers. We average the estimates we receive from the experts and adjust that average in light of the explanations given; the deviation from our own guess gives us an idea of how much confidence to have in our guess.

For now it suffices to note that when making the detailed estimate, the same basic approaches can be used. What changes is how the data is collected and how much you get. You may do year-by-year estimates rather than a quick CAGR, straight line, or exponential extrapolation. You may collect your year-by-year estimates by studying sales histories of competitors, interviews with experts, surveys of potential customers, more extensive literature searching, test marketing, etc. But inevitably, sooner or later you will have to make assumptions. The trick in any market research is to be very clear about the assumptions you are making, to justify why they are reasonable, and to indicate the level of confidence you have in the conclusions you are drawing. Then, if someone does not like the assumptions, they can always substitute their own.

ESTIMATING MARKET SHARE

Market share is a ratio of sales of a specific product, process, or service to the total sales of that product, process, or good in a territory (county, continent, etc.) and arena (or all arenas). It is usually expressed as a percentage of the total addressable market size. Estimating market share is always a bit of a dart toss, unless you are estimating it for a major player in an industry sector or market niche.

The global tire market was around $80 billion as of 2004.[39] There are somewhat over 150 companies that account for most of these sales, with 11 major companies each accounting for over $1 billion in sales.

Now, suppose you are trying to figure out the market share for an in-tire thin film air pressure gauge you want to license. Obviously the market share will vary depending on with whom you license. Suppose you license it to Michelin. They are the number one tire manufacturer in the world. So, you can probably get market share data for them. But what if you figure you can only license your gauge to a couple of the small fry in the industry. Obviously, one way to get a best estimate of market share is to ask them. Sometimes you can find it in Securities and Exchange Commission filings, or other documents that are required to be filed with government agencies.

Sometime the best we can do is figure out the shares for the big guys, subtract that from the total, estimate the number of smaller companies, and divide the remaining share up among them equally. If there are, for sake of argument, $40 billion accounted for by 50 companies that leaves $40 billion to divide up among the remaining 100 tire companies. If we plan on entering the market, in the absence of any other data, we might assume we too can end up with 1/100th of 50% or around .05% of the market. Other times we get lucky and can find data for some countries of interest. For example, the Slovak Republic tire and rubber company Matador had 1.9% of the United Kingdom tire market in 2003.[40]

Note that you can often get basic market share data for larger competitors by going to a data base like Hoovers (*www.hoovers.com*), Dun and Bradstreet (*www.DnB.com*), or Corptech (*www.corptech.com*) and looking at sales data. The problem is that the data is usually only reliable for publicly traded companies, and even for them, the rash of scandals like Enron have to give us pause.

One of the more reliable methods for estimating market share is to call the companies active in an industrial sector selling the products, processes, or services with which you will be competing. You ask sales representatives

[39] Davis, "Global Tire Industry Hits $80 Billion in Sales; High-Performance Tires, Growth in China are Key Factors in Success," *Automotive News* (October 4, 2004), http://www.highbeam.com/library/doc3.asp?DOCID=1G1:123070607&num=1&ao =&FreePremium=BOTH&login=1&ctrlInfo=Round16%3AProdCtrl%3ALogIn%3A LogIn, (accessed September 7, 2005).
[40] Slovakspectator.sk, "Tire-Maker Matador Expands to UK," *The Slovak Spectator* (September 6, 2004), http://www.slovakspectator.sk/clanok-17181.html (accessed September 7, 2005).

of each competitor about their market share. We focus on sales people because their job is to talk up the company and usually they are among the easiest to pump for data. If they cannot answer our questions, we have to go higher up the sales and marketing hierarchy, to a product line manager, or into management.

Usually it is possible to interview most or all of the players, as in most industrial sectors there just are not that many competitors, especially if we only focus on those that seem to be the major players. We seldom see more than 25 to 100 companies we have to call, and for more mature industrial sectors we can usually get away with less. Telephone interviews work best as they allow us to explore various ways of getting at share data. These ways include unit shipments and sales revenues. During the interview we also probe for whom they see as having any meaningful market share and ask for their best guess as to what that share might be.

Be aware that sales people may not know or may even intentionally mislead you. Typically you get more complete and accurate data if you promise to share with the respondent all the information you collect. You can also compare the answers from one company with the estimates concerning their share provided by others. If you can get price data, you can multiply the average price per unit by the number of unit sales to see if it matches the share data provided during the interview.

The current market share distribution should equal 100% of the market. Once initial estimates of the current market shares of competitors are obtained look at the market barriers and forces you have identified. These provide clues as to how to adjust those shares should you, or your technology, enter the market.

In making adjustments, be aware that others may also be entering the market. For example, organic solid state lighting holds the promise of providing low cost, long lasting, low energy consumption white light for general illumination use. A number of large and small firms, plus laboratories, are receiving federal R&D funds in this field (see *http://www.netl .doe.gov/ssl/pro_current_organic.htm*). Looking at the list of awardees, we quickly realize that several firms are positioning to enter the lighting market.

Some of these firms currently make more traditional light bulbs. Others do not. If we are interested in estimating the share that one of the small companies can grab (say Maxdem or Universal Display Corporation) we cannot simply figure out the market shares of current manufacturers of light bulbs and carve out a chunk for the technology of interest. We also have to consider that the other small companies listed on this web page are seeking to penetrate the market and may be grabbing share at the same time. Furthermore, we need to recognize that what we see on the U.S. Department of Energy site is only U.S. government funded awardees. We also have to consider the shares, which other domestic firms not receiving DoE money might grab and the shares foreign competitors might capture.

Whatever numbers you end up with, you still have to figure out where to toss your dart for your market share. As noted, the first step is to figure out who might partner with you or who you are striving to be like. By using their market share, you have a starting point for estimating your market share. If you are non-exclusively licensing, the starting point may involve adding the shares from multiple companies. As with market size, you take this best guess and call between three and seven experts and ask them if the estimate sounds reasonable. Usually by the time you call five people, you are starting to see a pattern in the answers. (Again it is advisable to ask the experts why they have made the estimate they give you.)

CONCLUSION

In this chapter we have seen that the key to estimating market size and share is determining who is in the specific market niche today and what the current buying pattern is. Even if our technology is something totally new—a Star Trek-like transporter—we can always find an analog to use. We then adjust that pattern in light of market barriers and forces on the one hand, and the like actions of ourselves and our competitors on the other. If we are using an analog, other adjustments have to be made that reflect the fact we are dealing with this technology and not that one.

Market barriers are factors that rigidify buying patterns. They can be identified by examining the buyers and sellers in likely transitions and the goods they are likely to trade. We look for factors that eliminate buyers (customer segments) from the market, limit the goods that can sold, or prevent a seller from competing.

Market forces are statistical trends that draw buyers or sellers into the market or drive them out. Forces may also affect the kinds of goods and the quantity of goods that are being sold. Player-based forces account for the lag in take-off that usually accompany radical and adaptive innovations when compared to incremental ones. The need to revamp the practice is a barrier that accounts for the delay in disruptive technology take-off.

PART **Three**
Strategy

CHAPTER 7

Positioning the Technology for the End User

INTRODUCTION

Strategy formulation can be viewed as a task sequence with three steps. The first step is to get clear how we might sell the products, processes, or services in which our technology is embodied. Positioning gives us a goal state, a picture of what a successful market entry looks like and when it might occur. Once we have that picture, we can look at where we are today and ask what we have to do to attain that positioning, the second step. The answer gives us our launch tactics. Finally, by looking at what we need to do to launch a product, process, or service, in light of our capabilities and capacities, we can figure out what kind of help we will need along the way. That is the key to figuring out who we want to do deals with.

There are always two possible customers for any technology. One customer is the end user, the person who literally puts their hands on the technology and uses it to accomplish a practice. The other possible customer is the target, the person who licenses, invests, joint ventures, enters into a strategic alliance, whatever in order to make money by moving the technology forward into the market.

Our emphasis in this chapter is how to position our technology for the ultimate end user. In Chapter 8, we will address launch tactics. Chapter 9 looks at targets, the people who will help us get into the market.

We assume, for the time being, that the technology is mature. We are concerned with how we can sell it once it is ready to go to market. After all, no sales, no money and no one interested in licensing, investing, partnering, etc.

Imagine a time-space continuum—our planet over time. Now overlay on it a socio-economic map—the flow of goods, industries, and people over the planet through time. Finally, add a map of knowledge and know-how. Now take a thumbtack, close your eyes, and stick it in. Look at where the thumbtack landed. It has landed in a position. What can you sell there? Alternatively, suppose the thumbtack is your technology. You have the option of sticking it anywhere you want, so long as that anywhere is in the future. Positioning is deciding where to place the tack. Generally, it is better to choose the position than to just close your eyes and stick it in. The latter sometimes leads to sticking it to yourself and no one wants to get stuck with a technology.

So how do we place the tack? Well, that depends on just what the tack is. The root of the word *technology* is the Greek word *technikos,* which means artistic, skillful, workmanlike, and, by extension, an activity done by rules of an art in a systematic manner.[1] This workmanlike approach is transmitted through *"logos,"* the root for the *"ology."* Logos means to give an account of; make a computation, reckoning; establish relation, correspondence, proportion; and provide explanation, utterance, and expression. Placed together we have the explanation of a precise, workmanlike way of applying skills. *Technikos logos,* technology is a way of doing that someone has thought about and then explained to us so we may also apply it.

A technology is a proven solution. This "solution" is not abstract. In *Art and Technics,* Lewis Mumford cites Emerson's phrase that life is more than just doing tricks. Mumford points out that *technikos* lives in the realm of cause and effect. *Technikos* is a way of self-creating ourselves because its proven solutions empower us to be more capable of living our dreams, purposes, and values.[2] So long as we respect the nature of the materials we use and the processes we work with, we can boil this water to make tea or flake this flint block to make an arrowhead that we will use to hunt for our dinner.

Positioning then is a matter of presenting the technology to end users that want the outcomes, the solution, that the technology offers. How we place the tack depends on the kinds of outcomes we want and that reflects the kind of problem for which we need a solution. The key distinction, as we shall see, is between consumer, industrial, and public goods. Industrial goods are positioned in terms of money-making potential. Consumer goods are positioned in terms of pleasure creation potential. Public goods are positioned in terms of risk reduction potential. As we have seen, we can use performance, ease-of-use, and price to measure a technology's utility for doing each of these.

TAKE-OFF

Our goal is to position the technology for take-off. Take-off typically occurs with between 5% and 20% market penetration, when sufficient market

---

[1] Liddell and Scott, *A Greek-English Lexicon* (Oxford: Clarendon Press, 1940), http://www.foreignword.com/Tools/dictsrch.asp?p=files/f_40_66.htm (accessed January 17, 2005).
[2] Mumford, "The Tool and the Object," *Art and Technics* (New York: Columbia University Press, 1952).

penetration is gained so the S curve starts to accelerate and the slope swings upward. The slope reflects an upsurge in the number of people buying. Usually word-of-mouth recommendations are kicking in to spur sales.

Now, to hit 5% to 20%, we need more than innovators as buyers. Those techno-weenies, nerds, and geeks who will buy the next greatest thing just because it is cool and neat and golly-gee-willikers are not enough people to kick start take-off. We need to get more mainstream buyers excited about what we have. We need the folks who are "opinion leaders" talking about what we have and why you should buy it.

Those opinion leaders are found in a number of places. Some are editors or writers for trade and business press. Others are officers or committee members of societies and trade associations. Yet others, and these are usually the most significant ones, are the guys and gals who when they buy something you think, "Hmm, if Mary is buying that maybe I should think about getting one too. After all, she is a pretty smart cookie."

Using Rodgers terminology, what we want is the early adopters excited and buying. (Usually *"best value"* buyers, they want performance, ease-of-use, at an affordable price; however *usually does not mean always*. As we shall see it all depends on how the technology actually is positioned.) Focusing on early adopters means we can use the same positioning to pull both the techno-weenies and the mainstream into our customer base, because if we are touting our performance and ease-of-use we will get the innovators and they will not complain if we can provide the technology for less than they thought they would have to pay to get their hands on it. At the same time, we are well on our way to an attractive value proposition for later adopters who focus on price. As more buyers enter the market, production has to ramp up, learning curve advantages and economies kick in, and the price comes down.

Bottom line: All things being equal, position new technologies for early adopters.

UMPF

But, here's the but: Without some kind of emotive *"umpf,"* there is no motivation for acquiring technology no matter how exquisite its yields and outcomes. This "umpf" can be anything. An example: the zipper. Zippers are a quicker, more secure, inexpensive way to bring two pieces of fabric or other pliable material together. The first patent for a zipper-like closing device was granted to Elias Howe is 1851, who also invented the sewing machine.[3]

---

[3] See Mary Bellis, "History of the Zipper," *About* (2005), http://inventors.about.com/library/weekly/aa082497.htm (accessed January 14, 2005).

Called by Howe an *"Automatic Continuous Closure,"* the "zipper" springs like Athena from the head of the Zeus of pre-Civil War American industrialization. First widely adopted in the 1930's, it is still in use today. The YKK factory in Macon, GA., for example, manufactures 7 million zippers each day. They produce 1,500 styles in more than 427 colors.[4]

The utility of the zipper is defined by its performance, price, and ease-of-use as a fastener.

But what makes us "want" to use zippers as consumers? Plato, for one, would reject consumption for its own sake. He would say the imperative should be stronger—the more the technology helps us live the "good" life, which is after all, the only life worthwhile living. We need not be so philosophic. It is enough for our purpose that whoever buys this technology feels it will make their life more *worthwhile*—however defined.

What is *worthwhile* is subjective, in the sense of belonging to each person individually. Nonetheless it also can be shared. This shared subjectivity, which we shall call inter-subjectivity, allows us to make predictions that concern whether a specific technology will have "umpf."

Consider what happens if you were standing at the south rim of the Grand Canyon at sunset. Struck by the scene you might you say "That is beautiful." You could look up and a group of strangers from around the world could be nodding their heads saying "Yep. It is." Umpf. Now consider what happens when you go to a rock concert and the music is good. Everyone is bopping to the beat. Umpf. (I once read in *Science News* that humans and fireflies are the only animals that can get their rhythms into phase without listening to a leader for each beat.[5])

Value propositions capture umpf. They should present the competitive advantage of a technology on price, performance, and ease-of-use metrics but they also should do more. A good one explains to people why there is umpf. For example, we recently did a project for the U.S. Department of Agriculture involving a straw and other grass-based insulation material that also has structural strength as boards, beams, and panels. The material has attractive price, performance, and ease-of-use characteristics. But its umpf comes from the fact that it makes it possible to build a house without any wood or metal at all. (The straw boards and beams are encased in stucco.) That umpf appeals to ecologists in the United States. The big umpf comes, however, in Third World countries that have been deforested.

[4] How Stuff Works, "Why Do Most Zippers Say YKK on the Pull-Tab?" 1998–2005, http://home.howstuffworks.com/question469.htm (accessed January 17, 2005).
[5] Milas, "U.S. Fireflies Flashing in Unison," *Science News* (March 13, 1999).

Let's go back to our zipper example. In 1893, Whitcom Judson, who was also the inventor of the "Pneumatic Street Railway," came up with a way to improve on Howe's fastener. He called his patented invention the Clasp Locker. It used an eye and hook. The Clasp Locker was the first commercially sold zipper precursor. The original niche for entry was shoes. It was introduced at the Chicago Worlds Fair but failed miserably in the market. No umpf.

Then, in 1913, the head designer at the Universal Fastener Company, Gideon Sundback, an electrical engineer, had an epiphany and re-conceptualized the locker as a smoothly sliding device. He increased the number of fastening elements and increasing the opening for the teeth so the two sides could be guided together for fastening by a slider that pulled between them. Pulled in reverse, it smoothly pulled them apart.

Like Judson's failure, this new iteration entered the market in shoes. B.F. Goodrich used it for a new line of rubber boots. B.F Goodrich renamed the invention a *"zipper"* as part of its advertising. (The name stuck—which certainly points out the potential benefit of trade marketing a clever name for a technology.) By 1917 it was used for shoes, tobacco pouches and U.S. Navy windcheater jackets—not a resounding success but enough umpf to generate positive cash flow in quirky little niches with unique performance requirements the zipper fit nicely.

Then, in 1928, everything changed. The hemline rose to the knee and the dress became more fitted. Clothing became more seductive. Women liked the look and so did the men.[6] Ahh, pleasure. The umpf of consumer goods. Pleasure is worthwhile. Ask any hedonist.

The new fitted-look, flapper-style dresses fasteners required a continuous lap that usually ran up the left side seam of the garment. Most clothes in the 20's used buttons, although snaps and hooks and eyes were found. These options did not create an elegant, tight and smooth line.

It was in this context, the zipper got its umpf. If you wanted the sleek, modern look, in the 1930s zippers gave it to you better than any other fastening option at an unbelievably low price (see Exhibit 7.1). The implicit argument was something like this: Take any dress and button it. Next pull the closure apart. The buttons will stretch; one may pop off. If the wearer is the slightest bit flabby, you can picture a bit of flesh seeping between the buttons of form-fitting dress that does not quite perfectly fit the form.

---

[6] This discussion is based on two primary sources: Carol Nolan, "Ladies Fashions of the Nineteen-Hundred Twenties" and "Ladies Fashions of the Nineteen-Hundred Thirties," *Women's Fashion History,* Southern California Lindy Society (1996–2003), http://www.lindyhopping.com/fashionhist.html (accessed January 17, 2005); and Pauline Weston Thomas, "1930s Fashion History–Stylish Thirties," *Fashion-Era.com* (2001–2004), http://www.fashion-era.com/stylish_thirties.htm#The percent20Zip (accessed January 17, 2005).

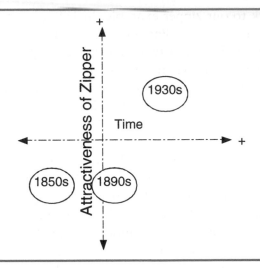

EXHIBIT 7.1   Zipper Timeline

Now do the same thing with a zipper! You cannot pull the dress apart. The zipper does not pop open as it distributes the force rather than focusing it at the button threads. The zipper smoothes the line along the seam into (at worst) a more discrete bulge. Pick your metrics: tensile strength, deformability, mean-time-between-failure—the zipper is attractive. But (there always is a but) more importantly, if you have one, you will be attractive too. Umpf.

Of course, someone had to make people aware that zippers could be used for clothes with umpf. That someone was Elsa Schiaparelli, an Italian designer of women's clothes. She made the zipper something women wanted.

In our jargon, Schiaparelli was an opinion leader. She mingled with modern artists like Marcel Duchamp, Man Ray, Salvador Dali, Jean Cocteau, Christian Berard and Francis Picabia. She had fabrics and accessories designed for her by associates. For Hollywood starlets and the rest of the rich and famous, she designed couture short fitted suits or jackets teamed with black dresses. She added colors like turquoise, shocking pink or hyacinth blue, creating an alternative to the pastel chiffon produced by Vionnet that was the rage for a while.

As a modernist, Schiaparelli liked the zipper. It was new and sharp. (Umpf.) She put plastic colored zippers in her clothes that combined decorative quality with functional utility. The result was dynamite. Incorporated as a design element, Schiaparelli popularized the zipper. That technology had become literally beautiful. Umpf.

(She was a master at umpf. She also designed a wide shouldered masculine suit for Marlene Dietrich that was widely copied throughout

Hollywood. Before WWII, Schiaparelli and Chanel, another umpfmeister, were great rivals for top designer fame. But as an Italian nationalist and supporter of the fascists, she had to flee when war broke out, leaving Chanel to dominate design.)

Of course, the socio-economic context on the one hand, and the cultural context on the other influence the ability to sustain umpf. They provide the macro-level context that supports or weakens value propositions.

The zipper's take-off as a product comes at a time when both the economic infrastructure and cultural orientations were in place. Economically, the U.S. garment industry was shifting to mass production of clothing for the general public. Sundback had invented the machines to make his zipper alongside the product invention. Distribution channels, in particular the strip mall, were spreading so consumers could have ready access to manufactured clothes. The simpler lines, like the flapper dress, which facilitated automated manufacturing, had seams where zippers worked well. Culturally, modernism emerged as an aesthetic trend across the applied arts from architecture to fashion. Chemically engineered fabrics like rayon were introduced, providing a new drape and feel for fabric and enhancing the shift to modernism to which the zipper contributed. Here was a new style of clothing different from what had been obtained from the local seamstress. It was Hollywood for the masses. Thus the cultural and economic infrastructure for rapid expansion of zipper demand was in place.

To summarize, positioning a technology is a matter of creating a value proposition that resonates with end users and buyers.

GOALS

Where does the umpf come from? As always, we begin with the end users, the people who put their hands on the technology. Now that we are doing market research, these people are no longer some Weberian ideal type. They are flesh and blood like the guy down the street getting on the bus who sweats when he works-out hard at the gym and that woman over there, jogging. Whatever else your technology does, if it is going to have umpf it has to improve their lives. Otherwise, what incentive do they have to adopt it?

Remember our discussion about wanting life to be worthwhile? It comes back in here. At least insofar as we are talking about technology, we almost always are also talking about applications with a purpose. We just don't turn on the stove for the heck of it. We want something. Like hot water for tea. Or stir-fry. Whatever. Because technology is a proven solution, it is useful for purposeful (that is, purpose-full) activities where for whatever the reason, we want it to work.

This *"whatever the reason"* is commonly called a goal. Goals are the outcome of thinking about our needs. Once we understand what it is we really want, we can set goals, translate those goals into objectives, design a task sequence, and set operational requirements for the skills, knowledge, tools and methods, and materials we need to reach those goals. In other words, we can develop practices. Alternatively, if we are engaged in a practice, we can ask what is the purpose of our activity.

> OK, maybe the boss says, "Hey, use this from now on." Then you want two umpfs: one to keep them from sabotaging the effort to introduce your technology; one to make the boss want to buy it for them. This situation is often the case when we are dealing with industrial goods. The umpf for the boss is making money. The umpf for the worker is a better job situation (i.e. easier, higher paying, safer).

Goals exist in relationships infrastructure and human capabilities. Thus we can infer the source of umpf by examining what infrastructure and capabilities exist in practices. An example helps here as always.

There were two basic paradigms for health care in the American colonies. The first was based on professionalism, the other on folklore.

The first paradigm had its origins in the Salerno School of Medicine in the period around 1000 A.D.[7] Building on the Greek view that the cosmos was made up of four basic elements: earth, air, water, and fire, early medicine saw the body as comprised of four *"humors:"* phlegm (earth), black bile (water) and yellow bile (air), and blood (fire). So long as these were in balance, the body was healthy. When they were out of balance, it was necessary to restore the balance by bleeding, enemas, and the like. Unfortunately, since this school of medicine believed each person had a dominant humor, maintaining balance sometimes was challenging and deadly.

Three aspects of this paradigm need to be highlighted for our discussion.

---

[7] See Wellness Directory of Minnesota, "The History of Medicine in America," 2003, http://www.mnwelldir.org/docs/history/history01.htm (accessed January 18, 2005).

First, the natural state of the body is presumed to be health. So the goal of doctoring is to restore health, because healthy people do not need doctors. Second, the physician as a professional is possessed of a body of technique and knowledge/know-how that are not available to the lay person. Third, because of the inequality of knowledge/know-how and technique, being healed means going to the doctor. As Plato notes in *The Republic,* like any other artisan, the physician must practice the art of money making in addition to the art of healing. Health care is tied to the ability to pay. Health care is *medical care,* that is, care based on the supervision of medical professionals.

The other paradigm was the one based on folklore. During the colonial period, many people were never treated by a physician during their entire life. Birthing was a communal event, conducted by midwives. Herbs and other local plants were plucked and prepared by family members or neighbors to make potions for healing. There were catalogs of herbs and roots and self-help books. For example, as early as 1652, in Great Britain Dr. Nicolas Culpeper published *The English Physician,* which described around 300 herbs and their medicinal uses. He also published *The English Midwife,* which dealt with birth and childcare. But there were also other sources of information. The natives had their own set of herbs for medicinal use. Many of these had properties unknown to the European physicians.

In our second paradigm, the natural state of the body is becoming either healthier or less healthy. If we take chamomile tea to calm the nerves, it does not mean there is "illness." Our goal is to maintain and regulate our body so it becomes ever healthier. In this paradigm, knowledge and know-how are more widely distributed. Local knowledge plays a role. Finally, being healed need not require an economic transaction. Family members, especially women, help other family members and neighbors help neighbors. Health care is *community care.*

Now, let's take a technology and position it by looking at infrastructure and the capabilities of the people who will put their hands on it. Our technology is an expert system that provides advice on best practices for preventive care for families. It was developed at a leading medical school with a strong family practice program.

The way this expert system works is you get on a computer and answer a series of questions. The questions are designed to guide you through a decision tree based on life style and symptoms in order to identify ways to better maintain health. The decision tree reflects how a trained professional processes the information and leads to the conclusions reflecting the consensus practices of family practitioners. Now, where's the umpf?

It clearly has little in Colonial America—kind of hard for something to

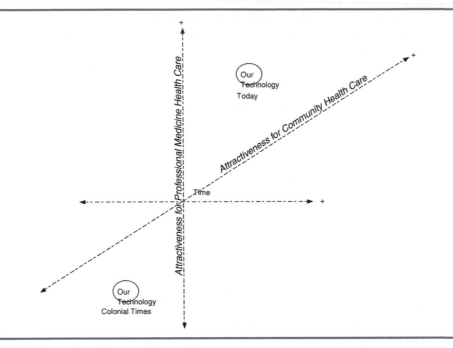

EXHIBIT 7.2   Infrastructure and Capabilities

have a lot of umpf if you cannot use it (see Exhibit 7.2). In the seventeenth and eighteenth centuries, to put it pedantically, there was a lack of computing infrastructure. (It is likely some people could understand what an expert system was and had the ability to develop the competencies. For example, Benjamin Franklin, who invented the battery, did have electricity in his house. But even Franklin likely would have been perplexed by how to type your input on a QWERTY keyboard or even how to adjust the contrast of the display, since neither existed.)

But there is another reason there is little umpf. As late as World War I, one in ten babies born in the United States died before age one.[8] If you live with the assumption, based on daily reality, that some of your children will die, then an expert system to prevent that makes little sense because you will not believe it can work. Such knowledge belongs to God maybe, but not to physicians. Until the causes of disease were understood, infectious respiratory diseases like pneumonia and influenza, gastrointestinal diseases like diarrhea, enteritis, and ulceration of the intestines, and tuberculosis

---

[8] Population Reference Bureau, "A Century of Progress in U.S. Infant and Child Survival," 2005, http://www.prb.org/AmeristatTemplate.cfm?Section=Mortality1& template=/ContentManagement/ContentDisplay.cfm&ContentID=7912 (accessed January 21, 2005).

were all illnesses you hoped did not take your infants. From the standpoint of the physician, it also makes no sense as there is no knowledge domain to underlie the development of rules. Buying one is just a waste of money.

Now, place that same technology in 2005. The attractiveness of the technology is totally different. What has changed? The obvious factor is advances in medical knowledge leading to a dramatic drop in infant mortality. The power of knowledge is now taken for granted.

> *In the past the natural history of disease has shown chains of causation. With the acute diseases, these chains have usually been quite short and easily broken. With the chronic diseases of today, they are far longer and more complicated. Often they involve patterns of behavior extending over half a lifetime. These patterns are, in turn, determined partly by genetic make-up, partly by family and social environment. The study of these chains necessitated both observation and social survey methods. The breaking of the chains entails the use of propaganda or mass education. By far the most effective educational agent is the spoken word, coming from someone held in respect.*[9]

Furthermore, computing infrastructure now exists. Computers are easy to buy. We can assume anyone reading this book has used the Internet and knows what it is like to have instant access to information about aardvarks or health care.

The consequence is that over the course of the past 100 years, what it means to make an "informed decision" has changed for both consumers and practitioners. The mythical rational man of legal and economic theory used to face limit in the exercise of his rationality from lack of access to information and lack of time for analysis. Now his descendants are limited by lack of time to wade through information so they want access to better analytical tools. Literally, what it means to act rationally has changed.

Now let's go back to inferring where we find the umpf to make a value statement for our expert system persuasive. We know many of the major causes of childhood death and illnesses are under our control, or at least influence. We know there is free data out there on the web that can help us understand threats to our children's health and how to counter them. Because we love our kids, we want to act rationally with respect to our kids' health. So, tools that help us sift through information make sense. Who wants sick kids? Umpf.

---

[9] Taylor, "The Natural History of Preventive Medicine, or Breaking the Chains of Causation," *British Medical Journal* (September 27, 1980), http://www.ncbi.nlm.nih.gov/entrez/query.fcgi?cmd=Retrieve&db=pubmed&dopt=Abstract&list_uids=7000280 (accessed January 20, 2005).

COMPETITIVE ADVANTAGE

OK, so we got umpf. But we still need a competitive advantage. How do we find where that lies?

To review where we are: Goal-driven activities are purpose-full. Where goal-driven activities are repeated, we call them practices. Practices provide openings for technology where part of their task sequence is repetitive. Where that is the case, it makes sense to develop methods and tools, *technikos logos,* in order to enhance productivity.

When I was a kid, you would go into the doctor's office and behind the receptionist was a wall of charts. Today, those charts can be on a disk. Electronic Health Records (EHR) systems, as of January, 2005, are used by 50 percent of the doctors in large practices and hospitals.[10] EHRs make it easier track patient symptoms, diagnoses, and treatments; prepare billing information; as well as a number of other benefits that increase the productivity of medical offices.

According to Dr. Blackford Middleton, chairman, Center for IT Leadership and director, Clinical Informatics R&D at Partners Healthcare and an assistant professor of medicine at Brigham & Women's Hospital, Harvard Medical School, the savings are substantial and the number of doctors involved are growing. In one study he did, billing errors accounted for 13% of savings from adopting EHRs, while billing capture increase accounted for another 14%, chart pull and transcription savings both accounted for 5%, radiology savings accounted for 15%, drug savings for 29%, etc. Assuming 50 doctors and 14.4% cost of capital, the five-year net return per provider could be as high as $108,100.[11] Insofar as making money is a goal for a medical group, EHRs are likely to have umpf.

Patents also benefit, According to the *Providence Journal,* electronic-medical-record systems tried in Indianapolis, IL and Santa Barbara, CA led to sharp falloffs in medical error.[12] (Of course, that should cut malpractice insurance costs as well as there is less chance of negligence.)

EHRs have become so important in the United States that a variety of organizations have sought to grab turf by developing standards, certifying

---

[10] Grant Gross, "Lack of Standards Hinders Electronic Health Records," *Infoworld* (January 10, 2005), http://www.infoworld.com/article/05/01/10/HNlackofstandards_1 .html (accessed January 20, 2005).

[11] Middleton, "Models of Cost Savings Enabled by EHR," *Healthcare Conference Administrators* (n.d.), www.ehcca.com/presentations/cahealthit2/middleton.ppt (accessed January 20, 2005).

[12] "Electronic Medical Records," *Providence Journal,* January 11, 2005, http://www .projo.com/opinion/editorials/content/projo_20050111_edrecor.16f4a7.html (accessed January 18, 2005).

procedures, and other quality assurance mechanisms—sure signs that the dominant design is being solidified. These include the American Academy of Pediatrics, Task Force on Medical Informatics, which has issued Special Requirements for Electronic Medical Record Systems in Pediatrics[13]; the Certification Commission for Healthcare Information Technology, which issues Electronic Health Record (EHR) certificates[14]; and the EHR reviews of the American Academy of Family Physicians Center for Health Information Technology.[15]

We can use the EHR to suggest how to gain competitive advantage when designing our expert system on pediatric preventative best practices. Much of the information we shall want is already in the EHR. Also, any responsible doctor will want to capture the information the patient offers in order to have better diagnostic data. Since we model our technology on the features and functionality of the EHR, we can say its design "dominates" our design decisions. Thus, we call it a dominant design.

Dominance is a consequence of a technology's centrality for the conduct of a task sequence. This centrality means you have to take it into account when designing products, processes, or services that embody your technology. At the same time, dominance does not mean that technology is ubiquitous. Take EHRs. Despite economic and patient care benefits, market penetration of EHRs has slowed. Cost and lack of standards are two barriers to market expansion. Converting from a paper-based records system costs between $10,000 to $30,000 per physician.[16] Converting can be risky if the system adopted is later out-of compliance with what standards do finally emerge. So, it is not surprising that over 90% of the medical practices with fewer than 50 doctors do not make significant use of information technology at all, according to Dr. Mark Leavitt, medical director of the Healthcare Information Management Systems Society.[17]

Nonetheless, to be dominant, adoption of technology design should be supported by strong market forces. Increased pressure from government

---

[13] "Special Requirements for Electronic Medical Record Systems in Pediatrics," *Pediatrics* (August 2, 2001), http://aappolicy.aappublications.org/cgi/reprint pediatrics;108/2/513.pdf (accessed November 14, 2004).

[14] AAFP.org, "Commission Appointed to Study Certification of Health IT Products," September 10, 2004, http://www.aafp.org/x29217.xml (accessed November 14, 2004).

[15] AAFP's Center For Health Information Technology, "Current Projects," August 9, 2004, http://www.centerforhit.org/x10.xml (accessed November 14, 2004).

[16] Projo.com, "Electronic Medical Records," *Providence Journal,* January 11, 2005, http://www.projo.com/opinion/editorials/content/projo_20050111_edrecor.16f4a7.html (accessed January 18, 2005).

[17] Grant Gross, "Lack of Standards Hinders Electronic Health Records," *Infoworld* (January 10, 2005), http://www.infoworld.com/article/05/01/10/HNlackofstandards_1.html (accessed January 20, 2005).

and private insurers to reduce medical costs is such a driver. For example, thirty-four major delivery systems and insurers in Massachusetts are collaborating through the Massachusetts eHealth Collaborative to build a state-wide medical information system. This system is designed to promote implementation of clinical information systems including electronic medical records, clinical decision support and data exchange applications. Blue Cross and Blue Shield of Massachusetts will give $50 million to help fund pilot projects.[18] At the same time, the federal government is also pushing adoption of EHR and related information technology tools as part of its National Health Information Technology Initiative. By executive order, the President established the National Coordinator for Health Information Technology.[19] That office has published a Framework for Strategic Action to ensure adoption of interoperable EHRs by the middle of the next decade. In addition, the Consolidated Health Informatics Initiative has issued standards for 20 areas involving electronic exchange of clinical health information. These standards will be adopted by the federal government. Other legislation requires the Department of Health and Human Services to promulgate standards and conduct pilot projects for electronic prescribing. Even money is starting to flow to support adoption. Thus, it is reasonable to expect another spurt of market expansion in EHR use.

Performance

Now let's go back to our technology, the expert system for preventive care for families.

We can leverage the pressures to adopt EHRs by positioning our technology as an adaptive technology, that is, as an extension for EHRs that provides added functionality with improved cost-benefits. For example, let's say you want to schedule a visit for your child for check-up. The receptionist on the phone asks you to go to the web and fill out an appointment form. This expert system pops up and collects whatever the doctors want and automatically uploads it into the EHR. (Alternatively, you could fill it out on a touch screen tablet at the office when you arrive.)

---

[18] Healthdatamanagement.com, "Massachusetts Plans Statewide Network," *Health Data Management* (December 20, 2004), http://www.healthdatamanagement.com/html/PortalStory.cfm?type=vend&DID=12211 (accessed January 20, 2005).
[19] This discussion based on Paul Smith, "Electronic Health Records and the National Health Information Infrastructure," *Find Law* (2004), http://library.lp.findlaw.com/articles/file/00010/009765/title/Subject/topic/Health_Medicare/filename/health_1_1163 (accessed January 21, 2005).

This positioning suggests performance features to emphasize in order to gain a competitive advantage. According to Toby Vandermark,[20] director of information and technology, American Board of Pediatrics, software like ours must work in a Microsoft Windows operating system. Since many electronic management and electronic health records systems use SQL and Oracle database systems, the software also should be capable of being easily integrated into an existing system stored in these programs. Rebecca Marshall,[21] health policy analyst at the American Academy of Pediatrics adds that the software must be easily adapted to meet the procedures of different offices. Part of adaptability is making it easy to integrate into a healthcare provider's current software and hardware infrastructure.

We end up with a design in which the data in the EHR is linked with our expert system and supplemental data entered by patients. We can anticipate that upon log-in, the system checks the patient's EHR and pulls up any relevant data. This information might be presented with check boxes, so it can be documented that the patient took a specific action to approve this data or change it. Based on the data in the EHR, it then requests supplemental data, as dictated by its rules. If this data triggers conclusions that indicate health issues, the expert system sends a copy to the nurse, who reviews the data and arranges for blood work, etc. The system suggests tests that can help resolve issues facing the health care team and the patient. Key data is automatically uploaded into the EHR. The system generates recommendations that are either sent directly to the patient or, where appropriate, to the nurse or doctor for review and approval before being sent to the patient.

What has happened is our expert system is no longer necessarily a free-standing system but may be an add-on and front-end for EHRs used by family practice groups. Our value proposition could be that it provides functionality that enhances the return-on-investment of EHRs by (i) directly capturing patient data, (ii) supporting decision making by the health-care team, and (iii) providing better patient outcome through enhanced family involvement in pediatric health-care.

If the practice is an economic activity, we also can look at the value chain and supply within which it occurs (see Exhibit 7.3). The practices elsewhere in these chains also create expectations for how practitioners in a specific task sequence will act, and thus what skills and capacities they have—if only because we can pin down what inputs have to be converted

---

[20] Personal correspondence with Vinay Thakur of Foresight Science & Technology on November 26, 2004.
[21] Ibid.

Input ⟶ Black Box ⟶ Output

EXHIBIT 7.3 Value Chain and Supply

into what outputs. Our medical expert system, for example, is a tool for the operations of medical practices.

Exhibit 7.4 is a workflow context for the medical expert system we have been discussing. Because the physician's office wants to be paid for its work, the requirements for submitting an invoice to the insurance company (or government agency) drive part of the record keeping. That requirement, in turn, drives some of the data items that must be collected during patient intake. ("Name: _____"). At the same time, the doctor needs data to conduct diagnosis, so this data requirement also influences the data being sought during intake. ("Where does it hurt, Mrs. Jones?") Another influence is requirements for treatment. ("What drugs are you currently taking?") In other words, there is a causal backward chain from data requirements later in the work flow to the patient data intake form. At each step, the outputs of one practice are the inputs for another.

In the case of the zipper, once it leaves the factory, it goes to the dress manufacturer (a supply chain relationship), who integrates it into the product, which is sent to the retail store. When we leave the supply or value chain, the constraints dissipate as the black box is not a process for created outputs that will be used by others. Rather the output is simply enjoyment . . . pleasure. The dress is sold to you, your girlfriend, your wife, whomever. While money changes hands, making this an economic transaction, the consumer transaction is leading to a non-economic use. The output may now be used in a leisure-time activity, like going out dancing. Nonetheless, we can still measure the desirability of the zipper as a tool for getting into a dress and keeping it on in terms of criteria like efficiency (resource use), efficacy (reliability of outcome and quality), or some other utility measure and compare it with buttons, snaps or Velcro®. Only when we look at taste do we lose the "objective" comparison.

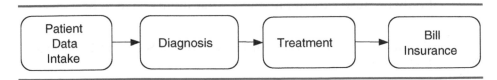

Patient Data Intake ⟶ Diagnosis ⟶ Treatment ⟶ Bill Insurance

EXHIBIT 7.4 Backward Chain in Workflow

Ease of Use

The people who will put their hands on our expert system or use our zipper did not suddenly climb out of a clamshell as in the Northwest Haidi tribes' creation myth.[22] They have skills and absorptive capacities, learned in other contexts. We can predict these traits with some degree of confidence if we know what their past and current activities are. Insofar as our concern is technology transfer, the activities that interest us most are the ones where our technology can be a "proven solution."

The skills and absorptive capacity constrain what features will provide ease-of-use. Technologies that are hard to understand or use are likely to be less attractive. As always, an example helps. Exhibit 7.5 plots computer skills and absorptive capacity in pediatric health care of physicians over time. The progression is admittedly crude, but it makes sense that doctors in the 1960s knew a lot more than the average Colonial American physician and had better computer skills.

The precise mix of skills, capacities, etc. are an empirical question. However, we can make an educated guess based on the contexts within which our end users engage in relevant practices so long as there is a dominant design. The reason we can make this guess is that the dominant design clarifies what is in the *"black box"* that converts the inputs into a practice into outputs. If we understand the skills and capacities it requires, we can assume they exist among participants in the practice who use relevant technology.

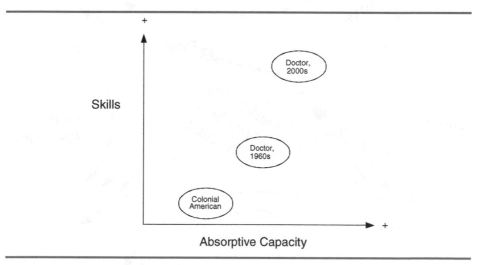

EXHIBIT 7.5 Absorptive Capacity

---

[22] Eldrbarry, "Raven Finds the First Men" 1997, http://www.eldrbarry.net/rabb/rvn/first.htm (accessed January 24, 2005).

We can now explicate a basis for making an educated guess about the mix of skills, absorptive capacities, etc. of our end users. What we are doing is looking at the current mix and projecting the likelihood of its continuation in time. This likelihood is a function of (i) how likely it is that the purpose of the activity will change, changing the outcomes being sought; (ii) what is the character of, and rate of, change in the dominant design, which influences what mix is required for successfully operating the in-place technology given the available inputs (and regrettably complicating things, their rate of change); and (iii) the skills, capabilities, etc. that the players bring to the practice in the first place. The result is a vector field that constrains the evolution of the skills, capacities, and other output related attributes of the players in practice upon which we are focused. They act upon them much as gravity fields act upon a spacecraft hurtling through the solar system. The gravitation forces of planets tug at the craft, affecting its direction and velocity of flight. It works pretty much the same here. Exhibit 7.6 illustrates this situation.

Conversely, we note in passing, the attractiveness of a specific technology for end users in a specific practice and the stability of a dominant design is constrained by the trajectories and rates of change of the attributes of

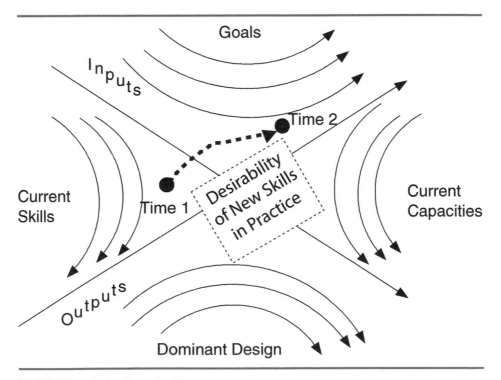

EXHIBIT 7.6   Market Force Field

the players who will work the technology and by the transactions that occur between practices in the value chains and supply chains to which they belong.

Where the force field constrains the evolution of skills, capacities, etc. in a direction favorable for our technology, ease-of use is not likely a barrier to entry (see Exhibit 7.7). This conclusion holds even if these attributes of players are changing so long as the change is in the right direction and at an appropriate rate. We can certainly envision a situation where skills and capacities have changed over time in such a way that a new technology that was previously viewed as very difficult to use is now actually viewed as easier than the currently used technology.

The participants in the practice affect what ease-of-use features will provide competitive advantage (see Exhibit 7.8). The people doing the billing have a certain skill set. If it is 1950, they can type, store a carbon copy in the patient's records, send one to the patient, and mail the original to the insurance company. If it is 2005, they can look up the record, update it, and hit send so the information goes out over the Internet.

Now, let's look at our expert system. If it is 1950, there is little utility in having a patient electronically enter a bunch of data, because no one farther down the chain can use that data. So there is a barrier to entry

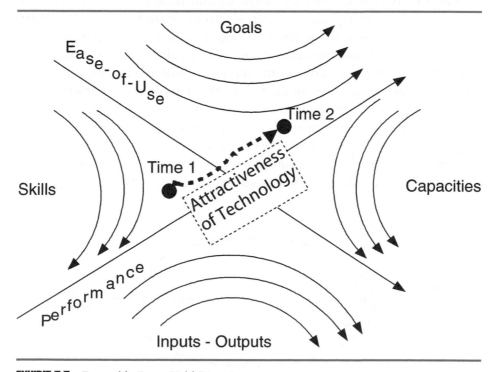

EXHIBIT 7.7 Favorable Force Field Direction

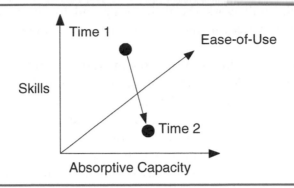

EXHIBIT 7.8 Skill Set

facing our expert system. One part of the barrier is the cost of training the office staff in computer literacy. The other part is the cost of buying the machines.

Hop to 2004. Recall that even in 2004, over 90 percent of the medical practices with fewer than 50 doctors do not make significant use of information technology at all. Let us assume computer literacy is not the problem. Let us further assume that cost is not an issue. What is the barrier? The barrier is how doctors do diagnosis and treatment. If the doctor is used to looking at a piece of paper, electronic data is less useful. If the doctor does not see value in the self-diagnostic activities of patients, why encourage them. Using the language of Porter's value chains, the way operations are conducted is a constraint on the way inbound logistics and infrastructure practices can be conducted. In other words, the paradigms for each practice in an organization's value chain place greater or lesser value on skills, capacities, and attitudes for other practices (see Exhibit 7.9).

Now hop to the present. On the one hand, preventative care is now seen as important as healing for professional medicine—a change in the paradigm. Thus, there is greater emphasis on making it easier to include patients

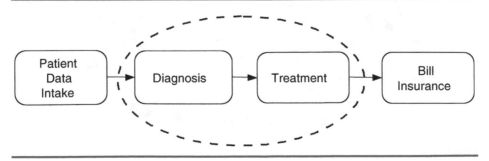

EXHIBIT 7.9 Inbound Logistics and Constraints

in their own health care, but in a way which does not increase burdens on, and thus costs for, the professional health care team. This shift also means that access to, and the ability to work with, data on prevention is increasingly part of the knowledge domain of physicians and nurses. On the other hand, medical record keeping is becoming increasingly electronic and the Electronic Health Record has emerged as a dominant design for medical practice administration, making computer skills increasingly common.

Price

There are three factors that need to be considered when determining price: comparables, the value generated by the practice in which the technology will be applied, and sticker shock. Let us take each of these and see how it applies.

The first factor is comparables. I go to the supermarket and buy cereal. Most cereals cost around $3 to $5 a box. In the middle of the aisle is a box for seven dollars. You gotta wonder what makes it so special.

Now, we have already discussed customer segmentation. So, the $7 box may be expensive because it is organic. Maybe it is expensive because it is made by exquisite chefs in a tiny kitchen in a small town in Alsace. Whatever. The point is that comparables are defined by what we want to buy. If we like Cheerios® we might compare the store brand and the organic brand of round oats. It is no different with expert systems or anything else.

The key point here is that we need to look at goods that have an equivalent performance and features mix. Two cautions. Be aware that comparables need not attain the performance and features in the same way, or even using the same technical approach as your technology. If I want to get from Providence to Boston by public transportation I can fly, take a bus, or take a train. Each is a competitor of the others. Also be aware that what is a comparable is sometimes defined by the practice. In the case of our expert system, it may be irrelevant what expert systems for damage assessment in nuclear power plants cost. What is relevant is expert systems for medicine, and in particular, for pediatrics or family practice.

Searching the web we find *http://www.computer.privateweb.at/judith/index.html*,[23] which lists a number of expert systems. DiagnosisPro™ is for family practice. It is made by Medtech and sells for around $100 for a single user copy and $1,000 for an institutional license. Other benchmarks can be found, and by looking at the mean and the range of deviation we can get a pretty good idea of how folks might respond to prices we set.

Note that depending on the doctors of interest, paper-based diagnostic systems may be of interest. These may be much cheaper. In some web

---

[23] Computer.privateweb.at (accessed August 30, 2005).

search I did, they appeared to be on the order of $10 to $40 . But that is misleading, because you first have to check to make sure they can be duplicated by the doctor without additional fees. Then you have to consider how much time is spent processing the data, and entering it into either paper or electronic patient records.

Hopefully, you are starting to suspect pricing comes in many variants. There is purchase price and life cycle cost. If the life cycle cost is lower, then the purchase price may be able to be higher. We say "*may*" because we have to take into account practice economics and sticker shock. If I only make $40,000 a year as an acupuncturist, I am going to think long and hard before buying a $5,000 piece of equipment. If I make $500,000 a year in my pediatrics practice, that $5,000 seems less threatening.

Thus, we see that the first factor, price, assumes a range of feasible pricing based on the second factor, the profit or net value generated by the activity. It has been a long time since my children were young enough to need a pediatrician and I am still years away from being a grandmother, so I have no idea what those doctors cost today per visit. But I recently went to the dentist and spent about $175 for a check-up and cleaning. So, at those prices it did not surprise me when the dental hygienist said her boss had the latest digital radiography system. In business practices, higher value activities can support higher priced product technology if that technology contributes to better profits.

Turning to process technology and practice economics, high throughput activities, such as production of commodities like paper, can support high priced production equipment if output is very high and the equipment provides economies of scale. (Paper making is one of the most capital intensive industries in the world.) In general, the greater the network economies or economies of scale or scope, the more buyers are willing to pay a premium for production technology over current pricing for technology lacking these economies. After all, it is all about profit. If I can reduce my costs, I can make more money.

Following Sanderson and Uzumeri in *Managing Product Families*, we can place practices along two continuums, depending on the characteristics of there outputs: variety of outputs and rate of change. At any given time, a practice can be placed in the chart in Exhibit 7.10. The chart alongside depicts the placement for the pediatricians to whom we want to sell our expert system. Pediatricians tend to see a wide range of problems, and thus to offer a range of services. The services they offer do change over time as medical knowledge advances and population preferences change, but these changes are not too rapid. By looking at the placement of a practice on this chart, we can make a pretty educated guess about what kind of process technology will have the highest value. For practices producing many outputs, technologies offering economies of scope will be attractive,

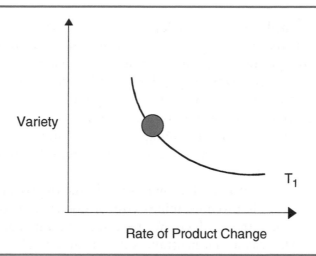

EXHIBIT 7.10 Variety of Output and Rate of Change

while for commodity-like production, technologies offering economies of scale are more attractive. An example of the former is technology for embedding chips inside printed circuit boards. An example of the latter is a better anode for aluminum production. However, even if the variety of outcomes is low, as the rate of change increases, economies of scope become more relevant. For low variety but high rate of change, design technologies are particularly attractive, such as CAD/CAM and chip design libraries. Where both the variety of outputs and the rate of their change are high, technologies offering network economies are attractive because they allow leveraging in place products and infrastructure while introducing new products. An example is drug discovery technologies such as genomics-based drug discovery. A similar analysis can be made for product technology. Thus, if we want to be on the high side of prices paid by players of specific practices for goods, it helps to understand how much leverage we provide them for recouping the money paid to us.

We were asked to find a royalty rate for embedded chip process technology. Royalty rates are a kind of price. Royalty rates for processes are often applied against revenues from sales of products made using the process.

What this technology does is enable placing the active and passive components inside the printed circuit board rather than on the surface. That increases reliability, facilitates miniaturization, and enables better performance in high frequency devices like cell phones. The

(Continued)

customer claimed that the technology would allow profits for adopters to soar from the industry average of around 4% to around 35%. Experts in the printed circuit board industry were incredulous.

Now, there are many ways of structuring royalties. The most commonly used way is to charge the royalty rate on net sales, which is defined as gross revenues minus discounts and returns. If I am buying this technology and I am running at a 4% profit, if the technology does not work as promised, I have a big problem. I do not have a lot of flex in my profit rate.

Another way that is well known is to charge the royalty rate on gross profits, that is revenues minus cost of goods sold (the cost of making and selling the product). We recommend a rate based on this calculation. The reason is it neutralizes the "I cannot believe it" argument. If the technology does not increase profits, our customer makes very little. If, however, it delivered as promised, they make a lot. If the buyer is still skeptical, the customer can always fall back and take a much larger share of any gross profits over the buyer's current profit margin.

As a quick FYI, there often are also upfront fees to compensate for consulting and know-how transfer so the learning curve in adoption is cut. Such a fee was charged here too. The fall back position was to forego the fee but raise the royalty rate. In other words, more risk, higher rates.

Returning to our pediatrician, the EHR seems well suited for his or her activities as it provides an economy of scope that, with add-ons like our expert system, can adapt to change. The ability to leverage the underlying EHR provides network economies.

Another way to get a handle on practice economics is to ask how long it takes to earn-back the cost of the investment. Technologies that start to pay off in less than a year are usually higher in value than investments that take more years, all other things being equal. The reason is the time value of money. The flip side of this is that investments that pay off quickly have a lower rate of return than those that take longer. Compare the interest on your bank savings account with the interest on a 15-year corporate bond.

So now we are running the numbers and we say, "OK the price seems fair given the market and I can make money off it and afford it." Will I buy it? Well, we still have to take into account sticker shock. I am always amazed what young women will pay for a pair of designer jeans. Sure, I could afford it. Perhaps if I wore them, my customers would say, "Wow, you look successful so I will hire you." But to pay $100 or more for a pair of blue jeans . . . no way!

In a similar vein, Gordon Bell points out that we tend to evaluate technology in terms or other goods with equivalent performance. He suggests there are seven price tiers:[24]

1. $10: wrist watch and wallet computers
2. $100: pocket/palm computers
3. $1,000: portable computers
4. $10,000: personal computers
5. $100,000: departmental computers
6. $1,000,000: divisional computers
7. $10,000,000: central headquarters or central lab computers

Sticker shock usually occurs when you hop orders of magnitude. Going back to designer jeans, say I am used to paying $30 or $40 dollars for jeans. OK, so maybe I would pay $60 for the ones that make me look trim, fit, and successful. But $100 jumps me into another order of magnitude. ("Aha," you say. "That is why so many things are $99.99.")

Pricing then is a matter of benchmarking against comparables, making sure the price makes sense given the economics of the practice, and avoiding sticker shock. Pricing has to be adjusted to take into account the customer segment.

Time

Before leaving competitive advantage, it is important to note that practices change over time and thus what enables having a competitive advantage also changes. Exhibit 7.11 is a simplified version of a graphic presented earlier. As we have discussed, over time a dominant design emerges for goods after which the rate of product innovation declines (what it is) and the rate of process innovation increases (how to make it). Here we are looking at the consequences of this interaction for what makes a technology attractive to buyers in a practice.

This exhibit tracks the interplay between market development, sales, and labor skill. We can draw a number of interesting conclusions from examining the chart. As markets mature, the emergence of dominant designs means process innovation is of more interest because the goal is to

---

[24] Bell, "Bell's Seven Price Tiers," *Computer Industry Laws, Heuristics and Class Formation: Why computers Are Like They Are,* (n.d.), http://www.americanhistory.si.edu/csr/comphist/montic/bell/tsld012.htm (accessed October 17, 2004).

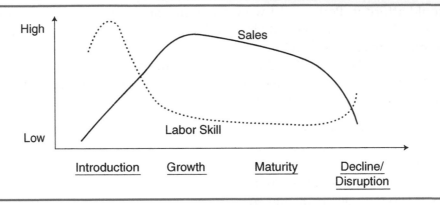

EXHIBIT 7.11   Relationship between Sales and Labor Skill

ramp up production. Correspondingly, there should be, and usually is, a move to standardize and simplify the product to make it easier to attain economies in production. My father once told me that his first job after graduating as an engineer was taking parts out of radios for Sylvania.

Similarly, there is usually a shift in the people working as more people are hired to keep up with demand. Early on, skilled craftsmen are needed to make the product as specialized machinery does not exist. Later on, larger production volumes justify buying dedicated process technology. But such machines and software means the locus of skill moves to some degree from the craftsman to the machine. It is only in declining markets, where skill once again becomes more important because someone has to know how to make things as the machines are getting older and it is not worthwhile reinvesting in high volume equipment.

We emphasize markets need not move linearly from one stage to the next. Nonetheless, time brings into the picture a realization that what constitutes competitive advantage is a moving target.

WINDOW OF OPPORTUNITY

We now can infer what performance functionality, ease-of-use features, and price will help us attain a competitive advantage. But when should we introduce our technology?

The window of opportunity is the period in which a new technology can be introduced into a market niche. The window of opportunity opens when something changes in either the immediate practice where our technology will be inserted or in the larger value and supply chains within which the practice is embedded.

It is in this context that market forces operate. As we shall see in

Chapter 8, market forces affect the distribution of attributes of players. What is happening here to create the window of opportunity?

First, malpractice costs are soaring. To the extent a well informed patient is more responsible for their own health care, the burden of God-like behavior on the doctor is correspondingly reduced. Further, if an expert system provides access to the collective wisdom of a field, using it is a defense against negligence. Also, consulting the expert system as another data source is an indicator that the doctor is practicing the diligence of a reasonable person seeking to avoid error. The attribute affected is risk aversion, an attitude.

Second, as preventative care becomes an accepted part of medical practice operations, the goals of physicians change. Preventative health care, where the concern is avoiding potential problems rather than avoiding recurrence or mitigating a condition, lends itself to *"telemedicine"* as here there are no symptoms to examine or physical to conduct. Since the goal is to change behavior long before traditional professional medical intervention is required, other people in the office can play lead roles in preventative case management. The patient can log in, fill out data, and be directed to other resources to better understand how to avoid future problems. A nurse or social worker can receive a copy of the data and recommendations, review them, and decide whether it is appropriate to respond with other resources or email/phone questions—much as consumer computer repair is now initially a help desk activity. The on-line interactive format allows preventative health-care to be provided even if the patient is far from home on another continent and concerned how to avoid a health hazard found there.

Note that the change that opens a window of opportunity need not be in the practice in which the technology will be introduced. For example, if insurers were to require electronic documentation during diagnosis and treatment that would spur adoption of hardware and software for use inside the examination room, which would in-turn, help overcome the barrier to entry that traditional paper-based practices there constitute for our expert system. Computer literacy, willingness to use electronic data, etc. would now become more highly valued skills, capacities, and attitudes, changing the context of practices along the value chain and opening the window of opportunity.

The National Health Information Technology Initiative is a federal effort to do just that. In an executive order issued on April 27, 2004, President Bush called for widespread deployment of health information technology within 10 years. NIH states:

> *This vision can be realized by making the health care industry consumer-centered and information rich, where information that is required for*

*good decision making is available whenever and wherever care is pro-
vided. . . . This information would be available to consumers and clinicians at the point of care whenever and wherever they need them and no
matter where it was originally gathered. Sophisticated decision-support
tools that help identify treatments that are best suited to a given patient
would be available to help reduce unnecessary treatments and to ensure
prevention procedures, both of which result in better outcomes. Medications would be ordered with computerized systems that eliminate hand-
writing errors and automatically check for doses that are too high or too
low. Information tools would also search for harmful interactions with
other drugs and for allergies. Prescriptions would be checked against the
health plan's formulary, and the out-of-pocket costs of the prescribed
drug would be compared with alternative medications. Patient information would be readily available for clinicians at the point of care and
would help patients improve their own care.*[25]

The change is so established that the next generation of doctors is
being trained with the aid of these information tools. For example, at
Duke University, PDAs have been loaded with PatientKeeper software to
give caregivers immediate, wireless access to patient data.[26]

What Exhibit 7.12 highlights is what we have is literally a generation
gap tied to whether or not you grew up using computers. Our expert system coheres with the computer skills and expectations of a generation
raised on the Internet. That is important as it reduces risk of adoption for
the end user.

> Recall that risk is the probability of regretting an action you have
> taken. Risk is the likelihood our value proposition stinks. I remember
> once being at the National Air and Space Museum with my children,
> my parents, and my grandmother, who was pushing close to 100 at
> the time. The docent was fascinated by her stories. She remembered
> reading about the Wright Brothers flight in the paper. She remem-
> bered seeing her first airplane. On the way out, my son was fascinated
> by the fact my grandmother remembered a world without airplanes.
> Then she told him about cars. She remembered reading about them
> being invented and recalls when she saw her first one. He was floored.

[25] U.S. Department of Health and Human Services, "Health IT Strategic Framework,
Vision for Consumer-centric and Information-rich Health Care," July 23, 2004,
http://www.hhs.gov/onchit/framework/hitframework/visionforconsumer.html
(accessed November 14, 2004).
[26] Michael Sciannamea, "Duke Caregivers Leveraging PDAs for Patient Care," *The
Telemedicine Log* (October 6, 2004), http://telemedicine.weblogsinc.com/entry/
1805781712401103/ (accessed November 14, 2004).

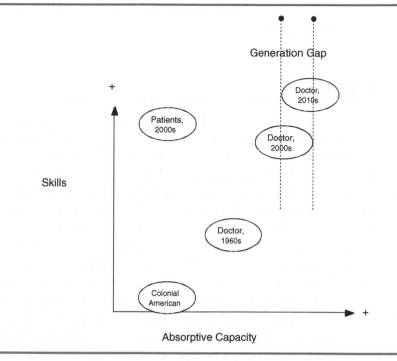

EXHIBIT 7.12 Computer Use Generation Gap

> I suspect my grandchildren will be surprised to hear stories about a world without computers. Kids who grew up playing video games and doing homework with Instant Messenger running are now in medical school. Trained in computer skills at school and comfortable surfing the web, their childhood experiences provide the "*Spielraum*" (literally *the playing room*) for a major paradigm shift in medicine. Risk is thus tied to attributes of the player that may have nothing to do with the practice into which our technology is being introduced.

Of course, just as windows open, they close. Four factors are critical here. The first is new technology that changes the competitive landscape. Going back to our zipper example, Velcro® is a technology that did that. Second, saturation will at some point occur. When everyone has bought, by definition the window closes. Third, when there are enough vendors and demand slows, the opportunities for entry shrink. Finally, just as changes in paradigms for practices can open windows, they can close them. In the airline business, the shift away from hub-spoke routing in the domestic U.S. airline industry closes the window of opportunity for large

747-like airliners even while widening the window for small aircraft to meet the needs of regional carriers.

VALUE PROPOSITIONS

A value proposition is the strategic framework for a value statement. The value statement is rhetoric. It tells the buyer why he or she should buy. A value proposition is the justification for the statement. It provides a perspective from which the technology should be viewed and within which the value statement makes sense and as such, both positions the technology vis-à-vis its competitors and suggests how a company seeking to commercialization their technology should orient its value creation activities.

According to Legrenzi, Girotto and Johnson-Laird, the initial specification of a decision acts as a focus for both the information that subjects seek and their ultimate decision, and they tend to overlook other factors which are not included in the original specification—factors that might well influence their decision in other instances.[27] Thus, in order to exploit the window of opportunity, we have to position our technology in such a way that end users are persuaded to look at factors that favor us and not the competition.

We can identify at least four logically distinct factors for value propositions, although the precise mix used in the value proposition for any specific technology is an empirical question tied to what end users and buyers want and with what technologies you are competing.

Cost leadership bases competitive advantage on price. The key here is often leveraging economies of scale. Temporary cost leadership can be gained through first mover advantage, which means that as the first competitor to be making, selling, and supporting a good, you are likely to attain know-how earlier concerning how best to accomplish these tasks. Typically, learning curve advantages are tied to a rising volume of goods sold, so the first mover advantage can be lost if a later entrant can ramp up volume more quickly. Process technology innovation is often combined with incremental product technology innovation for cost leadership. The process innovation is focused on specialized high volume production. Incremental innovation is attractive because it does not render obsolete the investment in process technology. Major product or service family transitions are carefully planned. Peoples Express, and later Southwest Airlines, are examples of this strategy. (Note that cost leadership is sometimes

---

[27] P. Legrenzi, V. Girotto, and P.N. Johnson-Laird, "Focusing in Reasoning and Decision Making," *Reasoning and Decision Making, Cognition Special Issue* (New York: Elsevier Science Publishers, 1993).

combined with hypercompetitive, predatory practices against competitors. Also, note it does not always work. People Express bellied up.)

Differentiation involves developing a family of services or features that meets divergent sets of end user needs better than the competition. It achieves a competitive advantage by building on *"platform"* technologies to provide the different price/performance bundles for different customer segments. The differentiated product or service family is a set of variations on a theme. For example, it is toothpaste with fluoride, toothpaste with fluoride and tartar control, toothpaste with fluoride and baking soda, toothpaste with fluoride and whiteners, etc. In other words, different customer segments have their needs satisfied through products that have variations that reflect how the needs of that segment impact the dominant design. Differentiation also can be provided through the packaging of a product. Better delivery, warranties, and enhanced customer services and repair services can meet requirements of different sets of end users. Procter & Gamble is an example of a company using this strategy. Adaptive innovations combined with process innovations are frequently used to gain sustainable advantage. Leveraging economies of scope is also a common tactic.

Focus is a strategy based on careful attention to buyers' and end users' specific needs. It is the kind of approach where close contact with the customer is maintained, so the products, processes, or services sold have been carefully developed to calibrate with the performance requirements and desired features of a customer segment. Focus strategies can be viewed as "loving them dearly." Adaptive and radical product innovation is more important than process innovation. Innovation is often focused on ease-of-use and performance more than price, so long as the value contribution to the customer is clear. Nextel is an example of a company using this approach with its business-oriented national walkie-talkie cell phones. Network externalities may be leveraged as a tactic to cut costs.

Rapid response is being the first to find a way to meet emerging end-user needs. This strategy works well in *embryonic* markets and enables selling to small numbers of customers. On the one hand, the dominant design is non-existent, and on the other, end-user needs are in flux. The number of products and/or services offered is large and rapidly changing, so it does not make sense to lock-in, and heavily invest in, a given product or service design until the market stabilizes. Rapid response also works where the life cycle of the dominant design is ending and an alternative technology may be able to hop in and capture market share. In either case, the competitive advantage lies in being agile so you can shift what you sell to meet changing and varying customer requirements. It is an approach sometimes taken by engineering consulting firms, such as CH2M Hill, who will custom design what the customer needs if they do not already

	Price Leadership	Differentiation	Focus	Rapid Response
Embryonic			X	X
Growth		X	X	
Shakeout	X	X	X	
Mature	X	X	X	
Declining		X	X	

EXHIBIT 7.13 Market Phases and Strategies

have it in their tool kit. Product innovation capabilities (often disruptive) are critical.

As noted in Exhibit 7.13, different market phases lend themselves to different strategies, due to the interaction of dominant designs with the skills and capabilities of the new buyers entering the market:

- In embryonic markets, the buyers likely do not have stable requirements as the dominant design is in flux, so rapid response or focus strategies are useful.

- As the market enters growth, the number of buyers is still relatively small. With the dominant design emerging, focus strategies can be used to provide best value for specific segments. Focus is attractive as the new users often lack methods and techniques for extracting maximum value from a technology because the dominant design is still new. The vendor plays a key role in disseminating know-how. Training, service, etc. enhance value as they cut adoption costs and speed progress down the learning curve. Later, as the flood of new users introduces definable customer segmentation, differentiation can be used to try to provide best value across these segments.

- As the goods offered converge around the features and functionalities of the dominant design, buyers now can find other sources of know-how. A good example is the *"For Dummies"* series of computer software handbooks. With increasingly commodity-like technology and easy access to know-how, price becomes more important. Differentiation continues to be attractive as a way segmenting the value proposition for different customer segments, but now it can also be used to leverage labeling as a way of charging different prices for the same goods in different customer segments. (Anyone who has ever shopped for Ralph Lauren clothes at both department stores and discount malls understands this intuitively.) This configuration encourages more buyers to enter the market. At some point, however, new entry of buyers slows, the rate of market growth slows, and shakeout begins.

■ Finally, as markets enter maturity, differentiation and price enable larger players to leverage economies of scale and scope or network externalities. Smaller players only thrive as niche players focusing on an underserved customer segments.

A small company can survive shakeout by focusing on a customer segment too small to attract the interest of larger players. An example is vector network analyzers. These are electronic metrology tools for test and analysis of waves. They track the phase, frequency, and amplitude of signals. Non-linear vector network analyzers add the ability to analyze the non-linear signal components of these waves. Only a non-linear analyzer can provide a complete picture of what is happening in a circuit. They present both the fundamental frequency and the harmonics. At present there is only limited demand for non-linear analyzers for cell phone base stations as bandwidth packing is not tight enough to require attention to the non-linear components of waves. Thus, there is only one company, Maury Microwave, that manufactures these analyzers. The company is named after its founder, who spun out of Agilent with a license to his invention. The market for these devices is just too small for a company of that size. Nonetheless, the expectation is that at some point in the future, bandwidth will become so tight that non-linear analyzers will become a booming business, At that time "Watch out," according to one expert we spoke with while doing a project on superconducting delay circuits for these analyzers. Agilent will pull back its technology and with some of the other big boys, they will enter the market. The lesson: If you are playing focus strategies, goodwill and a large enough customer base are critical for surviving shakeout and having the option to be acquired.

CONCLUSION

Positioning is a matter of determining the intersection between what your technology can do and what your end users need. We have seen the first step is clarifying what motivates buying behavior, what gives a product, process, or service "*umpf*." When umpf is clear, we can focus on the instrumental consideration of how to increase a good's attractiveness to buyers. The key to this activity is understanding the dominant design(s) used in the relevant practice(s) on the one hand, and what is happening in the practice itself as it adapts to market demand and socio-economic change on the other.

If we do our homework right, we end up positioning our technology at a Nash Equilibrium, which is a fancy way of saving, we position it where it makes more sense for buyers to buy it than to not buy it. Because markets are dynamic, this positioning may have to change over time, but what we hope to find is an equilibrium point that is likely to endure for at least five years *from the date of initial market entry.*

The reason for five years is most people in business do not have horizons longer than that. They need to show a good profit for the shareholders and some nice bonus for themselves. If a technology is not making money within five years of market introduction, the likelihood it ever will gets pretty slim.

Technikos

USING WEB SEARCH TO DEVELOP AND TEST HYPOTHESES

Web searching is more of an art than a science. One the one hand, there is the problem of knowing what to search for. On the other hand is the problem of the search terms to use.

What we are searching for is driven by the questions we are asking. Does a competitive opening exist for this technology? Is it competitive? Does a target exist? Is there technology in the patent literature that makes this technology redundant or will swamp it? We are seeking to make hypotheses that address the specific skills, capacities, and attitudes of people in order to make more general hypotheses about viable market niches for initial entry.

In making our hypotheses, frame your hypotheses in the positive and then seek to falsify them.[28] For example: This technology is unique in its ability to address these needs. Now we can search products, patents, and R&D literature to see if we can falsify our hypotheses.

In developing hypotheses, we are taking concepts and relationships out of our model and "operationalizing" them to the specific scientific-engineering domains of the technology and/or the context of the application. The set of concepts (and relationships between them) that can be derived from the model constitute an *ontology,* or a structure of being as depicted in the model. Exhibit 7.A1 presents a partial example. To develop hypotheses we take the concepts from the ontology and instantiate them using terms found in specific domains or contexts of interest. Once we have done that, we can begin to develop search terms and search strategies that allow us to sustain or falsify our hypotheses.

---

[28] This approach is openly Popperian. Whatever the philosophic argument, it is very useful for assessing technologies because ultimately we want solutions that work time and time again as promised. It is better to set the bar high. See Karl R. Popper, "Science as Falsification," 1963, http://www.stephenjaygould.org/ctrl/popper_falsification .html (accessed January 24, 2005).

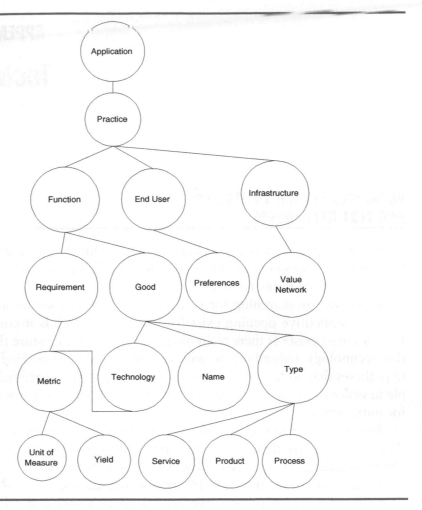

EXHIBIT 7A.1   Concept Map for Assessing Applications

For the Naval Surface Warfare Center, Carderock Division, we examined markets for a magneto-restrictive inchworm motor. In such a motor, in a magnetic field, a bar extends. When the field is removed, it contracts. We hypothesized it would be useful for automobile brakes. In Exhibit 7A.2, this hypothesis is used to construct a set of search terms based on a fragment of the conceptual ontology presented in Exhibit 7A.1.

Note that our initial selection of search terms may not be useful for one of three reasons:

1. A synonym of the term may be better for searching;
2. A term of more generality or specificity may be better for searching; or,
3. An instantiation for the concept may not appear on the web.

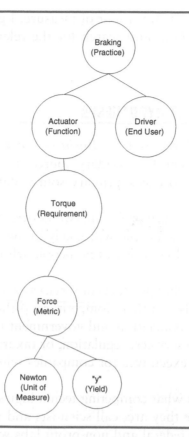

EXHIBIT 7A.2 Instantiation of Concept Map

If the last option exists, the hypothesis cannot be tested due to a lack of data. In either of the other two situations there are straightforward solutions.

> *To find new terms given known terms, several sources are useful. I usually begin with WordNet® at http://www.cogsci.princeton.edu/~wn/. Developed by Cognitive Science Laboratory at Princeton it is an on-line lexicon with synonym sets.[29]*

If I still do not have what I need, I search the web for Frequently Asked Questions (FAQs) and glossaries. To do that I use the string: NAME OR TERM and (glossary or FAQ or "Frequently Asked Questions") in Google™, which happens to be my favorite engine right now. If the

---

[29] "About WordNet," n.d., http://www.cogsci.princeton.edu/~wn/ (accessed January 23, 2005).

synonym I am seeking is for a unit of measure, I go to *http://physics.nist .gov/cuu/Units/index.html* and search for the relevant Standard International Unit.

INTERVIEWING TO TEST HYPOTHESES

Larry Kahaner was a reporter for *Business Week*. He notes that a good rule of thumb is to check secondary source data with primary source (interview) data and to check primary source data with data from secondary sources.[30]

In conducting interviews there are two key tricks that make things easier. First, only interview people who likely know what you are trying to find out. The way to do that is to find people whose job it is to know the data you are seeking.

If the question is what products or services exist, call salespeople. They will know their goods and their competitors. If the question is how big a market is, call trade association and government officials who track that data for membership services, regulation, or taxation. Another source for market data is sales executives for companies who are vendors for complementary goods.

If the question is what competing technologies exist, how they work, and how competitive they are, call scientists and engineers in university-industry centers and federal and non-profit labs with a large patent portfolio in the area.

The most important people to call are the end users who might purchase what you have. If you cannot find them, look for people who have purchased, or considered purchasing, one of the competing technologies.

Also providing insights into end-user needs are trade and professional society members from the most relevant committees and/or subcommittees.

(FYI: Marketing people at competitors are usually willing to provide performance and price information if you ask for it. Simply say you are collecting the information for a product comparison requested by a manager. Do not offer that you are a competitor, but if asked, do not lie.)

Whomever you call it is imperative to do two things in advance:

1. Know what you want to find out, and
2. What you will offer each person as an incentive to provide you the information.

---

[30] Larry Kahaner, *Competitive Intelligence* (New York: Touchstone, 1997), 56.

Plan your interview so you can collect everything you want to know in 10 minutes or less. If it is likely to take you longer to collect what you need, break up the survey into two or more interviews and direct each one at a different person in the company from whom you are seeking data.

The incentive usually is a non-proprietary description of the technology. This may not seem like much until you remember that these people are gatekeepers. Part of their job definition is to keep abreast of developments and your work could turn out to be a pretty big one if it is successfully commercialized.

There are two ways to conduct interviews: survey or case study. The case study method is more useful for most early stage commercialization market research as it can be done as a "quick and dirty" but scientifically, a valid study if conducted responsibly.

In a case study interview, the data to be collected has been identified in advance. Each data item contributes to answering a question. How each item will be analyzed to answer the question is also known. The interview schedule is simply a data collection form, used by the interviewer to make sure all the relevant data items have been collected. According to Bacon and Butler, typically three to six well-chosen interviews are able to resolve all critical issues and provide guidance as to subsequent commercialization activities.[31] That fits our experience at Foresight Science & Technology.

If more than one person is conducting the interviews, they should coordinate in advance and discuss what data they are collecting, why, and how they will describe what they are doing. This helps ensure a common presentation to each respondent, enhancing the ability to compare results from one interview with those from another.

---

[31] Bacon and Butler, *Planned Innovation* (New York:The Free Press, 1998), 83.

Presenting Your Technology

Regardless of how you plan to commercialize your technology, one of the three following scenarios dictates how much information to disclose in presenting your technology:

1. Pre-nondisclosure;
2. Post-nondisclosure (but pre-deal);
3. Post-deal (fully executed contract).

PRE-NONDISCLOSURE

As you begin to market your technology to interested parties you should prepare a high-level, non-confidential description of the technology and its benefits to the intended market. Think in terms of non-confidential abstracts, such as those that appear at the beginning of patents and technical papers. The wording should be simple enough so that almost anyone can understand it, since in many cases the initial reader of such a disclosure will not necessarily be on the same technical wavelength as you. For example: "A new cell-phone integrated circuit chip technology to create smaller, lower-power, cheaper cell phones. The basic idea is analogous to taking a 1 watt light bulb and 10 watt light bulb and effectively getting the power of a 100 watt light bulb." Such non-confidential descriptions may include identification of any relevant patents, published papers and abstracts as well as web-site information and press releases. If you are planning to distribute this information by electronic means, then make sure it can fit into the body of an email as text, as many email recipients currently delete any unidentified emails that contain attachments to prevent infecting their machines with unwanted viruses.

POST-NONDISCLOSURE (BUT PRE-DEAL)

Once a party has expressed interest in learning more about the technology and a formal nondisclosure agreement has been executed by both parties, then a more detailed description of the technology is required, frequently as a formal Power Point presentation (and possibly on-site technical discussion and facilities tour). The trick here is to present just enough information to entice the interested party into consummating a deal with you for access to the technology, but not so much information that he can either duplicate it on his own or is challenged to attempt to duplicate it without your assistance. Generally the how's are not discussed whereas the what's, where's, why's and who cares are. If you question whether or not you should disclose something, the prudent course of action is *not to do so* unless specifically requested, and even then if you feel uncomfortable in doing so, *don't.* If he asks for patents, and they have been issued, then it is okay to disclose that information, since they are freely available on the U.S. Patent Office's website anyway (*www.uspto.gov*).

INVESTOR PRESENTATIONS

In between the Pre- and Post-nondisclosure presentations is the never-never land of investor presentations. If you are looking for a venture capitalist or an angel investor, then you will need to put together a business case and executive summary. It's hard to write the executive summary without first having done a business or commercialization plan. A complete commercialization plan will likely include much of the information normally reserved for a Post-nondisclosure presentation. But most investors will not sign nondisclosure agreements prior to doing their own due diligence on a technology that captures their interest. Since only a very small percentage of new business proposals actually get funded by venture capitalists (less than 1% of those reviewed according to one source) the competition is extremely fierce. Hence the conundrum—what to do? The answer is to use an executive summary, which should not be more than 2 or 3 pages long, as the initial presentation package to potential investors. If an investor asks to see more information and/or a full business case, it is appropriate to ask that a nondisclosure agreement be executed first. Obviously, the executive summary will need to answer the what's, where's, why's and who cares at a high level and must be presented in such a way as to capture the reader's attention so that you get the desired call-back.

POST-DEAL (FULLY EXECUTED CONTRACT)

After both parties have signed the appropriate technology transfer or investment agreement, the other party will expect you to have a full-blown technology transfer package available (Note: This does not necessarily apply to patent license agreements, since in those cases you are simply giving them the right to *"infringe"* without penalty). Included in this package are a number of items, including (but not necessarily limited to) relevant written materials, patent applications, unpatented know-how, lab notebooks, manuals and drawings, as well as relevant certifications, licenses, approvals, pending applications, sales forecasts, pro forma income statements, manufacturing cost statements, existing and target customer lists and listing of any other relevant agreements. It should *only* be delivered after execution of the appropriate agreement(s) by all parties to the transaction.

Launch Tactics

INTRODUCTION

If no one knows about your goods, they won't buy them. If they don't like them, they won't buy them even if they do know about them. These common sense observations frame Chapter 8's problem. We need to bring knowledge of your good's competitive advantages to end users in a manner persuasive enough to stimulate buying.

We shall use two tools to help develop launch tactics: the SWOT and the 4 Ps'. SWOT stands for strengths, weaknesses, opportunities, and threats. We use the SWOT to figure out just what the 4 Ps' should be. The 4 Ps' are product, price, promotion, and place. The 4 Ps' are the launch tactics.

Product is what is being sold. It may be a product, process, or service. It may be a stand-alone good or a package that includes warrantees, financing, upgrades, you name it.

Price is what is charged to the buyer. The price may be paid at one time, as when you go to the store and buy a new shirt or blouse. Or it may be paid over time, as when you pay your utility bill each month. In the case of technology, usually payments over time are associated with licensing and called royalties.

Promotion is how the end users and buyers are made aware of the technology and how to buy it. Positioning provides the strategic framework or perspective for developing the content for promotion.

Place is how you get a good into the hands of the end user. It involves taking it from point A to point B and getting it into use at point B.

As we shall see, while our focus in this chapter is on figuring out the launch tactics to sell to the end user, in the process we also develop criteria for selecting our commercialization partner(s). The partner we want is a player that has capabilities and capacities that supplement ours so that we can pursue the 4 Ps'. If we cannot find what we need in one partner, then we need to string more than one together. For example, say you are introducing a new kind of production equipment. One partner, a contract manufacturer, may make the product, another partner, perhaps a sale rep organization, sells it, and yet a third, a contract repair operation, handles service in the event the equipment breaks. Any or all of these may help finance their piece of the action or the money could come from a third source, such as an investor or bank.

One note before proceeding. If you went to business school you may find the presentation here a bit odd. You will have to engage in what Samuel Coleridge calls "the willing suspension of disbelief."[1] If positioning is about finding Nash Equilibriums at which we can place our goods, launch tactics are how to make that positioning happen. The B-school methods have been adapted to that end.

SWOTS

SWOTs are a way of organizing the market research data we have collected in order to develop action consequences. What SWOTs do is help us figure out the 4 Ps'. We use them to extract the action implications from the research we have done.

We can illustrate the use of SWOTs with solid state lighting.

Solid state lighting is going to be big. Light-emitting diodes (LEDS) draw almost no power. They last years. With organic light-emitting diodes (OLEDs) they can be made by slapping the phosphor (or other material) on a piece of glass or plastic. This substrate can then be cut to any shape you want. If it is plastic, it can even be flexible.

OLEDs are much cheaper to fabricate than traditional LEDs because the emissive layer can be deposited in arrays on a substrate using simple inkjet printing methods. The result is a graphical color display for television screens, computer displays, or just general illumination. OLEDs create brighter images than traditional LEDs that can be viewed from wider angles. In addition, OLEDs require less power than the liquid crystal displays (LCDs) because LCDs behave like voltage-controlled translucent shutters while OLEDs are light emitters that do not need a backlight. As household or other building lights, OLEDs can provide diffuse sources of ambient light in comparison to inorganic LEDs, which are point sources. All in all, an attractive value proposition.

As production volumes ramp up, the supply chain for OLEDs is developing. For example, some semiconductor manufacturers are offering

---

[1] Mrs. Meese, one of my high school English teachers, loved the *Rime of the Ancient Mariner* and made us memorize it and a bunch of other Coleridge quotes. This one stuck.

power-converter integrated circuits (ICs) for OLED-bias supplies to give original equipment manufacturer (OEM) designers flexibility for designing the display power subsystem. Next will come power converter ICs strictly optimized for OLED power controllers.[2]

The United States accounts for about one third of the world's illumination. The U.S. Department of Energy concluded in 2003 that switching to OLEDs and LEDs from incandescents and fluorescents can save over 765 GW of energy over 25 years and eliminate the need for building 133 new 1000 MW power stations. It would reduce carbon emissions by 28 million tons annually.[3] According to the Society for Information Display, the global OLED market has grown from $251 million in 2003 to $408 million a year later. By 2008 the estimates range from as low as $3 billion to as high as $8 billion.[4]

Of course, a rising tide does not really mean all boats will rise. All sorts of barriers to entry exist. One barrier is competition. Big companies already are playing. These include household names like Samsung, Pioneer, and Kodak as well as less well known emerging tigers like RiTdisplay, AU Optronics (AUO), teco Optronics, Lightronik and Univision Technology in Taiwan.[5] So, if you are a small company commercializing an innovative material, you have to think about whether it is better to partner or go it alone. Another barrier is technology breakthroughs. Current approaches for making OLEDs include small vapor deposited molecules, polymers, fluorescent emitters, phosphorescent emitters. A new technology, quantum dots (semiconductor nanoparticles) may supplant all of these as luminescent down-converting materials. On the other hand, neither quantum dots nor any of the other materials has the lifetime at high illumination needed for general lighting. So, you have to pick your applications carefully and strive for rapid market entry in order to remain a player as everyone pushes the technology to higher performance. Other barriers highlighted by the U.S. Department of Energy include scaling manufacturing. It is not yet clear how to make defect-free large area OLEDs using continuous roll-to-roll printing. Encapsulation

---

[2] Joshua Israelsohn, "Organic-LED Graphics Displays Are Taking on LCDs for Image Quality and Low-Power Operation," *EDN* (November 24, 2004), http://www.edn.com/article/CA480492.html (accessed October 7, 2005).

[3] Milan Stolka, "OLEDs for General Illumination," March 2003, http://www.nrel.gov/ncpv_prm/pdfs/33586039.pdf (accessed October 7, 2005).

[4] Wikipedia, "Organic Light-Emitting Diode," October 7, 2005, http://en.wikipedia.org/wiki/OLED, (accessed October 7, 2005).

[5] Anita Li, "Taiwanese Vendors Focus on AMOLED Products," *Nikkei Electronics Asia* (May 2005), http://neasia.nikkeibp.com/neasiaarchivedetail/001111 (accessed October 7, 2005).

of materials against moisture while allowing transparency for light is still a challenge, as methods for packaging the OLEDs and connecting them to power sources.[6]

The SWOT is the tool we use to structure the data in order to extract launch tactics that allow us to leverage internal abilities and market forces to overcome barriers to entry. There are four steps to doing a SWOT.

1. Pick the Positioning

Actually we did this already, in Chapter 7. But if you skipped over that chapter, then you have to do it here. So, here is the short version.

Positioning is a matter of finding where our technology maps to end-user needs better than other offerings. Where that occurs we gain competitive advantage. If our technology does not have a competitive advantage we have a *big problem*. In that case, we have to stop and figure out how to get competitive advantage before doing the SWOT.

SWOTs are guided by how we are going to position this technology, which in turn is guided by how end users will literally touch, taste, smell, hear, and/or see it. So, like mariners at sea, our pole star is the needs of the end user, and we sail a course that leads the end users to realize we have what they want.

One key to positioning is to understand how our technology coheres with the dominant design in the practice. In the case of OLEDs, the challenge for positioning is whether to focus exclusively on general illumination or to step into the market by seeking interim applications with less rigorous performance, ease-of-use, and cost requirements. Most vendors have elected to step into the market, with the result that several firms compete for computer and device displays. One area of emphasis is cell phones. Several features of OLEDs make them attractive here, so much so that OLEDs could dominate cell phone displays in the next few years. The fact they do not need backlighting extends battery time. With the shift to camera phones, their wide viewing angle is attractive. Further, cell phones are costly, so the incremental cost for using an OLED instead of an LCD can be buried. Finally, as consumers tend to swap cell phones within a year, and they are not on all the time, the currently limited lifetime of around 10,000 hours is less of a factor in this application than in others.[7]

---

[6] Stolka, "OLEDs for General Illumination."

[7] Neil Savage, "Going Organic," *OE Magazine* (November 2003), http://oemagazine .com/fromTheMagazine/nov03/prodtrends.html (accessed October 8, 2005).

2. Determine the Strengths and Weaknesses

Strengths and weaknesses are internal to an organization. They are factors over which we have control, although exercising control might require tossing money at a problem. The primary factors we are concerned about are the technology and our organization. With respect to the technology, we typically are concerned about the maturity of our technology and its performance, ease-of-use, and price. With respect to our organization we are interested in knowing we have the capabilities and capacities to go to market and if we have the kind of people who will make it possible to do deals.

We have control over the maturity and specifications of our technology. Suppose our technology is a breakthrough, like quantum dots may be for white light OLEDs. **Strength.** Suppose we have a patent that has been issued for the material. **Strength.** Suppose we have a set of extending patents that cover ways of making and applying the material inexpensively. **Strength.** Suppose we are partnered with a bunch of leading universities here and abroad to further improve the technology. **Strength.** Suppose we are making limited product runs already. **Strength.** Suppose we have some happy customers for high value applications like cell phone displays. **Strength.**

Change the scenario. Now, suppose we know our technology is not yet mature enough to compete for cell phone displays. **Weakness.** We have to compensate for that weakness by hiring engineers to make it more mature. Toss money. Suppose we are using polymers but discover we cannot get the blue to illuminate long enough. With only red and green we cannot make a white light. **Weakness.** We have to go back into R&D and reformulate. Toss money. Suppose another problem is that although we can do batch manufacturing process in the lab, we have quality problems laying up a consistent thickness in roll-to-roll printing. **Weakness.** Toss more money.

Strengths make it easier to sell. Weaknesses make it harder to sell. Of course, strengths are not free. Usually they result from money wisely spent in the past. Still, if your focus is on the future, better to have a sunk cost behind you than a major expense in front of you.

It works the same way with organizational factors. Hey, we need a better lab. **Weakness.** Toss money. Hey, folks think our CEO is a genius. **Strength.** Whoops, they think he is a jerk. **Weakness.** Replace him. Toss money to hire that dynamite lady who built whosit's OLED business. Got her on board? **Strength.** How about brand loyalty and good will? **Strength.** How about a pipeline for labor, raw materials, components, sub-assemblies, you name it. **Strength.** How about supply chain problems? **Weakness.**

Often overlooked as a key strength is the personality of founders or champions. In the GE OLED story, Duggal's advocacy was critical. The story of petroleum jelly also highlights this point. Petroleum jelly was invented by Robert Augustus Chesebrough in 1859. When oil was found in Pennsylvania, this chemist decided to head to the fields to find his fortune. He found workers slapping something called rod-wax on cuts instead of bandages to stem the bleeding and help cure wounds. It also helped burns heal faster. Rod-wax was a paraffin like film that collected on pump rods and caused the drilling rigs to freeze up until removed. He developed a clean form of rod-wax that he called petroleum jelly.

R&D defined the product: petroleum jelly. The patent was issued in 1872. But there were clear weaknesses facing commercialization. There was no product awareness nor established distribution and sales channels to leverage. Intellectual property in the form of the patent alone was insufficient to sell a product no-one knew they wanted.

The personality of Chesebrough as an entrepreneur was the critical strength. Chesebrough used himself as his guinea pig during product development. He cut and burned himself in order to test the healing properties. Accepting the lack of awareness, Chesebrough used below low ball pricing combined with face-to-face promotion to build demand. He took the product on the road in his own medicine show, adopting the tactics of "snake oil salesmen." He traveled across New York State handing out free samples and demonstrating the product on himself. Six months later, he had twelve wagons distributing (placing) the product.[8] Within a few years, one jar per minute of Vaseline was sold.

With the post-Civil War industrialization of the American economy, trademarks became important corporate resources. By 1905 Congress had enacted a Trademark Act. Chesebrough used trademark to supplement his patent IP to promote the product. Urban myth says the name Vaseline emerged during the development phase, when he filled up every beaker in his lab with product so he began using his wife's flower vases to make the jelly. Adding a popular medical term *'line'* to *'vase'* gave him his trademark and positioning: the medical petroleum product, Vaseline Petroleum Jelly. Unilever, however, which owns the trademark, says Vaseline comes from combining of *Wasser,*

---

[8] Vaseline.biography.ms, "Petroleum Jelly," *Biography.ms,* n.d., http://vaseline.biography.ms/ (accessed October 8, 2005).

the German word for water with *elaion*, the Greek word for oil.[9] In 1877, Vaseline was registered as a trademark.[10] Whatever the source, the trademark itself was a strength as it put a name on the product that pulled attention away from the fact you were smearing oil on yourself.

Chesebrough's firm initially began as a manufacturer of kerosene, but after 1881 shifted exclusively to manufacturing Vaseline, thereby leveraging its intellectual property. This shift allowed Chesebrough to leapfrog into global sales and build strong market dominance for Vaseline.[11] Later, the emergence of Standard Oil in 1870 presented a new threat to Chesebrough Manufacturing. By 1878, Rockefeller had locked up around 80% of domestic refining capacity. Chesebrough responded by bringing his company into the Standard Oil Trust in 1882, adopting partnering to counter potential supply chain problems.

3. Determine the Opportunities and Threats

Opportunities and threats are environmental factors outside of our control. We find them by examining market forces and barriers as well as competition.

Unlike the case with weaknesses, with threats we cannot just toss money and make them go away. It is our inability to counter threats simply by tossing money at them that makes them so insidious. All we can do is seek to counter them by using our strengths to neutralize them while seeking to exploit opportunities.

Arthur Sicard invented the snowblower. Growing up in rural Quebec, Canada, he was eighteen when he first saw a thresher, a piece of farm equipment that gathers the wheat by pulling it in with rotating blades. Sicard adapted this idea to the problem of snow on roads. Unfortunately, his early attempts failed as machines bogged down in drifts. He was considered a crackpot. He left home and moved to Montreal,

(Continued)

---

[9] Unilever, "Vaseline," 2005, http://www.unilever.co.uk/ourbrands/personalcare/vaseline.asp (accessed October 8, 2005).
[10] Ibid.
[11] Harvard Business School, "Robert A. Chesebrough," n.d., http://www.hbs.edu/leadership/database/leaders/144/ (accessed October 8, 2005).

where after more trials and tribulations, in 1925 after a major storm he drove a truck with an auxiliary motor on the body of the truck that powered two rotating blades with a long ejection shoot behind for ejecting the snow. In this case, the critical factor causing an opportunity was the environment. The strength used to exploit the opportunity was a mature technology. By 1927, the town of Outremont had bought one and within decades the invention was in use throughout the world.[12]

General Electric's entry into OLEDs also highlights how strengths can be used to overcome threats as well as leverage opportunities, although here it is deep pockets and organizational clout that count even more than IP.

It was the fear of competition that drove GE into the OLED market. Anil Duggal, a GE chemist in corporate R&D realized that at some point OLEDs would supplant conventional incandescent and fluorescent lighting. He saw both an opportunity and a threat, depending on whether GE was leading or following the technology development. He was able to convince managers at his lab to support an initiative, and later found a champion in Greg Chambers, a business program manager. With Chambers help, GE obtained a grant from the U.S. Department of Energy, which spurred development by bringing in another revenue stream to help offset the cost of OLED development. In other words, the DoE funding program provided an opportunity that could be leveraged because the prior internally funded work created a strength to work from.

Then, in 2001, a new corporate CEO took over the reigns of GE from Jack Welch, who was less enthusiastic about investing in radical new technologies due to the risks involved. Jeffrey Immelt renewed GE's focus on innovation. Duggal and Chambers worked to build internal support for OLEDs, creating additional organizational strengths to supplement their technical strengths. The organizational strength resulted from linking R&D with marketing. (When it came time to pitch Immelt for support, Chambers said he told top management "GE should invent a new lightbulb every hundred years or so.")[13]

---

[12] Gilson Snowblower Shop, "Who Invented the Snowblower?" January 1, 2004, http://home.gwi.net/~spectrum/snowhistory.html#History (accessed October 9, 2005).
[13] Ryan Underwood, "Lighting the GE Way," *Fast Company* 85 (August 2004), http://www.fastcompany.com/magazine/85/ge.html (accessed October 8, 2005).

One way to get a handle on opportunities and threats is to use Michael Porter's Five Forces model. The web is full of discussions of Porter's Five Forces so we shall only briefly discuss them here.[14]

The forces are: bargaining power of suppliers (the entrenched competition); bargaining power of buyers (end users here); threat of substitute products (substitute technology here); threat of new entrants (you and other new entrants here); and competitive rivalry. Although Porter's presentation is often critiqued for being too static, that is less of an issue for us as we are using it as a heuristic tool and thus can compensate by remembering that what we are seeing is a snapshot out of a dynamic motion picture.

The bargaining power of suppliers and buyers mirror each other. In general, the higher the degree of consolidation and concentration (oligopoly or monopoly) on one side, the weaker the other side. The concentration ratio is the percent of output accounted for by the largest 4, 8, 20 and 50 companies. For the U.S. economy, this data is reported by the Bureau of Census at *http://www.census.gov/epcd/www/concentration.html*.

Similarly, the more dependent one side is on the other side for goods or sales, that is, the higher the percent accounted for, the weaker the dependent side. A classic example is the defense industry, where U.S. prime contractors are exceptionally dependent on the government. I once had a senior Boeing executive tell me that Boeing wanted to buy Bechtel as a diversification move years ago. The Secretary of the Air Force called the president of Boeing and said "No can do." When the president of Boeing complained, the Secretary of the Air Force simply said, "Well, we will take our business elsewhere then." Scotched that deal.

Other factors that affect relative strength are vertical integration of buyers and sellers, as that reduces dependency, the availability of alternatives (goods or customers) and the critical nature of what is being sold or bought for the survival of the entity.

Threat of substitutes is a function of both price and availability. All other things being equal, the more substitutes in a sector, the more likely price competition will emerge. As we have seen, substitutes need not be based on the same technology so long as they can provide equivalent functionality.

The greatest threats typically come from radical and disruptive technologies as they shift patterns for price elasticity, that is, the proportionate change in quantity demands given the proportionate change in price.

---

[14] Quick MBA.com, "Porter's Five Forces," 2004, http://www.quickmba.com/strategy/porter.shtml (accessed October 9, 2005).

Usually, for example, quantity demand drops when price increases. But consider the replacement of typewriters by word processors. The new technology offered such great savings with better labor productivity and enhanced efficiency that demand rose as prices rose. Similarly, broadband costs more than dial-up, but demand has grown for broadband access at home.

Availability reflects rates of product change. Typically sectors have a rate of product change that reflects buying patterns within the sector. Established vendors adjust to these rates and plan product replacement to coincide with buying cycles. However, the availability of substitutes also is shaped by how much an industrial sector is a net importer of technology on the one hand, and how open the sector is to innovations on the other. The more a sector imports and is innovation friendly, the easier it is for rates of new technology availability to increase in response to advances elsewhere as it is easier for technological substitutes to enter the sector from unanticipated places.

We have already discussed barriers to entry. Barriers that are commonly mentioned in the context of Porter's model include patents and other intellectual property rights, government regulation, restricted distribution channels, the needs to be able to afford large or expensive facilities to address market demand, and difficulties in switching brands (e.g. hopping from a Windows® platform to a Unix platform).

These four factors influence the fifth factor, which is rivalry or how vicious is the competition in an industry. Factors affecting rivalry include the number of firms in a sector (more firms usually means more competition), slowing market growth (shakeout), high strategic importance of the sector for the firms involved, high fixed costs that require competitors to produce at near capacity, low switching costs (which means buyers can easily substitute one product for another), high storage costs or very perishable items (which means inventory has to be turned quickly), and high exit barriers (which leads firms to fight more vigorously as they are stuck and have to compete.) Exit barriers include specialized assets that are hard to sell, integration of one business with other business units, which makes them hard to sell off without adverse impact, and high exit costs, such as the need to cover pensions or outplacement of displaced workers.

4. Look at the Intersection

Usually we only want three or four factors in each category. We want to focus on the important ones, not on some exhaustive catalog. De facto what we are doing is an ad hoc sensitivity analysis, choosing only those factors that are likely to have a significant impact on the outcome. Once we have these strengths, weaknesses, opportunities, and threats identified, we can figure out how to launch the technology.

Recall that the 4 Ps' are product, price, promotion, and place. To determine launch tactics we simply look at the intersection of the factors and draw out the consequences for how we conduct one or more of the 4 Ps'. Let's see how this works. Suppose we are positioning an OLED innovation for the general illumination white light market.

	Strengths: Working OLED, strong IP, can do batch production	Weaknesses: No highly reliable volume production
Opportunities: Rapidly growing market		
Threats: Competition from major U.S. and Asian firms; DoE funding start-up competitors		

Now we look at the intersecting cells. There is always an element of serendipity here as all we have is a heuristic tool. There is no intrinsic order to which cells are used to address which one of the 4 Ps' nor is there any formula for finding an acceptable solution for launching a product, process, or service to sell to end users.

We are stuck with the fundamental reality that we are practicing an imperfect science. All we have to guide us is the algorithm of coherence that says given the data we have collected during market research, does the solutions we propose fit with that data. If they do, choose the one that makes the most sense—however you determine that. Otherwise the only guidance we have is to make sure we have addressed all of four of the 4 Ps' and that the manner in which we have addressed them compensates for our weaknesses and neutralizes our threats in such a way as we think we actually sell something.

The following is an example. For sake of argument, let's assume our technology is a quantum dot material that we will manufacturer ourselves, targeting "high end" applications. An example of such a firm is Nanosys, Inc., which has an exclusive license to U.S. Patent Nos. 6,890,777 and 6,914,265, Quantum Dot White and Colored Light Emitting Diodes, from the Massachusetts Institute of Technology. The patents cover the technology underlying the use of semiconductor quantum dots for down converting phosphors for white and colored light emission. Although Nanosys appears to be targeting displays, as the lifetimes required are shorter, the technology could be applied to general illumination down-stream. Companies such as Evident Technologies are focused on this market, using funding from the New York State Energy Research and Development Authority.[15]

In the following table we focus on how a company like Evident might enter the general home illumination market. In the following example, we will focus on how a company like Kodak might enter the same market. Our intent is not to be historically accurate. We use these two examples strictly for illustrative purposes.

	Strengths: Working OLED, strong IP, can do batch production	Weaknesses: No highly reliable volume production
Opportunities: Rapidly growing market	*Product and Price:* Initial product for lighting is high end designer lighting, sold at premium prices as the designs are driven by aesthetic considerations. The customer is rich home-owners, and key stakeholders are interior designers. To enhance the designer quality, license trademarks from leading designers like Kate Spade or Vera Wang. Stay away from overused designers like Ralph Lauren. As the market builds, if you retain rights in the designs you help develop and the ability to use the trademark for a higher volume line, you may be able to develop a product family for more mainstream buildings and the homes, much as you can now buy Ralph Lauren paint at Home Depot. This artsy product family can be	*Promote:* The initial designer focus gets you in the market with a premium product whose pricing helps build cash flow. Promotion should emphasize design shows and high end, but popular magazines like *Architectural Digest* as well magazines presenting new technologies to wealthier audiences, like *Smithsonian.* Assuming this strategy makes sense, the initial production is batch based, which the more mainstream family used roll-to-roll continuous production As sales build and demand starts to outstrip batch capacity, you will be well placed to do an IPO to fund manufacturing technology and build volume facilities that lets you keep up with demand. Note that for investors you need to promote yourself as providing a proven solution

[15] Evident Technologies, "Evident Technologies Receives NYSERDA Funds for High-Efficiency Lighting Products and Demonstrations," June 2004, http://www.evidenttech .com/resource-center/resources/Evident%20Technologies%20Collateral%20and%20 Articles/Evident%20Product%20Collateral/Press%20Releases/quantum-dot-led-pr .pdf (accessed October 8, 2005); and http://www.evidenttech.com/applications/ quantum-dot-ssl.php, 2005 (both accessed October 8, 2005).

	Strengths: Working OLED, strong IP, can do batch production	Weaknesses: No highly reliable volume production
	used to differentiate you from other competitors that will emerge for home lighting.	being sold today. The focus of the IPO is money for scaling, not market entry as is the case with less advanced competitors.
Threats: Competition from major U.S. and Asian Firms; DoE funding start-up competitors	*Promote:* Start major campaign focused on interior designers with theme: Tomorrow's lighting here today. Thus the emphasis on the "*hot*" fashion designers, not the old standards. Use first mover advantage to build brand loyalty so designers will spec your lighting. Show up at meetings like those of the American Society of Interior Designers and the International Interior Design Association. Promote the fact you will protect your IP position by vigorously pursuing infringers. This builds the mystique of the product as well as scaring off competitors. As you are positioning for the high end to middle range, consider when to begin licensing materials to lower end manufacturers, although what can be sold will have to be carefully defined.	*Place:* If the product can be plastic, it should be a very light weight product so consider drop shipping via airborne express. One advantage is that you can offer next day delivery. Otherwise it makes sense to offer just-in-time delivery so units do not have to be stored till needed. Consider ways to stimulate awareness like providing free samples to designers and journal editors that can be placed in their own offices for general illumination. Service can be handled by pick-up as a new unit is being shipped out, enabling you to use "no hassle" service to help build brand loyalty. Obviously, rigorous quality control is critical as OLEDs should be very robust. You may want to think about special designed packaging to product units in shipping.

If our positioning or the factors change, we end up with different recommendations. Let's use the same factors, but this time, as noted, we shall very loosely use Kodak as an example. Kodak discovered OLED materials in the late 70's and by the late 1980s was patenting them. There are more than 150 Kodak patents in the field. Kodak's emphasis has been on licensing, but it also has been building production capacity with an emphasis on displays and signage, as that can leverage the company's roll-to-roll production expertise.[16] Unfortunately, it has been harder than anticipated to drive down manufacturing costs while improving yields OLEDs. Exacerbating matters is that the materials remain relatively short lived compared to inorganic LEDs and LCDs.[17]

	Strengths: Working OLED, strong IP, can do batch production	Weaknesses: No highly reliable volume production
Opportunities: Rapidly growing market	*Promote:* Promote yourself as a clearinghouse or pipeline for OLED licensing by expanding your relationships with both engineers and product line managers on the one hand and in-licensing executives on the other. Being active in the Product Development Management Association, Licensing Executives Society etc. is one way to network to new relevant companies.	*Product:* The product being sold is actually IP, which is where the focus has been in the past. (For example, in May of this year Fuji Electric Holdings Co. Ltd. of Japan licensed Kodak's technology to develop its own full-color OLED displays.[18] Fuji joins over 15 other major corporations licensing Kodak OLED technology.) In order to diversify into general illumination, your technology pipeline has to be refilled. One way to do that is to shift from product to process technology, as it appears that roll-to-roll and other OLED processes can be generically applied. That enables addressing core issues that hinder the industry as a whole. Either internally or through the existing joint venture with Sanyo this process technology can be pursued, possibly in connection with emerging active matrix 40 inch amorphous silicon

---

[16] Eastman Kodak, "Display and Components Group," n.d. http://media.corporate-ir.net/media_files/IROL/11/115911/reports/display.pdf (accessed October 8, 2005).
[17] John Latta, "Dice Roll Gamble in OLED—Lowering Expectations," *Wave Report* (March 1–3, 2005), http://www.wave-report.com/conference_reports/2005/DisplaySearch2005.htm (accessed October 8, 2005).
[18] "Fuji Licenses Kodak OLED Technology," *Electronic News* (May 23, 2005), http://www.reed-electronics.com/electronicnews/article/CA603347.html (accessed October 8, 2005).

	Strengths: Working OLED, strong IP, can do batch production	Weaknesses: No highly reliable volume production
		displays and 14-inch solution-processed displays.
Threats: Competition from major U.S. and Asian Firms; DoE funding start-up competitors	*Product:* Competition will only intensify as new materials and devices are introduced. The DoE Small Business Innovation Research Program is an example of one place to find new materials (and possibly process) technologies better suited for general illumination. Consider using early Phase III partnering to gain access to technology. By leveraging DoE and other federal agency funded research, you may be able to add more advanced device configurations and better materials to counter the threat from Asian and other competitors. These technologies can refill your product pipeline in order to supplement next generation process improvement licenses. Then you can license either as stand-alone process technology or bundle it with materials sublicenses.	*Price:* With patents expiring in 2007,[19] it is time to milk the current core patents for whatever you can get. At the same time, better process technology presents the downstream option of refocusing exclusively on manufacturing rather than licensing as a source of revenues. Assuming you can make major process improvements, consider using gross profits as a basis for calculating royalties rather than net sales. To the extent you use your own generic process technology (e.g. roll-to-roll) to make displays for your own products, the ability to calculate the savings should be better. (In 2003, Kodak announced it would use its OLED brand NuVueon its EasyShare LS633 digital camera.[20]) Such use also proves the value of the technology, enhancing the value that can be derived from licensing.

Again we emphasize that the SWOTs here are strictly illustrative and we are not trying to accurately reflect any firm's actual strategies. Having said that, we can note that the emphases resulting from the two examples is dramatically different.

---

[19] Bill Roberts, "Big Bucks from Little Screens," *Electronic Business* (November 1, 2004), http://www.reed-electronics.com/eb-mag/article/CA475428?text=big+bucks+from+little+screens (accessed October 8, 2005).
[20] Jack Mason, "Kodak and Dupont Launch an OLED Brand Land Grab," *Small Times* (July 17, 2003), http://www.smalltimes.com/document_display.cfm?section_id=46&document_id=6368 (accessed October 8, 2005).

The first example focuses on promotion. The reason is companies like Evident are not yet in the market. To get in, they have to show up on someone's radar screen. They need to find a way to get a toehold that can be rapidly secured from cut-throat competition by larger firms already selling product. Often technology is not enough for that, especially in a fast moving field like OLEDs. Thus, loosely following the approach of Chesebrough, trademark IP is used to supplement product IP to build a competitive advantage and brand loyalty. This positioning as a technology innovator is tied to a focus strategy oriented towards a very narrow customer segment able to pay premium pricing.

The second example places emphasis on finding new product. This is the major launch tactic issue. The reason is Kodak is already established in the market. The challenge is to regain technology leadership to continue to pursue its strategic thrust and positioning as a vendor of general illumination OLED technology to manufacturers in that market just as it has licensed into the display manufacturers. This positioning as the technology validator and broker is tied to a differentiation strategy oriented toward a broader set of customer segments in order to become a clearinghouse.

LOOKING FORWARD: LAUNCH TACTICS AND FINDING THE TARGET

So far our launch tactics have focused on how to sell to the end user. These launch tactics provide a path into the market. Once we have plausible ones, we can reasonably argue our technology has value. The reason is simple, value only exists where revenues can be earned and now we can explain how those revenues can be earned.

Once we do have a path for realizing revenues, that path points toward a de facto Schelling point when selecting targets for licensing, venture, joint ventures, and so forth. The reason is again simple. By examining our 4 Ps' we discover places where our capabilities and capacities are weak. Just like the bays on a jigsaw puzzle piece, these weaknesses point out the strengths we want our targets to have. Furthermore, the target has to be a player able to help us implement the path we have selected, but one who is weak in certain critical areas where we are strong, most notably in technology.

Although there is no simple formula, common sense does apply. Thus, if you are in a position where you have all the assets you need, you have strong IP protection, and there is little competition, it makes sense to take the technology to market yourself, as that way you can capture the entire revenue stream generated. Where you do not have all the requisite assets, but a strong IP position and few competitors, partnering makes sense.

Where you lack assets, there is competing IP, and there are many competitors, licensing looks increasingly attractive as it enables you to monetarize the IP rapidly.

There are always two factors at play when looking at our assets for weaknesses. On the one hand is our absorptive capacities. Do we have enough product and process technology familiarity (domain capacity) and market familiarity (context capacity) to produce, sell, distribute, and support the goods and services in which our technology will be embodied or in which our technology will be used? On the other hand are our capabilities and resources. Do we have the complementary assets (capabilities, financial strength, and people) to pull it off? (See Exhibit 8.1.)

The first factor, absorptive capacity, is a function of organizational strengths. Thus, the greater our weaknesses on either dimension, the more likely it is we will need help to accomplish successful market entry unless we have very deep pockets, in which case we can buy the capacity we need.

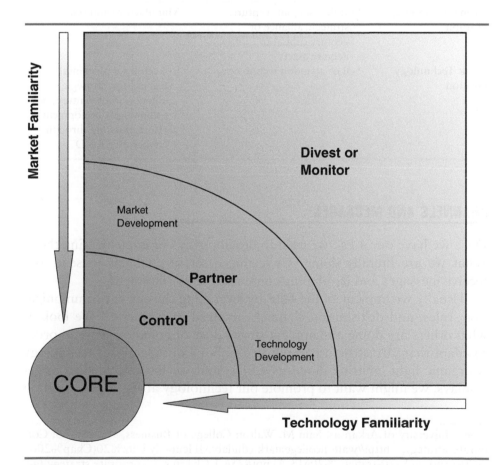

EXHIBIT 8.1 Technology and Market Familiarity

Alternatively, where capabilities and financial resources are lacking, it makes sense to find partners who can carry the technology forward to the market. Where deep pockets do exist, technology and core competencies can be leveraged through acquiring people, other companies, and/or supplemental technology. Horizontal integration mergers are a good example. For example, Tyson, the largest U.S. chicken producer, acquired IBP, the largest U.S. beef producer because similar distribution and marketing channels were used in both companies, so strong market familiarity (context capacity) made it plausible to gain synergies while hopping across product families (domain capacity). A similar logic applies to the Hewlett Packard–Compaq merger, where there were both market and technology synergies.[21]

The following table adapted from Megantz's *How to License Technology* depicts the choices.[22]

	Weak Complementary Assets	Strong Complementary Assets
Strong Technology Position	Out license, joint venture, strategic alliance or venture capital to acquire assets	Manufacture and sell
Weak Technology Position	Sell or abandon technology	In-license supplemental technology, strategic alliance, joint venture, new technology development effort, possibly through cooperative R&D

CHANNELS AND MESSAGES

Once we have our 4 Ps', we need to develop ways of implementing them. What we are literally doing is selecting a set of channels to send and receive messages and developing content for those messages.

Usually we implement the 4 Ps' by leveraging the current communication, sales, and distribution channels involved in a practice. We look at what others are doing and apply a strong dose of common sense in order to adapt that infrastructure to our needs. For example, if our technology is organic light emitting diodes (OLEDs) and we have decided to target displays, we might want to promote our technology at the annual meeting

---

[21] See University of Arkansas, Sam M. Walton College of Business, "Chapter 6: Corporate Strategy," http://waltoncollege.uark.edu/lab/MHennelly/blitz%20(Chap%20on%20corporate%20strategy,%20M&A).ppt#256,1,Chapter 6: corporate strategy (accessed October 9, 2005).

[22] R. Megantz, *How to License Technology* (Hoboken, NJ: Wiley, 1996).

of the Society for Information Display. If we are interested in selling to military contractors, we might advertise in defense publications.

> We usually can find an Internet channel simply by popping a relevant term into a browser. Sometimes all that is necessary is to pop the term between "*www.*" and "*.com.*" But because you get a hit does not mean that the channel is monitored by the people you are trying to reach. Nor does it mean it is authoritative. For example, if you insert display you end up at *http://www.display.com/*. Clearly a portal, but whose? Who monitors it? How do companies get listed? Is it accurate? What we want is not just any channel, but the main ones.

Promotion and sales channels may overlap, although they do not have to. If you want to buy a MP3 player, you crank up your computer and search the Internet for reviews. Often a site with reviews (e.g. CNET, ZDNET) has a link to a buying guide where not only do you get URLs for vendors, you also get the price (with shipping if you enter your zip code). You click the link and buy. Of course, other channels are multifunctional as well. Telephone solicitors, trade shows, and door-to-door traveling salesmen, all are examples of dual function channels.

The selection of promotion and sales channels is usually determined by the number of buyers. The smaller the number and the more "custom" or "advanced" the good, the more likely direct sales will be used. There are around 15 manufacturers of cell phones.[23] It is not a big deal to have a sales engineer and marketing executive travel to each one to explain the advantages of our OLEDs for displays. Where goods are more commodity-like and/or the number of buyers larger, however, sales via catalogs and the web make more sense. In between use of distributors and VARs are likely channels. Clearly, what is at play is how much hand-holding and education is required to land the sale.

	Small Number of Buyers	**Large Number of Buyers**
Commodities	Sales representatives	Catalogs and portals
Custom Goods	Sales engineers	Value add resellers

A similar logic applies to placement. On the one hand, there are physical considerations; on the other, hand-holding and education again comes into play.

---

[23] About.com, "All Cell Phones Sorted by Manufacturers," 2005, http://cellphones .about.com/od/phonemakers/ (accessed October 9, 2005).

Physical considerations have to do with what it takes to get a good from point A to point B undamaged. If the display is sensitive to moisture, we have to pack it according. If electrical interference is an issue, the packaging has to be designed to mitigate that. If it is food, maybe we want refrigeration to mitigate spoilage. If it is small we can use air freight. If it is very big, we may need to ship by rail and truck.

The other consideration is ease-of-use. Let's Say we are Kodak. If we go to *http://www.kodak.com/eknec/PageQuerier.jhtml;jsessionid= I144LDQEL52O1FW4FBEHWEMW1YUBI4L4?ncc=au&lcc=&pq-path= 1473/1481&pq-locale=en_AU&_requestid=1253* we find the homepage for Kodak's Nu-Vue displays. If we are selling these displays to companies for cell phones, we can just drop ship the displays as the engineers and production workers at the factory will know what to do with the product. However, Kodak also licenses its OLED technology. (See *http://www.kodak .com/eknec/PageQuerier.jhtml?pq-path=1473/1481/1490&pq-locale=en_ US*). Taking a license for a manufacturing process or a material is not as easy for the end user to deploy. We may have to provide more support as part of placing the technology via the license. In that case, our placement method may involve a year long consulting contract under which we help the licensee design the factory, buy the equipment, install it, and optimize the production.

Message content should reflect the general enterprise strategy of the player commercializing the technology as applied to the technology as positioned. We shall call this constraint the strategic thrust. Thrust is set by management.

Building upon Sanderson and Uzumeri, we can distinguish competitors in a market on the basis of how many goods they sell and how rapidly their product families change.[24] Clearly, different combinations lend themselves to different thrusts.

	Small Number of Goods	Large Number of Goods
Slowly Changing Product Families	Price	Differentiation
Rapidly Changing Product Families	Focus	Rapid response

What the content contains is a persuasive argument that either explains why our technology fits with what the end user wants (and what people who buy for the end user want), or it is designed to convince a stakeholder to change their behavior so that end-user requirements evolve and our technology will fit. Exhibit 8.2 illustrates this point.

[24] Sanderson and Uzumeri, *Managing Product Families* (Scarborough, Ontario: Irwin, 1996).

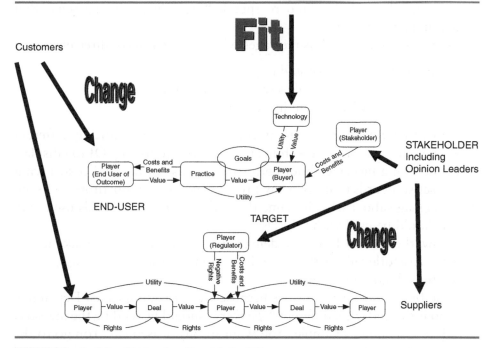

EXHIBIT 8.2   Building Technolog Fit with End Users

RHETORIC AND MESSAGES

If the discussion of what is a good begins with Plato in the Grand Tradition of Western thought, the discussion of how to persuade people to buy goods in the Grand Tradition begins with Aristotle. Following Aristotle we can distinguish between three kinds of persuasive speech: political, legal and ceremonial, or as we shall call them, pitching, rationalizing, and appealing.

Political speech is focused on decision-makers and the object is usually to move the audience to do something. The argument is in terms of expediency. Aristotle sees this as a moral-ethical kind of speech, however for our purposes, it is simply selling. The point is we are framing the argument to say do this and you will be better off in the future because of that. We shall call this kind of speech "*pitching.*"

Legal speech is focused on the past and has to do with what has or has not happened. The object is to determine the truth. For Aristotle, this makes it very logical in nature. For us, logic is supplemented by scientific data. The point is that when pitching, legal speech supports the claims of expediency. We shall call this kind of speech "*rationalizing.*"

Aristotle's final type of speech is ceremonial, which addressed honor and dishonor, praise or blame. Ceremonial rhetoric is aesthetic, in the sense that for Aristotle, it is concerned with what is beautiful. For us, it suffices to say it is about taste. It supports the pitch by giving the "*umpf*" for buying. We call this kind of speech *"appealing,"* in the sense that something appeals to us.

What we end up with is messages whose content have three elements:

1. A pitch or what you should do;
2. A rationale or why it makes sense to do it; and,
3. An appeal or why we will like doing it.

Note that a message sent to an end user may be dramatically different than one sent to another stakeholder. I want you to use my OLED display, so I send you a message about performance, ease-of-use and cost. I want her to set standards that favor my product over my competitors so I send her a message about why the same IEEE interconnect standards used with LEDs should be used with OLEDs.

Now, the content has to be delivered in such a way as to make it persuasive. Aristotle tells us there are there modes for accomplishing persuasion: ethos, logos and pathos.

The first, ethos, persuades us because we trust the speaker. Depending on who is the audience, different *"speakers"* should be sending the message.

Here is a simple example: You want to buy a used car. You go to the car lot and the salesman pitches you. You are cynical. You go home and check *Consumer Reports*. You trust the message because it is from a neutral third party. It is no different with technology. You pitch your OLED technology in a presentation at the Society for Information Display: great. Someone from the U.S. Department of Energy is a keynote speaker at a meeting and says you have the best OLED material she has ever seen: much better. Authoritative expert *and* independent third party.

Logos is the Greek term for both logic and nature. Logos persuades because of the way the argument is constructed. It uses enthymeme (simplified logic) to make deductive and inductive arguments. (Enthymeme merely means taking part of an argument for granted as when we assume brighter displays capable of being viewed from wider angles are a good, rather than establishing that fact.) It also uses example (*"nature"*) to illustrate from experience.

Again a simple example: One of the nice things about OLED displays is the wider viewing angle. Suppose you are with your parents and aunt and uncle at lunch when your sister calls and drops the news she is getting married. Only she is marrying this cheapskate, so you are not that happy about it. That's when you discover the real advantage of OLED displays. She shows you a picture of her engagement ring snapped with her cell phone. Your mom holds it up and everyone sees the diamond. Let me tell you, the smaller the diamond, the more you appreciate brightness and contrast or it would just wash out.

Pathos convinces by tweaking the emotions of the audience, whether positive or negative. Pathos only works if you understand the "hot buttons" to push. For example, suppose you want to sell displays to the Department of Defense for use by soldiers in Iraq. You argue one reason for buying your OLEDs is that ours are made in the United States, not outsourced to Asia. This kind of argument is not rational, which is the case with logos. Outsourcing has nothing to do with how well the display will work in combat. You are simply playing to fear.

Following Aristotle we can distinguish three elements in persuasive speech: the speaker, the audience, and, of course, the speech itself. Depending on the channel we use, we need to select a "speaker" who will be seen as persuasive and have that speaker convey a message that contains a pitch, a rationale, and an imperative. The rationale should support the pitch with logos and the imperative play to the pathos of the audience.

CONCLUSION

In this chapter we have seen that launch tactics is a matter of framing messages that are sent through channels to various players. The key players are the end users and buyers, but other stakeholders are also important. Examples of such other stakeholders are journal and business media editors and authors, members of professional and trade associations, government regulators, members of standards bodies, other companies in supply chains, and the like.

We begin developing our launch tactics by focusing on the requirements of our end users and the positioning we want. We also need to consider how general organizational goals apply with respect to those customer segments, which we call strategic thrust. With this orientation, we then examine our strengths, weaknesses, opportunities, and threats in order to discover a path into the market. We describe this path with the aid of the 4 Ps': product, price, promotion, and place. The 4 Ps' are our launch tactics. If they are plausible, they should lead to sales.

The 4 Ps' do more than suggest how to sell to end users. They also provide criteria for identifying commercialization partners to help us enter the market. The criteria reflect where we lack capacity and capabilities to execute the 4 Ps'. What we want are partners who share our view of how to succeed and bring strengths where we are weak. Finding those partners is the subject of Chapter 9.

Four
Going Back

Finding the Target

INTRODUCTION

Doing deals is how technology gets monetarized. The deal is a transaction in which money, or something fungible enough to be turned into money, gets traded for rights in the technology. In this chapter, we focus on with whom we will do the deal. In Chapter 10, we will focus on how much money we should ask for. In Chapter 11, we will discuss how to negotiate deals.

We shall call the player with whom we want to do a deal the target. Finding targets is pretty straightforward if we have done our homework. There are three steps.

First, since we know who the customers are, we want a target who sells into the relevant market. Strong market familiarity is a plus. An even greater plus is a significant customer base with strong brand loyalty. Alternatively, we can target players who can credibly enter the relevant market should they so desire. For example, Procter and Gamble made a decision that they wanted to enter the men's skin care and shaving market. So they bought Gillette. (Deep pockets and strong brand loyalty in related markets are a good basis for a credible claim to be able enter a closely related market.)

Second, we need a target that has relevant absorptive capacity. Not only should the target be able to understand and work with our technology, they should be able to do so in the context of the markets we are seeking to penetrate. That means if we are developing technology for military recon, we do not take an acoustic technology to a company specializing in optics, even through it may make reconnaissance pods for military aircraft.

Finally, in the context of our SWOT we have had to do some hard thinking about our weaknesses when it comes to completing the R&D and bringing the technology to market. We need a target with relevant capabilities and capacities to compensate for our weaknesses or enough money to enable us to buy what we need. Ideally, it should also be able to help us leverage our strengths.

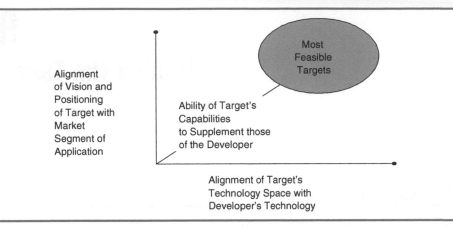

EXHIBIT 9.1   Target Alignment

From a game theory standpoint, what we are doing is looking for a target with whom doing a deal represents a Nash equilibrium for us both. Exhibit 9.1 uses three dimensions for qualifying targets Although there is no reason why more could not be considered, usually these suffice. We want a target that will align with our understanding of the market and how our technology should be positioned so that the 4 Ps' can be implemented (see Exhibit 9.1). Its technology space, that is, its technology portfolio and absorptive capacity, will align with our technology in such a way that we fill a current gap or provide a strategic asset for the future. Its capabilities will compensate for our weaknesses and leverage our strengths. That way its best possible strategy is to team with us. See, simple: a Nash equilibrium.

If the target has a positive attitude towards taking the risks associated with bringing new technology to market, even better. Of course, as another old saying goes, "the devil is in the details" so it is to the details we now turn.

MARKET ALIGNMENT

The easiest thing to determine is market alignment. The first thing to determine is just who is, or wants to be, selling to the customers you have targeted. This is easy to figure out because all you have to do is plunk the customer segment in a browser and see who the relevant vendors are. You go to web sites, if they look good, you delve deeper. You look at annual reports, especially the chairman's and president's statements as they will present the "*vision*" under which the company is operating. Of course, for publicly traded companies, it is useful to look at Securities and Exchange

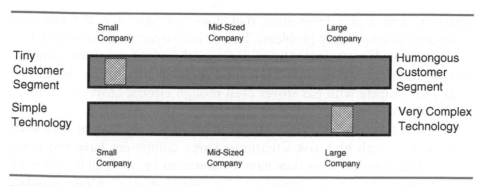

EXHIBIT 9.2   Positioning and Complexity of Technology

Commission (SEC) 10K filings and analysts reports in order to get a fuller reality check.

Just who aligns is more difficult to answer. For example, the size of the target has to be appropriate given the size of the customer segment for which you are positioning and the complexity of your technology (see Exhibit 9.2). You need a big company to make and sell airplanes. You need a big company to make and sell toasters for a different reason. In the former, it is the complexity of the product that drives size, not the number of customers. In the latter, it is the number of customers, and not the complexity of the technology.

But size and complexity cannot be used as a hard and fast metric for selecting what size of company to target. You also have to take into account the phase of the market. As we have seen, phase is driven by the number of buyers in the market and the criteria they use for making buying decisions. These factors relate to the emergence and solidification of dominant designs. Let's use toasters as an example.

Toast goes way back. Bread was toasted in Roman times. In fact our word toast comes from the Latin word "*tostum*," which means to scorch or burn. When the first electric toaster was invented in 1893 by Crompton and Co., a British firm, the toaster market was embryonic. Further, it only toasted one side of the bread, which meant you had to stand there and flip the bread after turning off the machine. Not the best ease of use. Another problem was the wires burned out rapidly, so performance had some problems. Further, there was not a lot of electricity around. In the United States, the first commercial power station did not open until 1879. (It was located in San Francisco. Electric power had been around for awhile however. The first utility in the United States was founded in 1816.[1]) Classic

---

[1] About.com, "Timeline of Electricity—Electronic Inventions," 2005, http://inventors .about.com/library/inventors/blelectric2.htm (accessed October 15, 2005).

situation with a new innovation that does not have a well established dominant design: supply problems, lack of infrastructure, and mixed ability to meet end-user needs. (To provide another data point for comparison, it was not until the late 1920s and early 1930s electric stoves first began to compete with gas stoves even though electric stoves were being sold by the 1890s.[2])

Usually it is small companies that can afford to experiment with what will work in such high risk situations. Large companies have too many pre-existing commitments they have to honor to be as flexible, although some firms set up venture subsidiaries or *"skunk works"* whose mandate is to push the envelope. These exist outside the inertia of the rest of the operation. A review of 23 empirical studies by Damanpour reported in the *Academy of Management Journal* found that managers at middle or lower levels most often introduced incremental innovations but that radical innovations were typically initiated and developed in units created for this purpose, such as R&D and new ventures.[3]

In 1905, Albert Marsh patented a chromium-nickel alloy that could be used to make long-lasting resistance wire. The invention was hot enough that he formed Hoskins Manufacturing Company to develop and sell the alloy. Within a year, George Schneider had invented a toaster using the new wire. American Electric Heater Co. of Detroit, where Schneider worked, ended up in the toaster business on the basis of his patent. For us the lesson is that in embryonic markets, targets are firms with relevant abilities, but it is not necessary that they are already selling into the relevant niche as no well defined niche may exist.

Let's look at this from a dominant design perspective. Schneider leveraged the dominant design for making toast over a fire and transferred into the dominant design for a toaster by mechanizing it with the aid of a heating element. You still applied heat to one side till it was brown enough and then turned over the bread and heated the other side till done.

The emergence of his (and Crompton and Co.'s) design defined the market. Now we know what a toaster is. And knowing what one is, invites others to copy that design, especially if growth in demand presents attractive opportunities for a return on investment. General Electric entered the market in 1909 with an appliance based on a competing wire alloy with which they sought to work around the Marsh patent. (This workaround failed. GE's alloy was found to infringe the Marsh patent in a suit brought by Hoskins. The lesson is that infringers often make easy

---

[2] Bellis, "The History of Stoves and Ovens," *About,* 2005, http://inventors.about .com/library/inventors/blstoves.htm, (accessed October 15, 2005).
[3] Damanpour, "Organizational Innovation: A Meta-Analysis of Effects of Determinants and Moderators," *Academy of Management Journal* 34, no. 3 (1991).

pickings as targets.) Westinghouse entered in the 1909–1910 season with what might be considered the first toaster oven, a stamped sheet-metal flatiron-like device. Pacific Electric Heating Company entered with a toaster sold under the Hotpoint brand, claiming it actually invented the toaster in 1905.

When bigger firms enter an early stage growth market, sales heat up due to brand loyalties and marketing clout. This is a classic scenario for a market transitioning past the take off growth phase. Now adaptive innovations start extending functionality as the big companies position vis-à-vis each other on the one hand, while smaller new entrants seek to enter and grab a share of the growing sales on the other hand. The innovations are used to support claims to have a *"best value"* solution for customers. Alonzo Warner invented a better way of holding the bread, an efficient pincher. This innovation launched Landers, Frary & Clark into the toaster business as it improved ease-of-use. Design for aesthetics also becomes an increasingly important factor. In the toaster market it is George Curtiss of Landers, Frary & Clark who leads the pack, designing products whose aesthetic quality lets them be sold for up to 15 years.

Another focus for innovation was mechanisms for turning the toast so both sides could be easily browned. Spencer Wiltsie patented a turning mechanism that was sold by the Coleman Electric Stove Company. Edwin Rutenber invented an alternative and simpler slice-turning mechanism, introduced by his own firm in 1917. By the end of the 20s there are a set of players in the market, each of whom is seeking innovations to gain competitive advantage. Note also that as automatic turners and other adaptive innovations are added, the paradigm for toasting is starting to change.

Then in the mid-20s, Frederick Hummel and John Noeth patented a toaster that has a timer that tips the rack out when the cycle ends. This adaptive innovation represents a definitive break with the dominant design going back to Roman times. Now, not only can the bread be toasted on both sides without intervention, you do not have to watch it to ensure the toast does not burn, In 1919, a new paradigm is established by Charles Strite's pop-up toaster (a toaster with a timer and a spring plus elements on both side) is the basis for a new dominant design—one still in use today. By 1926 it was in the market, being sold by Waters Genter of Minneapolis under the brand name Toastmaster. Toaster sales skyrocketed until market saturation was reached in the 1960s, with almost every U.S. household having a toaster.[4]

---

[4] A number of sources were used to collect data. Particularly helpful for patents was Charles Fisher, "Hazelcorn's Price Guide to Old Electric Toasters 1908–1940," *Toaster Articles* (2003), http://www.toaster.org/patent.html (accessed October 15, 2005).

Now, the purpose of this digression was to explain our qualifier about who makes a good target. While higher levels of complexity likely will always make correspondingly larger companies more attractive as targets, due to the financial and diverse capacity resources required to handle complexity, market size only counts to the extent that both infrastructure and a dominant design is in place. Otherwise, the benefits of economies of scale and scope that accrue to size cannot be brought into play. Further, as the economists will tell us, there is some level of output above which the benefits of size have diminishing or no marginal utility. Another way of putting this is that who makes a good target depends on what the actual market size is, not on what the potentially addressable market size is. As we have seen, the actual market size is correlated with the phase of the market. Large companies become relevant only in growth, shakeout, and mature phases and in the growth phase only once the transition to take-off in demand occurs.

As the toaster example points out, a supply chain needs to exist (alloy wires, electricity) that can support scaling. Thus, as breakthrough innovations enter in one sector, opportunities exist elsewhere for technologies that enable companies in those sectors to reposition themselves to leverage the new competitive situation. We focus on suppliers of materials, components, subsystems, etc. to the sector in which the innovations are occurring. The prime instance in the toaster's history is Nichrome, the nickel-chromium alloy that made resistive wire longer-lasting.

A similar logic applies to shifts in dominant designs. No dominant design, no way to determine just what process technology provides as a competitive advantage because you do not know what you are making. Small vendors with low overhead and flexible equipment are likely to dominate.

We conclude innovations present challenges and opportunities for vendors in the supply chain for the practices in which the designs are changing, making them feasible targets to the extent they lack what we offer. These vendors may well be smaller niche players as their customer base is the manufacturers of the end-product, which can be substantially smaller than the ultimate end-user base.

Several years ago we looked at a technology for remote monitoring of emissions from cars that was being funded by the U.S. Environmental Protection Agency. At the time, there was strong pressure to monitor for NO_x emissions both at emissions testing stations and as part of highway monitoring programs in communities out of compliance with the Clean Air Act. The problem was the current technology, based on an invention by the University of Denver, could measure CO_2, O_2 and some other gases but not NO_X. Aerodyne Research, the EPA awardee, had developed a field spectrometer that could measure NO_X and the other desired gases in an open path system. The question was, who might be Aerodyne's customer?

Aerodyne wanted to either license their technology or make it as an OEM and have someone else sell it. The solution was to look at who was active in the emissions monitoring business and at who was trying to expand into remote monitoring. That gave us the end users. Then we worked back up their supply chain to the monitoring equipment manufacturers to identify who might be a target.

Changes in dominant designs also open up opportunities for hitherto non-existent synergies for what are called platform goods. Platform goods are products and services that are sold to make it possible to use a good (film for traditional cameras) or to use it better (software for computers).

There is an old adage about an idea being "the best thing since sliced bread." Sliced bread and the toaster are intimately connected and are part of the same paradigm shift we saw earlier with the zipper. After World War I, the United States had excess manufacturing capacity and in sector after sector, home and local based production of household and personal items was replaced by industrially made goods. In the case of sliced bread, the story begins in 1912, when Otto Rohwedder starting thinking of ways to automatically slice bread, which of course would make it easier to get the bread into the frame that holds it in the toaster. (Sandwiches were already a popular food, dating back to the fourth Earl of Sandwich in the late 1700s, who loved to eat beef between slices of toast so he could have a free hand for card playing.) Rohwedder initially tried holding the bread for slicing with hit pins. This approach failed. After a while he developed an industrial bakery oriented machine that could slice and wrap the bread to prevent the slices from going stale. The timing was good. By 1926 the pop up toaster was in the market. His patent was filed two years later. And he formed Mac-Roh Sales & Manufacturing to manufacturer and sell machines. Within 2 years, 1930, Wonder Bread was selling pre-sliced bread; toaster sales skyrocketed as now the size of slice was standardized. By 1933, U.S. bakeries produced more sliced than

(Continued)

unsliced bread.[5] In other words, shifts in dominant designs make companies with platform goods targets because they will be trying to figure out how to leverage the new designs for their own benefit.

Alignment also requires compatibility with your vision of how the market needs to be approached. This compatibility is a matter of how the potential target is positioned and how it currently sells.

There are various categorizations for how companies compete. Our model highlights technical leadership, best value, price, and availability as bases for competition due to their coherence with the dominant design driven phase of the market. Larry Kahaner presents an alternative classification, based on how reporters often describe company strengths.

- Product
- Financial
- Technology
- Manufacturing
- Marketing/advertising
- Organization
- Alliances
- Goodwill/brand loyalty/reputation[6]

Whatever the categorization, from a tactical perspective we want to do a deal with a player for whom our technology will be seen as enhancing and reinforcing their ability to compete.

We have already indicated the utility of websites and annual reports for getting a window on how a company views the market. Even better if they sell relevant goods is to look at their advertisements; then call them up and let them pitch to you. If you can afford to, visit their booth at a relevant trade show. As always, talking to people who have just left their booth is as important as talking to the people the company sent. You also can ask a competitor at trade shows how they differentiate themselves from your potential target. Asking reporters authoring the annual "industry overview" for trade publications is also useful.

Assuming basic alignment, the next issue is the strategic importance of the technology for the target. This determination has three parts.

---

[5] Mary Bellis, "The History of Your Toaster," *About.com* (2005), http://inventors
.about.com/library/inventors/bltoaster.htm (accessed October 15, 2005); and "Otto
Frederick Rohwedder," *The Great Idea Finder* (n.d.), http://www.ideafinder.com/
history/inventions/breadslicer.htm (October 15, 2005).
[6] Kahaner, *Competitive Intelligence* (New York: Touchstone, 1997), 101.

The first part involves determining if what you have to offer is redundant given what the target has and where its product plans are likely heading. Making this determination requires looking at the product mix of the potential target in light of demand trends for the customer segment. If a sector association has developed a road map, even better. The road map will place along a timeline the technologies that are likely to be important for success in the sector and the performance targets for those product technologies (and thus for the process and service technologies needed to support products).

Redundancy can be determined by conducting a gap analysis. Previously we used gap analysis to find applications for our technology. This time gap analysis is used to determine the likely impact of your technology for your target over some period of time—usually either the next five years, five years from the date of market introduction or both. There are two questions. First, are they missing the piece that you have to offer? If the answer is yes, then it makes sense to ask the second question: How important is it for them to have that piece? Obviously, if the conclusion is in line with the second slider in Exhibit 9.3, the target should be more interested in your technology than if the conclusion is in line with the top slider.

Note that in Exhibit 9.3, we are using hedge to refer to an offensive hedge. Offensive hedges are developed in order to respond to uncertainty about what goods customers will be seeking in the future. By contrast, defensive hedges are obtained either to keep products off the market that compete with products currently sold by the acquirer or they are obtained to have something to respond with on the off chance a competitor moves in an unanticipated direction. The core distinction is that offensive hedges

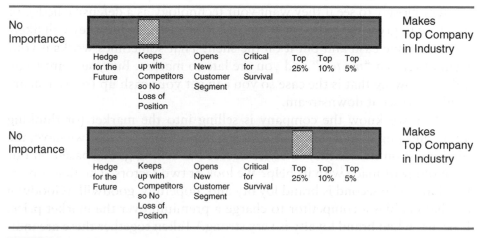

EXHIBIT 9.3 Offensive Hedge

are obtained in order to be able to exploit opportunities; defensive hedges are obtained in order to eliminate threats.

The second part has to do with timing. The timeline to finish development of your technology has to align not only with the timeline of the end user for purchasing the good, but with the product replacement cycle of the target. The issue is optimizing return on investment. Replace a product too early and you do not ride out the growth phase of its life cycle. Replace it too late and you lose market share.

> I remember meeting Jacob Rabinow, the inventor of the reading machine used by the U.S. Post Office, around 1980 while he was Inventor in Residence at the National Institute for Standards and Technology (then the Bureau of Standards). He told me this great story about how he invented the machine, then sold his company to Control Data. He became a vice president of Control Data. He quit in frustration. He told me the reason was he kept on going into Bill Noyce, the CEO at the time, with these brilliant ideas for improving the reading machine. Noyce was excited too but had to keep on saying, "Jacob, we just trained the sales engineers on the last improvement. Let's sell this one for a while to make some profit before we obsolete it."

The final part has to do with the role of the customer segment(s) you are targeting in the overall enterprise strategy of your target, and for larger firms, the business strategy of the relevant division or group. The more significant the customer segment, the more likely the target will be interested in your technology. But, and this is a big but, you have to look at the strategy closely to see if they want your technology as a defensive hedge or as a way to grow the business. If it is just a defensive hedge, they will likely pay you some cash and put it on the shelf. That sometimes works if your technology is a "*me too*" and you are late to market. But you want to do a deal knowing that is the case so you can get your cash up front. You are unlikely to see it downstream.

Once we know the company is selling into the market (or thinking about entering it) and there is a strategic importance to what we have, the final question is: Are they likely to succeed at selling goods based on our technology or made with its help? We look at two factors. The first is market share. The second is brand loyalty and, hopefully, goodwill. (Goodwill is what enables a competitor to charge a premium over the market price. It occurs when brand loyalty is very strong.) Taken together these are indicators that a target "*owns*" a piece of one of the customer segments of interest. Since you want to sell to that segment, having a piece of the action to build from is a good thing.

A potential source of precise data is generic market research reports, such as those from Frost and Sullivan, Freedonia, etc., or from custom market assessment firms like Foresight Science & Technology. If you have a broker, they can usually tap into stock analyst reports, but for larger multi-product family companies, analysts are pretty useless unless what you are interested in is a major product family for the company you are considering targeting. Along the way, you can collect some pretty good information on brand loyalty by asking about that as well.

Be careful when using generic market reports: You have to make sure that what the report is discussing is actually relevant for your technology. A few years back we were doing a market assessment of the need for high security file servers for a company in Finland, that had developed a very low cost secure architecture for a stand alone file server. We found all sorts of data on file servers and the need for better security. But we also found that this need was not a high priority at large companies, universities, or government agencies because they had already put solutions in place and our customer was looking for immediate sales, not sales in three to five years, when the next cycle of upgrading might begin. The conclusion we came to was if they wanted immediate sales, they would do better focusing on the underserved smaller and mid-sized firm customer segment. These firms had generally not been active in the round of buying recently completed by larger organizations because they did not have a lot of Information Technology (IT) infrastructure, staff, or budget.

We knew there were firms selling security solutions to such end users. Because file servers are computers, not surprisingly information on the need and the firms trying to sell goods to meet it was all over the web. Indeed, there are so many of them, the question was who really was a player. We looked at a few reports from Frost and Sullivan and Gartner but concluded we could not trust the data, because when they reported on vendors, they did not report vendors by the size of companies they serviced. Just because IBM had a lot of market share did not mean it had it in the customer segment in which we were interested.

We ended up calling local and regional value added resellers and IT support firms in selected cities across the United States with large, small, and mid-sized high tech companies. We knew that protecting proprietary information at high tech firms was a big issue at the time

(Continued)

and we also knew smaller Value Added Resellers (VARs) and IT firms tended to service small and mid-sized companies, so we assumed people servicing such companies might be a good source of data. They were. We asked owners whom they saw as the key players and why. Then we called sales managers at Dell, Gateway, Hewlett-Packard, and other major vendors showing up in *PC Magazine,* our surrogate for a small business focus, and asked them to estimate roughly how much of their file server business was with small companies. Putting these two sources together we came up with a first cut hit list of potential licensees based on who was already in and who was trying to build in this customer segment.

Although precise data is not always readily available, you can always call up major distributors and retailers and ask their sales or buying people how important a specific company is in the industry when compared to others and how much brand loyalty their customers have. Market size estimates on the order of less than or greater than or about some increment of 25% or 33% can be obtained by asking for people's gut reactions. Similarly, you can get reactions as to whether a competitor is in the top 5%, 10%, 25% or in the few guys at bottom. You can get "a lot, some, a little, none" estimates for brand loyalty using this approach.

If all else fails, look at who is being aggressive among your potential targets. Companies working to build market share are far more like to be successful than those struggling to hold on to it.

TECHNOLOGY ALIGNMENT

As noted in the introduction to this chapter, it is hard for a company specializing in acoustics to have the absorptive capacity required to handle optical technology. That said, how can we determine technology alignment so we know whether we have it or not?

The first step is to be clear just what technical capabilities and intellectual property is required to move our technology into the market. A useful tool for determining that is quality function deployment (QFD). The house of quality is simply a tool for translating end-user needs into functional requirements. It is called a house because the shape resembles a house. The quality label comes from the fact that quality should be defined by end-user needs.

Exhibit 9.4 is a QFD house of quality for a battery powered toaster for camping. The concept is to make a toaster that is small enough to carry in a pack that can be recharged by being plugged into an automobile lighter

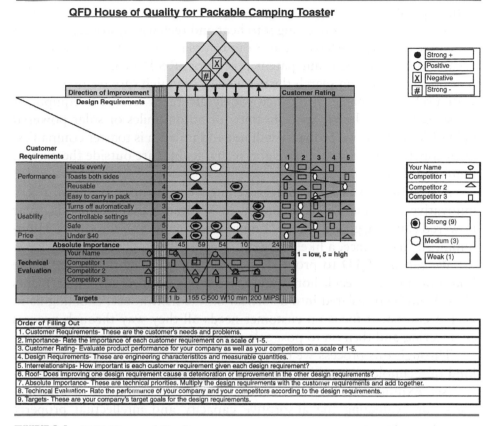

EXHIBIT 9.4 QFD House of Quality

outlet. We also provide on the bottom of the exhibit some guidance on how we made it.

One importance of these kinds of exercises is that they force us to translate our end-user needs into technical performance parameters on which we can measure our progress versus our competitors. But even more significant here is that they highlight the kinds of technology space we are looking for in our targets.

The targets for this technology are not likely traditional toaster companies, unless we find some indication that they are interested in entering the camping market. Instead our targets are likely to be manufacturers of goods for backpackers, tailgate campers, the military, remote field offices, and the like. These are the firms likely to have high market familiarity and to have brand loyalty among the customer segment we are focused on. However, we cannot rule out a traditional toaster company as one of them certainly is a candidate for expanding into this niche—especially if our toaster can be positioned as the first member of a product family bringing in the home conveniences to "that table in the woods."

In any case, from a technology perspective we are looking for targets with capabilities relating to making light weight goods that use power very efficiently (both converting it to heat and recharging storage) and can control heat. Once we have these as our criteria, we can start searching for organizations with relevant patent portfolios, R&D programs, and current products. We can search the net widely, in which case we may end up with a set of companies from such widely divergent sectors as equipment for spacecraft to electric space heaters for automobiles or solar powered field offices. What we probably will not end up with is toaster companies, as the operating constraints (weight, rechargeable) are outside the current dominant design.

After a bit of web and patent searching we come upon Brunton, a very innovative camping goods company in Wyoming that is making solar powered camping goods as well as more traditional camping stoves. Hummmm. At first glance, a likely target.

We can use QFD to probe deeper. One of the nice things about the house of quality is each horizontal (the design engineering requirements above) can be translated into a vertical on the next house, enabling us to keep a consistent focus on customer needs all they way through process engineering and then on to post-sale repair and customer service.

Through this process we end up with a more complete picture of the kind of technology capabilities that are required to bring a good to market (see Exhibit 9.5). We can then use this set of capabilities as a benchmark for evaluating the absorptive capacity and intellectual property portfolio of targets.

We now want to delve even deeper in order to understand just how our technology fits into their technology space. To do that, we develop a profile of the relevant capabilities by searching databases with patents and patent applications, R&D, and if we have not done so already, products. We use the target's name as a search term. Because companies sometimes try to hide their R&D and product development efforts, we also search on the name of subsidiaries as well as on the names of key researchers and engineers if we know them. In smaller firms, we use the names of the founders and key executives as they may hold the patents in their own names yet.

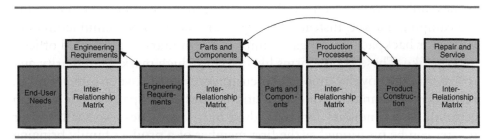

EXHIBIT 9.5   QFD Chain of Houses

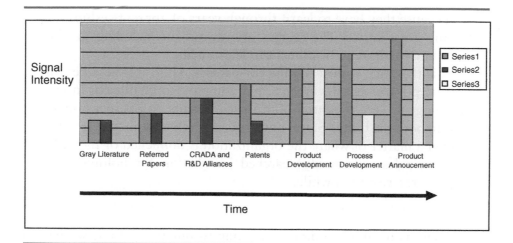

EXHIBIT 9.6 Analysis of Absorptive Capacity

The first use of this data is bibliographic analysis to identify areas of technological interest. The more patents in a specific patent subclass, the more likely there is interest in that field. Similarly, the more staff of the target presents papers at professional meetings or authors publications that appear in referred journals or trade publications, the more interest there likely is in a field. References in business, trade, and general media also are useful for gaining insight.

We can take bibliometric analysis one step further by looking at what is contained in documents and where they appear. We do this with the same method introduced for examination of competing technologies in Chapter 4. By tracking when messages about the technology occur, and their frequency, we gain a window into what is happening within a target. In this static snapshot redraw of an earlier graphic, the first series in Exhibit 9.6 represents a typical distribution as a technology goes to market. The second series represents a technology development effort that fails to transition to product. The final series represents an in-licensed technology where the process technology is already in place at the company and only requires modest adaptation.

I recently heard a story about how one Indian family passes on its recipes to the next generation. The woman (for in this family the women did the cooking) never teach their daughters to cook. They never write down or orally describe a recipe. All they do is allow their daughters to help in the kitchen if they so chose. Only those daughters interested enough to put up with this silent treatment became cooks.

(Continued)

But because they have to learn through years of apprenticeship, they became great cooks. The recipes are always there, hiding in plain sight, but you have to be diligent to learn them.

It is the same with searching for patents. They are there because they are government documents, but you have to be diligent in your searching. Be sure to search both issued patents and patent applications in both the United States and abroad as where someone files first is often a matter of where the organization is domiciled or the utility of using a less commonly searched jurisdiction for holding cards closer to the vest for a while.

If there is no IP nor initiative relating to our technology, we have a potential gap we can fill. However, even if there is an initiative, we may still fill a gap. What we have to do is delve deeper yet and try to characterize the product and process technology the potential target uses and where they are on the Bohn Knowledge Levels with respect to these technologies (see Exhibit 9.7). Sometimes the information we need can be found by searching the web and fee for service data bases. Sometimes it is in market research reports, scholarly publications, or trade publications. Sometimes we have to go to trade shows, call experts, or network through professional societies.

However the data is collected, technology space profiling and associated gap analyses help us understand what we are bringing to the picnic and what the target is likely to be bringing. Regardless of how deep we have to go, alignment is a matter of our technology filling gaps for the tar-

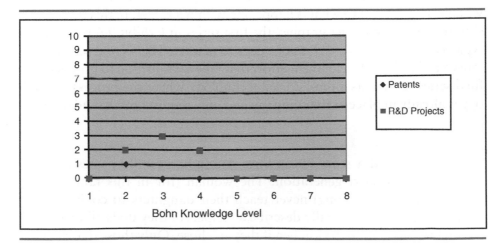

EXHIBIT 9.7 Bohn Knowledge Levels

get, where the target has enough absorptive capacity to take our product to market. Sometimes, in order to get the full range of capacity needed, we may have to partner with more than one target; however, that changes nothing in the basic approach for determining who those targets might be. Between us all, we still have to have all the product, service, and process technology we need to go to market and succeed there.

The second step is to determine whether the target is an importer of technology. Following Hanel, we can note that the greater the proportion of intellectual property a competitor or industry in-licenses from the outside, the more dependent it is on IP inflow to sustain its competitiveness. We can use the formula NETOUT, which is the difference of all patents owned by the company versus those out-licensed or otherwise exported, to identify firms focused on exporting rather than exploiting their technology: NETOUT = (PI – PX), where PI is patents used internally and PX is patents exported. Major exporters make poorer targets usually. NETIN gives us those that import or other acquire their technology or NETIN = (PI – PA). The ratio NETIN/NETOUT allows us to identify firms likely to be importers.[7]

Also relevant for companies actively patenting is whether the target is a pioneer or an imitator. According to Mary Ellen Mogee, pioneers are leaders building a pool of IP in a new area. As such they tend to cite their own patents. Imitators rely on the work of others as a basis for their own work. As such they tend to cite patents developed by others more frequently.[8] Imitators in fields relevant to your technology are likely to be more receptive to outside technology.

Analogous to the case with marketing, the third step for determining alignment is assessing how important the intellectual property we are bringing to the deal is for the target with which we want to the deal. Let me remind you intellectual property is different than technology. Property is a bundle of legally enforceable rights. What we want to know is how our patents, copyrights, trade secrets, trademarks, etc. fit with the targets.

The first dimension for determining importance is to understand the function of our technology for the target. Exhibit 9.8 presents three options.

Core technologies are critical for how players compete today. It is Windows for Microsoft. Nobody acquires a technology that competes with its core technology unless it is to kill it.

Strategic technologies are critical for how players want to compete in the future. It was Windows back when Microsoft was selling DOS.

---

[7] Hanel, "Interindustry Flows of Technology: An Analysis of the Canadian Patent Matrix and Input-Output Matrix for 1978–1989," *Technovation* 14, no. 8 (1994).
[8] Mentioned in Kahaner, *Competitive Intelligence*, 117.

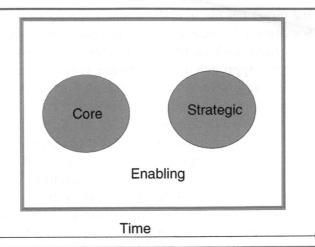

EXHIBIT 9.8   Types of Technology by Use

Players will acquire strategic technologies but they will want exclusive rights to them.

The final kind of functionality is enabling. Enabling technologies are those that make it possible to better use core and strategic technologies. You do not have to control them, but you do want access if your competitors have access. Windows is an enabling technology for almost everyone except Microsoft, Sun (who owns Java), and the companies developing Unix based operating systems like Red Hat Linux.

Companies that use patenting of process and other enabling technologies to protect a core technology are said to be pursuing clustered patenting illustrated in Exhibit 9.9. The enabling patents are like concrete barriers set in place to stop those who would seek to sneak onto the core technologies turf. Competing technologies may be added to upset the ability of competitors to use them as safe harbors. The cluster creates a maze that has to be navigated by setting road blocks of potential infringement. Both design and utility (or plant) patents can be used in this IP strategy.

The second dimension for determining functionality is to determine the way in which your technology will be used within that category. There are two primary roles for core and strategic technologies. A technology can extend another, in the way that a battery pack extends the utility of a toaster by enabling us to make toast in the woods. A technology can also supplant another technology. The dual element frame supplanted swinging doors for toasters by removing the need to flip the bread over.

Companies that build patent portfolios based on extending the functionality of a core are said to be pursing bracketed patenting. What they

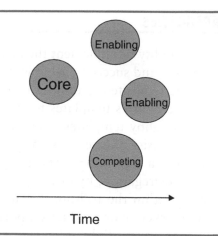

EXHIBIT 9.9 Clustered Patenting

are doing is pushing out the space around their core by using the extensions as brackets for it. Supplanting technologies may be added to provide stepping stones to a new bracketed set, as Exhibit 9.10 indicates.

Obviously, these patent protection strategies are not mutually exclusive. From the standpoint of choosing targets, the real issue is what you have and what you need. If you have an extension and no ability to productize your technology (perhaps you work for a university or federal lab), then you probably want a company pursuing a mixed strategy as you need receptivity to owning extensions but you also need capabilities in production that may be found in enabling patents.

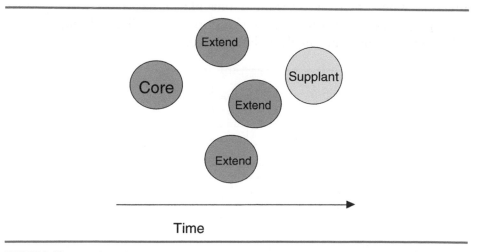

EXHIBIT 9.10 Bracketed Patenting

ALIGNMENT ON CAPABILITIES

Capabilities address the ability to implement the tasking needed to get the technology into the market and succeed once it is there. A helpful starting point for determining the requisite capabilities is the U.S. Department of Defense's Defense Science Board's templates for transitioning R&D production. Called the Willoughby templates after the man who headed up their development, they consist of a set of steps that are commonly conducted when transitioning a technology. The template can be run at a higher or lower level of aggregation, by drilling down from roll-up steps to the component steps within the roll-up. Because DOD was not concerned with things like marketing or product support, Foresight expanded the templates to include these (see Exhibit 9.11).

At the highest level, there are three basic activities:

1. Transitioning, which involves taking the technology out of R&D and into production;
2. Penetrating, which involves entering the market and expanding market share; and
3. Financing, which involves determining how much money is needed to pull the other two steps off and obtaining it.

Each step in these task sequences can be defined in terms of outputs, what processes can be used, inputs and other resources required, IP utilized, costs, ownership of an emerging IP, and things that can cause delays or cost overruns (i.e., risk factors). Once we have identified what we can do, we know what we need from our targets. To the extent we supplement each other and have little overlap, we are in alignment, so long as all the tasking needed to get into the market and grow market share once there is present. Where there is overlap, if one player has a clear competitive advantage when performing the tasking, there is still good alignment as allocating tasking is not likely to be an issue.

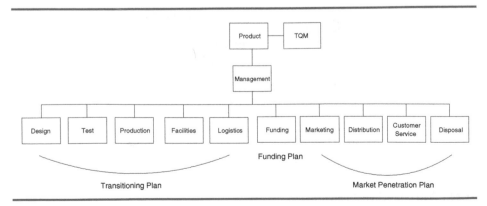

EXHIBIT 9.11   Allocating Tasking

For each step or substep we can flow chart out the activities if we need to further allocate tasking. What we are doing is simplified variant of productability analysis. For example, suppose we are going to sell our battery-powered toaster over the web. One party to a joint venture or strategic alliance may handle taking the orders and processing payments, while the other party may be responsible for manufacturing the toaster and shipping it to the customer. In other words, once we have the task analysis, we can match up tasks with the capabilities of the party who is best prepared to handle the tasking.

Capability data is often hard to get in any detail. For publicly traded U.S. companies, SEC filings are perhaps the best source for data. Reports of stock analysts may also be helpful shortcuts. Unfortunately, it often is a matter of searching press releases and that way you can at least find out when factories are built and major equipment bought. Also easy to obtain for public companies is general financial information, which can be used to assess the potential depth of their pockets. Revenue data for smaller firms can be obtained by searching Dun & Bradstreet or Corptech, but self-reporting tends to skew the information, suggesting pockets are deeper than they really are.

ATTITUDE TOWARD RISK

Risk is the fear you will regret a decision. In business, we can measure attitudes towards risk in terms of how players select options given their expected payoffs, that is, the fair market value of an uncertain payment. Expected payoff is a function of the sum of the payments expected times the probability of obtaining each payment or

$$\sum (\$_1 \times p_1) + (\$_2 \times p_2) + \ldots + (\$_n \times p_n).$$

As in game theory, we can distinguish between three kinds of players: risk loving, risk neutral, and risk adverse. The risk loving player will choose a less certain payoff over a certain payoff, even if the certain payoff has a higher expected value than the risky one. The risk adverse player will choose the certain payoff over the less certain one, even though the certain payoff will have a lower expected payoff. A risk neutral player will simply choose the payoff with the highest expected value.

Since at least the early 1990s, attitudes toward risk have been discussed as a factor favoring or discouraging innovation in firms. At that time, the willingness of companies to adopt innovations was shown to be related to a range of organizational characteristics in various studies. Some examples are:[9]

---

[9] Damanpour, "Organizational Innovation: A Meta-Analysis of Effects of Determinants and Moderators."

Characteristics of Organization Used	Impact on Innovation
Specialization	Positive
Functional differentiation	Positive
Professionalism	Positive
Formalism	Nonsignificant
Centralization	Negative
Managerial attitude toward change	Positive
Managerial tenure	Nonsignificant
Technical knowledge resources	Positive
Administrative intensity	Positive
Slack resources	Positive (but weak, which suggests there is a distinction between absorbed and unabsorbed slack, i.e. the more slack is liquid assets, the less it is positive)
External communications	Positive
Internal communications	Positive
Vertical differentiation	Nonsignificant
Size	Nonsignificant

Other studies have confirmed that the attitudes of managers are themselves an important factor. These attitudes also can be correlated with objective factors. For example managers with a history of working in jobs that are externally facing, such as R&D and marketing, tend to be more supportive of innovation. Managers who read widely, travel, and are in general scanning the environment for opportunities are also more willing to support innovations. Solid production and financial expertise, plus participating in planning and control activities are another set of factors correlated with support for innovations.[10]

Any deal involves allocation of risk. What we want is a target whose willingness to bear risk is compatible with the level of risk we want to unload (see Exhibit 9.12).

While it is hard to determine how a target might respond to any specific technology, usually it is easy to determine their attitudes towards the risks in general. According to Larry Kahaner, behavior profiling should

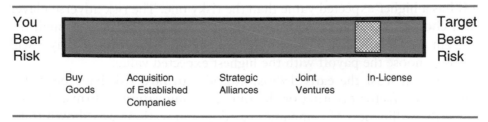

EXHIBIT 9.12   Willingness to Bear Risk

---

[10] Hoffman and Hegarty, "Top Management Influence on Innovations: Effects of Executive Characteristics and Social Culture," *Journal of Management* 19, no. 3 (1993).

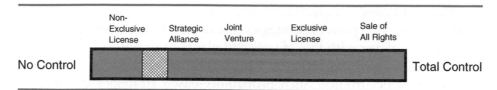

EXHIBIT 9.13   How Much Control to Demand

include at least three elements: past successes and failure because, like Pavlov's dogs, people tend to repeat successful behavior but try to avoid mistakes they have made before; overall behavior traits, because habits are hard to break; and the internal and external environment the player is in, because people do respond to stimuli and the environmental pressures on them may constrain or open up options for new behavior.[11]

Past successes and failures can be garnered by reading the press (especially profiles of, and interviews with, senior managers), company press releases, annual reports, and government filings. Behavior traits sometimes can be found in gossip columns and society pages. Stimuli and environmental pressures are usually easiest to study as they reflect business conditions and events.

There are two behavioral traits that are important to try to determine. The first trait has to do with how much control a player will demand. In general, the greater the control over a situation, the less the risk. This control can be sought over the knowledge and know-how involved in a technology, over how the technology is used, or both (see Exhibit 9.13). Fortunately, management decisions in the past are indicators.

The second trait has to do with how a player seeks to minimize risk. We can describe two polar extremes which minimize risk. One pole, called maximin, focuses on seeking outcomes that selects the minimum risk options and then determines which of these gives the highest level of benefits. The other pole, called minimax, seeks the smallest risk outcome from among those providing maximum benefits. Clearly, we would prefer our target to lean as far as possible towards minimax strategies unless our technology is mature and well proven (see Exhibit 9.14). Career path and past decisions can provide insights.

Maximin ▨ Minimax

EXHIBIT 9.14   Risk Strategies

---

[11] Kahaner, *Competitive Intelligence*, 117.

The significance of attitude is clear. Just because a Nash equilibrium exists between two players' strategies that favors deal-making, a deal may not occur. A player with lots of time and plenty of resources can examine potential outcomes and make an assessment of their benefits and his/her likelihood of occurrence. Such probability-based strategies can lead to pure plays, by which we mean do it or do not do it. But even in game theory, players are free to adopt less than optimal strategies, so it makes sense to factor that in. No wonder, when people do not have lots of time and plenty of resources, they shoot from the hip based on the data and analysis they do have plus instinct. The best we can usually do is put a behavior profile together with objective indicators favoring innovation in order to make a reasonably educated guess about how much risk our targets might bear.

CONCLUSION

In this chapter we have discussed how to select targets for deals. We have seen feasible targets are aligned with you on three dimensions: market, technology, and capabilities. But alignment is not enough; the target also has to have an appropriate attitude towards risk given the technology readiness level of your technology and the strengths and weaknesses of your company, university, or lab.

In general, it helps to think of alignment using slider bars. The more you can slide the market to the high side, the better the target appears.

Background research only takes you so far. At some point you have to pick up the phone and call someone, asking "any interest in doing a deal" and explain why they should be interested and would be silly missing out on what you have to offer.

CHAPTER 10

Valuing the Technology

You cannot do a valuation until you know what you are going to use it for. Valuations are always a guesstimate. We have to make assumptions, if only because we are projecting revenue and expense streams that will only occur in the future. The number of assumptions we make reflects how much money is at stake. The more money involved, the more we try to pin down our assumptions. Which ones we can leave unpinned is a matter of how critical they are for the final outcome.

A thought experiment can drive home the importance of assumptions. Suppose it is 1979 and you work for Carter-Wallace Inc., who makes Trojan prophylactics. Someone has come to you concerning whether to in-license a new material that makes rubbers that are able to block viruses and do not have leakage problems. They want to know the potential value for the company. So, you do a discounted cash flow analysis. You talk to manufacturing and get estimates to use for production costs. They say the new material will add 50 cents to one dollar to each prophylactic. You buy some market research reports. You get out your spreadsheet and start cranking numbers. And you come back to management and say, "These market research reports suggest no one cares about viruses. We want to block bacteria and sperm." So, it does not look like a big hit because there is no reason to pay the premium. So, the company passes. Ten years later, on June 29, 1988, you are hoping no one remembers you shelved a better prophylactic for preventing AIDS, because the *Los Angeles Times* is running a story on how a UCLA study has found Trojan Ribbed Natural and Trojan Ribbed are among the worst condoms in the country, having only questionable effectiveness for stopping the spread of AIDS.[1]

Could you have foreseen AIDS? Maybe. Maybe not. But that is irrelevant. The point is you would not have had to have that kind of foresight to know, even twenty years ago, that sooner or later a viral disease would be transmitted during sex. So you should have concluded your firm would

---

[1] Allan Parachini, "Condom Study Finding Wide Differences among Brands," *Los Angeles Times,* June 28, 1988, http://www.aegis.com/news/lt/1988/LT880613.html (accessed October 22, 2005).

explore in-licensing this patent as a hedge in case a viral-based sexually transmitted disease emerged in the future. Of course, you would not recommend rushing it into production. After all, it is pretty hard to justify running a factory and trying to sell a product for which there is no demand.

Now, you can tear this example apart and a fundamental fact remains. In doing valuations we are not calculating absolute value but expected value, that is, we are calculating revenues (whether gross or net) times the probability of realizing those revenues. The probability, as we shall see, is captured in the discount rate. To do valuations we have to make assumptions about the future.

The quality of these assumptions rests on two things. The first is good market research designed to reduce ambiguity concerning key assumptions. The better we can pin down our numbers, the more reliable our projections are likely to be. The second is instinct. Some people just have better instincts. The first can be taught, the second comes with practice. In this chapter, we look at three sets of critical assumptions: revenue, expense, and risk.

THE BASICS: DISCOUNTED CASH FLOW

All valuation methods rely upon discounted cash flow analysis (DCA). In a DCA you calculate the revenues by period. (Sometimes you only calculate out some period of time you can foresee with reasonable certainty and use a residual or terminal value to represent the rest of the period for which revenues are possible.) Then you calculate the expenses. Next you subtract expenses from revenues. That gives net cash flow. Finally, you discount the revenues for the out years to the present. Exhibit 10.1 is an

Inputs							
Period	0	1	2	3	4	5	
Current Investment	$100.00						
Future Cash Flows		$21.00	$34.00	$40.00	$33.00	$17.00	
Discount Rate		8.0%	7.6%	7.3%	7.0%	7.0%	
Net Present Value Using a Time Line							
Period	0	1	2	3	4	5	
Cumulative Discount Factor	0.0%	8.0%	16.2%	24.7%	33.4%	42.8%	
Cash Flow	($100.00)	$21.00	$34.00	$40.00	$33.00	$17.00	
Present Value of Each Cash Flow	($100.00)	$19.44	$29.26	$32.08	$24.73	$11.91	
Net Present Value	$17.42						

Cumulative Discount Factor on date t = (1 + Cumulative Discount Factor on date t-1) * (1 + Discount Rate on date t) - 1
Present Value of Each Cash Flow = (Cash Flow on date t) / (1+ Cumulative Discount Factor on date t)
Net Present Value = Sum over all periods of the Present Value of Each Cash Flow

EXHIBIT 10.1   NPV General Discount Rate

Inputs						
Period	0	1	2	3	4	5
Current Investment	$100.00					
Future Cash Flows		$21.00	$34.00	$40.00	$33.00	$17.00
Inflation Rate		3.0%	2.8%	2.5%	2.2%	2.0%
Real Discount Rate		5.0%	5.5%	6.0%	6.5%	6.5%
Net Present Value Using a Time Line						
Period	0	1	2	3	4	5
Nominal Discount Rate	0.0%	8.2%	8.5%	8.7%	8.8%	8.6%
Cumulative Discount Factor	0.0%	8.2%	17.3%	27.4%	38.7%	50.7%
Cash Flow	-$100.00	$21.00	$34.00	$40.00	$33.00	$17.00
Present Value of Each Cash Flow	-$100.00	$19.42	$28.99	$31.39	$23.79	$11.28
Net Present Value	$14.87					

EXHIBIT 10.2   Real and Inflation Net Present Value with General Discount Rate

example I built a few years ago using instructions provided by Professor Craig Holden of Indiana University.[2] The discounting reflects the risk in actually realizing the net revenues. If you get fancy, you adjust the discount factor to reflect the change in risk over time.

Sounds pretty simple, doesn't it? It is. You can get fancier by adding in inflation, which also reduces the value of the money your will make in the future. Then if you want to get really really fancy, you adjust both the discounting and the inflation rate, as is done in Exhibit 10.2.

APPROACHES TO VALUATION

There are five main ways of valuating technology. Three of them make sense. Two are stupid. Obviously, you want to use the ones that make sense unless you are negotiating with people even stupider than you would be if you used one of the stupid approaches.

Not Stupid Methods

The most widely accepted is the *market approach*. In this approach, the value of a technology is represented by its market value, that is, the value

_____

[2] The spreadsheets were built with the aid of Craig Holden's instructions at http://www.bus.indiana.edu/cholden/smcf/Instruct.htm. That link is no longer active, but Holden, associate professor of finance at the Kelley School of Business at Indiana University, has a series of books on using Excel modeling to learn financial subjects, including valuation, at http://www.excelmodeling.com/. I highly recommend the approach.

of the net revenues it generates, discounted to the present. As we often do not have sales data to use as a basis for forecasting the revenues for a new technology, a common technique is to use a benchmark or set of benchmarks, constructed by looking at sales for similar products, and building the revenue side of the forecast by adapting the benchmark to fit this specific technology. We can, for example, do two SWOT analyses to compare our benchmark technology and its market penetration with our current technology and its situation in order to have some basis for making this adjustment.

The *income approach* focuses on creating a ground up determination of the income generating potential of technology. In this approach, the value of a technology is a residual in an analysis of how a firm uses its assets to generate net cash flow in its on-going operations. To use this approach we either need an ongoing entity or the ability to construct some generic organizational entity that is the *"typical"* firm. We also need to either assume how intellectual assets that have contributed in the past will be related to how they contribute in the future or how an industrial sector average performer would use their assets.

In either case we are relying on the formula:

$$\text{Net Cash Flow} = \text{Economic Performance} = x(\text{Physical Assets}) + y(\text{Financial Assets}) + z(\text{Intangible Assets})$$

where x, y, and z represent the contributions of a unit of asset to the performance. With this formula, what we do is strip away the known contributors, that is the physical assets and the financial assets (money – cash on hand). That leaves us with the unknowns, which are the intangible assets.

To find the value of these assets, we can use the calculated intangible value (CIV) method. It works as follows:

Step 1: Calculate average pre-tax earnings for some reasonable period, say three to five years. This is found on a company's income statements.

Step 2: Take the average year-end tangible assets for that period. This number comes off their balance sheets.

Step 3: Calculate ROA. Return on assets (ROA) is a commonly used measure for how profitable a company is relative to its total assets. It is calculated by dividing the company's annual earnings by its total assets, giving us a percentage. A simple formula is ROA = net income/net assets. Typically ROA varies by industry and by company. More precisely we can add the interest expense back in to the calculation so we can use operating costs for ROA = EBIT(1 – tax rate)/Total Assets = [Net Income + Interest Expense(1 – tax rate)]/Total Assets, where EBIT is earnings before interest and tax.

Step 4: For the same period, find the industry's average ROA. This is a look-up found by searching the web.

Step 5: Calculate the company's excess ROA, which is (the industry average ROA times the company's tangible assets) minus the pre-tax earnings from Step 1. That gives us how much more or less the company makes from its assets.

Step 6: Calculate the average income tax rate for this period and multiply that by the excess ROA. Subtract this result from the excess ROA, which gives us the after-tax premium due to intangible assets.

Step 7: If you want a current value, calculate the discounted value of the result by using the company's weighted average cost of capital.

The problem is we still have to parse the return to intangible assets to find what share of it is attributable to intellectual property in general. So we start eliminating more things, this time taking off percents due to things like goodwill, supplier reliability, professionalism of staff, etc. till we end up with the contribution from intellectual property for the company of interest. Of course, we are not done yet, because the residual is for all intellectual property. We now have to determine if this "*average*" return can be used as a basis of calculating the value of our specific technology. We have to adjust for any unique aspects of this set of intellectual assets from those that were the basis for the CIV.

Bottom line: However you look at it, doing a ground-up analysis is a big headache and still a bit of a black art. But sometimes it is all you can do and sometimes it makes more sense to do it than use market value, as when you are figuring out the contribution of IP to a company seeking venture capital or a joint venture.

The final way that makes sense is *auctions*. Auctions should only be used where the seller of the technology has bargaining power, the technology is easy to apprehend by many buyers, some base or participation fee can be set (because it would be a real bummer to auction off your technology and get nothing for it), and the process has "*integrity.*" By integrity we mean it can be trusted. For example, if you use sealed bids, there is a standard form used by all the bidders so apples are being compared to apples and not to oranges, and you provide a prototype licensing or other deal agreement to all bidders so they can factor the terms of the deal into how they bid.

What an auction does is literally build a market place. By definition, if enough players bid, a fair market value emerges.

Stupid Methods

The *cost approach* asks what it would cost to replicate the technology. It is based on the notion of replacement value, something well known to anyone who had insurance and then totaled a car in accident. Of course, what something costs today is probably not what it cost when it was developed. After all, there generally is progress in science and engineering, and there also is "*leakage*" of ideas. So replacement value is usually below the original cost of developing the technology.

Unfortunately, the cost of replacement is irrelevant. Worse, it is stupid. As we have repeatedly discussed in this book, as a buyer all I care about is what net utility the good I am buying creates for me. Your cost of creating it has nothing to do with its value for me. The value for me is tied to how I can use it. That, and how badly I want it for whatever reasons, determines what I will pay. So your price of acquiring or creating any asset is not necessarily commensurate with the economic value of that the asset for any downstream acquirer.

> Suppose you play the piano. You decide you want a piano in your apartment, so you monitor the want ads, find an upright, and buy it. But you get flustered and instead of negotiating the price down, you negotiate it up. Just because you paid a negotiated price does not mean it was a good deal. Maybe you are a lousy negotiator. Maybe you are in that class of people who Abe Lincoln said can be fooled part of the time.

Another method used sometimes is the *25% rule*. This rule is a rule of thumb that assumes that an IP asset's value is around 25% of the gross profit, before taxes, from the operations in which the asset is used. Again, this is pretty stupid. In an article entitled "Use of the 25 Per Cent Rule in Valuing IP," Robert Goldscheider, John Jarosz and Carla Mulhern looked at a bunch of transactions across many industries and concluded that there was a lot of variation in royalty rates across industries and that the 25% rule only applied as a rough rule of thumb for all transactions aggregated.[3]

> If you are having trouble understanding why this is stupid, imagine a TV sitcom, kind of like *Leave it to Beaver*. The husband gets home after a long day at work. He is tired and hungry. He opens the door and the baby has just spit up, the two year old, Jamie, is running around with his diaper off, Mary the four year old is drawing with crayons on the wall, and the wife is telling Johnny, the eight year old, "Sit down and do your homework. I have to finish making dinner and I do not have time to keep telling you to turn off that TV." Perfect timing. Being the suave loving husband, he says to his spouse. "Darling, I'm, home. I missed you as much as the average of all men missed all women for all times." "Hello! Read my lips! Make your own dinner." Slam. (That was the door to the bedroom. Crying is heard.)

Just as we do not love in the average, we do not do deals for an average technology across all industries or even within an industrial sector. The deal is for this technology in the here and now. So while it makes sense to figure out how to apportion value generated between the things that contribute to that value, rules of thumb based on over-aggregated averages can lead to some pretty bizarre results.

Non-Revenue Value and Its Valuation

Be aware that the *"value"* for both you and the other party may not be fully captured by any of the preceding methods. Indeed, the full *"value"* of a patent, trade secret, etc. is likely to never be fully captured by revenues because part of the asset's utility resides in the negative right to prevent others from doing something they would otherwise be legally permitted to do. As we have said before, value, which is a monetary concept, is only roughly equivalent to utility, which is an instrumental concept.

Consider this scenario. You have a technology. You introduce goods into the market and they are a big success. Your technology is protected by

---

[3] Robert Goldscheider, John Jarosz, and Carla Mulhern, "Use of the 25 Per Cent Rule in Valuing IP," *les Nouvelles* (December 2002).

a very strong patent, and you have a reputation for vigorously defending your IP turf. A competitor thinks about trying to design around your patent. The problem is they cannot figure out how to do that. So your IP scares off this potential competitor and they do not embark on a plan to develop and sell goods encompassed by your patent's claims.

Take another scenario. Suppose a competitor reverse engineers one of your goods and decides you are infringing them. They start thinking about suing. Then someone over there realizes, "Whoops, if we hit them, we may be vulnerable to being hit back because this product of ours may infringe that patent of theirs." So your patent portfolio has added utility because it makes competitors cautious about enforcing their intellectual property rights against you for fear of retaliation.

In both cases, you may never know how close you came to having competition. Even if you did know, because it did not happen, forecasting the economic impact on your revenue stream would be very difficult. Would the competitor have knocked your socks off or would they have flubbed? How badly?

One way to get at these non-value utilities is to use a scorecard. In scorecard approaches, the various components of intellectual assets that create utility are defined and indices (often ordinal) are created and used to create a scorecards presentation. A composite index with weighting, etc. may or may not be included in the process.

REVENUES

There is a great line, somewhere in Damodaran's *Investment Valuation*, that goes: "Much of the tedium in valuation is a direct result of having to estimate cash flows."[4] Clearly to estimate revenues we need to know how much money is being made, when, and for how long.

In general, we expect to see a J-curve. During R&D and product development, the revenues are negative. Over time cumulative revenues grow, until, all other things being equal, at market saturation the revenue growth levels out as the only buying that remains is replacement buying. Exhibit 10.3 is a J-curve.

Depending on for whom we are doing the valuation we may or may not care about the negative revenues. For example, if we are doing the valuation for a licensee, we do not care about losses prior to the time we acquire the technology. Not our problem.

We can use the ballpoint pen as an example to illustrate this point. The

---

[4] Aswath Damodaran, *Investment Valuation* (Hoboken, NJ: Wiley, 1996).

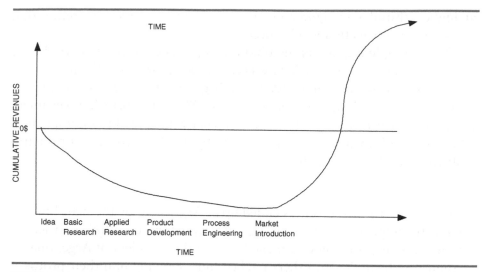

EXHIBIT 10.3 J-Curve of Revenues

ballpoint pen was invented by John Loud, an American leather tanner. He invented a device with a reservoir of ink and a roller ball that could be used to apply the thick ink to leather hides. The patent was issued in 1888, but his pen was never produced. Over the next 30 years, around 350 other patents were issued for similar devices, but none of them made it to market because of the ink used. (How many of you are old enough to remember pocket protectors?) Some inks were thin, causing the pens to leak. Others were too thick and they clogged the pens. Yet other ink was temperature sensitive and both leaked and clogged.

Ladislas and George Biro solved the ink problem, but even their pen succeeded after years of losses. Ladislas was an editor in 1935, when he got fed up with fountain pens that smudged, needed to be refilled, and due to their sharp tips, often ripped the newsprint. Their pen, however, was not made until after they fled Hungary for Argentina at the beginning of World War II, applying for a new patent in Paris as they fled. Unfortunately, their experience also highlights the importance of getting end-user involvement early in development. Their pen relied on gravity to pull the ink, so it had to be straight up and down to work. Gravity feed also meant if you paused to think, you got a glob of ink in one spot. The first Biro pens were a market disaster. However, the brothers went back to the lab and devised a capillary action pen in which the ball acted like a sponge, enabling the pen to be held at a slant. Within a year, this pen was being sold throughout Argentina. Even then they ran out of money. Real success did not come until the British government licensed rights to their patent in order to have writing devices that British Royal Air Force pilots could use at higher altitudes in fighter planes. It was the success with pilots that make the Biro pens financially successful.[5]

The example highlights the ubiquitous presence of the J-curve. In the case of the ball point pen, which was easily recognized as a *"better mouse-trap,"* it still took about a decade to really get the design down, pass break even, and start making sustainable income. When the British government licensed it, their basis for valuation was what was needed to fight a war in a Spitfire, not how money had been spent by the Biro brothers nor the travails they had been through.

> The reason the Biro brothers ended up in Argentina, by the way, highlights the importance of having a good elevator speech. While on vacation at the seashore, they happened to meet the President of Argentina, Augustine Justo. The brothers pitched him, showing him their prototype ballpoint pen, President Justo urged them to come to Argentina and make the pens there. By 1943, they had and were in production.

Of course, we already have a basic revenue estimate from doing our market size estimate earlier. It is this estimate that we are adjusting here. There are three kinds of adjustments we need to make.

The first set have to do with how distributed in time are our data points. The size of the deal will determine if we need to do a year-by-year estimate for the life of the patent or the useful life of the intellectual property. The smaller the deal, the more liberties we can take. For example, we can estimate annual sales through break even and on to take off. Once we turn the curve up we can make some straight line or exponential growth assumptions and run those out until the curve starts to level off or breaks due to saturation or competition or obsolescence. For a tiny deal we can take some market estimate and just apply a straight line or exponential growth rate appropriate for that customer segment based on overall growth in demand.

We also want to adjust for the rate at which products are changed by the target, which will influence when and for how long sales will occur. In Exhibit 10.4, a move to either P_2 or P_3 from P_1 will affect the rate of product change.

Another adjustment needs to be made to reflect how much of the price paid by the buyer is attributable to this technology.

There is an old Zen Buddhist story about a monk walking along the

---

[5] Idea Finder.com, "Ballpoint Pen," February 2005, http://www.ideafinder.com/history/inventions/story055.htm (accessed October 23, 2005).

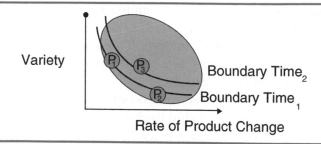

Variety

Boundary Time₂

Boundary Time₁

Rate of Product Change

EXHIBIT 10.4   Product–Market Interaction

road when a prince drives by in a chariot. The prince stops, turns the chariot around, and comes back to the monk. "You there," he says, "who are you?" The monk answers. "You could call me Pramaha, but that is not who I am." The prince says angrily, "Monk, why do you mock me? I will have your head cut off." The monk says calmly, "What are you riding in?" "Why, a chariot." "If you took away the wheels would it still be a chariot?" "Why of course!" replies the prince. "And if you put the wheels back but took away the reins, would it still be a chariot?" "Yes, yes," says the prince impatiently. "And what if you put back the reins but removed the yoke?" "Of course," says the prince, slower as he is starting to see the pattern. "That is why my name is Pramaha but that is not who I am," smiles the monk.

Now, the point of the parable is that the whole is different than the sum of the parts. By functionally decomposing the product, process, or service, we can explore how much of the value of the whole is attributable to the part our technology represents. The wheel is not the chariot, but without it, it would be a darn poor device. So the value is likely substantial as the functionality likely is critical in the eyes of end users. By contrast, the reins may be possible to replace. Perhaps the horses can be trained to respond to voice commands. In that case we would suspect the value of the reins is less than that of the wheels. Note that what we are doing is comparing each item to all other items and asking how important it is. This method is called analytical hierarchical comparison or AHP.[6]

(More important: 1-Less, 2-Equal, 3-More)	Yoke Compared to	Wheels Compared to	Reigns Compared to
Yoke	N/A	3	2
Wheels	1	N/A	1
Reins	2	3	N/A

---

[6] See "Spatial Decision Analysis," n.d., http://www.gpa.uq.edu.au/courses/GEOM/3002/w8_decisions.pdf (accessed October 26, 2005).

Other methods exist, such as the multiattribute tradeoff system or trading cards, which can be used.[7]

If the functionality is already present in the good, then we can use the value of the current functionality as a starting point for the percentage of value our technology might represent.

We did a project that involved electro-optical chromophores for small scale optical interconnects from chip to chip and chip to board in telecom boards. Optical interconnections replace the metallic traces that provide the electrical connections on printed circuit boards. Because of increased functionality of components at the same time that device dimensions are shrinking, it is increasingly difficult for the traditional copper interconnects to meet microelectronic circuit design requirements of delay, thermals, noise, power, and bandwidth.

We knew, from market research interviews, that the industry was price sensitive, so it was important to introduce the optical interconnect for roughly the same price as the current interconnects. Unfortunately, we could not find the price for electrical interconnects. What we could find is the average price for boards with components and interconnects on them. By speaking with a number of experts, we did a quick survey on the percentage of completed board price attributable to the interconnects. Knowing the price of traditional boards traditional electronic interconnects, we could calculate the revenues for our interconnect. However, we needed to adjust that figure because electro-optical chromophores are likely to be important for passive interconnects, which involves passing information rather than for active interconnects which perform calculations. Once we had an estimate of the proportion of active to passive components, we were able to calculate the value of electro-optical chromophores as we knew the cost of manufacturing them. Interestingly, because they are cheaper to make, their value will likely be greater than the electronic interconnects they will replace.

Where the functionality is new, we can obtain an estimate by asking people what they would pay for that functionality. Often they do not know, as they have never thought about it before. In such cases, it helps to ask them what they might pay if they could have their "wish list" price. That price at least gives us a floor.

We can also take each functionality, component, or feature of a product, service, or process and ask how important it is to the end user. We ask

---

[7] See Bureau of Reclamation, "Multi-Attribute Tradeoff System (MATS)," n.d., http://www.usbr.gov/pmts/guide/toolbox/mats.html (accessed October 26, 2005); Bureau of Reclamation, "Trading Cards," n.d., http://www.usbr.gov/pmts/guide/toolbox/tradingc.html (accessed October 26, 2005).

that end user how much, or what percent, of the value of the good would be lost if the functionality, component, or feature was missing. (We can call them up and literally ask them or we can do market research to try to estimate their response.)

Be aware there is a presumption in Western civilization that the whole is greater than the sum of the parts. When it comes to IP, occasionally the part is greater than the whole. That occurs most commonly with flexible process technology.

Suppose you are making printed circuit boards for telecom. To take a historical example: a fine pitch surface mount machine—the machine which lets you put components on a board without needing through holes. Surface mounting enables drastic reduction in the size and weight of such products. (For that reason it has been widely adopted.)

In the printed circuit board industry, companies work on very narrow margins. So, they do not like to invest unless they have a customer who needs a specific process technology and is willing to pay enough to get it if the cost of the equipment is covered by the contract. Suppose you have a cell phone customer who wants components surface mounted. You buy the machine and make the boards. The value of the technology is initially equal to the incremental revenues you made on that contract because you did surface mount rather than through-holes. But, the actual value is much greater as you still have the machine and having it makes it easier to win other contracts as well as to garner larger revenues during performance. If the increment is large enough, the value added by the surface mount machine may exceed the value of the rest of your production line, which will be reflected in a dramatic upswing in profitability.

A specific technology also may create value across a wide range of products for the licensee (or other partner). Where a good has synergies with existing products, its introduction stimulates sales of those other goods. So, some incremental value is added for its contribution to marketing each time a synergistic good is sold.

The same approach works for stacking and bundling. Stacking occurs where several pieces of IP need to be licensed in order to bring a good to market. In biotechnology, patents are often stacked. A trademark might be stacked with a design or utility patent, as would occur if a licensee of U.S. patent 6,951,499, Toy Sword with Contact Indicator, licensed the trademark Star Wars from Lucasfilm prior to selling the sword.[8] Bundling is used where a portfolio of IP is desired, as when Boeing hired us to

---

[8] See Cecile B. Corral, "The 'Star Wars' Licensing Empire Strikes Back," *Discount Store News* (June 7, 1999), http://www.findarticles.com/p/articles/mi_m3092/is_11_38/ai_54943702 (accessed October 25, 2005).

examine markets for a portfolio of noise reduction technology or Corning asked us to look at a portfolio of carbon technology. In such case the portfolio is reshuffled into sets or bundles that meet a common need. Bundling can be used as a way of circumventing time limitations on a revenue stream. Copyright might be bundled with a patent in the case of some software. The patent is only 20 years, the copyright much longer. If a trade secret for know-how is bundled with a patent for a manufacturing process, the trade secret portion of the deal could still generate revenues after the patent expires.

In either case, the question emerges: How much value does each component of the stack or bundle add to the value of the whole? A Hasbro figurine is worth less to a kid who loves Star Wars if it is just a big furry beast rather than Chewbacca.

The second set of adjustments has to do with whom we foresee partnering. In our earlier discussion of market size, we explored how market share is based on the perceived desirability of our technology for its end users. Here we need to take into account the market power of our target as a supplier or technology (or goods), either on their own or in some kind of partnership with us. We adjust our previous estimate for the market share of our target as well as for their brand loyalty. If there is strong premium pricing for their products and services, goodwill adjustments to revenues may be appropriate.

The third set of adjustments has to do with customer segmentation. Different customer segments likely will view the value added by features, functionalities, and components differently. So, we may want to calculate the value by segment to correctly value a technology. Take the narrow angular share of the cheap hexagon clear plastic BIC® Cristal® pen. Some people would pay more for a more comfortable pen, like the BIC® Select, which mimics the shape of the fountain pen, but not others. So, we actually have two distinct customer segments.

So much for the easy part. Now we have to pin the numbers so we can have confidence that they make sense. Probably the easiest way is to call up a bunch of experts and ask them what they think of your projection, then take some average of their estimates on how to correct what you have, and apply it. The problem is you may end up with a bunch of people who have not examined their own assumptions. So, you may just be forecasting the collective folly, like in 1948, when many newspapers ran headlines reading "Dewey Wins," only to find out when the votes were counted he lost.[9]

---

[9] See PBS.org, "Truman versus Dewey," 2002, http://www.pbs.org/wnet/historyofus/web13/segment5_p.html (accessed October 22, 2005).

My favorite personal misjudgment is the fax machine. When I first read about fax machines I thought to myself, "What a stupid idea. Who would want to type up a document on a computer, print it, transmit if over phone lines, and then re-enter on a computer on the other end. Why not just transmit it electronically using FTP (file transfer protocol for you young folks)." Of course, I was wrong. My instincts were fine. Ten years from now kids will ask what is a fax machine. But I failed to check my assumptions. If I had, I would have rapidly realized I would be one of the tiny number of very early adopters of computers and the Internet. Fortunately, no one had hired me to assess the market size for, or value of, fax machines. Of course, if they had, I would have checked my assumptions about computer use and Internet access and hopefully not have made the mistake.

The challenge is to correlate the assumptions with actual buying behavior. As indicated earlier, the easiest was to find a relevant comparable and then adjust the comparable for the differences between that situation and yours. For that, a SWOT is helpful. As before, we examine the strengths and weaknesses of our commercialization strategy with the one pursued in our benchmark.

For example, if we are trying to value the ball point pen as a technology, we might look at the fountain pen as a benchmark. A successful fountain pen was patented in 1884 by L.E. Waterman, an insurance salesman in New York. It became the dominant design for a permanent writing instrument for the next sixty years.[10] As was the case with the ball point pen, Waterman was not the first one to come up with the idea. The oldest surviving fountain pen was made in France in 1702. John Jacob Parker patented a self-filling fountain pen in 1831. However, as was the case with ball points, early fountain pens had ink spills and other problems. What Waterman did was add the air hole to the nib. He also placed three grooves inside the feed mechanism, thereby controlling the leak rate. He was motivated as he had destroyed a valuable contract with a leaky pen. What followed was a period of adaptive innovation such as the use of a pressure sack with a button-like device for filling the pen, which provided the basis for Parker and lever filling, which provided the basis for Schaeffer.[11]

---

[10] Mary Bellis, "A Brief History of Writing Instruments, Part 3: The Battle of the Ballpoint Pens," *About* (2005), http://inventors.about.com/library/weekly/aa101697.htm (accessed October 23, 2005).
[11] Mary Bellis, "A Brief History of Writing Instruments, Part 2: The History of the Fountain Pen," *About* (2005), http://inventors.about.com/library/weekly/aa100897 .htm (accessed October 23, 2005).

Note that this class of SWOTs, by definition is different than the prior ones we did to figure out launch tactics and partners. This time we assume we are partnered with the target we are about to engage in negotiations. Then we compare the opportunities and threats in our situation with that of the benchmark. This time, the intersection of the rows and columns contains adjustments that need to be made to adapt the baseline to our situation.

One caution: Sometimes it is necessary to use more than one benchmark. For example, a few years back we were projecting the revenue flow for introduction of farm-raised artic char into the United States. We used two benchmarks: tilapia, which was unknown in the U.S. market prior to its introduction like the char; and salmon, which was known in wild form, but was closer in taste and texture to our fish. Our final projections took into account both sets of data in order to develop the projections for char.

EXPENSES

Expenses are cash outlays that need to be made on the way to market and once there. Exhibit 10.5 gives an idea of the kinds of tasking that eats up this cash. The exhibit is an extension of a set of tasking developed by the U.S. government's Defense Science Board and called the Willoughby templates. We have extended these as commercialization was not a DOD issue at the time they were developed.

(One justification for the 25% rule is the fact that the closer a product or service comes to market, the more the expenses are incurred. The argument is that developing the technology only brings you about 25% of the way with respect to cost. We emphasize that what really is involved is an empirical question. You have to look at the actual process and calculate the percentages from that examination.) The simple way to estimate costs is to examine the tasking needed to bring a technology to market. Each box in a tasking chart like the one in Exhibit 10.5 can be viewed as a black box in a giant input-out model. For each box we determine the kind of processes we can use, the labor and other resources those processes require, and the likely outputs. If we know the throughput for the box, we can thus calculate both some absolute minimum fixed cost and the variable cost as the number of units fluctuates. We can also calculate how long it will take us to complete the process.

We can link processes in two ways. Some processes fall along a critical path. Outputs of earlier boxes are required as inputs for later boxes. Other processes can be conducted when convenient, at least within some range of time. Thus, we can string together the boxes in one or more sequences that give us budgets and a basis for calculating cost of goods sold.

An example of an incremental innovation market entry task sequence

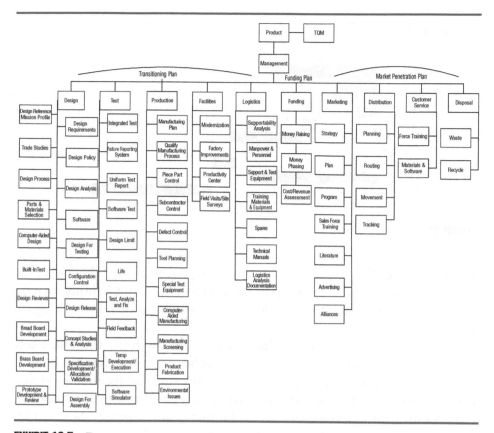

EXHIBIT 10.5 Expenses

is Exhibit 10.6. The example comes from a Foresight Science & Technology tool called the virtual deal simulator™ (VDS™). The VDS™ maps how a technology gets to market and provides a common framework for determining how best to allocate the tasking among the various parties. What concerns us here is that the more incremental the technology, the more the VDS™ output looks like a traditional project Gantt chart.

As the technology becomes more disruptive and revolutionary, the process develops loops as iterations of research, design, engineering, and test are integrated into various pre-prototyping experiments until a viable solution is discovered. This is what should have happened with the ball-point pen. Instead, the expenses skyrocketed because the factory was built before the gravity fed design was fully validated.

Regardless, the tasking, given the schedule, drives the costs (as Exhibit 10.7 suggests) as well as the timing of expenses. Obviously, it is easier to determine the timing of and amount of expenditures with greater certainty for evolutionary technologies than revolutionary ones because they are closer to being repetitive, variations on what has been done

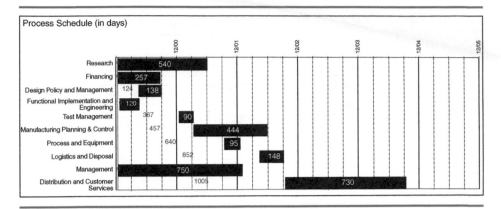

EXHIBIT 10.6 VDS™ Output

before. Indeed, the very nature of repetitive processes lend themselves to application of Six Sigma and other such quality control methods focused on reducing errors due to deviation from procedures or poorly designed procedures.

By contrast, the more revolutionary the technology, the less likely there are to be established production and other processes that can be used as a baseline for development. Indeed, Iansiti's study of technology development at major firms found that revolutionary technology development requires different approaches than evolutionary development. Some of his findings are summarized in the following table.[12]

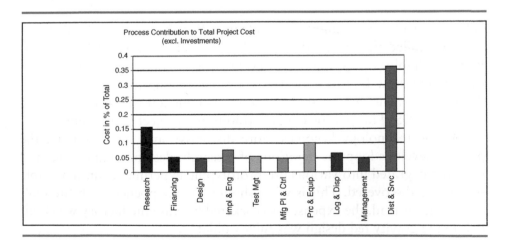

EXHIBIT 10.7 Tasking Drives Cost

---

[12] Iansiti, *Technology Integration* (Boston: Harvard Business School, 1998), chap. 7.

	Revolutionary	Evolutionary
Focus	Strong research focus and emphasis on external knowledge searching for novel solutions	Commitment to architecture of current production process and emphasis on optimization of technology
Experimentation	Extensive use of parallel approaches involving simulation, mock-ups, and alternative models as part of experimentation	Selective prototyping, rapid targeted series of iterative experiments
Project Team	Mixed teams with participation by partners from universities and other companies or new hires. Success associated with strong research experience. Prior project experience in development of early products, services, or processes not significant	People with extensive experience with existing approaches and goods drawn primarily from within the company

As with revenues, expense calculations can be generic or specific for the targets. A generic expense calculation can be made by conducting producibility analysis for each box. The quick and dirty way to do that is to simply call up a couple of potential vendors and ask them what it would cost to outsource the activity. But this method of cost detail needs does not account for economies, learning curve advantages, etc. So, the initial estimates have to be refined to take into account the changing capacities and capabilities of the actual targets (and yourself) as well as how changes in yields affect costs.

Again, the ballpoint pen can be used to illustrate how scale of product can affect expenses on the one hand and price on the other. In October, 1945, Gimbels Department Store in New York sold 10,000 pens at $12.50 each in what is widely viewed as one of the most successful new product launches in U.S. history. Over 5000 people jammed the entrance of the store to buy the pen, made in a makeshift factory by 300 workers employed by Milton Reynolds. Reynolds was a salesman who saw the Biro pen in Argentina while vacationing. He set up production without a license from the brothers on the grounds the patents had mostly expired. In the first three months of product, Reynolds sold over two million pens in 38 countries, attaining total revenues of $5.7 million and a net income of $1.6 million. Those kinds of numbers brought competition. By March of the next year, Eversharp and Eberhard Faber, who had teamed to license the Biro patents, entered the market by selling through Gimbels' rival Macy's. Their pen sold for $19.95. Within two years, competition brought the price of a pen down $0.94. A year later they were down to $0.39.

The lesson is that as sales build, it becomes economically feasible to bring in more specialized methods and equipment. A modern example is Gillette's disposable ballpoint pen hopper designed to funnel thousands of pens into two channels.[13] Another example is a German ballpoint pen factory machinery capable of manufacturing 2,100,000 ball point pens using 3 shifts over 25 days. The core assembly, stamping, and refill assembly machine has stations feeding extruded barrels from hopper magazine to chain transfer, hot stamping, planish the front side, chamfer the front and rear sides, fill the ink from a stainless steel ink tank, feed and insert the tip/metal point, sense the ink and point, ejection of incomplete refills and eject the good refills/ball point pens into a container and count them.[14]

Of particular interest for valuation is a subset of expenses called cost of goods sold (COGS), sometimes called cost of sales. COGS is such as the amount paid to purchase raw materials, components, subassemblies, etc. and turn them into finished goods. COGS is of interest because net sales (sales − returns and discounts) minus COGS equals gross profit. Gross profit is often used as a basis for calculating royalty payments, especially where process improvements are involved.

The reason for using COGS is twofold. First, these are the direct expenses needed to make a product or service. Second, these expenses are seen as more "objective" than others:

- More subjective, like how much marketing to do or how much interest to incur;
- More easily manipulated, like taxes or general and administrative costs; or,
- In the post Enron world, such potential slush funds as legal and accounting.

QUICK RECAP

We have now addressed revenues and expenses. With these two we have everything we need to calculate value of a technology over its life, defined

[13] WorkingModel.com, "Prototyping High Volume Production Equipment at Gillette Corporation, n.d., http://www.workingmodel.com/success/ss_gillette.html (accessed October 23, 2005).
[14] "Ball Point Pen Factory Machines," Genu Industries Private Limite, 2005, http://www.alibaba.com/catalog/10897971/Ball_Point_Pen_Factory_Machines.html (accessed October 23, 2005).

as the period from its inception to the end of its income generating days. Note, we can stop our calculations at any point and declare the result to be the value of the technology, so long as we are clear about just what number we are using.

Net Sales – Manufacturing Costs (COGS) = Gross Profits

Gross Profits – (R&D Expenses + Marketing Expenses + G&A Expenses + Selling Expenses) = Operating Profits

Operating Profits – Income Taxes = Net Income

Net Income + Depreciation = Gross Cash Flow

Gross Cash Flow – Additions to Working Capital + Additions to Fixed Plant Investment = Net Cash Flow

Net Cash Flow = Value (prior to discount)

The value of an asset over its life is not the present value. The present value represents the value over its life reduced down to a single number that is the value in today's currency of the multi-year *forecasted* net revenue stream. In short, it is what you can sell the technology for today if you wanted to just unload all your rights. It is the equivalent of selling your house in fee simple, that is, without retaining any legal rights.

RISK

There are three components to risk when doing valuations: firm-specific, technical, and market. Typically these are lumped together in the discount rate, but to be more precise, only the first two should be. The reason is that the first two are under our control, which means if we have enough money, we can make the risk go away. Market risk is different. No matter how much money we toss at it, it eludes control.

We shall look at these different kinds of risk in a second. What concerns us here is why we care. From looking at Exhibit 10.8, the answer is obvious. Risk affects value. Value is based on revenues minus expenses. Risk either delays when we can get revenues (or even worse, means we get none) or it increases our expenses. Either way, risk reduces value. So, if we want to maximize the value of our technology, we want to figure out how to reduce risk.

Technical risk has to do with whether or not the technology can attain the desired yields on metrics of interest. In general, the more mature the

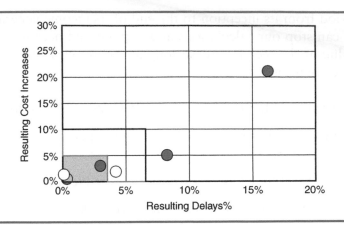

EXHIBIT 10.8   Cost versus Delays for All Risks along Value Chain

technology (the higher its technology readiness level) the less risky the technology. As we move up the TRL levels, either the technology works or it does not. Unfortunately, there comes a time when the risk may not be small enough, yet the cash required is increasingly substantial. This zone is called the *Valley of Death*. (See Exhibit 10.9.) Nonetheless, so long as we have money to toss at the problem, we can get a definitive answer as to whether the technology can be matured.

Similarly, we can toss money at production. We can use NASA's engineering manufacturing readiness levels (EMRLs) to measure production maturity and thus the benefits of tossing the money. EMRLs measure

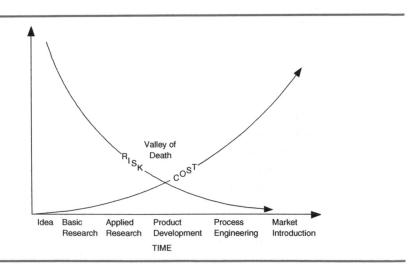

EXHIBIT 10.9   Valley of Death

process maturity, just as TRLs measure product maturity. EMRLs are measured on an ordinal scale from one to six.[15]

1. *Product design/definition.* To develop a production process for a system, component or item, we need to have an idea of what we want to produce. Thus, EMRLs begin only after a relevant engineering application has been selected and a bread board or brass board has been developed, that is, a bench top proof of concept. At this phase we can make a core component that suggests a prototype is possible. Production is an informal activity and done as part of the research and development by people in the lab.

2. *Product integration.* We are doing one of a kind production, but this time we are doing it on an alpha test level prototype. Again, this is informal and done in the lab.

3. *Systems engineering.* Using the prototype, a more formal product analysis is conducted. Basic production requirements can be validated and further defined, even though process changes will need to be made as the product is refined as a result of alpha and beta testing. The materials to be used later for production and manufacturing can be evaluated, as can the production equipment itself. That allows developing a budget and planning process for making the goods. The production process may be a new one, developed for the specific good(s) of interest, or existing production processes may be adapted to make these goods. Whatever the case, since the production process can be mapped out, inspection and test equipment can be selected and preliminary quality and reliability levels set. In other words, we are now designing the production process so low rate batch or pilot production can be planned.

4. *Product demonstration.* Beta testing is occurring. At this point, it is clear what is being made, so planning for scale up of the production process is underway. It is critical that all quality and reliability requirements and other key process characteristics are now identified, although not necessarily under control. As the underlying system, component or item reaches advanced development, the physical and user interfaces have to be clearly defined.

5. *Low rate initial production.* As beta testing winds down, the final production process design can be finished and itself pilot tested. Either a pilot line for a new process will be set up or it will be

---

[15] Adapted. For complete definitions of each level, see Thomas Fiorino, "Engineering and Manufacturing Readiness Levels—Fundamentals, Criteria and Metrics," November 2002, http://www.onr.navy.mil/sci_tech/industrial/nardic/docs/emrls.ppt (accessed October 4, 2004).

demonstrated that the good can be made using an existing production process.

6. *Full rate production.* The production process is now fully implemented. Systems, components or items are made under a process that includes continuous product/process improvement. This is the highest level of production readiness and by this time, there are almost no engineering/design changes. Six-Sigma or other advanced quality methods can be deployed.

Like product risk, production risk has two components. The first is how mature is the process, that is, have we done it before and if so, with what degree of replicability. The second is how certain is our knowledge about what we are doing, which as we saw earlier can be measured with the Bohn Knowledge Levels. There is a world of difference between 300 guys working for Milton Reynolds in a makeshift factory assembling ball point pens out of spare aluminum not needed for the war effort and a fully automated dedicated piece of production equipment that pumps out 2.1 million ball point pens in 25 days. In the first case, we may have high replicability, but it is due to craftsmanship. Craftsmanship is learned through apprenticeship. It is expensive and difficult to duplicate. In the latter case, replicability is a consequence of solid engineering. As the Bohn Knowledge Level rises, the locus of replicability shifts from the worker to the machine.

Note that certitude of replicability is an issue for components and materials manufacturing as well as for the finished product. Recall a major barrier for the initial introduction of the ballpoint pen was discovering an ink that would flow evenly in a wide range of temperatures. Another ink issue that emerged in the 40s. The pens did not work as advertised. They did not write smoothly, the ink dried slowly, it faded, and God forbid you forgot your pocket protector, it did not wash out of clothes when the pens leaked, other times the ink just did not flow. As a kid I remember holding matches to pens, trying to get the ink flowing without melting the plastic casing of the pen. Clearly low replicability—some pens worked, some did not. Indeed, by 1951, consumers were fed up and sales of fountain pens surpassed those of ballpoint pens as innovations like ink cartridges made fountain pens almost as convenient to use as ball point pens.

Enter Patrick J. Frawley Jr. and Fran Seech, who was an unemployed chemist who had worked for a ballpoint pen company that went bankrupt in the big pen bust in early 1950's. Working out of his house, Seech invented a new ink formula. In 1949, Patrick J. Frawley Jr. bought Seech's formula and started the Frawley Pen Company, introducing the first retractable ballpoint tip and the first no-smear ink. So confident was Frawley of his ink that he came up with one of the more audacious marketing campaigns in history. Called Project Normandy, Frawley's salesmen were trained to be very pushy. They would go into the offices of retail store buyers and literally scribble on the shirts of the buyers with their pens. Then they would offer to buy the executive a more expensive shirt if the ink did not wash out. But the shirts did come clean and the "Papermate" pen was a huge success, soon selling hundreds of millions per year.

Now, if we want to reduce technical risk, we know what to do. We get a bunch of smart people and we beat down the problem. There are all sorts of resources to tap for technical risk reduction. My personal favorite is the Best Manufacturing Practices Program, *http://www.bmpcoe.org/*. Developed by Ernie Renner in 1985 as a U.S. Navy Program, BMP is today a partnership among the Office of Naval Research's BMP Program, the Department of Commerce, and the University of Maryland. Of particular interest is the Program Manager's WorkStation.

> *The Program Manager's WorkStation (PMWS) is an electronic suite of tools designed to provide timely acquisition and engineering information to the user. The main components of the PMWS are KnowHow, the Technical Risk Identification and Mitigation System (TRIMS), and the BMP Database. These tools complement one another and provide users with the knowledge, insight, and experience to make informed decisions through all phases of product development, production, and beyond.*[16]

BMP's TRIMS is based on the Willoughby templates.

Still other solutions exist. If traditional risk reduction methods do not work, we design an R&D program and gnaw away at the problem. If internal or extramural R&D does not have answers, there are still tools like TRIZ (Teoriya Resheniya Izobreatatelskikh Zadatch or, in English, Theory of Inventive Problem Solving) we can try to help to get outside our box and discover alternatives to explore. Or we hire consultants and hope they can help us.

A few years back we were hired by a major food company. At that time there was a calcium craze going on. Consumers wanted calcium in all sorts of food from orange juice to yogurt. Our customer, responding to market demand, wanted to add calcium to one of their products. The problem was the preservative they used leached out the calcium they were trying to add. So, they came to us and asked us to find a new preservative, that was tasteless and did not need U.S. Food and Drug Administration approval. We found the preservative in Australia. It was a by-product of milk and cheese production and as natural as what you got from your mother's breast.

[16] Best Manufacturing Practices, "Systems Engineering—PMWS Software: Overview," n.d., http://www.bmpcoe.org/pmws/index.html (accessed October 25, 2005).

Firm-specific risk is similar to technical risk in that we can often mitigate it by tossing money at it. After all, the assumption behind paying all that money for an MBA is that you are somehow going to end up a better manager or corporate leader and because of that you are going to be worth more in the marketplace for labor because better managers reduce firm-specific risk. (Of course, it is an empirical question if this assumption of superiority for reducing firm-specific risk is sustained by the data.)

When it comes to firm-specific risk, the critical issue is people. We did a project for a major university that had developed a bioinformatics-based drug discovery platform. The question was whether license it or spin it out. The technology could support a spin-out, as drug discovery activities are outsourced by big pharmaceutical firms. Indeed, we had data that indicated outsourcing is growing at a rate of 15% to 20% per year and should be around $2 billion by 2007.[17]

The spin-out would have been run by a senior faculty member who was getting ready to retire. He had run a research lab, complete with post-docs, grad students, and some undergraduates. But he had never met a payroll and he had never manufactured anything beyond a benchtop breadboard. As configured the spin-out had way too much firm-specific risk. Without a management team with skills to run and market the business, success was unlikely. We recommended making the professor a CTO and identified a venture capital firm interested in investing and building the rest of the management team.

Compare that situation to the founding of Intel. In the 1960s, Bob Noyce was passed over for CEO of Fairchild Semiconductor. So he left. Gordon Moore left with him. They called Arthur Rock, a venture capitalist, and asked him for $2.5 million to start a new company. Rock asked for a business plan. Noyce typed up a page that said we are going to do interesting things in silicon like semiconductor memory, we are the guys who built Fairchild, and we will put up $500,000 for one half of the company. Based on the success of Fairchild, which introduced the silicon transistor, Rock raised the other $2 million.

As before, there are tools galore. These range from large scale systematic programs, such as Six Sigma or ISO 9000 family certification to simpler approaches such as the U.S. Bureau of Reclamations "How to Get Things Done."[18] Associated with the methods are statistical and statistical and logic tools like histograms, critical path analyses, error models and

---

[17] Kerry A. Dolan, "The Drug Research War," *Forbes* (May 28, 2004), http://www.forbes.com/insights/2004/05/28/cz_kd_0528outsourcing.html (accessed October 25, 2005).

[18] U.S. Bureau of Reclamations, "How to Get Things Done," www.usbr.gov/pmts/guide/ (accessed October 25, 2005).

effects analyses, or Ishikawa diagrams (see Exhibit 10.10). Also, as before, there are consultants you can hire.

Again, the point is not to get hung up on the specifics. What is important is that firm-specific risk can be mitigated. First, you make sure you do not put clowns in charge. Then you make sure whoever is in charge has a process to get everyone on the same page and moving in the same direction.

Market risk is different. Following is our J-curve. But in Exhibit 10.11 we have added a box around the curve to indicate a range of possible variation that increases in width over time as uncertainty is greater the farther out you go. We need to "*fuzz*" our revenue projection because we cannot control the market. Someone may introduce a new technology that prematurely obsoletes ours. Or a competitor for one reason or another may start a price war. A government may decide to regulate our goods. In other words, market risk exists because any projection is actually a probability distribution in which the precise revenues earned in any year is a bit like rolling dice with loaded dice. Some numbers have greater probability, but any could turn up. Monte Carlo simulations can be used to fuzz the projections to account for this uncertainty.

Indeed, a study by Agarwal and Bayus on "Market Evolution and Sales Take-Off of New Products" highlights the uncertainty that faces any single firm introducing an innovation. Their data suggests new competition is a very important factor in the market evolution and take-off of product innovations. In examining 30 product innovations for which good time series data exists, they found sharp increases in the number of

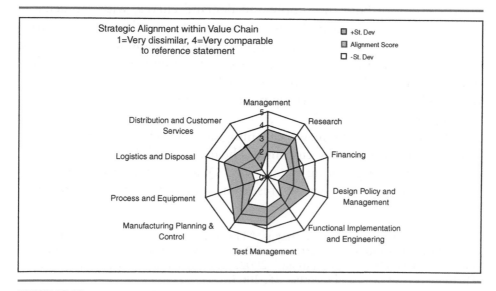

EXHIBIT 10.10 Strategic Alignment along the Value Chain

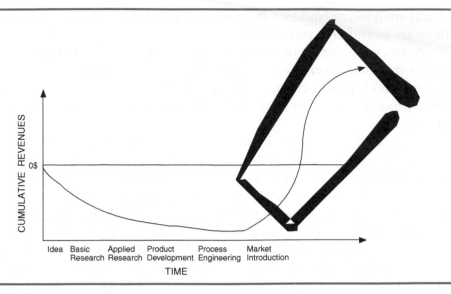

EXHIBIT 10.11   J-Curve with Probability Distribution

competing firms in a new market usually preceded sales take-off. Higher entry rates by competition were associated with quicker sales take-offs. They found that price reductions accounted for less than 5% of the variance in sales take-off times whereas entry into the market by new firms explains almost 50% of the variance. The ballpoint pen was one of their examples.

They explain this result by arguing that sales take-off results from outward shifting of both the supply and demand curves, with the demand curve being pushed out by firms entering the market because new firms will advertise, introduce product improvements, expand distribution, and generally increase consumer awareness of the innovation. The product improvements tied to promotion, etc. help to overcome consumer reluctance to buy due to the relatively poor performance of the initially introduced product or service.[19]

Of course, once again we can mitigate risk. The first method is to make sure the voice of the customer is heard (see Exhibit 10.12).

Concurrent engineering is one way. Quality function deployment is another. Focus groups, survey research, and test marketing are other

---

[19] Rajshree Agarwal and Barry L. Bayus, "The Market Evolution and Sales Take-Off of Product Innovations," Department of Business Administration, University of Illinois at Urbana-Champaign, January 2002, http://www.business.uiuc.edu/research/020104paper.pdf (accessed October 25, 2005).

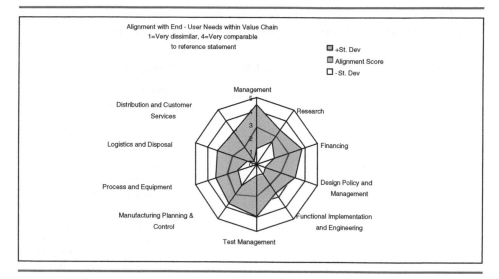

EXHIBIT 10.12 Alignment with End-User Needs within the Value Chain

methods to ensure we listen to the voice of the customer and bring it into the development process. Equally important is structuring the transitioning and penetration plan to ensure a consistent view of customer needs informs the practices that comprise the value chain.

Since we know the initial buyers will usually focus on technical performance based buying while the next set will want a best value proposition, we can design for best value as well as performance by focusing on how to leverage dominant designs and practice paradigms where they exist. Indeed, the more revolutionary and disruptive the technology is likely to be perceived, the more we want to balance that risk by focusing on (1) a well established market niche with (2) clearly articulated needs and buying criteria even if these niches are tiny. After all, the hardest sales to get are the first ones and so better to enter a sure market than to go after a speculative "*big hit*"—especially if you lack deep pockets.

OK, now that we understand the types of risk, we can ask how they affect the value of our technology. If we are being precise, technical risk and firm-specific risk should be the basis for our discount rate when calculating value. Because we can control for these, and at some point say, "Yep, they are gone," our discounting should have some downward slope or step function over time (at least assuming we are ignoring inflation). On the other hand, market risk should not be included in our discounting. Instead, we should account for it by calculating the probability distribution of outcomes for revenues. As a practical matter, however, almost everyone globs them together.

The following table is from Richard Razgaitis' *Early-Stage Technologies: Valuation and Pricing.*[20] It provides typical ranges for discount rates.

Risk Level	Approximate DR (%)	Description
Risk Free	10–18	Existing product, high demand, building more of the same
Very Low Risk	15–20	New well-understood technology for an existing product
Low Risk	20–30	New features, well-understood technology introduced into an existing market
Moderate Risk	25–35	New product, well-understood technology introduced into market with competition
High Risk	30–40	New product, not well-understood technology introduced into an existing market
Very High Risk	35–45	New product, new technology, new market
Extremely High Risk	50–70	New company, unproven technology, new market

CONCLUSION

In this chapter we have discussed how to value technology. There are any number of fine books on how to do valuations. It is a stable of B-school curricula. So, it does not make sense to spend a lot of time on it. So, although we present the basics of discounted cash flow analysis, our discussion has focused on three sets of assumptions that have to be made to do valuations: assumptions about revenues, assumptions about expenses, and assumptions about risk.

The take-aways are simple:

- First, keep it as simple as possible as this is somewhat of a black art. Do market-based valuation if possible because (a) it makes sense and (b) it is a lot cheaper than the alternatives.
- Second, mitigate as much risk as you can with the budget and time you have available. The more risk you mitigate, the more your technology is worth. Cut risk and you cut the discount rate. (It usually is wise to

---

[20] Richard Razgaitis, *Early-Stage Technologies: Valuation and Pricing* (Hoboken, NJ: Wiley, 1999).

do three scenarios—a high, medium, and low and to use sensitivity analysis to identify the factors which influence the differences—that way you know where to focus risk mitigation.)

- Third, adjust your revenues and expenses in light of who your partner is likely to be. Consider their ability to leverage what you have and to mitigate risk. That pops the value up more as hopefully they can help you sell on the one hand and leverage economies of scale, scope or network plus some learning curve advantages to cut costs. Since you probably are doing the valuation to show them what a good deal this is, you want the value of your technology as high as is possible while maintaining solid academic integrity and good data.

There is a final take-away that we have not discussed in the body of this chapter because it is obvious. But in case it is not: Check your spreadsheet.

Why Real Options Are a Waste of Time

As with relationships with spouses, significant others, parents, children, and anyone else you may love including your dog, there are all sorts of ways to make things more complicated. In valuation for technology transfer deal-making, the best way to make things unnecessarily complicated is to use real options. The reason is simple: They are very costly to do right and even then they do not give you very good data. They require a reference portfolio with a known value, which is pretty hard to create. Further, the value of the option will vary depending on who holds it, that is, depending on who is the buyer of your technology. While this is true for any valuation, real options are complicated and expensive enough to calculate that you feel you should get something a lot better than the usual methods of tossing the dart. So, unless you really are curious, skip the rest of this section as you probably will never use it.

Well, you are one of the curious ones. Here is the two-minute overview. After that, get a book specifically on them and do all the exercises.

Real options make sense where there is substantial uncertainty as to net cash flows making a pure discounted cash flow (DCF) valuation sketchy. Calculating a real option assumes you create the option value by comparing the value of your technology to a reference portfolio whose value is known. And there lies the rub, technology, especially when you are moving it across organizations, is a lot less liquid than financial options. It is even less liquid than commodities like oil (where real options are used for deciding when to drill oil wells) or real estate (where you can use multiple listings and court records to find comparables).

Following Damodaran, the price of an option is equal to the price of a known replicating portfolio, which usually is a combination of risk-free bonds that creates the same cash flows as the option being evaluated.[21] Thus, to calculate a technology option you need:

---

[21] See Damodaran, *Investment Valuation*.

- The value of underlying asset, that is the net present value of product(s) introduced, discounted to address uncertainties;
- The variance of asset value, that is the anticipated variance in value of the preceding goods based on data from comparables or probabilities we have assigned to market scenarios associated with our forecasts;
- The time to expiration of option, which is the time at which IP protection expires or the window of opportunity for market entry closes;
- The strike price, which is the development and other costs required to commercialize the technology;
- The riskless rate, which is usually set to the rate for U.S. treasury bonds of a suitable time period; and,
- The revenue stream or dividend yield lost each year, which is equal to the annual cost of cash flows for years lost due to delay in failure to exercise the option or, after exercise, because we let competition enter and grab some of our market share.

Needless to say, it is a pain to pin down the assumptions you need to use real options. Since the whole process assumes management is free to exercise the option or not, real options work a lot better for planning internal R&D or developing IP management strategies, which are outside the scope of this book, than for deal making, where the degrees of managerial freedom start collapsing rapidly. As the old saying goes, it takes two to tango.

The value of the option at any time is basically the upside potential gain minus the initial investment and the current cost of further realization (development costs, etc.). The upside gain is influenced by the amount of market risk that exists. After all, the more uncontrollable the risk, the greater the value of an option. On the flip side, technical or firm-specific risk reduce the value of an option. That is because these are risks that can be mitigated by tossing money at them. So they can be reduced depending on management's degrees of freedom to do just that and to do it wisely. If you can reduce the risk, why buy the hedge.

The nice thing about options is any negative outcomes, beyond initial investment, can be avoided by not investing further where the upside value is less than the costs. In that case you do not exercise the option.

Be aware there are two methods usually used for calculating technology real options: the binomial and the Black-Scholes methods. Black-Scholes has serious problems as it assumes there is a limiting distribution of revenues that is normal (Gaussian) and that the price of the goods being commercialized is continuous. It assumes there are not any jumps in their IP or other asset-based price. As Robert Clarkson notes, simplifying assumptions such as these are blatantly inconsistent with real-world behavior. That makes them dangerous to use and folly to rely on as a way of recognizing, measuring, and managing risk in the real world.[22] Unfortunately, the binomial method is equally suspect, as binomial lattices use a discrete-time approach that assumes that the value of the asset will go up or down with a specified probability. Further, we need to make some assumptions concerning the diffusion parameters such as variable volatility over time. So again we end up with a false sense of certainty with respect to the results.

My own personal belief is you might as well just create a decision tree and assign probabilities to the branches. Note that by doing so, all we are doing is sketching out the decision nodes in a game in extensive form. Options exist at information sets, which are the decision nodes with more than one branch. The issue then becomes selecting, if it exists, the path that contains the dominant strategy, that is, the strategy that yields the highest payoff. When each player follows their dominant strategy, we have a dominant strategy equilibrium. Ideally, there is a Nash Equilibrium at the point where each player is following their dominant strategy.

[22] Robert S. Clarkson, "Financial Risk and the Markowitz and Black-Scholes Worlds," *Actuarial Approach for Financial Risks,* Colloquium Proceedings, Cairns, Australia, August 13–15, 1997, http://www.actuaries.org/AFIR/colloquia/Cairns/Clarkson.pdf (accessed October 26, 2005).

CHAPTER 11

Doing the Deal

Deal-making is about using an intellectual asset package to build relationships that are economically beneficial to all parties to the transaction. As we have repeatedly seen, there are a variety of ways to do deals. You can sell a finished product, you can sell an idea you just had, and you can do a whole lot things in between. Our discussion will not be specific to any kind of deal vehicle, like licensing, strategic alliance, joint ventures, equity investment, etc. What we shall be focusing on is what makes a deal worth doing, and how to put it together, regardless of the specific legal vehicle used.

Deals allocate part of the value a technology generates between the parties. This part of the value is the cash the buyer pays to acquire the technology. Some of this cash is captured by the party that developed the technology. The rest is captured by the parties taking it to market and supporting it there.

Deal-making is like managing water rights. The picture in Exhibit 11.1 is the Yangtze River in 2000.[1] Three Gorges Dam construction site is to the left side. Notice that there are two ways to allocate the flow in this river. One is to allocate water. Some of the water flows downstream to towns and cities. Some is used for agriculture along the way. This allocation concerns water rights. In an analogous manner, each party in a technology transfer deal wants to get their fair share of the (cash) flow.

Dams, like the one being built in the photo, can be used to extract electric power from the flow of the river. Again, there is an analog in deal-making. At least one of the parties (the acquirer), and usually both parties, want to extract some horsepower from this deal that can be used to drive other business operations or sales forward.

The goal of deal-making is to find a solution where everyone gets what they need and at least some of what they want so the deal is worthwhile signing. Deal-making is not usually a zero-sum game. Because the objectives

---

[1] NASA, Jet Propulsion Laboratory, California Institute of Technology, "Yangtze River and Three Gorges Dam," September 7, 2004, http://asterweb.jpl.nasa.gov/gallery-detail.asp?name=Yangtze (accessed October 27, 2005).

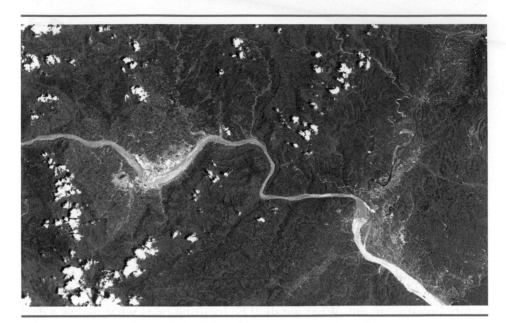

EXHIBIT 11.1   Yangtze River Photo
Source: NASA/GSFC/METI/ERSDAC/JAROS, and U.S./Japan ASTER Science Team

of parties usually overlap synergistically, the whole is often greater than the sum of the parts.

These objectives are usually financial. "I need to make so much money with so much net profit." There may be other objectives. "I need to enter this or that market niche in order to expand this business," or "I need to beat that son-of-a-pup over there to market." There is no intrinsic reason why the various objectives have to conflict unless one party is being greedy or someone has seriously misestimated the value of the technology and it turns out there is not enough value to divide up.

Each deal, by definition, involves a legal relationship because deals are made with contracts. Contracts are deliberate agreements between two of more parties that create or modify a legal relationship. Sometimes, contracts are used to end legal relationships.[2] By deliberate, we mean the parties are assumed to have thought about them before signing them. From a game theory perspective we can say that technology transfer contracts are simply ways that parties make binding commitments to coordinate strategies for transforming ideas into useful things so they both make money or garner other benefits.

Each contract binds the parties to do, or abstain from doing, the certain

---

[2] Henry Campbell Black, *Black's Law Dictionary,* 4th ed. (West, 1968), 394.

and specific things that are spelled out in the agreement. Since what is spelled out is action that will occur in the future, contracts are promises. They are ways of shaping the future to what the parties see as their mutual benefit—at least at the moment of signing.

The way we shape the future is to transfer rights, which is of course the "consideration" for signing the contract. Each of these rights is a power, a privilege, a faculty, or a demand that belongs to one party to the contract and limits the other party.[3] Do an exclusive license and for the field of use within which that license is granted, you can no longer practice your invention. In other words, rights are permissions to freely act.

Rights give the holder of that right the capacity and power to control the actions of others to the extent that the right reaches to them either by contract or law. If a party decides later to take back their consent to the exercise of the capacity and power implied by the right, then the holder of the right can call upon the coercive power of the state to make the bloody bastard do what they promised to do.

Of course, in order to understand what is really going on in a contract, we have to look at the underlying human experience being reified in the legal language. There is something substantive and real the parties are seeking to enshrine as a quasi-ethical imperative capable of guiding their collective behavior.

So much for the basics. Fortunately, we can leave the basics to the lawyers.

Our job in this chapter is to figure out what we want to do and to see what we can get the other side to agree to. Once we do that, the lawyers can make sure the agreement captures what the parties want in a way that can be enforced in a court of law. If the deal is well designed, the net costs for breaching the contract will be greater than the net costs of supporting the deal even if many of the assumptions the parties had when agreeing to it have changed.

From a game theory perspective, if we do our job well, we will create a coalition supported by an enforcement mechanism. Once that has been done, supporting the deal should be a dominant strategy for both parties. A Nash Equilibrium with a Schelling point should exist for the term of the agreement. The coalition acts as a team, at least to the extent the agreement defines behavior, in order to pursue its shared objectives in the larger non-cooperative game called the global economy.

In this chapter we focus on two topics: preparing to negotiate and negotiating. In preparing we will explore how to examine the relationship sought, the intellectual asset package needed to sustain that relationship,

---

[3] Ibid., 1486.

and how to work the economics of the deal so it pencils. We end with a discussion on how to negotiate deals that explores two sets of activity: setting the stage and pulling it off.

PLANNING FOR NEGOTIATIONS

There are three issues in planning.

The first issue is: What do I need? This is not a metaphysical question. It is a nuts and bolts query concerning why you want a deal rather than just going it alone. We will use personals to illustrate the point.

> Hello,
> I am social, intelligent, and spontaneous. I recently moved back to RI after being away for a while and I am still readjusting. I am a single, attractive female, and I am looking for someone to be friends with, possibly more in the future depending on the person. I am 5'5", brown skinned African American, shoulder length brown hair, brown eyes, nice smile, average weight, I work out. If I have to describe what physical qualities I want in a man they would have to be: 5'10" or taller, nice smile (teeth), nice eyes. Creativity, sense of humor, and confidence are also qualities I am looking for. I haven't been out too much so it has been difficult for me to meet new people. I like movies, music, games, outdoors, traveling, talking, etc. What are you looking for??????????[4]

Compare that with:

> hi,
> i'm actually posting this for my gf . . . i'm far away for a couple years, and she needs a guy to have sex with . . . strictly physical relationship . . .
> she's wild . . . she's 5'4", 120 lbs, dark blonde hair, 34c's, brown eyes, loves everything, loves to please and be pleased . . .
> you should have your own place . . . and be drug and disease free please include pics . . . i will be forwarding this to her[5]

Just like people, universities, labs, and companies often lack something. As we saw in our discussions of launch tactics and finding targets, by being clear about that something you know what you are looking for in a partner. That allows you to plan for the kind of relationship you want.

---

[4] Craigslist.com, "Let's Enjoy Each Other's Company—25," October 26, 2005, http://providence.craigslist.com/w4m/106850532.html (accessed October 28, 2005).
[5] Craigslist.com, "Sweet Girl Seeks Strictly Physical Relationship—20," October 23, 2005, http://providence.craigslist.com/w4m/106149802.html (accessed October 28, 2005).

The second issue is: What do I have to give, in order to get what I need? This time we will use eating as an example. Let's say you want a healthy body. What should you eat? According to the USDA: "One size doesn't fit all. My Pyramid Plan can help you choose the foods and amounts that are right for you."[6] USDA notes that factors influencing what you need to eat are your age, sex, and activity level.

A similar dynamic exists when planning for technology transfer deal negotiations. Once we know the relationship we want, we can figure out what intellectual assets we should transfer to make that relationship work. Understanding what assets are needed allows us to plan the IP package we will offer. We can also determine whether we have all the assets needed for that package or whether we should be looking for additional assets to fill gaps.

Finally, we need to determine if it is really worthwhile doing a deal. Let's use friendship as an example. Suppose you are trying to figure out what to do tonight and your friend calls us and says, "Hey let's watch a movie." "OK, which one?" And they give you the name of some really stupid flick that well maybe you would watch it on DVD but to pay $9 to go to the theater . . . I think not. So you say "Well, I'd love to get together but I am not really into going to the movies. How about seeing if there is any jazz tonight?"

Again, we have an analogous situation in planning for technology transfer negotiations. There is some minimal net benefit calculus that has to be met or it just is not worthwhile doing the deal. So, we have to examine the economics of the deal in order to plan the negotiations so we end up with a deal we want.

Relationships

There is always a business reason for doing a deal. The reason has to do with weakness. After all, if a player is entirely self-sufficient and capable, there is no reason to share the cash flow stream from the technology.

A player may be unable to conduct all the task sequences (and constituent tasks) needed to get a product, process, or service out of R&D and into the market. (See Exhibit 11.2.)

Or the player may not be able to structure and manage the sequences and constitute tasks in order to get them done on time, within budget, and on schedule. (Following Porter, we can ask how we will construct the value chain in Exhibit 11.3.)

---

[6] U.S. Department of Agriculture, "Steps to a Healthier You," n.d., http://www.mypyramid.gov/ (accessed October 28, 2005).

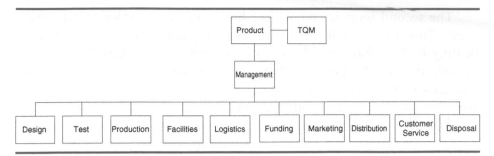

EXHIBIT 11.2   Task Sequences

There is, of course, no necessity for all the task sequences nor all the
practices in the value chain to exist inside the same player. Not surprisingly,
most deal vehicles involve distributing the tasks or task sequences across
various players, that is, across a supply chain like the one in Exhibit 11.4.

The question becomes: How do we determine who should do what
tasking? Because we are dealing with multiple entities, we also have to
address how the movement of inputs and outputs between tasks is structured in order to ensure everybody gets as much utility from the deal as
possible.

We will use a two party deal here, but the technique works with any
number of parties. All we need is a piece of paper and some magic mark-
ers. (We can also use software.)

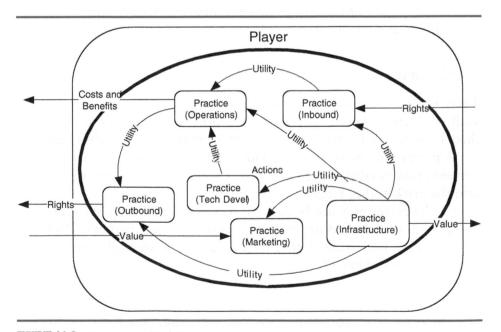

EXHIBIT 11.3   Structuring Task Sequences

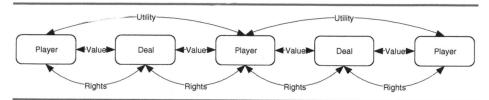

EXHIBIT 11.4 Distributing Tasks across Various Players

We use one color or shading for each party. Assuming we already know the sequences and discrete tasking, we look at each task and ask who can do it. If there is a cell that only one party can perform, we color it with that party's marker. If both parties can do it, we leave it blank.

Suppose we end up with a sequence like the one in Exhibit 11.5. Assuming both parties are equally capable of conducting the white discrete task cells, it makes sense to give the whole sequence to the Gray party as it simplifies management of the sequence.

Now, suppose we have the configuration shown in Exhibit 11.6. Again, let's assume both parties are equally as capable of doing the white cells. Looking at the cells there is a relatively coherent division. Gray seems to have better capabilities for test and evaluation, where as Black has better development and fix capabilities. So, it makes sense to let Gray manage the test program, collect the feedback and put together the reports, and then pass that to Black, whose job it is to solve problems that emerged during testing.

Why does this make sense? It makes sense so long as we assume both parties are acting like rational players in neoclassical economics. We assume that everyone wants to maximize their rewards. Since we know the total net value is the result of both revenues and expenses, by giving tasking to the party best able to accomplish it, we should minimize expenses, thereby increasing the overall value left over to divide up between all the players. Just who should do what is a question for internal soul search on the one hand and competitive intelligence on the other hand.

From a planning perspective, we want to know what we should be doing, what the other party or parties should be doing, and what that means from a budgeting and risk management standpoint. Once we divide up the tasking using the preceding technique, we can get a pretty good handle on budget and risk by treating each task as a gray box—that is, as a box that is a more transparent than a totally black box, but not necessarily fully defined. (See Exhibit 11.7.) It suffices for planning purposes to know, for each box of interest, what the inputs are likely to be, and what outputs we can expect. If we have these, we can string the boxes together and identify the critical path.

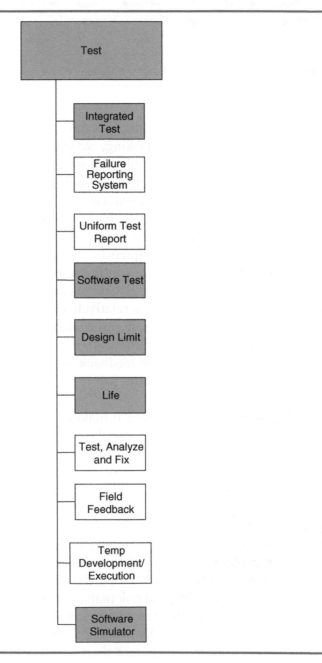

EXHIBIT 11.5 Two-Party Deal: Test A

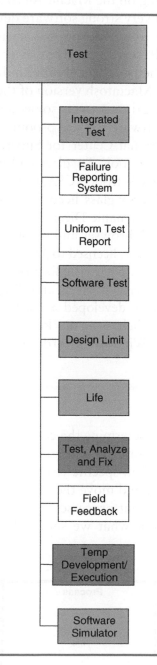

EXHIBIT 11.6 Two-Party Deal: Test B

We supported a deal that brought three dimensional scientific visualization software running on the Macintosh to Spyglass, Inc. Our customer, Visualogic, had very strong software development capabilities. They had won awards from the National Science Foundation's Small Business Innovation Research program to support development of the software. We had helped them obtain funding from Apple to support development of a Macintosh version of the software. So, looking at capabilities, the logical target was someone with market presence who wanted to add software to their product family. Spyglass was a spin-out from the National Center for Supercomputer Applications focused on selling NCSA tools. Spyglass had licensed the technology and trademarks for Mosaic from NCSA, so it clearly had market presence. It was a good fit. Spyglass licensed Visualogic's software and sold it for years under the name Dicer. (Spyglass later ended up producing both its own web browser and its own scientific visualization software. Their browser was licensed to Microsoft, where it became the basis for Internet Explorer. Their visualization package did less well. As Spyglass licensed out its crown jewels and disappeared as a company, Visualogic went to plan B developed as part of the licensing negotiations. They developed their own marketing capabilities and ported their software back to Windows in order to expand the addressable market.)

We can also begin to determine the cost of goods sold and the technical and firm-specific risk for discounting. The technical risk relates to can we do the process. The firm-specific risk relates to manage the process, obtain the inputs needed, and move the outputs to where they need to be next. If we are unclear about processes, we use quality function deployment (QFD) to figure out what we should be doing and producibility

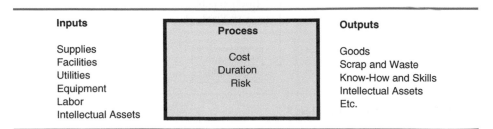

Inputs	Process	Outputs
Supplies	Cost	Goods
Facilities	Duration	Scrap and Waste
Utilities	Risk	Know-How and Skills
Equipment		Intellectual Assets
Labor		Etc.
Intellectual Assets		

EXHIBIT 11.7   Budget and Risk

analysis to find some way of doing it. That allows us to guesstimate cost and technical risk for the process. If we know what we are doing, have a reliable supply chain and have good sales, distribution, and customer support capabilities, firm-specific risk is low. By the time we get done with this exercise, we have a basis for estimating cost of goods sold, throughput, and risk.

In planning the relationship, however, we have to also consider the ability to manage firm-wide risk. Suppose one of the players has exquisite capabilities but is on the verge of bankruptcy and things at the company are just a mess. If the other player has decent capabilities, deep pockets, and has a well run shop, under those circumstances we may prefer it do more tasking. Why? Because if we want to maximize value, the level of firm-specific risk makes it too likely we shall have delays, which will push the time to market back, which will delay revenues, or horror of horrors make us so late that we miss the window of opportunity and fail to grab a share of the market altogether.

Once we have an idea of how the task sequences can be organized, we can explore our options. We can create scenarios based on different divisions of labor. We compare these scenarios to a baseline consisting of how the tasking would be conducted if we did the commercialization on our own, possibly with the aid of contractors. Obviously, we are only interested in scenarios that leave us better off than doing it ourselves.

When in doubt, a baseline based on doing it ourselves provides a floor for negotiations. If we show no improvement in gross profit via partnering, it does not make a lot of sense to enter deal-making. On the other hand, the scenarios that allow us to capture the most gross profit is the one we want to have as the basis of the deal. How much better off we need to be than the floor is a question for management, but once we have that goal established, we can select a set of acceptable scenarios that we can use as options for negotiation. Once we get to the table, if we do not end up with something as good as one of these scenarios then, all other things being equal, it would be time to agree to disagree, shake hands, and walk away.

Now, we added that "all things being equal" clause. So far we have treated the planning as if we are planning for a one time event. But that is not usually the case. Usually what we want to do is find a target with whom we can build a pipeline through which a series of technologies can flow to market. So, we need to factor in which scenarios we will accept for a one time deal and which ones we need for a more enduring relationship, if that is, in fact, a goal.

Different relationships will likely force different changes in our operations and focus. In Exhibit 11.8 we map out possible impacts on the

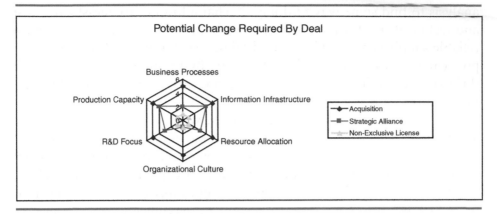

EXHIBIT 11.8   Potential Change Required by Deal

developer of a technology from three different kinds of vehicles: an acquisition, a strategic alliance, and a non-exclusive license. Zero is no impact. Five is maximum impact.

With an acquisition, everything is up for grabs as the control of the company has shifted from one set of owners to another. In a strategic alliance for OEM production, the downstream buyer often demands changes in order to be able to better integrate the supplier into their enterprise resource planning and ensure the flow of technology they will want in the future. This kind of control is most common where large platform integrators are involved, as in supply chains for automobiles and aircraft, although some large retailers—like Wal-Mart—are notorious for forcing changes on their suppliers. Vendors may be required to expend large sums of money to become ISO 9000 certified or to adopt a specific CAD/CAM or enterprise resource planning (ERP) software that allows transmission of designs and production scheduling back and forth. Non-exclusive licenses are closer to the other extreme. The amount of impact is limited by the arms length nature of the relationship. Only direct sales likely would have less impact. As always, the precise rankings are an empirical question that is answered with the aid of competitive intelligence.

We can now reexamine our scenarios and consider how flexible and open to change we want to be. Our willingness to change depends on a range of factors, but probably the most important ones are the mission statement and vision for the company, university, or agency itself. Changes that move us further along our strategic thrust make sense. We need to think long and hard about those that divert us. While it is obviously difficult to figure out the changes we need to consider before they have been proposed during negotiations, what we have built is a tool we can use for that evaluation.

Intellectual Asset Package

Once the task sequences are defined and scenarios for division of labor developed, it is easier to determine the precise intellectual asset (IA) package to transfer. The package obviously needs to include everything required for a given scenario and should offer nothing more as it does not contribute value. Ideally, the package works for a range of preferred scenarios.

Exhibit 11.9 is from U.S. Patent 636,272, issued to William Middlebrook, of Waterbury, Connecticut in 1899. It is for a machine that makes gem paperclips. The patent includes both the basic design for an improved paper clip that was less likely to tear paper *and* the way of making it.

A number of paper clip patents had preceded Middlebrook's. In 1867 Samuel Fay was issued patent 64,088 for a Ticket Fastener. The patent specified the clip was for paper in general as well as for holding tickets to garments. Over 50 other designs were patented prior to 1899. The modern wire paper clip was never actually patented. It was made in Britain by the Gem Manufacturing Company in the early 90's. But what makes Middlebrook's significant is not just the design, but the fact it was bundled with a machine that produced it in quantities. In other words, it had the asset package needed to go into production of paper clips.

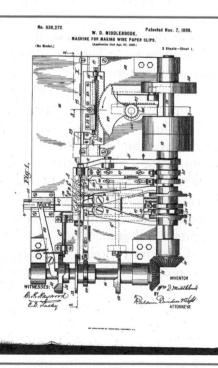

EXHIBIT 11.9 Paper Clip Machine Patent

Cushman and Denison, a manufacturing company making paper clips, recognized its value and acquired the patent that same year. They added a trademark, *"Gem,"* to Middlebrook's paper clip. Within five years their Gem brand swept the market.[7]

We caution that an *asset package* is different from a *property package*. An intellectual property (IP) package transfers patents, copyrights, trade secrets, trade marks, and other legally recognized property. The intellectual asset (IA) package includes property such as the drawings, design blueprints, manuals, software programs, data bases, and the like, which themselves are property because they can likely be protected by copyright, but it also includes more. It usually also includes know-how concerning methodologies and processes important for implementing the technology. The asset package, in other words, can include uncaptured art as well as the captured art, science, and engineering. This component of the art may not even be well enough captured to constitute a trade secret. How much know-how needs to be transferred is a function of the relative absorptive capabilities of the parties to a deal.

Years ago I had a fellow work for me, Stan Goddard, who told the story of being on a destroyer that was steaming off the coast of San Clemente Island, where the Navy had a live fire range. They were testing a new shell for naval guns. Stan was an observer on the ship, representing the Navy lab developing the shell. Also aboard were a bunch of retired admirals as San Clemente is by San Diego, a major naval base and a nice place to retire out.

The target was a shack on the side of a mountain on the island. There was a spotter on the top of the mountain. The ship fired the first salvo. Boom. "Too high, a little lower," radioed in the spotter. Boom. The shell landed even higher up the mountain. "Whoa! Other way! Too high," radioed the spotter with a touch of concern in his voice. Boom. " G-d #*!^ idiots! Cease Fire! Cease Fire!" The captain of the ship was clearly embarrassed and stormed down into the belly of the destroyer where the fire control computer was. Behind him came the retired admirals and Stan. When they got there he went to the chief in charge of the fire control computer. "What the heck is going on here? Are you deaf?" "No sir!" the chief replied, snapping to attention.

_____

[7] The Great Idea Finder, "Paperclip," September 28, 2005, http://www.ideafinder.com/ history/inventions/paperclip.htm (accessed October 27, 2005).

> The fire control computer was an old machine with an analog dial. Basically you turned it, one way was higher, the other way lower. The chief was a young kid who had grown up in a digital world. The knob was located at the bottom of the computer, by the deck, so you had to lay on your belly to read it. When you did, even with a flashlight, you discovered that the machine was so old that all the markings had worn off. So the kid used common sense. Up should turn things up. Down should turn them down. Unfortunately that was not the case: a classic undocumented know-how problem.

Undocumented know-how is particularly important for process and service technologies. For this reason, transfer of these technologies commonly involves consulting contracts in order that the recipients not have to agonize their way through the learning curve.

Returning to our task sequences, with the aid of the sequence we diagrammed out for this deal, we can identify what specific components of our package need to be transferred when in order to enable the process with reduced technical risk. (Hence the concept of just-in-time knowledge™ illustrated by Exhibit 11.10.)

An example: In 1998 MEMC Electronic Materials, Inc. of the United States signed a non-exclusive agreement with Posco Huls Company Limited (PHC) of South Korea for use of all the technical information to manufacture, promote and sell silicon wafers of sufficient purity and crystalline structure for use in advanced semiconductor processes, and specifically excluding processes and materials for producing polycrystal silicon.

At the time of this agreement, MEMC was practicing its process in the United States to make silicon wafers. A key component of the agreement was that MEMC furnished PHC the information and consulting necessary

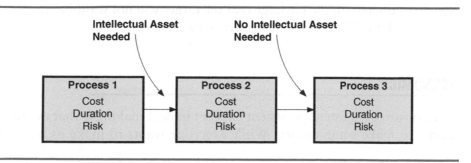

EXHIBIT 11.10 Package Components to Be Transferred to Reduce Risk

to *"design, construct, and operate"* a plant in South Korea with an agreed on capacity and agreed on initial capacity.

> *Within six months of signing, MEMC would furnish a consultant to PHC who reviewed what was to be done by PHC and their readiness. This consultant would work up a set of specifications for the factory that would be mutually agreed upon by both parties. Once that was done, another six months was provided to develop the engineering manual for the design, equipping, and layout of the facility. Next PHC would prepare its own detailed drawings, which had to be approved by MEMC. Within four months after that, MEMC would provide the operations manual and arrange for the training of up to 12 PHC personnel at MEMC's factory in the U.S. for a total of 72 man months. To support actual construction, set up, and initial operations, MEMC agreed to provide one or more engineers for up to 48 man months. MEMC also agreed to loan 2 engineers to PHC for a limited period, who would become on-site employees of PHC during the initial start and ramp-up of production. To address continuing improvements, each party agreed to provide the other such improvements it may make for a five-year period from the date of first commercial production by PHC. In addition, each party agreed to allow reasonable on-site inspections and examination of documents by the other party so know-how could be transferred.*[8]

By transferring the IA in stages, the risk on both sides is reduced as payment can be tied to deliverables. In the MEMC-PHC deal, the technology fee of $7.8 million was paid in installments. One twelfth of the fee was paid by the end of the calendar quarter in which signing occurred. One twelfth of the fee was then paid in each of the eleven following quarters. (An additional running royalty was charged for the process technology.)

Note that the utility of our IA may be limited if other IA, which we do not own, are required to use our IA effectively and efficiently. During the planning process we first figure out what is the complete package needed to support the tasks. Then we take out of the package the items we cannot provide. If our target does not need them, fine. If they do, we may have to gain access to those assets in order to do the deal. Next we look at what assets we do have in the package that the target will not want because they are redundant. The end result may vary by scenario.

ECONOMICS

The consistent insistent persistent existent in deal-making is that everyone wants to make some money. While everyone wants to make as much as

---

[8] 10-K405 filing with the U.S. Security and Exchange Commission, December 31, 1998.

possible, they always have some floor. At the end of the day each party is going to look at its share of the revenue stream, its costs of goods sold, subtract one from the other, discount the result to the present, and decide whether there is enough money to be made to justify doing a deal.

Three things needed to get all the parties above that threshold: a big enough pie, a way to divide it up that gives people at least the floor they want, and a division that seems fair so they are willing to accept their share.

Partnering can make the pie bigger by making it more likely you will sell. It can also lead to cost reductions (which makes the net bigger) by enabling the partners to leverage economies of scale and scope or network economies; offering learning curve advantages; guaranteeing access to supplies or the ability to drive supply costs down by buying in volume; giving access to previously expensed or depreciated facilities and equipment that still have productive life left; offering internal capital at below market rates; and on and on.

Now, all of this is fine and good but the kids need shoes, your car needs gas, and the boss wants to show the shareholders a return on their investment. So, the real issue in planning the economic negotiation is who gets what share of the net present value when. The calculation is conceptually straightforward. We treat the post deal situation as a free-standing entity and run a series of annual profit and loss statements for it for as long as revenues are anticipated. Then we divide those up.

We begin by using one of the scenarios concerning what needs to be done in order to get the technology into the market and sell it. We have already explored who is going to do what, so we can make up a budget for each party. This budget has to include inputs, so IAs are included that way. We can play around with the budgets by examining risk and the impact of various risk mitigation strategies.

Next we discount to the present so we have the net present value (NPV) of the budgets for each party. We can see we are going to have spend "x" and the other parties are going to have to spend "$y_{1 \ldots n}$." So, if we are going to go forward, everyone has to make those investments. If we were starting a new company or partnership, we likely want the proceeds as they are realized in accordance with the ratio of the investments.

In theory, every IA has a fair market value. So, if we are giving the other party our IA, they need to compensate us for that. We will use side payments to handle that, in other words, the payoffs to the parties are adjusted to ensure a fair distribution. The situation is analogous to transfer pricing for IP being moved from one division of a major corporation to another division.

Unfortunately, in reality we seldom have a clear fair market value. We are back at the problem of contribution, discussed in Chapter 10. (If all we are doing is licensing or selling goods, our problem just went away.)

To figure out contribution, we focus on the tasking. If there is no deal, the other party will have to do this tasking without this IA. That set of activity has a cost. Now pretend the deal has already been done. If the IA has value, the cost should be less. The difference between the two present values is the value of the IA in the context of that tasking. As long as that value is greater than my net profit objective, I am fine with a side payment equal to that sum.

This *less* cost after the deal has two components. On the one hand, there are out-of-pocket expenses. It takes one hour to train someone rather than five hours if the developer provides a trainer. On the other hand, the risk of failure is lower, which reduces the discount rate associated with the value of the process over time. That increases the value of the IA as it takes into account the greater likelihood of the process working with the aid of the developer's know-how than without it.

We will have to take less than the full discounted value of our IA in order to make a deal happen. Some value has to remain for the other party or the deal may not make sense for them. They are essentially running the same calculation. It will cost them this much to replicate the technology. They need this kind of return on investment. Whatever we offer, they can do their own ROI and calculate if they can get it cheaper from me than via internal development. If we have strong IP protection, we probably can make it more expensive for them to infringe than to do a deal.

From this perspective, planning for the economics of a deal revolves around the cost of doing business and the revenues to be made. (Surprise, surprise.) The more we can document how our technology reduces costs or raises revenues, the better off we are. Similarly, the more we can show that risk is minimized, the higher the NPV, the better off we are. (Remember, this is true even though the absolute value does not change with the discount rate. What does change is the odds of realizing the profit.)

The second question in planning the economics is when we want the money. The answer is dependent on how badly we need the cash and how likely it is that the other party (or parties) will be around (that is, not bankrupt or liquidated) to pay us downstream. It also has to do with what the contract says. If we sell all our rights as happens when we sell a product, it does not make sense to wait around for the money if we do not have to.

Even where we take money over time, we may want to seek up-front payments or initiation fees. These fees have two functions: accelerating payment and compensating for risk reduction (see Exhibit 11.11).

Payments get accelerated when the developer is cash short or the acquirer desires to cash out the other party early in order to limit payments downstream. By moving downstream payments up front, all or part of the future payments is captured immediately based on their present worth value. In this case it is simply a matter of discounting future revenues.

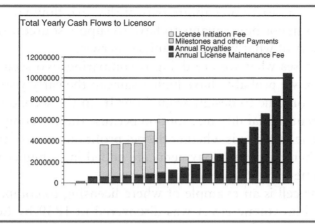

Total Yearly Cash Flows to Licensor
- □ License Initiation Fee
- □ Milestones and other Payments
- ■ Annual Royalties
- ■ Annual License Maintenance Fee

EXHIBIT 11.11 Total Yearly Cash Flows to Licensor

Compensating for the transfer of know-how at the time it occurs can be handled in two ways. The parties could sign a supplemental consulting contract or they can build the payment into the license. Regardless, consulting can be valued at the cost per hour for the people providing the know-how or on the basis of the value generated. The consulting's contribution to value reflects how much more the technology is worth with that expertise tossed in rather than without it.

Where initiation fees are used, there are various rules of thumb. I remember reading one approach that said figure out what it would take to develop the technology today and take 15% of that. OK. Why? It makes more sense to base the fee on the value acceleration occurring due to risk reduction for the buyer. This acceleration due to risk reduction is a matter of how much the discount rate has been reduced, which in turn increases the net present value, and thus represents what supplemental is garnered at the time of initiation of the deal as opposed to value garnered over the life of the deal. How much of this is captured in the fee itself is a matter of negotiation skill.

Of course, the big question for us is are we likely to make enough money out of this deal to meet our internal hurdle rate (our desired return on investment). Obviously, if the hurdle rate is not met, one thing we can do is to engage in risk mitigation, thereby bringing the discount rate down and increasing our chances of clearing the hurdle rate. Or we can argue we need a larger chunk of the revenues. If that does not work, we have to walk away.

Be aware when planning for negotiating the economics of a deal there are other reasons for allocating value between entities. For example, suppose the market is growing very fast. It may be difficult for one player to capture all the opportunity. Thus, it makes sense to bring other players in as licensees so at least you capture part of the cash flow you would miss. Or perhaps a major buyer wants to have to supply sources. Again, better to capture part of what you would miss otherwise.

In such cases what we are doing is comparing two scenarios. In the first scenario, we probably have higher sales in the early years as it takes the competition time to design around our IP. In the second scenario, we have a different probability distribution because there is competition from the get-go. The question is whether the net profit outcome of the latter distribution, when the royalty payments are added in, is higher than the net profit outcome of the former distribution.

The solar cell is an example of where licensing to competitors made sense. The photovoltaic effect was discovered in 1839 by Edmund Becquerel, a 19 year old French experimental physicist. He was playing with an electrolytic cell with two metal electrodes at the time. In 1883, Charles Fritts, an American, made the first functioning solar cell by creating a device by coating selenium with an extremely thin layer of gold. Almost a decade later, in 1941, Russell Ohl, an American who also invented the transistor, made the first silicon solar cell at Bell Labs. In 1954, three of his colleagues at Bell Labs, Gerald Pearson, Calvin Fuller and Daryl Chapin, designed the first practical solar cell, which had a 6% energy conversion efficiency when in direct sunlight. This cell was the first one marketed. In 1955, a Bell solar battery was placed in service by Western Electric to telephone carrier system in Americus, Georgia.[9] In 1962, 3,600 Bell solar battery cells powered the world's first communications satellite, Telstar I.[10]

Now, clearly AT&T (which owned both Bell Labs and Western Electric) had the capability to do everything needed to bring the solar cell to market. Yet by 1955, Western Electric was licensing solar cell technologies commercially. In doing so, Western Electric was following an established strategy of out-licensing selected breakthrough innovations from Bell Labs. In 1952, for example, they had licensed the semiconductor transistor to Texas Instruments.[11] Western Electric had begun its own production only one year earlier.

---

[9] Mary Bellis, "Definition of a Solar Cell—History of Solar Cells," *About* (2005), http://inventors.about.com/od/sstartinventions/a/solar_cell.htm (accessed October 27, 2005); and "History: Photovoltaics Timeline," *About* (2005), http://inventors.about.com/library/inventors/blsolar2.htm (accessed October 27, 2005).

[10] Lucent Technologies, "Bell Labs Celebrates 50th Anniversary of the Solar Cell—Timeline," 2004, http://www.bell-labs.com/news/2004/april/anniversary50_timeline.html (accessed October 27, 2005).

[11] Texas Instruments, "History of Innovation: Semiconductor," 2005, http://www.ti.com/corp/docs/company/history/semiconductortimelinelowbandwidth.shtml (accessed October 27, 2005).

Planning the Game in Extensive Form

The results of these examinations need to be captured in a form conducive for use during negotiations. The extensive form for representing a game in game theory is essentially a decision tree. As such, the extensive form is a useful way to represent what we have learned.

Exhibit 11.12 is an example of a game, resulting from a planning process associated with licensing. Once we have drawn out the options, we can assign outcomes and probabilities to each step in order to determine what are and what are not acceptable paths at each node.

In negotiations, what we actually are planning is a game comprised of a number of subgames. That means that the solution (the Nash Equilibrium) for the game requires finding a set of subgame equilibriums, called a *subgame perfect equilibrium.*

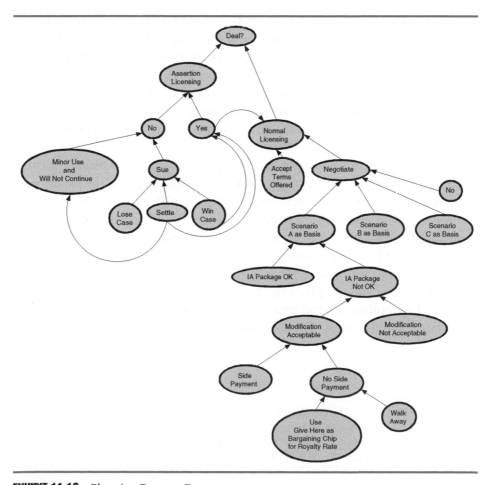

EXHIBIT 11.12 Planning Process Game

We try to find this equilibrium by using backward induction. We examine the lowest level subgames at the end of each branch of the tree. We find their equilibriums. These equilibriums provide values we can use as the payoffs for the next higher level subgame. The chain is worked until we can solve for the equilibrium of the most complex game. The sequence of Nash Equilibriums is the subgame perfect equilibrium.

In planning for negotiations, we *"think forward"* to develop the structure of the decision tree and its subgames and then we *"reason backwards"* to figure out what our best response strategy is at each branching node.[12] Of course, either party can use the imbedded game structure to change the outcomes. For example, what if considerations relating to larger business strategy affect this negotiation. One is that the other party or parties are viewing this negotiation as just one in a chain of future negotiations over other technology we (or others) may bring them. For them, each negotiation is nested in a larger game the company is playing. (This was clearly the government's case when it initiated antitrust proceedings against Microsoft.[13]) Or cash flow may not be the primary motivation for doing the deal. A major corporation seeking to enter a new market may go shopping for companies that have strong market presence or for strategic alliances with established firms. For example, Agile Software, a maker of Product Life Management software, bought Cimmetry Systems, a maker of visualization software, for $41.5 million to get its hands on its customers and enter a new niche.[14]

Where we suspect nesting is occurring, it is wise to reexamine the other parties' behaviors in similar contexts. We may discover that the other party has nefarious reasons for entering negotiations with us. These may include pumping us for information, trying to stop us from doing business with their competitors, trying to steal our ideas, or figuring out how to enter our market and compete with us.

One big caution before moving on to the next topic. You can blow through a lot of money planning. So, it is always important to match the level of data collection and analysis to the size of the deal being negotiated. For a small deal, which is not likely to generate significant revenues,

---

[12] McCain, "Sequential Games," in *Game Theory* (Mason, OH: Thomson South-Western, 2004), chap. 14.
[13] See Antitrust Case Filings, Antitrust Division, *United States v. Microsoft*, n.d., http://www.usdoj.gov/atr/cases/ms_index.htm (accessed October 29, 2005).
[14] Aberdeen Group, Market Alert, "Agile Continues 'Growth' Vision with Cimmetry Acquisition," February 8, 2005, http://www.agile.com/news/2005/aberdeen%20_020905.pdf (accessed October 29, 2005).

sometimes the best thing to do is figure out what you need to make it worthwhile economically and then shoot from the hip.

NEGOTIATING

Negotiating technology transfer deals is ultimately about trust. No matter how well drafted the agreement, both parties have to feel good about it. They have to feel that both of them want this to happen so when they do sign, they are not signing on for a long winter of headache.

> Years ago I saw comedian Bill Cosby in a club. He told this joke about the difference between dogs and cats. You go to your dog and say, "Hey dog, get the paper." The dog says "Sure" and brings it back. You go to your cat and say, "Hey cat, get the paper." The cat says, "You talking to me? Nuts to you."
>
> You can negotiate like you want to do a deal with a dog or you can act like you expect to be dealing with a cat. If you are negotiating like you are dealing with Cosby's cat you have to wonder why you are negotiating in the first place.

Setting the Stage

Because trust is so important, trust building has to start early. One way to do that is to engage potential targets long before you are ready to do a deal. Concurrent engineering is one such opportunity. You send your technical people to relevant professional society and trade association meetings, where they meet their colleagues from firms who might be targets. They talk to them about their needs and about their requirements with respect to your technology. The ones that get excited about what you are doing, you are invited to join an informal advisory committee. (You ask them to sign nondisclosure agreements of course and you check out their companies to be sure they do not have a reputation for stealing technology.) Presto chango! You are building champions for your technology.

At each step of the commercialization process, there are relationships you can build that will facilitate deal-making. While R&D and product development need not be a linear process, and often is not, the point is that you always want to be building ties to stakeholders you will need a year to three years downstream, rather than waiting until you must find them in order to succeed.

	Exploratory/ Fundamental Research	Applied Research and Development	Design and Production Engineering
Relationships to Build	Technical experts, research partners	End users, opinion leaders, potential investors, suppliers of platform or complementary goods, downstream targets	Lead customers, targets, vendors in supply chain

If you do build these ties, you have time to convert the stakeholders to advocates, thereby creating champions and a climate of support for your technology when you actually do go to do the deal. By choosing your potential advocates wisely, the channels your targets are likely to monitor will be carrying messages about the utility and merit of your technology before you even contact those targets.

Depending on the target's absorptive capacity and technology space, at some point it is time to pick up the phone and initiate discussions. Exhibit 11.13 depicts our view of the importance of personal contact. It is based on our experience and a graphic I once saw years ago in a presentation by someone from Boeing explaining how they structured concurrent engineering on the 777.

Once you do pick up the phone, be blunt. Explain the value proposition you have to offer. Ask them if they are interested. Figure out what you need to do to get a deal. You want to ask questions like:

- Are we correct in our understanding of why you are interested in this technology?
- How do you see this technology fitting into your product, service, or production?
- What criteria will you use to evaluate this technology?
- Is it at an appropriate level of maturity for you, and if not, what do you like to see?
- What information would you like about it and the developer?
- How long is it likely to take to find out if you are seriously interested?
- Who will be doing the evaluation to determine interest?
- What kind of deals do you like to do?
- Have you acquired technology analogous to this in the past and if so from whom?
- Are you willing to participate in concurrent engineering and/or test and evaluation of the technology?
- Who is (or are) the ultimate decision-maker(s)?

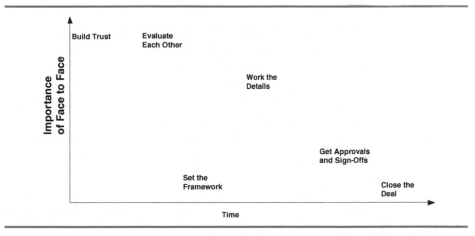

EXHIBIT 11.13   What Do You Need to Deal?

If interest exists, and they are willing to test, it is worthwhile arranging a face-to-face. The reason for insisting on a willingness to test is no one buys technology without kicking the tires. Even if all you have is a bench top lab brassboard, they are going to want to be sure there is something other than vaporware or non-obtainium.

Before meeting, do a quick version of planning for negotiations. As part of this planning, conduct competitive intelligence market research in order to confirm or falsify your assumptions about what choices the other party (or parties) might see and how they will evaluate those options.

Ideally, the face-to-face takes place at your facility. You want to see if they will spend money, because the more money they are willing to spend, the more likely they are to be seriously interested buyers rather looky-lou's. But if you want the deal and they have a reason for asking you to visit, go. Examples of good reasons include, "We want our VP to meet you and we are a Fortune 500 company." and "We will have a team of engineers to meet with you as well as our product line manager." In the first case, it is the time of a person whose hourly cost is very high. In the latter case, it is a lot of people's time.

At this meeting you should be prepared to present your case. The case has three parts. The first part is why your technology will make them money. This part has to do with the end-user needs you meet and the size of the market. The second part is why what you have is better than what anyone else has. Hopefully, this part includes why your IP protection is so strong it blocks others from entering your turf or designing around it. The final part is they can convince higher management that what you have is the best thing since sliced bread. This part includes things like synergies with other products, the utility of your IP for their IP portfolio, and the utility of your technology for building brand loyalty among their current customer segments or for opening up new ones. The latter argument presumes your competitive intelligence indicates that is a goal of theirs.

If the meeting goes well, push to put together a schedule for evaluation of your technology in more detail and negotiations. The trick at this point is to get them to commit to deadlines, not decisions.

They will go off and do what they have to do. As the deadline approaches, re-engage and see how it is going. See if they need more information, data, etc.

Assuming the results are good, the next step is to put together a framework for these discussions. The framework has three components: a term sheet, an agenda, and a list of participants.

Before drafting the term sheet, revisit your decision tree and back-up data. Issues to reconsider in light of the interaction with the target to date include:

- Type of deal you want
- Determine long versus short term
  - Cooperativeness of partner(s)
  - Likelihood of improvements and new technologies
- Technology
  - What level of control you need to retain
  - Bundle of intellectual assets required
- Revenues—costs of implementation and risks
- Timing of payments
  - How badly you need cash
  - Total amounts and anticipate payouts
  - Upside and downside risk
- Factors suggesting exclusivity is reasonable
  - Limited use / narrow range of applications or territorial relevance
  - Economies exist
  - Market success record
  - Oligopolistic sector with high barriers to entry
  - Capabilities
  - Likely willingness to pay
  - Non-dependent on standardization for market acceptance
  - Performance targets for exclusivity

The term sheet is a draft framework for the offer. I emphasize *draft* because a term sheet only covers key points, so you want to label it clearly as a discussion draft so it is not construed to be an offer that, if accepted by the other side, suddenly puts you in a contractual relationship you never intended. All you want to do is provide overview of what kind of deal you would like so the other party can determine if it looks like it is worthwhile negotiating.

Depending on the kind of deal sought, the sheet will be different, but common points include:

- Name of owner and points of contact
- Technology
  - Name
  - Maturity
  - Description of intellectual property protection
- Recipient of term sheet
- Property to be sold
  - Description
  - Derivative works and other intellectual assets included, if any
  - Scope of what is being sold (rights)
- Type of deal vehicle
- Coverage (exclusivity)
  - Field of use
  - Use specification
  - Territory
  - Rights retained
- Duration
- Deal vehicle specific terms (license example—it would be different for other types of deal vehicles)
  - Fees & royalties
    - Upfront/initiation
    - Running
    - Calculation method
    - Minimums
    - Supplemental know-how fees if any
  - Other key terms
    - Milestones and other obligations (if any)
    - Maintenance and enforcement
    - Grant backs
    - Improvements
    - Sublicensing
    - Jurisdiction and law for dispute resolution
    - Indemnifications and warrantees

The agenda describes how the negotiations will be conducted. Usually it makes sense to focus briefly on where consensus lies so those issues can be set aside. Further, by starting with the positives, a climate of success is encouraged. The agenda should define milestones for the negotiations and indicate at what points approvals and sign-offs should be sought.

The timing is also important. Negotiations should not drag on. So, if the issues cannot be resolved in an initial face-to-face, video/Internet conference, or conference call, then times and dates should be set for email exchanges or follow-up calls.

Almost always at least three people are involved in negotiations. There is the lead negotiator. Where face to face meetings or video or phone conferencing is occurring, a second person is there to watch for body language and provide perspective. (That person's presence also gives you the opportunity to use a need to huddle or take a bathroom break to slow down the pace or halt temporarily to let tension bleed off.) As the size of the deal increases there also may be a more senior person involved who may not participate in the actual negotiations, but has the sign-off authority. (Ideally, you want to avoid that. Better to have them in the room so the deal can get done.) Finally, there is always a lawyer or a team of lawyers. (Deals are contracts, after all.)

War gaming is a useful technique for checking your term sheet, agenda, and team. In war gaming a negotiation, two teams are created. One team pretends to be you (the folks actually selected for the negotiation usually). The other team plays the party you are negotiating with. Both teams are provided the best data possible on the party they are gaming.

The actual game is a series of mock negotiations. Each game ends with a debriefing. Both teams rethink their approaches and decision trees. Additional data may be collected where its absence weakened the negotiating posture. Then the game is replayed over and over again until the margin utility of lesson learned shrinks too low. A final wrap-up is conducted and the decision tree modified one last time to reflect the results.

Pulling It Off

If the term sheet and agenda is seen within the realm of reasonableness, it is time to work the details. Here is where the "*craft*" of negotiation comes into play. The craft has five critical components.

First, be fair. Unfair deals tend to fall apart.

Second, terms should place tasking and burdens on the parties who are best able to perform them while controlling the risk involved. So, if you are a developer of technology and the other party is going to make and sell it, you are not going to indemnify them against product liability as that is something they are better able to control. If they insist you indemnify them, only do it if they will make a substantial enough side payment that ensures you can purchase a very large and bulletproof liability policy. The corollary is that if neither party can control the risk nor insure against it, no-one should promise to bear the risk. For example, never warrant that your patent is valid because it may turn out that someone really did invent your gadget before you did. All you can warrant is that you are unaware of any reason it is not valid at the time you make that statement.

Third, do your best to help the other side meet their hurdle rate and other key requirements. (Of course, it is an open question if they will be up front about these.) After all, if they cannot satisfy these necessities, they will have to walk away.

Fourth, be honest. Who wants to do a deal with dishonest people? The last time I saw Bill Cosby, he was the commencement speaker at my son's college graduation. He had a great line: "The truth will set you free, but first it will piss you off."

Finally, follow the agenda. As you move through the agenda, send out memos to all participants that summarize points of agreement as well as issues to work later. Ask for feedback to be sure you have captured the consensus. These memos become the basis for modifying the term sheet so you have a consensus document to send to the lawyers

Now, this advice is really just common sense. In implementing it, common sense continues to be useful.

Work to keep the emphasis on problem solving in a mutually supportive climate. If you want a relationship after the deal, act like it exists before the deal and negotiate from that perspective. That means you have to respond to requests for information, empathize with concerns the other side raises, treat their negotiators with respect, and be willing to engage in provisionalism—which means you need to be able to say things like, "Well, let's explore a couple of options here and see what works best for all of us."

Use questions as well as statements, but do not act like Socrates or a professor before a law school class who is seeking to show the student what an idiot he or she really is. Questions should be used to draw attention to items of concern or confusion in a non-threatening way. Their goal should be to elicit information or an explication of the analysis that information has received.

Be willing to compromise. For each item that is not critical on your list, be willing to give so long as there is a tit for tat as they give on items not critical for them.

My favorite way of compromising is to use an adaptation of Benjamin Franklin's decision algorithm. Franklin recommends drawing a line down the middle of a piece of paper. You put the positives favoring a decision on one side and the negatives on the other. Then you start crossing off items. This positive is about equal in value to me as that negative. That negative is more significant, maybe it is equal to these three positives. By the time you get done, there is something left on one side—be it positive or negative. So, you have a decision.

In a negotiation, take all the stuff you agree on and set it aside. Instead of positive or negative, put the issue positions you each are pushing on that party's side of the line. Then start horse trading. This process helps remove those issues that can be traded away.

What are left are the sticking points. Usually these go to the money and the assumptions behind where revenues come from, what costs must be incurred, and where risk lies. My preference is to use what I call data initiative to address sticking points. For example, at Foresight we use a royalty calculator to justify our position on rates (see below).

Factor	Rate	Weight	Impact
Industry norm		0.0	0%
Significance (breakthrough add 5–10%, major add 0–5%, minor subtract 0–3%		3.0	0%
Refinement/maturity of technology (high add, low subtract)		2.0	0%
Breadth and strength of ip protection (yes add, no subtract)		2.0	0%
Portfolio, not single patent being licensed (yes add, no subtract)		2.0	0%
Exclusive market position in field of use gained (yes add, no subtract)		3.0	0%
Immediate utility in market (yes add, no subtract)		2.0	0%
Commercially successful (already successful in market add, not yet proven in market subtract)		3.0	0%
Competition exists which will inhibit ability to exploit (yes subtract, no add)		1.0	0%
Foreign rights (yes add, no subtract)		3.0	0%
Sales Conveyed or highly likely (yes add, no subtract)		2.0	0%
Duration (over ten years add, under three years subtract)		1.0	0%
Upfront payment required (yes subtract, no or conditional add, standard neutral)		2.0	0%
Minimum royalties (yes subtract, no add, standard neutral)		2.0	0%
Know-how included in deal (yes add, no subtract, standard neutral)		3.0	0%
Support/training provided after initial transfer (yes add, no subtract, standard neutral)		2.0	0%
Maintenance and enforcement burden (licensee subtract, licensor add, standard neutral)		2.0	0%
Exposure to liability (yes subtract, no, standard neutral)		2.0	0%
Total		37	0%
Add to industry norm			0.00%
RATE			0.000%

To get the industry standard rate, first we review fee for service data bases, books with royalty rates, and SEC filings to determine what seems to be the range for the kind of technology we are supporting. Next, we interview licensing executives from both universities and companies. We work to ensure we get perspectives on what a fair rate would be from both out- and in-licensing people. Using this data we come up with an industry rate we can justify. Then, we bump it a bit to allow for convergence. (If asked we will admit this—perhaps ironically it is a moment of humor that allows everyone to start focusing on what is really fair).

We adjust the industry average for the specifics of this technology. The factors we use in our royalty calculator are those from the Georgia Pacific case and that have been shown to be important in empirical studies. We weight the factors, using our best judgment in light of the market research data we have. We also assign adjustments on that basis.

Now, I would love to say the moment we pull out the royalty rate calculator the folks on the other side of the table say "Wow. You're right. OK." Sometimes, but not always. What it does do, however, is frame the discussion. Now they start coming back with their data, which usually they have been holding back. The reason is they have to. Otherwise it is our data against their bald assertion.

The great thing that has happened is we no longer are at an impasse. Recall that in our discussion of economics above, we were able to take a set of tasking, put numbers to it, and figure out net cash flow and who contributes what to that flow. We are back in that mode, only this time collectively with the other side. The negotiation is no longer about who gets what so there take that. It is instead about who has good data we can use and let's plunk it in, crank the formula, and see what comes out. Even if your data is somewhat speculative, so long as the assumptions are clear and grounded in a way reasonable for the size of the deal, the other party has to come back with data or they look silly even to themselves.

The point is this: Where there is an impasse, it behooves us to provide a solution path. That path should focus on what any reasonable person would find persuasive. Now, clearly the most persuasive solution would be one that meets everyone's needs. If we cannot have that, then we want a solution that represents *"fair market value"* or *"industry standard,"* because the whole premise of a market economy is that markets work. Barring that, we fall back to splitting the difference or some other heuristic which seems fair given there is an impasse and both parties agree we want to do a deal despite that impasse.

A couple of other quick pointers:

Whenever you do put forth a position, listen. You have made your offer. It is time for them to accept it or counteroffer. Do not undercut yourself by falling back to your last resort position if they are silent. Give them time to reply. If they want to think, that is OK. Wait. If need be, suggest a break so they can discuss how to reply in private.

Negotiations can get pretty heavy and tense. So chill. Tell jokes when appropriate. Never push so hard that the other side cannot save face. When you do change positions, explain why you are doing that so the other side gets clued into how you think. Ask them to explain why they change so you can understand better how they view things. Sometimes it is just corporate or national or ethnic cultural habits that are the hang-up.

Be aware that we are all people, so look for nonverbal cues. If the other party is doodling they likely are either bored or lost. Watch for body language. Even on the phone you can listen to the tone of the voice, the pitch range and register, loudness, tempo, and duration of words and sentences. Changes are clues that something is happening. The way people act when face to face are signs to what they are feeling, for example:

- Defensiveness (arms crossed on chest, pointing of fingers)
- Considered evaluation (head tilted, stroking chin, taking off glasses)
- Suspicion (looking away, glancing sideways)
- Readiness and interest (sitting on the edge of the chair, moving closer)
- Nervousness (clearing throat, "whew" sound, fidgeting, jingling change in their pocket, covering the mouth with their hand when speaking, perspiring)
- Frustration (short breaths, "tsk" sound, running their hand through their hair or on the back of the neck, wringing their hands)
- Boredom (doodling, blank stare, drumming)

In email, we have to fall back on language choice cues, unless the other party is using capitals, bold, italics and the like. Be sensitive to everyday phrases that slip in and suggest meanings and intent. "Kick it around" carries a lot less support for a suggestion that "have to give it to you."

Avoid making the negotiations more difficult. Do not spring surprises on the other side. Do not grandstand, yell, engage in theatrics, threaten, haggle, etc.

When the other side is speaking, be a good listener. Do not interrupt. Do not cross-examine like you are Perry Mason in a courtroom. Periodically summarize what you heard to make sure you correctly understand.

Finally, it is important to keep making headway, so do not be afraid to suggest mutually setting deadlines or time limits for discussions, so long as there is enough time for each side to state its case. Sometimes you can use an event to provide an external deadline. For example, there may be PR utility in announcing an agreement at a trade show or conference. Regardless, if there comes a point where headway cannot be made and will not be made within a reasonable time—accept it, shake hands, and walk away.

CONCLUSION

Deals allocate the net revenues generated by a technology between at least two parties: the current owner of the technology and a party acquiring part or all of the rights the owner possesses. What the deal does is put these two parties into a relationship. There are all kinds of relationships that can emerge, running from one time, short term, arms-length relationships, as occurs when a product is sold, to the enduring one that occurs when a firm is acquired.

Leaving direct sales of goods aside, from the standpoint of the owner of technology, the deal is important because some help is needed to get the technology to market. So, the deal involves allocating tasking, and thus costs and risks, between the parties to the deal. This allocation is the basis for negotiating a fair deal. Who does what gives us one side of the equation each party brings to the deal: the expenses and discounting. The other side, revenues, can be viewed as set by the market on the one hand, and the success of the relationship being built by the parties on the other hand. At the end of the day, each party puts these two sides together and decides if there is enough money being made to make the deal worthwhile.

Because the deal does institutionalize a relationship as a legally enforceable set of rights held by each party, the deal has to make sense as a business relationship. Common sense dictates that relationships built on trust and honesty are easier to maintain than those built on lies and deception. This simple realization is all that is needed to negotiate a deal. Everything flows from it. In negotiations you act the same as you will act after the deal is inked. If the other party is not willing to do the same, it probably will not work whatever the contract says and you might as well save time and headache and walk away now.

Now, this sounds pretty Pollyanna. But if you stop and think about it, if the technology is good, if you have customers lined up, if you know how to launch it, and you select the right target, then the convergence of interests should support this kind of behavior. Sure, there will be some dickering around the margins as everyone tries to get the best deal possible. But so long as there is good money to be made, everyone should be able to compromise and still come out ahead.

CHAPTER 12

The Twelve-Step Program

I'm one of those people who collect Chinese fortune cookie fortunes. Earlier this year I got one that said "Begin, the rest is easy." At the time I thought it was pretty pithy.

The beginning is hard, but so is the ending. You want to say something that ties it all together and leaves the reader with a moment of epiphany. So, here are my concluding thoughts. Throughout this book I have tried to use web sources whenever possible. I want you, the reader, to understand the big problem in technology transfer is not finding information, but knowing what to do with it.

Since Alcoholics Anonymous, twelve-step programs have stood for an approach in which members of a support group acknowledge problems and then work together to solve them and share their victories.[1] Technology transfer is like that. If you are in this business and have not attended a meeting of the Association of University Technology Transfer Managers or Licensing Executives Society, you really need to go. People are glad to share insights and wisdom. Talk about win-win. Another great resource is Techno-l, a listserver, currently hosted at *http://www.techno-l.org/process .cfm?pageID=1*.

So, let me leave you with this twelve-step program for technology transfer success:

1. Find the end users.
2. Understand their needs, both today and as they change over time.
3. Determine the market forces so you take into account market dynamics.
4. Find the competition that can hurt or swamp you within five years of market entry.
5. Identify your barriers to market entry.
6. Figure out where your competitive advantage lies and, if you cannot, find another set of end users where you do have a competitive advantage.

---

[1] Wikipedia, "Twelve-step program," October 24, 2005, http://en.wikipedia.org/wiki/ 12-step_program (accessed October 28, 2005).

7. Be honest about your strengths and weaknesses when it comes to development and commercialization.
8. Figure out the launch tactics so you can sell to your end users.
9. Identify the capability and capacity gaps that keep you from developing your technology and launching it.
10. Find targets who can fill those gaps and want to sell to your end users but lack a technology like yours.
11. Map out how to work with those partners to move your technology to market and attain take-off.
12. Do the deal.

Of course, the precise number of steps is somewhat arbitrary. Exhibit 12.1 is a depiction of how we view the process at Foresight Science & Technology. You can begin or enter the path at any point, depending on the maturity of your technology and what market research and concurrent engineering has been done in the past.

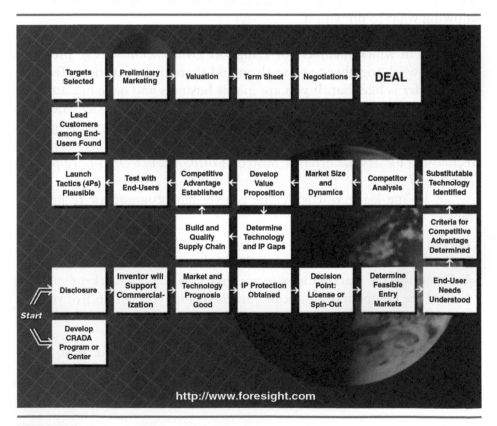

EXHIBIT 12.1   Foresight's View of the Process

However you view the process, there are two critical take-aways I would like to leave you with. First, be responsible. This is our planet and if we do not take care of it, who will? Second, when you do technology transfer you get to see a lot of really cool stuff. All we have to do is help make it useful. So go ahead and have fun. It's supposed to be fun.

Nothing happens without a sale.
David Speser

If opportunity doesn't knock, build a door.
Milton Berle

A well-defined imagination is the source of great deeds.
Chinese Fortune Cookie

Cost leadership, 49, 50, 60, 63, 232

CRADA, 89, 90, 94, 285

Criteria, 8, 9, 14, 18, 31, 32, 37, 38, 46, 50, 72, 75, 76, 85–92, 95, 96, 122, 140, 143, 159, 160, 167, 218, 245, 267, 273, 283, 317, 323, 352

D

Deals, 7, 20, 22, 36, 38, 40, 41, 55, 58, 62, 64, 67, 68, 74, 82, 88, 100, 102, 157, 203, 249, 269, 270–364

Deal vehicle, 70, 85, 89, 90, 92, 94–96, 102, 329, 334, 355

Differentiation, 49, 50, 60, 63, 141, 233, 234, 260, 264, 292

Discounted cash flow, 295, 296, 324, 326

Disruptive technologies, 75, 84, 85, 195, 253

Dominant design, 21, 24–27, 38, 51, 70, 74–77, 79, 82, 84–86, 95, 96, 101, 121, 136, 143, 155, 159–162, 167, 194, 195, 215, 219, 220, 223, 227, 233–235, 248, 273–275, 278, 284, 309, 323

E

Early adopters, 142, 143, 191, 195, 205, 309

Ease of use, 9, 11, 16, 18–20, 22, 26, 27, 33, 38, 63, 65, 69, 74, 76, 70, 80, 82, 96, 97, 115, 133, 135, 156, 158, 162, 165, 169, 204–206, 219, 221, 222, 228, 248, 249, 264, 266, 273, 275

Enabling, 52, 119, 257, 284, 288, 289, 303, 345

End users, 17–20, 22, 25–27, 32, 38, 40, 50, 51, 55, 58, 61, 63, 67, 69, 72, 73, 75, 76, 78–81, 96–98, 107, 112, 113, 115, 117, 120, 122, 125, 133–139, 144, 155, 159–161, 166, 204, 209, 219, 220, 232, 233, 235, 240, 245, 248, 253, 255, 265, 267, 277, 281, 305, 308, 352, 363, 364

Expense, 21, 131, 168, 249, 295, 296, 299, 310–316, 324, 335, 345, 346, 361

F

Features, 4, 11, 18–20, 25, 26, 69–71, 75, 77, 79, 81, 82, 84, 105, 117, 118, 120–122, 133, 135, 140, 144, 148, 177, 189, 194, 215, 217, 219, 221, 223, 228, 233, 234, 248, 308, 324

Functionality, 18, 21, 26, 32, 69, 70, 75, 77, 79, 81, 82, 84, 105–107, 112, 121, 123–125, 128, 131, 133, 135, 136, 144, 162, 187, 215–217, 228, 253, 275, 288, 305–307

G

Gap analysis, 279

Goals, 17, 18, 23, 24, 27, 32, 33, 36, 37, 59, 67, 69, 73, 74, 80–82, 85, 88, 97, 169, 209, 210, 220, 221, 229, 265, 267

Goods, 3, 4, 7, 9, 13, 17, 22, 24, 25, 26, 32, 42, 44, 48, 52, 55, 60, 62, 63, 65, 70, 79, 98, 100, 118, 134, 139,141, 144–146, 149, 161, 163–165, 171, 180, 182, 185, 187, 199, 200, 203,

Printed in the USA/Agawam, MA
October 21, 2021

783185.004